Contents

Part III. Emerging Youth Cultural Forms and Practices

Part IV. Negotiating and Affirming Identity, Space, and Choice

Acknowledgments

It is a distinct pleasure when a project merges both professional and personal interests, and this volume reflects such a combination. As scholars who conduct research in the areas of immigration, the new second generation, and race/ethnicity, we hold a keen interest in the Asian American population and in Asian American youth in particular.

The Asian-ancestry population in the United States has made an indelible mark on the nation's demographic scene, multiplying eightfold from 1.4 million in 1970 to 11.9 million in 2000, and is projected to increase to 20 million by 2020. Although Asian Americans constitute only 4 percent of the country's population, they are the fastest growing racial/ethnic group in the United States, outpacing every other group in the rate of population growth in recent years. Moreover, Asian Americans comprise a significant portion of today's new immigrants, accounting for one-third of all new arrivals since the 1970s. As the twenty-first century unfolds, the children of Asian immigrants—who are often referred to as the 1.5 generation (foreign born arriving in the United States prior to age 13) and the second generation (U.S. born of foreign-born parentage)—are coming of age in record numbers. Surprisingly, there has been relatively little research on Asian American youth, and virtually none on the topic of Asian American youth culture.

This void is all the more astonishing considering that Asian American youth are highly visible on college campuses on the East and West coasts, and in metropolitan areas in between. Their presence is discernible in elite private universities such as Harvard and Stanford, in small liberal arts colleges such as Pomona and Wellesley, and in large public and private campuses including the University of California campuses, the "Big Ten" universities in the Midwest (Indiana University; University of Michigan; University of Iowa; Purdue University; University of Minnesota; University of Wisconsin–Madison; Michigan State University; Northwestern University; Pennsylvania State University; and Ohio State University), and in state and community colleges across the nation.

As professors at the University of California campuses in Irvine (UCI) and Los Angeles (UCLA), respectively, where the Asian American student body makes up significant proportions of the total undergraduate enrollment (nearly 60 percent at UCI and 40 percent at UCLA), we come into contact with Asian American youth every day. We teach Asian American students in our classes, meet with them during our office hours, and participate in many of the activities they organize. Being in such close relationships with them affords us the unique opportunity to understand what issues they find most pressing, most interesting, and most salient in their daily lives. Keeping in mind what they have told us, we have collected a number of original chapters that speak to a host of issues that are directly relevant for today's Asian American youth. We hope that the Asian American youth who read this book find that it accurately reflects their lived experiences, and moreover, that they find it as meaningful to read as it was for us to write.

On a more personal note, as a former Asian American youth who grew up in the United States, and as the immigrant mother of an Asian American youth, we cannot deny that the topics of Asian American youth culture, identity, and ethnicity hold personal significance for both of us. Hence, in gathering material for the book, we selected chapters that resonated not only with our students' experiences but also with some of our own. Although we have certainly raised more questions than we have answered, we hope that this book motivates a new generation of researchers to delve further in the area of Asian American youth culture, since there is yet much to uncover in this fertile and underexplored terrain.

Like all projects of this size, this one owes manifold debts. First and foremost, we would like to thank all of the contributors who saw merit in our project and agreed to contribute their original ideas to it. The chapters reflect the diversity of their interests and disciplines, including Asian American studies, sociology, history, anthropology, political science, criminology, law, and other professions. Together, the volume provides a foray into Asian American youth culture, identity, and ethnicity, and has turned out to be much greater than the sum of its parts.

We are also grateful to former editors at Routledge, Vikram Mukhija and Ilene Kalish, whose keen eyes saw promise in our book proposal and whose enthusiasm for the project reaffirmed our commitment to it; to Salwa C. Jabado who helped to steer along the project to completion; and to Amy

Rodriguez at CRC Press, whose meticulous editing made the book more readable. We thank the anonymous reviewers for their insightful comments and suggestions. We would also like to thank Philip Jia Guo, Chiaki Inutake, Jina Jung, and Angela Sung for their research assistance.

We also express our sincerest gratitude to both of our professional institutions, UCI and UCLA, for giving us the time and support to complete the book. A fellowship from the Center for Advanced Study in the Behaviorial Sciences, which was generously supported by the William Flora Hewlett Foundation Grant #2000–5633, was awarded to Jennifer Lee during the academic year 2002 to 2003, providing unencumbered freedom to develop and work on the volume. The project was also supported by multiple research grants from the Asian American Studies Center, the Social Science Division of the College of Letters and Science, and the Academic Senate at UCLA.

Our families have been unwavering sources of support for both of us. Jennifer Lee wishes to express her deepest gratitude to her parents Sangrin and Wonja Lee and her sister Jeena Stephanie Lee for their unconditional love and endless encouragement. Min Zhou wishes to thank her husband Sam and son Philip for their love, understanding, and wholehearted support.

Finally, we wish to convey our appreciation to our students, especially those at UCI and UCLA, who inspired us to conceive of this project, and motivated us to complete it in a timely manner. Through their inquiries, they challenged us to grapple with and understand the meaning and content of Asian American youth culture, identity, and ethnicity. Hence, to our students—who continue to push us to become better teachers, mentors, and researchers—we dedicate this book as our sincerest and humble form of gratitude.

Jennifer Lee and Min Zhou

CHAPTER **1**

Introduction:
The Making of Culture, Identity, and Ethnicity among Asian American Youth

Min Zhou and Jennifer Lee

This volume centers on Asian American youth, focusing specifically on the way in which they create and practice a culture that is distinctively their own. In turn, this distinctive Asian American youth culture has powerfully shaped Asian American youth's daily lives and ethnic identities. Until recently, social science research rarely treated Asian American youth as a distinct analytical category. In fact, when we discuss Asian American youth culture with academic and lay people, we are often met with puzzled looks, followed by questions such as: "Is there such a thing as *Asian American youth culture?*" "Do Asian American youth have a culture of their own?" "If so, what is it like?"

To many Americans, Asian American youth do not fit into any of the popular images typically associated with youth culture or subcultures, such as hip-hop artists and rappers, hippies, skinheads, punks, graffiti writers, low riders, ravers, or suburban "mall rats," with the exception, perhaps, of gang members. For a long time, Asian American youth have been neglected or at best homogenized into a social group widely celebrated as the "model minority" while derogatively stereotyped as "nerds" or "geeks." As such, they are considered a uniform group and deviant from "normal" teenage Americans.

Through the chapters in this volume, we counteract this one-dimensional portrait, showing the diversity among Asian American youth and illustrating how they have created a culture of their own through "grassroots cultural production" (Bielby, 2004). Moreover, in the process of creating a distinct culture, they have also redefined the Asian American community. This collection comes from the original work of scholars from diverse disciplines such as Asian American studies, sociology, history, anthropology, political science, psychology, criminology, and law as well as by practitioners. It illustrates how Asian American youth create and define an identity and culture of their own against the backdrop of contemporary immigration, continued racialization, and the rise of the new second generation (the U.S.-born of foreign-born parentage). Before turning to the chapters that make up the volume, we first offer a brief literature review of the research on youth and youth cultures. Then, we establish an analytical framework for understanding Asian American youth and the way in which they have successfully carved out a cultural niche for themselves.

RESEARCH ON YOUTH AND YOUTH CULTURES

Youth and Culture

In preindustrial societies, one's life course was roughly marked by two discrete stages—childhood and adulthood. However, in postindustrial societies, the duration of childhood has been prolonged and also includes the distinct, yet overlapping stages of adolescence and youth. Today, youth generally refer to those between the ages of 16 and 24 (and sometimes even 30). These young people are at the stage in their life cycles where they strive to find their own spaces, make their own choices, and form their own identities, while at the same time deterred by certain norms, rules, regulations, and social forces from accepting the myriad responsibilities that accompany full adulthood.

The delayed entrance into adulthood stems from two sources: on the one hand, societal constraints prohibit youth from partaking in certain adult activities; and on the other, youth also prolong this stage in their lives. For instance, while American youth may legally enter the labor force, those under the age of 18 are considered minors and therefore banned from participating in electoral politics or purchasing a pack of cigarettes. In addition, it is a criminal offense for an adult to have sex with a minor, even when the sex is consensual. Furthermore, while accorded the full rights of citizenship at the age of 18, those under the age of 21 are prohibited from buying or consuming alcoholic beverages and entering nightclubs that serve alcohol. While societal constraints play an active part in delaying the entrance into adulthood, American youth themselves are increasingly active participants in prolonging this stage of their lives. For instance, it is becoming increasingly more common (and to some extent necessary in today's economy) for those under the age of 25 to continue with school full time after graduating from high school. Consequently, seeking higher education delays the transition to adulthood, which is typically characterized by a stable job, marriage, home life, and parenthood.

Today, to be young is to be hip, cool, fun loving, carefree, and able to follow one's heart's desires. As a significant social group, this age cohort is inherently ambiguous as it juxtaposes and strives to find balance between the dialectics of parental influence and individual freedom, dependence and independence, innocence and responsibility, and ultimately adolescence and adulthood. It is precisely the tension arising from this ambiguity that drives the public misrepresentation of youth as deviant, delinquent, deficient, and rebellious or resistant.

Culture, on the other hand, is defined as the ways, forms, and patterns of life in which socially identifiable groups interact with their environments and express their symbolic and material existences. Young people experience the conditions of their lives, define them, and respond to them, and in the process, they produce unique cultural forms and practices that become the expressions and products of their own experiences (Brake, 1985). Thus, youth culture is broadly referred to as a particular way of life, combined with particular patterns of beliefs, values, symbols, and activities that are shared, lived, or expressed by young people (Frith, 1984). As social scientists, our goal is not only to identify young people's shared activities but also to uncover the values that underlie their activities and behavior. As early as 1942, Talcott Parsons coined the phrase "youth culture" to describe a distinctive world of youth structured by age and sex roles with a value system in opposition to the adult world of productive work, responsibility, and routine (p. 606). While youth culture may oppose the adult values of conformity to adult culture and responsibilities, it also serves as an invaluable problem-solving resource—the development and use of day-to-day practices to help make sense of and cope with youth's shared problems (Frith, 1984).

The study of youth culture has a history that dates back to the turn of the twentieth century with roots in the field of criminology. Below, we trace its history from the Chicago School to the Birmingham School, and to more recent research on American youth. What becomes glaringly apparent from this review is that Asian American youth have been virtually omitted from broader studies of youth, illustrating the vacant niche in the study of American youth culture.

The Chicago School and Classical Sociology of Youth

With its roots firmly implanted in the field of criminology at the turn of the twentieth century, research on youth and youth cultures flourished amidst sweeping social changes in the United States and Britain after World War II. Even before "youth" and "youth culture" were analytically defined, earlier research focused almost exclusively on delinquency and deviance rather than on young people as a whole. Prewar youth were largely regarded as "gang" members, or groups of working-class young men hanging out in slums on the streets. Thus, many studies of youth prior to World War II implicitly and explicitly framed them (especially those who were working class) as undisciplined, unruly, lawless, and violent. The distinct styles of dress, leisure habits, and behavioral patterns that young people exhibited in public made them appear, both individually and collectively, as deviants from the norm.

The criminological inquiry about youth can be traced to the Chicago School, which was mainly concerned with the negative consequences of urbanization. Urban sociologists considered urban problems as inherently youth problems because, compared to rural communities, cities had more young people and more activities that both targeted and engaged them. However, much of the earlier work, including classical studies such as Frederick Thrasher's study of urban gangs (1927), Paul Cressey's taxi-dancers (1932), and William Foote Whyte's street corner society (1943), did not directly place youth at the center of analysis. Rather, these studies were concerned with how changes in human habitats induced by urbanization led to consequences associated with youth. More specifically, they focused on the ways in which urban life disrupted traditional ties to kin and community, and posited that the loss of a tightly knit system of family and community control led to the breakdown of moral values. The collapse of moral values, in turn, spawned a rise in juvenile delinquency, deviance, mental health problems, and organized crime.

Although most classical studies of youth adopted a macro urban perspective, another important strand of research emerged from the Chicago School—symbolic interactionism. Unlike the previous studies that focused on the roles of community and urbanization, studies born of the symbolic interactionism tradition focused on micro-level social processes, and in particular, on the way in which deviants and deviant behavior were defined by social groups and by society at large, and in turn, on how deviants coped with their labeling. Perhaps the most prominent study of this tradition is that of Erving Goffman (1963) who described how an individual whose physical traits and behavioral characteristics did not fit the "norm" was labeled as a deviant and stigmatized by an imposed identity, also referred to as the "spoiled" identity. Furthermore, Goffman illustrated how such an individual who was labeled as deviant "managed" his or her spoiled identity, either by retreating from social interactions or by passing for "normal." In contrast to Goffman's study, Howard Becker's (1963) classic study of "outsiders" focused more on the people who did the labeling than on those who were labeled. Becker demonstrated how groups who occupied positions of power and privilege successfully labeled marijuana and alcohol use as deviant, and benefited from such labeling not merely on moral grounds but also on political and economic grounds, consequently enhancing their control over the working class.

Sharply diverging from both macro and micro traditions of the Chicago School, Robert K. Merton (1949) took an entirely different approach to the study of deviance. In his classic essay, "Social Structure and Anomie," Merton argued that deviance is a response to anomie and resulted from an imbalance in the social system between socially approved goals and the availability of socially approved means of attaining those goals. According to Merton, individuals responded to the system's imbalance in five distinct ways in terms of acceptance or rejection of the socially approved goals and/or the means of achieving those goals: conformity (accepting both); innovation (accepting the goals but rejecting the means); ritualism (rejecting the goals but accepting the means); retreatism (rejecting both); and rebellion (rejecting both). "Innovation" was the most common form of deviance. Taking a middle-range approach, Merton located the source of deviance squarely on the social structure and the culture it produced rather than on macro structural forces or on the micro-level processes in which the deviants themselves came to interact with others and with societal institutions. Adopting Merton's middle-range approach to the study of deviance, Albert Cohen's study of urban gangs (1955) illustrated how gang membership provided lower-class boys (who could not achieve respectable social status through normative means) with the opportunities and means to attain respect and other forms of achievement.

The Birmingham School and Youth-Centered Approaches

While the Chicago School dominated studies of youth prior to World War II, during the postwar years, social scientists and cultural critics began to develop new models of understanding youth and youth culture. Spearheaded by the Centre for Contemporary Cultural Studies at the University of Birmingham (known as the Birmingham School), scholars and critics adopted a more holistic approach. Rather than focusing solely on the causes of youth-related problems, they attempted to map the meaning of youth and document the rich experiences lived by youth (Hall and Jefferson, 1976). Influenced by the Marxist conception of cultural production, Birmingham School researchers redefined youth as cultural producers and consumers rather than as delinquents. Moreover, they regarded youth cultures as the distinct ways and patterns of life in which socially identifiable youth groups come to process the raw material of their life experiences and give expressive forms, or "maps of meaning," to their social and material existence (Clarke et al., 1976: 10). By centering on youth, with a particular focus on the "look" of various youth cultures, the Birmingham School perspective located the subject matter in relation to three broader cultural structures: the working-class parent culture; the dominant culture; and the mass culture (Gelder, 1997).

First, youth cultures were considered a part of the working-class parent culture, similarly subjected to the structural constraints of the working class. During the postwar years, broad economic and urban shifts had an enormous impact on the lived experiences of youth, in particular, urban revitalization, economic restructuring, and formal schooling. These changes disrupted the dense cultural space for working-class life and polarized the working class into two distinct groups: the highly skilled suburbanites and the low skilled trapped in urban ghettos, which included the majority of working-class youth. Hence, youth culture was born of the structural constraints associated with working-class life, and moreover, the culture itself was viewed as a means of expressing and resolving the crisis of class.

With this conception of working-class youth culture, the Birmingham School regarded the youth's public display of nonconformist styles and deviant behaviors as more than simply a rebellion against their working-class parents. More fundamentally, the unconventional styles and behavior of youth were considered a means of expressing working-class youth's resistance to middle-class authority. For example, Birmingham School scholars regarded the skinhead phenomenon as a symbolic attempt to reaffirm the traditional working-class core values of "community" rather than simply an act of senseless rebellion (Clarke, 1976).

Second, the Birmingham School also situated youth cultures within a hegemonic relationship to the dominant culture. Developed by Antonio Gramsci (1971), the concept of "hegemony" refers to the power of a society's ruling class to exert total control—state power, economic resources, and ideas—over subordinate classes. Rather than excluding the subordinate classes, the dominant class incorporated them into key institutions such as the family, school, church, and other cultural institutions in order to prevent them from erecting alternate institutions. By incorporating them into such key spheres of life, the dominant class not only ensures that the subordinate class will adopt its ideologies and values, but in the process, it effectively reproduces class subordination.

Youth from the subordinate classes (the working class and racial minorities in particular) introduced a repertoire of strategies, responses, and ways of coping and resisting the dominant class authority that had clearly articulated collective structures. Working-class youth constructed distinct subcultures around their living environments, representing the appropriation of the "ghetto" as well as a class-conscious struggle to negotiate identity and to carve out a "space" of their own. However, as a consequence of creating their own space, their class-based culture served as a mechanism in their alienation from society at large (Clarke et al., 1976: 60).

Third, youth cultures were viewed as a form of mass culture because youth were both consumers and simultaneously producers of mass culture. On the one hand, the postwar employment opportunities afforded working-class youth a substantial amount of disposable income, making them the first targeted consumer group (Benson, 1994). Their newly acquired affluence allowed them to consume mass culture in a new way, leading to the need to produce new cultural forms. Mark Abrams posited that young people should be defined not by their delinquent behavior, but rather in terms of their market choices (Abrams, 1959). In effect, Abrams argued that their consumption patterns and market choices reflected a new "teenage culture" defined in terms of leisure goods and activities. This, in turn, generated distinct youth cultures that transcended both class and racial boundaries. For example, while working-class youth (mostly people of color) appropriated the ghetto to create their own distinctive cultural forms and meanings, middle-class youth (mostly white) gravitated to the "ghetto" and imitated the cultural forms of their working-class counterparts as a way of expressing their own experience (Clarke et al., 1976: 60).

Although the development of youth cultures transcended the boundaries of race and class, the Birmingham School insisted that youth culture was not classless since youth continued to be manipulated by big businesses, advertisers, marketers, and distributors of the dominant class culture. In short, the Birmingham School perspective underscored the role of class and hegemony in shaping the experiences of youth and youth culture, even within the realm of a seemingly "classless" mass culture.

Recent Youth Research in the United States

Both the Chicago School and Birmingham School traditions have had a profound influence on youth culture research in the United States, especially between 1950 and 1970. While the studies from the Chicago School focused on the macro social forces that led to deviance among youth as well as the micro interactions among those labeled as deviant, and the Birmingham School focused on the role of class and hegemonic social structures, recent research on youth cultures has veered in a different direction altogether. Contemporary research on youth culture reveals a tendency to move youth out of class-based categories, and instead, emphasize the diversity of youth cultures as well as the multidimensional nature of resistance. The resurgent literature on youth culture, especially since the 1980s, turns our attention to the distinctive characteristics of youth, with a particular emphasis on the impacts of class, race/ethnicity, gender, and geography on their cultural expressions, signs, symbols, and activities.[1]

Significant collections of youth culture include *Rave Off: Politics and Deviance in Contemporary Youth Culture* edited by Steve Redhead (1993), *Generations of Youth* edited by Joe Austin and Michael Nevin Willard (1998a), *Youth Culture* edited by Jonathon Epstein (1998), *Digital Diversions* edited by Julian Sefton-Green (1998), and *Cool Places* edited by Tracey Skelton and Gill Valentine (1998), to name just a few. Also noteworthy are numerous book-length case studies, thematic works, and comparative studies such as *The Gang as an American Enterprise* by Felix M. Padilla (1992), *It's Not about a Salary ... Rap, Race and Resistance in Los Angeles* by Brian Cross (1993), *Youth: Positions and Oppositions* by S. J. Blackman (1995), *Young and Homeless in Hollywood* by Susan M. Ruddick (1995), *New Ethnicities and Urban Culture* by Les Back (1996), *Gangsters* by Lewis Yablonsky (1997), *Popular Music and Youth Culture* by Andy Bennett (2000), *Renegade Kids, Suburban Outlaws* by Wayne Wooden and Randy Blazak (2001), and *The Hip Hop Generation* by Bakari Kitwana (2002), to name some prominent monographs.

We highlight several significant conceptual advancements in the recent literature on youth culture as they help provide some contextual background for our understanding of the Asian American youth culture. First, instead of placing youth within a class framework or portraying them as delinquents, new research on youth in the United States focuses on the interactive processes between various macro and micro social forces in the formation and practice of culture and identity. Going beyond analyses of class, contemporary work recognizes the diversity of youth cultures, examining differences across a wide range of social categories, including class, race/ethnicity, gender, sexuality, and geography, and sometimes even making further distinctions within these categories. For example, the experiences of white and nonwhite youth, boys and girls, and heterosexuals and homosexuals are now presumed to have distinct characteristics that interact with structural forces such as hegemony, racism, sexism, and homophobia. Their experiences shape their socialization, which in turn affect the ways in which members of each respective group express, represent, and identify themselves.

Second, informed by the Birmingham School tradition, new research highlights the role of agency on the part of youth, and focuses on the proactive approaches toward the cultural production and consumption among youth of different class, racial/ethnic, and gender backgrounds. For instance, Andy Bennett (2000) views youth as a culture in its own right, asserting that youth themselves are capable of generating norms and values. Youth use their bodies, ghetto walls, city streets, as well as the press, television programming, and online publications as sites for cultural expression and practices. In doing so, youth present their experiences and aspirations to society at large, often making use of the most advanced forms of technology to introduce their views.

Newer studies do not regard the emergence of youth cultures simply as a form of resistance to class subordination, but also as a form of engagement with the dominant culture to articulate and reaffirm their own multifaceted lived experiences and identities. For instance, Bakari Kitwana (2002) points out that while black hip-hop culture has become commercialized and popularized in mainstream American culture, it has continued to be expressed both publicly and privately in a myriad of ways. More than just graffiti-writing, break-dancing, dee-jaying, and rap music, black hip-hop culture now includes verbal and body language, along with a certain attitude, style, fashion, and proclivity toward activism. This wider repertoire has redefined the meaning of black youth identity and worldview not only from other Americans but also from an older generation of African Americans. However, rather than remaining exclusively within the domain of black youth culture, today's urban hip-hop culture attracts and is appropriated by white and other racial/ethnic minority youth in the United States and beyond.

Third, while the research that emerged from the Birmingham School in postwar Britain placed class at the center of analysis, newer research has replaced class with race/ethnicity. Differential opportunities exist along racial/ethnic lines, affecting fundamental social and economic spheres including education, housing, healthcare, and employment. Moreover, although the nation's social problems are largely the consequences of economic restructuring and unfulfilled promises of equality of opportunity, racial/ethnic minority youth are often held accountable for problems as wide ranging as single motherhood, urban youth gangs, and high school dropouts. However, rather than blaming minority youth, George Lipsitz (1998) argues that youth research should be located within the racialization of social crises such as unemployment, poverty, ghettoization, school failure, alcohol, drug, and gang violence. Furthermore, Lipsitz contends that understanding social crises will be incomplete if scholars fail to pay attention and learn from the lessons that young people are trying to teach the broader society through cultural expression such as dance, music, and visual imagery.

RESEARCH ON ASIAN AMERICAN YOUTH AND YOUTH CULTURE

Asian American youth as a group have been almost entirely omitted from research on youth and youth culture in the United States. This omission has not been accidental, but rather, deeply rooted in the legacies of racism and legal exclusion. From the first significant wave of Chinese immigrants reaching America's shores in the late 1840s to the outbreak of World War II, Asian Americans were made up mostly of Chinese and Japanese, with significantly smaller numbers of Filipinos, Koreans, and Indians. Because of various anti-Asian immigration laws, the earlier Asian immigrant groups were small in size and, with the exception of the Japanese, dominated by foreign-born men, with few traditional families. Not only isolated by national-origin groups, Asian Americans were also segregated from other Americans at work, in school, and at their place of residence, essentially ensuring that they would be excluded from fully participating in American life.

During the exclusionary era, people of Asian descent were viewed as clannish, unassimilable aliens, and their cultures backward, corrupt, or simply negligible. The only images that most Americans held of Asians were those promoted in the media: the yellow peril personified in the evil of Fu Manchu; feminized and asexual Chinese men such as Charlie Chan (and later kung-fu masters and fighting machines); exotic geishas, China dolls, and seductresses; or the dragon ladies. These distorted images carried and perpetuated the Eurocentric perception of Americans of Asian ancestry as the exotic Oriental—"foreign" and non-American (Hong, 1993). Asian American youth of the time were all too aware of such misrepresentation, and as a result, they attempted to combat the negative stereotypes by redefining the meaning of being American and expressing their experiences through various forms of cultural practices, such as forums, dances, and ethnic presses. However, exclusion, segregation, and the disrupted community life constrained their cultural practices and limited their voices to the margins of their own ethnic communities (see the chapters by Chun, Matsumoto, and De Vera in this volume).

Even when the racial stereotypes were challenged during the ethnic consciousness movements, including the civil rights movement of the 1960s, new stereotypes of Asian Americans emerged, most prominently that of the "model minority." The new stereotype—the model worker, the overachiever, the math maniac, or the science/computer nerd—carried with it a new set of distorted images of Asian-origin Americans and characterized them as anything but "normal."

This time, however, Asian Americans took their struggles beyond their ethnic communities into mainstream America. For instance, since the late 1960s, Asian American literary work, mostly by U.S.-born or U.S.-raised young Asian American writers and critics, aimed to counteract the misrepresentation of Asian-ancestry Americans and reclaim their place in America. Spearheaded by Jeffrey Paul Chan and his associates in their groundbreaking collection *Aiiieeeee!: An Anthology of Asian American Writers* (1974) and Maxine Hong Kingston in her autobiography *The Woman Warrior* (1976),

Asian American cultural works—first in literature and then in film, theater, and the English-language press—have not only flourished but also have become visible in mainstream America. Most of the work recounts the personal and communal histories and experiences of growing up American in immigrant households, in ethnic communities, as well as in mainstream America—all from the perspective of youth.

Although these works have undeniably made significant cultural advancements in understanding the experiences of Asian Americans, studies of Asian American youth still remain on the margins of youth research in the social sciences. Hence, the goal of this collection is to place the experiences of Asian American youth at the center of analysis. In doing so, we first propose a framework for analysis.

"Asian American" as a Meaningful Social Category for Analysis

Before developing a framework for studying Asian American youth and youth culture, we must first ask whether "Asian American" is a meaningful analytical category. Our answer is affirmative. In the United States, race often overrides many major socioeconomic and cultural factors—including education, occupation, language, and religion—to affect the everyday lives of all Americans. While social scientists generally agree that race is a social and cultural rather than biological category, there is often a tendency to racialize others into a limited and discrete set of racial categories such as white, black, Hispanic, American Indian, and Asian. Furthermore, those who do not neatly fit into one of the readily available categories are either overlooked, ignored, or may even cause anxiety for those who do the labeling (Kibria, 1996; Omi and Winant, 1994). Hence, while race is a social construct, the lived experiences of race are real and consequential (Lee, 2002).

Coined by the late historian and activist Yuji Ichioka, "Asian American" was a term initially used to describe a politically charged group identity in the ethnic consciousness movements of the late 1960s. This self-proclaimed category emerged to reject the Western-imposed category "Oriental" and to fight invisibility. Today, "Asian American" is widely considered an umbrella term that includes native- and foreign-born U.S. citizens and permanent residents from Asia (east of Pakistan) or who have ancestors from this region. Asian-origin Americans, especially those of East Asian origins who have long been dubbed Oriental, adopt the pan-ethnic label because of convenience and because other Americans cannot and often do not even try to make ethnic distinctions, despite vast differences in national origin, religion, language, and culture. Moreover, the pan-ethnic label has become instrumental for political mobilization and activism (Zhou, 2004).

Although the category "Asian" is both convenient and instrumental, behind closed doors, few Americans of Asian ancestry actually identify themselves as Asian, and even fewer as Asian American. Instead, they identify with their specific countries of origin such as Chinese, Japanese, Korean, Filipino, Indian, Vietnamese, and so on. For example, in a study of Vietnamese youth in San Diego in the mid-1900s, 53 percent identified themselves as Vietnamese, 32 percent as Vietnamese American, and only 14 percent as Asian American. Moreover, nearly 60 percent of these youth considered their chosen identity as very important to them (Zhou, 2001).

Not only do Americans of Asian ancestry not identify themselves as Asian or Asian American, in private they often contest the imposed pan-ethnic identity for a myriad of reasons. First, Asian Americans are a group predominated by the first generation (or foreign born) from diverse national origins. While some have family histories in the United States that date back further than those of Eastern or Southern European origins, most Asians arrived in the United States after the liberalization of immigration laws in the late 1960s. To put this growth into perspective, in 1970, there were only 1.4 million Asians, and in 2000, this figure soared to 11.9 million, now accounting for 4 percent of the total U.S. population.

Before 1970, the Asian-ancestry population was largely composed of Japanese, Chinese, and Filipinos. Now, Americans of Chinese and Filipino ancestries are the largest subgroups (at 2.8 million and 2.4 million, respectively), followed by Indians, Koreans, Vietnamese, and Japanese (at more than one million each). Some 20 other national-origin groups, such as Cambodians, Pakistanis, Lao, Thai, Indonesians, and Bangladeshis were officially counted in government statistics only after 1980 and together amounted to more than two million residents in 2000. Except for the Japanese who are proceeding into the fourth generation, all other Asian-origin groups (including the Chinese and Filipinos) are disproportionately made up of the first generation (for more details, see Zhou in this volume).

Diverse national origins lead to differences in language, religion, food-ways, customs, histories of international relations, contexts of emigration, reception in the host society, and patterns of adaptation. Moreover, for some national-origin groups, such as Chinese and Indians, internal differences in language, dialect, and religion are substantial. While such differences persist most prominently in the private domain and mainly affect the immigrant generation, they also have a significant impact on the second and succeeding generations. Even though the ethnic distinctiveness associated with homeland traditions and cultures blur with each succeeding generation (due to acculturation and rapid and high rates of intermarriage), the experiences of growing up among Asian American youth are intrinsically linked with immigration. Today's Asian American youth balance their time and attention between the larger society and their immigrant families and ethnic communities as well as their parents' ancestral homelands, making this balancing act uniquely Asian American.

In addition to the diverse national origins among the Asian immigrant population, Asian Americans also hail from diverse socioeconomic backgrounds (unlike earlier immigrants from Asia and Europe who were mostly low-skilled laborers who came to the United States in search of work). Today's immigrants from Asia migrate for a number of reasons: to join their families; to invest their money in the U.S. economy; to fulfill the demand for highly skilled labor; or to escape war, political or religious persecution, and economic hardship. The diverse socioeconomic backgrounds give rise to varied settlement and mobility patterns. Whereas middle-class immigrants are able to start their American lives with high-paying professional careers and reside in comfortable suburbs, low-skilled immigrants and refugees often have to endure low-paying, menial jobs and settle in urban ghettos, creating a bifurcated distribution of the Asian American population along class lines. The sharp divergence along class lines is likely to lead to fragmentation within the larger Asian American community, making the rise of a pan-Asian identification ambiguous and questionable.

Class bifurcation has direct implications for the identity formation of today's second generation. Unlike the second generation of the 1960s and 1970s—most of whom grew up in segregated urban enclaves—a visible proportion of today's second generation grows up in affluent middle-class suburban neighborhoods, making their experiences distinct not only from yesterday's second generation but also from their contemporary working-class counterparts. Members of the suburban middle class maintain little contact with their working-class co-ethnics in urban enclaves, and show limited interest in working-class issues. In short, socioeconomic diversity marks yet another unique characteristic of today's Asian American youth.

Last but not least, intergenerational differences among Asians complicate intragroup dynamics and family relations. Most notably, native-born children and grandchildren of Asian ancestry feel a sense of ambivalence toward newer arrivals. Because about two-thirds of the Asian American population is first generation, native-born Asians must now confront renewed images of Asians as "foreigners." Resembling the new immigrants in phenotype, but not necessarily in behavior, language, and culture, the more "assimilated" native born find that they must actively and constantly distinguish themselves from the newer arrivals. The "immigrant shadow" looms large for Asian American youth and can weigh heavily on the identity formation of native-born youth. However, native- and foreign-born youth react differently to the "immigrant shadow." For instance, comments about one's "good English" or inquiries about where one comes from are often taken as insensitive at best, and offensive or even insulting at worst, to native-born Asian Americans. By stark contrast, similar encounters tend to be interpreted or felt more positively among foreign-born Asians. Different lived experiences between the native and foreign-born are thus not only generational but also cultural.

Similar to other Americans in speech, thought, and behavior, native-born Asian Americans and their foreign-born counterparts often hold contradictory values and standards about fundamental issues such as individualism, civil liberties, labor rights, and ultimately, the ideology of assimilation. While they are infuriated by their unfair treatment as foreigners, native-born Asian Americans find themselves caught between two vastly different social worlds and at ease with neither. The ambiguity caused by the contradictory perception of "forever foreigner" and "honorary white" further pushes native-born Asian Americans into a dilemma of whether to include or exclude immigrants in their struggle for racial equality (Zhou and Gatewood, 2000). The uncertainty of their status, along with bicultural and intergenerational conflicts, marks a third unique feature of today's Asian American youth.

While recognizing the vast diversity among Asian Americans, we argue that intragroup dynamics and their consequences render the Asian American experience unique, and the imposed pan-ethnic category meaningful for analysis. However, we do not lose sight of the fact that "Asian American" is an imposed identity and most often, not adopted by either the first or second generation who are much more likely to identify with their national origins than other Americans.

For the second generation, ethnicities based on national origins will recede under the pressure of assimilation, but assimilation does not necessarily lead to diminishing ethnic distinctiveness as predicted by the classic model of acculturation and assimilation conceived by Milton Gordon (1964) decades ago. Instead, the process of assimilation may give rise to a heightened sense of nonwhiteness or a "pan-minority identity" that may be expressed in a variety of ethnic identities rather than a single one. Thus, as members of the second and later generations become more fully incorporated into America's racialized social system, a pan-ethnic identity may become more salient, more inclusive, and more quintessentially American in everyday practices. It is precisely from this point of departure that we study Asian American youth culture and its effect on identity and ethnicity.

UNDERSTANDING ASIAN AMERICAN YOUTH: OPPORTUNITIES AND CONSTRAINTS

Given the complexity of Asian American experiences, we argue that research on Asian American youth and youth culture should be located first and foremost within the dual processes of international migration and American racialization. These dual processes unfold two distinct yet intertwined social worlds that every Asian American child must confront, and present the dialectics of opportunities and constraints for the younger generation who continue to create a culture of their own.

Immigration

Immigration is the most immediate process that shapes the cultural formation of Asian American youth. As noted earlier, Asian Americans are a predominantly immigrant group, which in turn has an enormous impact on the experiences of Asian American youth. As they grow up, they are intimately influenced and often intensely constrained by the immigrant family, the ethnic community, and their parents' ancestral homeland. Research has illustrated how the immigrant family and ethnic community have been the primary sources of support as well as the primary sites of conflict (Zhou and Bankston, 1998).

Asian American children, despite their diverse origins, share certain common family experiences—most prominently the unduly familial obligation to obey their elders and repay parental sacrifices, along with the extraordinarily high parental expectations for educational and occupational achievement. Many Asian immigrant parents (especially those who had already secured middle-class status in their home countries) migrated to provide better opportunities for their children. As new immigrants, the first generation often endure difficulties associated with migration such as lack of English-language proficiency, American cultural literacy, and familiarity with the host society. Moreover, those who gave up their middle-class occupations often endure downward occupational mobility, relative deprivation, and discrimination from the host society (Lee, 2000). In their directed quest to achieve socioeconomic mobility, the first generation appears to their children as little more than one-dimensional hard workers who focus too much on material achievement and too little on leisure.

Although their children may feel that their immigrant parents have a narrow vision of success, the first generation are all too aware of their own limits in ensuring socioeconomic mobility for their children, and hence, turn to education as the surest path to move ahead. Thus, not only do they place an enormous amount of pressure on their children to excel in school, but they also provide the material means to assure success. For example, they move to neighborhoods with strong public schools, send their children to private after-school programs (including language programs, academic tutoring, and enrichment institutions in the ethnic community), spend time to seek out detailed academic information, and make decisions about schools and majors for their children (Zhou and Li, 2003).

Although the parents feel that they are doing what is best for their children, the children—whose frame of reference is "American"—see things differently. From their point of view, their parents appear rigid and "abnormal," that is, unacculturated, old-fashioned, and traditional disciplinarians who are incapable of having fun with them and unwilling to show respect for their individuality. The children view the immigrant family and ethnic community as symbols of the old world—strictly authoritarian, severely demanding, and overwhelmingly stifling.

At the same time, however, the children witness at first hand their parents' daily struggles as new immigrants trying to make it in America, and consequently, develop a unique respect and sensitivity toward them. One of the most prominent ways that they demonstrate their respect and sensitivity is through a subtle blend of conformity to and rebellion against their parents. Asian American youth are less likely to talk back or blatantly defy their parents than other American youth. For example, in her study of Nisei daughters during the years of Asian exclusion, Valerie Matsumoto (this volume) depicts the tension between native-born daughters and their immigrant parents in the way they defined womanhood. However, rather than challenging their parents head-on, running away from the family, or leaving the ethnic community, the native-born daughters judiciously negotiated the roles assigned to them by their parents and the tightly knit community by creating various cultural forms—dances, dating, and courtship romances—to assert a gender identity that was simultaneously feminine, "Americanized," and "Japanese." Although this delicate balancing act may take a heavy emotional toll on Asian American youth, it is precisely their ambivalence toward their immigrant families that makes the youth culturally sensitive, which, in turn, expands their repertoire for cultural expression.

Racial Exclusion

Along with the experiences associated with immigration, racialization is a second important process that shapes the cultural formation of Asian American youth. The youth confront the consequences of racialization in a number of ways, the first of which is their encounter with racial exclusion. During the period of Asian exclusion, Asian Americans—who were considered an "inferior race"—were confined to ethnic enclaves. The youth who grew up in this era had few social, educational, or occupational options beyond the walls of the ethnic enclave and were barred from full participation in American life. Consequently, some Asian American youth turned their attention overseas to their parents' ancestral homeland for opportunities that were denied to them in the United States. For example, frustrated by their limited mobility options in America, native-born Chinese youth in the 1930s promoted the "Go West to China" movement to seek better opportunities in their ancestral homeland. As Gloria Chun (this volume) illustrates, second-generation Chinese youth strongly advocated for and disseminated the information regarding the move back to China through public forums and ethnic presses.

Cultural forms and expressions such as ethnic presses, dances, and beauty pageant contests (see De Vera's chapter in this volume) not only affirmed ethnic identities but also inadvertently reinforced Asian Americans as the foreign "Other." While the days of racial segregation in ethnic enclaves have long since disappeared, the effects of racialization still remain a part of growing up in the United States for Asian American youth. For instance, today's Asian American youth develop an awareness of their nonwhite racial identity that functions as a marker of exclusion in some facets of American society, as Nazli Kibria (2002) describes in her study of second-generation Chinese and Korean Americans.

Racial Stereotyping

Another way in which Asian American youth face the consequences of racialization is through racial stereotyping. Excluded from fair representation in mainstream American media, most portrayals of Asian Americans have been either insidious stereotypes of the "foreign" *other* or celebrated images of the "super" *other*, setting Asian Americans apart from other Americans (see Nancy Yuen's chapter in this volume). So pervasive are racial stereotypes of Asian Americans that Asian American youth culture is, in part, produced within the context of counteracting these narrowly circumscribed, one-dimensional images, most prominently that of the model minority.

The celebrated "model minority" image of Asian Americans was born in the mid-1960s, at the peak of the civil rights and ethnic consciousness movements, but *before* the rising waves of immigration and refugee influx from Asia. Two articles published in 1966—"Success Story, Japanese-American Style," by William Petersen in the *New York Times Magazine* and "Success of One Minority Group in U.S.," by the *U.S. News and World Report* staff—marked a significant departure from the portrayal of Asian Americans as aliens and foreigners, and changed the way that the media depicted Asian immigrants and their descendants. Both articles extolled Japanese and Chinese Americans for their persistence in overcoming extreme hardship and discrimination in order to achieve success (unmatched even by U.S.-born whites) with "their own almost totally unaided effort" and "no help from anyone else." The press attributed their winning wealth and ability to get ahead in American society to hard work, family solidarity, discipline, delayed gratification, nonconfrontation, and disdain for welfare.

Although the image of the model minority may seem laudatory, it has far-reaching consequences that extend beyond Asian Americans. First, the model minority stereotype serves to buttress the myth that the United States is a country devoid of racism, and one that accords equal opportunity for all who take the initiative to work hard to get ahead. The image functions to blame those who lag behind and are not making it for their failure to work hard, their inability to delay gratification, and their inferior culture. Not only does the image thwart other racial/ethnic minorities' demands for social justice, it also pits minority groups against each other.

Perhaps one of the most devastating consequences of the model minority stereotype is its effect on Asian American youth who feel frustrated and burdened because others judge them by standards *different* from those of other American youth. Their rebellion against the image manifests itself in their adoption of cultural forms and styles that are influenced by other racial/ethnic minority youth, especially African American youth. For example, many Asian American youth adorn hip-hop style clothing, listen to rap music, and frequent hip-hop clubs. However, it would be a mistake to assume that Asian American youth simply imitate other youth cultures. While they borrow elements from other minority youth cultures, they consciously create unique Asian-American-style cultural forms and practices that manifest themselves in import car racing, DJ-ing and emceeing, raving, and film and theater (for example, see the chapters by Namkung and De Leon in this volume).

A case in point is the recently released all-Asian-cast Hollywood film *Better Luck Tomorrow*, directed by Justin Lin (2003). Defiantly turning the model minority image on its head, the film exposes the dark side of living up to the meek, studious, overachiever stereotype. Moreover, it depicts a series of shocking scenarios that illustrates that Asian American adolescents are just as confused and disturbed as other disaffected American youth who are bored with life. The multifaceted portrayal of Asian American youth proves that they can be good-looking, smart, funny, susceptible to drugs and alcohol, prone to violence and other vices, capable of self-destructive behavior, and completely lacking in morals all at once. While the model minority stereotype still endures in the media and popular culture, Asian American youth use cultural expression to show that they are far more multidimensional, complex, and, in fact, normal than the stereotype allows.

Invisibility

Yet another way in which Asian American youth confront the consequences of racialization is with invisibility, or the lack of public/media exposure. While all American youth are marginalized in society, they are nevertheless highly visible in mainstream American culture. Stereotypical or not, images of white and black youth permeate the media—from high culture on television, film, theater, music, dance, and fashion, to low culture on the street. However, images of Asian American youth are virtually absent, and perceptibly so. Hence, their expression through cultural forms and practices is an avenue through which Asian American youth make their presence on the American scene.

For example, Asian Americans have never had a significant place in the American recording industry as performers, producers, or consumers. By contrast, whites and blacks, and more recently Latinos, have been highly visible in and targeted by the recording industry. To counter the invisibility, many Asian American cultural workers believe that "just by being there" is the first step to being recognized, but beyond that, Asian Americans need to take active steps to realize their full political and artistic potential (Wong, 1997). So invisible are Asian Americans in the recording industry that many Asian American cultural workers consider making a mark on this scene as an urgent political and revolutionary project.

Whereas cultural workers agree that Asians are invisible in the arts, they do not agree on the means by which to assert their presence. For instance, Fred Ho (1999), an Asian American jazz artist, argues that "just being there" is not enough. Moreover, Ho contends that because Asian American cultural work is revolutionary in nature, Asian Americans should be in control of the means of cultural production by establishing their own production companies. Only by establishing their own means of cultural production can Asian Americans problematize the ideology of assimilation, reject Eurocentric and essentialist forms, and draw upon the rich Asian, immigrant, and working-class traditions of Asian Americans.

Globalization and Transnationalism

Globalization and transnationalism provide yet another means through which Asian Americans confront the effects of racialization. Advancements in digital technologies and the Internet allow today's generation of Asian American youth to communicate and stay in close contact with their respective ancestral homelands through visual imagery, music, sounds, and words beyond the imagination of earlier generations (for examples, see the chapters by Chiang-Hom, Sandhu, and Võ and Danico in this volume). Globalization beyond national borders widens the cultural space in which Asian American youth are able to maneuver at relative ease to create new opportunities for cultural production and expression.

Cultural forms such as styles, music, dances, desires, and dreams among South Asian American youth, for example, are shaped not only by American influences but also through diasporic influences to create an empowering sense of identity (Maira, 2002). The opportunities presented by globalization for the identity formation of Asian American youth are not reserved only for the native born. Christy Chiang-Hom's research (this volume) shows how foreign-born Asian American youth cope with the hostile reception from native born Americans (including their more acculturated coethnic peers) by turning to their homeland cultures—to which they remain close through technology—in order to forge a positive identity.

In sum, Asian American youths' adoption of cultural forms are the products of both opportunities and constraints presented to them from the larger processes of immigration and racialization. Because many Asian Americans are foreign born, the experiences of Asian American youth are inextricably linked to immigrant adaptation, the immigrant family, and the ethnic community, thereby making their experiences distinctive from those of other American youth. And while other racial/ethnic minority youth also experience the racialization of their identities, the effects of racialization and the way they manifest themselves in cultural expression are distinctive. Racial/ethnic minorities in the United States have suffered and continue to suffer from exclusion and stereotypes, but the stereotypes of each group are different and affect minority youth differently. The stereotype of the Asian model minority constrains and frustrates youth, pigeonholing them into a one-dimensional, superhuman mold. In other realms, Asian American youth experience the pangs of invisibility and attempt to make their mark through unique cultural practices such as import car racing, dance, theater, and clothing styles. Finally, today's advancements in technology offer Asian American youth influences beyond America, and also broaden the scope of their cultural terrain.

Asian American Identity and an "Emergent Culture of Hybridity"

A diverse lot, today's Asian American youth often adopt a number of different identities—ethnic, hyphenated-American, pan-ethnic, or multiracial—and these identities are not necessarily mutually exclusive. However, unlike white American youth whose choice of ethnic identities is symbolic, the identity choices among Asian American youth are far more limited and consequential. Previous research indicates that nativity, generational status, bilingualism, gender, neighborhood context, and perceptions of discrimination are important factors in determining the identity choices among today's Asian American youth (Lee and Bean, 2004; Portes and Rumbaut, 2001; Xie and Goyette, 1997; Zhou and Bankston, 1998). Perhaps most importantly, as nonwhite racial/ethnic minorities, Asian American youth are subject to outsiders' ascription, meaning that how others perceive them has a profound effect on the way they choose to identify themselves. Joane Nagel (1994) has long noted that the choice of identities is a dialectical process that involves both internal and external opinions and processes, that is, what *you* think your identity is versus what *they* think your identity is.

Stating that ethnic identity is simply a matter of choice ignores the structural context in which ethnic identities emerge. For instance, African American youth are most vulnerable to outsiders' ascription. Black youth may make intraracial distinctions based on nativity, ethnicity, or skin tone, but the power of race as a socially defined status in the United States makes these differences irrelevant or less important than the racial label *black* (Waters, 1999). Though perhaps less constrained than African Americans, Asian American youth may also find it increasingly more difficult to retain a strictly ethnic identity when outsiders identify them pan-ethnically as Asian. Few Asian American youth embrace the pan-ethnic label as their primary source of identification, but they understand that outsiders do not necessarily make (or even try to make) ethnic distinctions, lumping them into the catch-all category "Asian."

The construction of a pan-Asian American culture or identity is not simply a reaction to externally imposed racialization. It also involves a complex process of internal socialization of Asian values, shared experiences of growing up Asian, and an Asian upbringing within the context of the larger racial stratification system. Even the "model minority" stereotype serves to heighten the sense of being Asian rather than being "Chinese," "Japanese," or "Korean" (Kibria, 2002). Asian American youth may strongly cling to identities based on national origins, but, with time, their ethnic identities may become less salient and more symbolic in nature (Gans, 1979; Waters, 1990).

Yet another distinctive feature of Asian American identity is that Asians are neither black nor white, but occupy a position in between, at least at this moment in time. In a society that has long been divided by an impenetrable black-white color line, it is not at all clear that today's Asian Americans see themselves (or for that matter that others see them) as either black *or* white. While Asian Americans may be considered "people of color," the degree to which they view themselves and are viewed by others as closer to black or white is highly ambiguous (Lee and Bean, 2004). On the one hand, they are minorities and therefore subject to racial discrimination and prejudice. On the other, some Asian ethnic groups have achieved social status on a par with—and in some arenas, superseding—whites. Consequently, the "in-between" and "dual status" of Asians may provide greater flexibility in the identity choices for Asian American youth, especially for Asian multiracials (see the chapter by Lee and Bean in this volume).

Although the centrality of race, outsiders' ascription, and the black-white color line has a powerful effect on the identity choices of Asian American youth, also relevant is the fact that most Asian American youth are either immigrants or the children of immigrants. Hence, their identities are inextricably bound by the experiences of immigration, the immigrant family, and the ethnic community, as well as their interactions with mainstream institutions such as schools. However, rather than stating that racial ascription and the influence of the immigrant family and ethnic community leave few ethnic identity options for Asian American youth, or that they freely choose their identities, we avoid either/or explanations. Instead, we attempt to offer an integrative framework for understanding how Asian Americans create a sense of identity given the opportunities and constraints before them.

Asian American youth feel they are both a part of and yet apart from mainstream America. Asian American youth have successfully carved out a unique cultural space for themselves that is, in part, a consequence of their constant negotiation between the traditions of their immigrant families and the marginalization and exclusion they experience from the larger society. This does not mean that Asian American youth divorce themselves entirely from mainstream American culture. However, the unique dual status of Asian American youth combined with their immigrant backgrounds prompt them to actively craft a culture of their own that is distinctive both from their ethnic communities and from other American institutions and youth. In doing so, they negotiate between "American" and "Asian" traits, which often results in an "emergent culture of hybridity" that mixes elements of both worlds. By carving out a space and culture of their own through "grass roots cultural production" (Bielby, 2004), Asian American youth have been able to adopt an identity apart from the restraints imposed by the roles and expectations of the family, the ethnic community, work, and school. Consequently, this culture offers young Asian Americans a collective identity—a reference group from which they can develop an individual identity (Brake, 1985).

As the chapters in this volume demonstrate, youth culture is not static; it changes with time and adapts to different structural and historical contexts. Certain forms of youth culture that were meaningful and salient in an era of Asian exclusion are no longer relevant today. It is difficult, if not impossible, to predict which forms of ethnic and pan-ethnic youth culture will fade and which will persist for generations to come since predictions are inconsequential when made in a social and cultural vacuum. As the work in this volume exemplifies, Asian American youth cultures are not only the creative innovations of the young people but also the responses and products of larger forces. We demonstrate how Asian American youth have asserted and continue to assert the multidimensionality of their lived experiences. The chapters that we have selected for the volume address some of the most pressing issues underlying Asian American youth culture, identity, and ethnicity.

AN OVERVIEW OF THE CHAPTERS

Asian American youth have played a critical role as producers, consumers, and distributors of an emerging Asian American youth culture. Despite tremendous intragroup diversity, certain aspects of that culture transcend ethnic, gender, and geographic boundaries. We have carefully selected a range of original work conducted by scholars from different academic disciplines and by practitioners. However, our selection does not claim to be "representative" of the lived experiences of all young Asian Americans. Rather, it focuses more broadly on the diverse cultural practices of Asian American youth and the emergence and development of a distinctive Asian American youth culture. Going beyond the discussion of deviance, delinquency, masculinity, oppositional culture, or marginality that are often the foci of prior research on youth cultures, *Asian American Youth* examines how these youth have created, practiced, and negotiated culture, identity, and ethnicity for themselves throughout American history and in contemporary multicultural America. The chapters that follow are organized around four key thematic issues: population dynamics; historical patterns of cultural practices; emerging cultural forms and practices; and negotiating and affirming identity, space, and choice.

Part I contains two background chapters, familiarizing the reader with important demographic trends—immigration, and intermarriage and multiracial identification in the Asian American community. In Chapter 2, Min Zhou highlights two notable facts about contemporary Asian American youth: the predominance of the children of immigrants (1.5 and second generation) who are just coming of age at the turn of the twenty-first century and the vast differences in migration histories, national origins, settlement and adaptation patterns, and socioeconomic achievements. A simple pass of the census data shows clear inconsistencies with the image of a homogeneous social group that is often celebrated as the model minority. Zhou reminds the reader once again that the experiences of Asian American youth are shaped by both their immigrant and their American experiences.

Chapter 3 adds another level of complexity to the population dynamics, calling attention to the increasing number of Asians who claim a multiracial background. Based on analysis of the 2000 U.S. Census data, Jennifer Lee and Frank D. Bean find that more than one out of every four Asian Americans intermarry, and one in eight Asians report a multiracial identity, which is more than five times the national average in the United States. Moreover, given the trends and patterns of Asian intermarriage, the Asian multiracial population is projected to soar to one in three Asians by the year 2050. Lee and Bean also explain that the rise in multiracial identification has direct implications for the Asian American population and for America's changing color lines. They conjecture that a new divide may emerge that separates blacks and nonblacks, most prominently in parts of our country that have become increasingly racially and ethnically diverse from the new immigration.

The four chapters in Part II provide a glimpse of Asian American youth culture through a historical lens, taking the reader back to the era of Asian exclusion in the late 1920s to the nation's postwar golden years of the 1950s. In Chapter 4, Arleen de Vera examines a unique form of cultural expression, that of Rizal Day Queen contests and their relationship to nationalist and gendered discourses in the Filipino immigrant community. With the onset of tensions over U.S. colonization of the Philippines and the racial exclusion of Filipino immigrants in the United States, Rizal Day celebrations were used to promote nationalist visions of an idealized Filipino community. They provided a way to build unity, reaffirm ethnic pride and tradition, and present the best in the Filipino to the American public. Rizal Day pageants also presented opportunities and constraints for young Filipinas. On the one hand, the cultural events granted young women a forum through which they could contest gender ideals by engaging in small acts of defiance and expressing their own desires for self-fashioning and deportment. On the other, the pageants also restrained the individuality of young Filipinas by holding them to an impossibly high standard of sacrifice and duty in a community dominated by immigrant men.

In Chapter 5, Valerie Matsumoto describes the debates over the shifting gender roles that emerged regarding the "New Woman" in the early twentieth century. Focusing on Japanese American women in Los Angeles's Little Tokyo, Matsumoto finds that their synthesis of "modern" femininity was complicated both by the racial discrimination they faced from the larger society and by their ethnic community's views regarding appropriate female behavior. Under the watchful eyes of the immigrant community,

Matsumoto details how Nisei women experimented with cultural forms of socializing and courtship, and introduced popular mainstream elements into the ethnic enclave while retaining certain aspects of their parents' customs.

In Chapter 6, Shirley Lim uses the lens of Asian American ethnic presses and sororities to portray Asian American women's youth culture during the post–World War II golden age of American consumption. Perhaps most intriguing about the emergence of Asian American youth culture is that young Asian American women, in particular, represented the Asian American consumer. Exercising cultural citizenship in an attempt to claim a place for themselves, Asian American females continually fluctuated between public displays of assimilation into white, middle-class America and Asian ethnic pride, and sometimes managed to forge a sense of cultural hybridity. As Lim notes, the negotiation between "American" and "Asian" traits were key steps in claiming a place in the American nation and would later form one of the bases for the Asian American movement.

In Chapter 7, Gloria Chun examines how ethnic identities and consciousness shifted among native-born Chinese American youth in two critical historical periods: the 1930s and 1950s. In the earlier period, Chinese Americans experienced blatant racial discrimination, legal exclusion, and blocked employment opportunities, leading many native-born youth to consider *returning* to or going *back* to China. However, their orientation changed dramatically when China turned communist in 1949 and the U.S. government considered any links to China as treacherous. In this political climate of growing anti-Chinese sentiment, Chinese Americans severed all ties to China, publicly disavowed communism, vocally adopted American ideals, and shed their cultural heritage in order to adopt an unequivocally American identity. Chun argues that the dramatic shift in ethnic identity among Chinese Americans during the two time periods were bound by shifting social, economic, legal, and geopolitical constraints.

Part III includes seven chapters on contemporary Asian American cultural practices that offer vivid details about how youth spend their time, what they value, and how they interact with other youth as well as society at large. While many of these contemporary cultural forms transcend race, gender, and geography among today's youth, the way the youth practice these forms are distinctively Asian American. Sabeen Sandhu examines the underpinning of commercialization of Asian Indian culture in the United States, raising a broader question about cultural and social acceptance. As Sandhu depicts in Chapter 8, Asian Indian culture has become enormously popular, mass-marketed, and easily consumed in mainstream America. It has become chic to wear *mehndi*, adorn a *bhindi*, smoke a *beedi*, and practice yoga. All of these practices of exotic ethnic cultures enable white Americans to indulge in "instant karma." However, Sandhu points out that Asian Indians are largely missing from the depiction and commercialization of these trends. In addition, the trends weigh on the ethnic identities of Asian Indian youth since they retain their traditional meaning regardless of how Asian Indian youth may view these trends. Sandhu argues that unlike the instant karma that is easily worn and discarded by other Americans, karma is not instant nor easily discarded for Asian Indian youth who constantly straddle two cultures and struggle to gain acceptance into mainstream American culture that only partially accepts them.

Christy Chiang-Hom examines the transnational cultural practices of Chinese immigrant youth and parachute kids in Chapter 9. Unlike the second generation who were born and raised in the United States, immigrant youth and parachute kids spent the majority of their formative years in a different culture, were schooled in a different language, and now find themselves categorized and ridiculed as racialized minorities and "F.O.B.s" by their U.S.-born peers, including their acculturated coethnics. Chiang-Hom examines the academic, psychological, and social adjustment of foreign-born adolescents, including the subgroup of foreign-born youth known as *parachute kids*, youth who initially came to attend school in the United States without their parents. Immigrant and parachute youth face enormous challenges, especially because they move to the United States during or after adolescence—a developmentally sensitive period during which all youth experience significant physical and emotional changes. In their quest to adjust to their new host society, these immigrant and parachute youth create their own cultural and social space in which they forge a positive identity.

Chapter 10 takes the reader into the world of import car racing in southern California, detailing how Asian American youth carve out a distinct ethnic niche in the American car culture. Victoria Namkung reveals that the import scene is wildly popular, attracting tens of thousands of Asian American youth, and, as a consequence, has propelled a historically invisible racial group onto center stage of the previously Anglo-dominated consumer market and culture. Namkung shows how the import car culture and racing events provide a cultural space for Asian American youth to nurture a sense of empowerment, pan-ethnicity, and community. Furthermore, Namkung argues that import car racing directly challenges the negative stereotypes associated with Asian American males by allowing them to construct and assert an unequivocally masculine, hyper-heterosexual identity.

In Chapter 11, Linda Võ and Mary Danico take the reader into "PC rooms," "PC Bangs," and "Cyber Cafés"—the fastest-growing business in Asian ethnic enclaves in southern California. For low-income Asian

American teenagers who reside in southern California's urbanized suburbs, cyber cafés not only offer an affordable and accessible form of entertainment, but they also provide a diversion from the boredom, stresses, and problems of everyday life. Although some critics argue that video games such as Counter-Strike (and cyber cafés more generally) encourage violence and are addictive—referring to them as "on-line heroin"—Võ and Danico argue otherwise. Rather than promoting violence, cyber cafés offer a safe space where Asian American male youth can form friendships, gain a sense of empowerment, and reclaim their masculinity. In cyber cafés, players are judged by their gaming skills rather than their race, class, or status, and provide a way for young men to display their virtual masculine abilities.

Lakandiwa de Leon gives the reader a tour of the hip-hop scene in Chapter 12 and shows how young Filipino Americans have played a prominent role in all aspects of this culture from DJ-ing to graffiti-writing to break-dancing to emceeing. De Leon focuses on how pioneering Filipino DJs and club promoters provided Filipino American youth a safe and positive cultural space, thereby allowing them to build coalitions and forge a collective identity. By inspiring Filipino youth to envision new possibilities, the DJ scene and broader hip-hop culture present role models who have created an original, distinct, and positive culture with which Filipino youth can identify.

Chapters 13 and 14 introduce the reader to the subculture of Asian youth gangs. Though a far cry from the model minority stereotype, Asian American youth gang members are not simply criminal deviants looking for a thrill. In Chapter 13, Diego Vigil, Steve Yun, and Jesse Cheng present a case study of Vietnamese youth gangs in Little Saigon in Orange County, California. The authors note that the gang members they studied are second-wave refugees whose families were often torn apart by the migration experience to the United States. The authors argue that the loosening of family control and the stressful problems at home push some Vietnamese youth out onto the streets. Street gangs provide a "surrogate" family for those who fall astray, providing both recognition and a sense of self-esteem and social support that youth desperately seek. In the eyes of some Vietnamese youth, the gang holds appeal as a provider of affiliation, community, material well-being, protection, and guidance—for many, all-too-scarce sources of security and comfort in a strange, foreign land. Moreover, gang membership and activities appear to provide a faster and seemingly surer path to the American dream of success.

Sody Lay presents a similar case of youth gangs of another national origin in another American context in Chapter 14. He examines the reasons behind the emergence and growth of Cambodian American youth gangs in Providence, Rhode Island, a place where few Asian immigrants have settled in the past. Lay explains that Cambodian American gangs initially emerged to protect refugee youth from harassment and victimization by other ethnic gangs, and were later transformed into the more permanent, often violent, and dangerous form found today. Lay also reveals that gang membership appeals to some Cambodian youth because they must contend with issues such as estrangement from their parents, leaving a void within the child's life that can be filled on a variety of levels by gangs. In gangs, Cambodian American youth find those who speak a common language, older gang members who may fill the role of surrogate parents, and camaraderie with individuals who share the common experience of straddling two cultures yet feeling a part of neither. Gangs offer opportunities for protection, companionship, excitement, romance, money, a sense of identity, and, not least of all, acceptance. However, Lay reminds the reader that although Cambodian youth may find individual acceptance in gangs, gang members still remain outcasts in the larger society.

Part IV shifts the focus to examine how Asian American youth negotiate identities, social spaces, and choices in today's multiethnic America. Asian American youth forge identities for themselves through community building, tactical manipulations of mainstream stereotypes, dating strategies and partner preferences, and political activism. The youth also create distinct identities and spaces by establishing ethnic organizations, performing race, gender, and sexuality, and pursuing choices in a myriad of ways that are uniquely Asian American. Chapter 15 takes the reader onto college campuses, an important site for Asian American youth to reconnect and reconstruct their own identity that is distinct from the immigrant generation. Rebecca Kim's case study of Korean American evangelicals suggests that second-generation Korean Americans (and Asian Americans more generally) do not enjoy as many "ethnic" options as the children of European immigrants and cannot simply practice symbolic ethnicity like white Americans. For second-generation Korean Americans, ethnicity is neither primordial (inherited from the first generation) nor assimilative (holding little meaning or consequence). Instead, the growth of ethnic evangelical fellowships on college campuses reflects an "emergent ethnicity" that is made and remade in America—a product of second-generation Korean Americans' continued interaction with their ethnic community and the broader American society. Kim predicts that as long as ethnic group members feel a sense of social exclusion, ethnic associations will persist, and ethnic ties will remain strong beyond college.

In Chapter 16, Nancy Wang Yuen investigates the intersection of personal and professional identities through an examination of how young Asian American actors perceive and act, and react, in Hollywood's entertainment industry. Yuen shows that Hollywood plays a significant role in creating and perpetuating stereotypical images of Asian Americans by lumping distinct ethnicities into a single racial category and pounding them into particular molds with racial signifiers such as phenotypes, accents, and distorted behavioral characteristics. In an industry heavily dominated by whites, Asian American actors continue to struggle to achieve Hollywood stardom. However, Yuen finds that Asian American actors actively work behind the scenes to contest the racialized and racially-gendered stereotypes through various performative and coping strategies such as challenging and resisting phenotypical, verbal, and behavioral stereotypes.

In Chapter 17, Mark Ng takes the reader into a social world that is often rejected by the Asian immigrant community and marginalized by white America. Ng examines the way in which gay Asian American youth "search for home" and seek a safe haven where they can feel both secure and welcome. Gay Asian American youth often find themselves leading double lives—the racial versus the sexual—which is particularly difficult in light of the "model minority" stereotype that has completely ignored diversity in sexuality. Zooming in on some popular gay social spaces in West Hollywood, Los Angeles, Ng relays how these physical sites have become the playground, meeting ground, training ground, and battleground for individuals who identify themselves as gay and strive to establish a safe haven for themselves. West Hollywood has been considered a safe "place" for gay white men, but Ng raises the question of whether such a "space" exists for gay Asian Americans. He argues that even within identifiable queer places, social and power relationships reproduce, and the sense of belonging and community varies by race. Ng explains how gay Asian Americans negotiate identity, confront racialization, and contest marginalization and exclusion.

Sara Lee studies the partner preferences among second-generation Korean Americans in Chapter 18. She finds that, contrary to popular opinion, class and gender complicate their choices and often override race and ethnicity. Middle-class Korean Americans prefer coethnic partners because they are socially networked to coethnics, the majority of whom are middle class. By contrast, growing up in more racially and ethnically diverse and less affluent neighborhoods, working-class Korean Americans feel closer to other working-class minorities, such as blacks and Latinos, than to middle-class Koreans or Asian Americans. Because their class status is more salient in their daily lives than their ethnic identity, working-class Korean Americans are more open to dating and marrying across racial and ethnic lines. Furthermore, Lee finds that gender matters. The cultural perceptions and negative stereotypes of Asian males affect the partner preferences and dating patterns of both Korean American men and women. While Lee argues that individuals may have the will to choose marriage partners, she also reminds the reader that social and cultural factors play a significant role in constructing intimate relationships.

In Chapter 19, William Wei provides a thought-provoking commentary on young Asian American activists from the 1960s to the present. Wei takes a critical look back at the Asian American Movement in the 1960s. He also focuses on one of the most enduring legacies of the movement—the creation of Asian American Studies as an academic field. Reflecting upon Asian American activism over the decades, Wei argues that, although it may have declined in the 1970s and 1980s, political activism has revived in the last decade of the twentieth century. He points to the active responses from the Asian American community to the Wen Ho Lee case, the Abercrombie & Fitch tee-shirt incident, and the offensive comments made by Shaquille O'Neal regarding Yao Ming. That young Asian American activists quickly and strongly reacted to such incidences illustrates that they are willing to defend themselves and their community against those who question their American identity or deprive them of it. In this regard, Wei argues, young Asian American activists of today and the Asian American activists of yesterday have much in common despite differences in time and space.

Chapter 20 synthesizes the work of the volume and underscores how Asian American youth have successfully created alternative spaces and negotiated new identities for themselves. We also reiterate why Asian American is a meaningful category of analysis, and illustrate how Asian American culture is distinct from other minority youth cultures. We close by providing fruitful directions for future research since we are keenly aware that research on youth in the emerging, multidisciplinary field of Asian American Studies is just beginning to gain momentum and that much work awaits to be tackled.

Notes

1. We do not attempt to provide a comprehensive review of the contemporary literature on youth culture. Rather, we highlight some of the theoretical approaches helpful in establishing an analytical framework for the study of Asian American youth and youth culture.

PART I

Population Dynamics and Diverse Contexts of Growing Up American

CHAPTER 2

Coming of Age at the Turn of the Twenty-First Century:

A Demographic Profile of Asian American Youth

Min Zhou

The Asian-ancestry population constitutes the fastest growing and most ethnically diverse group in the United States. As of 2000, this population made up 4 percent of the total U.S. population, or 11.9 million, an eight-fold increase since 1970, when the number was only 1.4 million. Though still relatively small compared to other groups, Asians are enormously diverse in national origins and socioeconomic backgrounds. Americans of Chinese and Filipino ancestries are the largest subgroups, followed by Asian Indians, Koreans, Vietnamese, and Japanese. At least 20 other national-origin groups have become a visible presence in the United States in recent years; these include Cambodians, Lao, Hmong, Thai, Indonesians, Bangladeshis, and Pakistanis. Owing to the recent arrival of many Asian immigrants, approximately two-thirds of the Asian population, or 64 percent, is foreign born (the first generation). Another 27 percent are U.S. born with foreign-born parents (the second generation), and less than 10 percent are U.S. born with U.S.-born parents (the third generation or higher).[1] Because of the historical circumstances of legal exclusion and contemporary immigration, only since the late 1980s have Asian Americans begun to mature into the second generation in large numbers; exceptions are the Japanese, who are into the fourth generation.[2]

Differing from their foreign-born parents, many immigrant children and children of immigrant parentage lack meaningful connections to their parents' homelands. Thus, they are unlikely to consider a foreign country as a point of reference, and they are much more likely to evaluate themselves or to be evaluated by others by the standards of their country of birth or the one in which they are raised (Gans, 1992; Portes and Zhou, 1993; Zhou, 1997). Given that Asian American youth are overwhelmingly first or second generation and will represent a crucial component of future American society, Asian American youth face distinct challenges in growing up American.

This chapter provides a demographic profile of Asian American youth cohorts using the U.S. Census and Current Population Survey data. It begins with an overview of Asian Americans' diverse cultural origins and their encounters with mainstream American society and culture. It follows with a descriptive analysis of the demographic and socioeconomic characteristics of different-generation cohorts. Finally, the chapter examines how ancestral cultures, immigrant family dynamics, and socioeconomic status interact with American cultures/subcultures to affect the adaptation of Asian American youth and discusses the implications for the development of Asian American youth culture, identity, and ethnicity.

A HISTORICAL LOOK AT ASIAN IMMIGRATION AND DEMOGRAPHIC TRENDS

Labor Migration, Anti-Asian Exclusion, and Distorted Community Development

There has been an Asian American presence and community in the United States for more than 150 years. It is a vastly diverse ethnic community consisting of people whose ancestors, or who themselves, were born in more than 20 Asian countries. Until World War II, immigration from Asia had originated primarily from China, Japan, and the Philippines, with a much smaller number from Korea and India. Even as late as 1970, the Asian American community was largely composed of three ethnic groups— Japanese (41 percent), Chinese (30 percent), and Filipino (24 percent). The "other" category, which included Koreans and Asian Indians and insignificant numbers of others, constituted less than 5 percent of the total Asian population (see Table 1.1).

A series of anti-Asian exclusion laws—particularly the Chinese Exclusion Act and the laws that excluded immigrants from the "barred zone" (known as the Asian-Pacific triangle), as well as the national origins quota system established in the National Origins Act of 1924—severely distorted natural population growth and community development. As already noted, pre–World War II immigrants from Asia represented only a tiny fraction (less than 5 percent) of the total number of immigrants admitted to the United States, and most of them originated from China and Japan, and after the 1920s, from the Philippines. These earlier Asian immigrants, like the "tired, huddled masses" from Europe, were typically poor and unedu-

Table 1.1 Asian American Population: 1970–2000

	1970*	%	1980	%	1990	%	2000	%
Chinese	435,062	30.2	806,040	22.7	1,645,472	22.6	2,879,636	23
Filipino	343,060	23.8	700,974	19.7	1,460,770	20.1	2,364,815	19.9
Japanese	591,290	41.1	700,974	19.7	847,562	11.7	1,148,932	9.6
Asian Indian	—	—	361,531	10.2	815,447	11.2	1,899,599	16
Korean	—	—	354,593	10	798,849	11	1,228,427	10.3
Vietnamese	—	—	261,729	7.4	614,547	8.4	1,223,736	10.3
Other**	70,150	4.9	364,598	10.3	1,091,015	15	1,161,535	11
Total	1,439,562	100	3,550,439	100	7,273,662	100	11,906,680	100

* Asian Indian, Korean, Vietnamese, and other Asian-ancestry subgroups were not tabulated in the 1970 census.
** The "other" category included Pacific Islanders.

cated peasants, and many were male, leaving their families behind in their respective homelands. They came to the United States with the hope of making a quick fortune which they would bring back home after a few years of back-breaking labor. The Chinese were the first group to arrive in the United States in large numbers as sojourning laborers, and the Japanese came to fill the need for labor after the Chinese Exclusion Act went into effect in 1882. Filipinos, being American nationals not subject to immigration quotas, answered the labor demand after the door to the United States was closed with the enactment of the 1924 National Origins Act.

Partly because of the sojourning orientation of early Asian immigrants, and partly because of the anti-Asian bias and the restrictive nature of U.S. immigration legislation, Asian American communities across urban America in the late nineteenth and early twentieth centuries were overrepresented by single adult males. They were primarily bachelors' societies with relatively few women, families, and children (Chan, 1991; Takaki, 1989). The gender ratio for Chinese was nearly 27 males per every female in 1890, and dropped to 9:1 by 1910. Although the gender ratio evened out over time, by the 1940s, males still outnumbered females by more than 2:1 (Zhou, 2003a). Like the Chinese, the Filipino population was heavily skewed toward males, and in 1910, the sex ratio was 10:1. It grew more uneven in 1920 but slowly improved to 4:1 in the 1940s (Agbayani-Siewert and Revilla, 1995).

Unlike the Chinese and Filipino populations, the Japanese did not suffer from a severe gender imbalance. Owing to the 1908 Gentlemen's Agreement, which aimed to curb labor migration from Japan, the wives of Japanese laborers already in the United States were allowed to join their husbands. As a result, from the beginning Japanese immigrants settled in the United States as families and developed family-based communities, mostly in farming in Hawaii and on the West Coast (Nishi, 1995). The Japanese settlement pattern was quite distinct from that of other Asians, which suggests clearly that the "old" second generation (children of pre–World War II Asian immigrants) began to come of age only after the early 1930s. The proportion of second-generation Chinese adolescents was relatively small, and even fewer second-generation Filipino Americans were present prior to World War II.[3]

Contemporary Immigration

The trend of slow population growth and the invisibility of the second generation in Asian American communities began to reverse itself only after the late 1960s, despite the repeal of the Chinese exclusion laws in 1943, the passage of the War Brides Act in 1946, and further relaxation of Asian exclusion laws in the early 1950s. The Immigration Act of 1965, known as the Hart-Celler Act, abolished quotas based on national origins, established a seven-category preference system for the unification of families and for persons with needed skills, and set an equal 20,000 per-country limit. The enactment of this act in 1968 marked the beginning of the contemporary era of Asian American community development. Although the Hart-Celler Act has had a significant impact on Asian American population growth, other factors such as global economic restructuring, rapid economic development in Asia, and the failed Vietnam War have been among the most important in fueling Asian immigration into the United States (Cheng and Yang, 1996). As a result, the share of contemporary immigrants from Asia as a proportion of the total immigrant population soared from 5 percent in the 1950s to 11 percent in the 1960s to more than one-third of all arrivals since the 1970s. Between 1970 and 2000, nearly seven million immigrants were legally admitted to the United States as permanent residents from Asia. Among the Asian immigrants, 21 percent come from the Philippines, 18 percent from China, Hong Kong, and Taiwan, 12 percent from India, 11 percent from Korea, 11 percent from Vietnam, 3 percent from Japan, and the remaining 24 percent from other Asian countries (USINS, 2002).[4] Although the majority of contemporary Asian immigrants are either family-sponsored migrants (close to 80 percent), or employer-sponsored skilled workers (about 20 percent), Southeast Asian refugees have constituted a significant share of Asian immigration. Since 1975, more than 900,000 refugees have arrived from Vietnam, Laos, and Cambodia as a direct result of the failed U.S. intervention in Southeast Asia.

Consequently, the Asian American community has grown rapidly and expanded to include at least 24 national-origin groups officially tabulated into the census since the 1980s. As table 1–1 shows, by the year 2000, Americans of Chinese and Filipino ancestries had increased to 2.9 and 2.4 million, respectively, while the numbers for Asian Indians, Koreans, Vietnamese, and Japanese broke the one-million mark. Many other national-origin groups made a visible presence in the United States only after the 1970s. As of 2000, there were 206,000 Cambodians, 204,000 Pakistanis, 198,000 Lao, 186,000 Hmong, 150,000 Thai, 63,000 Indonesians, and 57,000 Bangladeshis in the United States. Although the Asian population includes other national origins, their numbers are far smaller, at under 25,000.

Diverse Socioeconomic Backgrounds and Settlement Patterns

In addition to the diversity in national origins, the most distinguishable characteristic of post-1965 immigration from Asia is perhaps its enormous heterogeneity. Unlike earlier immigrants from Asia or Europe, who were mostly low-skilled laborers, today's immigrants from Asia include those who come to join their families, invest their capital in the U.S. economy, fill the labor market demands for high-skilled labor, and escape war, political, or religious persecution, and economic hardships. For example, scientists, engineers, physicians, and other skilled professionals tend to be overrepresented among Chinese, Taiwanese, Indians, and Filipinos, while less educated, low-skilled workers tend to be overrepresented among Southeast Asians, most of whom have entered the United States as refugees. Given their pre-immigrant education and skills, many middle-class immigrants are able to start their American lives with high-paying professional jobs and secure a comfortable suburban living, while low-skilled immigrants and refugees endure low-paying menial jobs and live in racially segregated inner cities. The 2000 U.S. Census shows that, on the whole, Asian Americans have made remarkable socioeconomic achievements. Their overall median household income is $55,525 (the highest of all racial groups, even surpassing that of whites), and their poverty rate is a low 10.7 percent (the lowest of all racial groups). These averages, however, mask the vast heterogeneity among the Asian ethnic groups. Although highly skilled and professional Asians boast high median household incomes, Southeast Asians, especially Lao, Hmong, and Cambodians, trail far behind.[5]

Despite the geographical concentration in historically gateway cities, settlement patterns among Asian Americans are diverse. However, as in the past, Asian Americans are heavily concentrated in the West, and California alone accounts for 35 percent of all Asians (4.3 million) in the United States. California is also home to the largest number of each of the six main national-origin groups. Second behind California is New York State, which accounts for 10 percent, or 1.2 million, of all Asians. Chinese, Indians, and Koreans are heavily concentrated in New York, but not Filipinos,

Japanese, and Vietnamese. Several other states are home to large populations of specific Asian-origin groups. For example, Texas has the second largest Vietnamese population, next to California. Illinois has the third largest Filipino population, next to California and Hawaii. Washington has the third largest Japanese population, next to California and Hawaii. And New Jersey has the third largest Indian and Korean populations, next to California and New York. Among cities with populations that exceed 100,000, New York City, Los Angeles, and Honolulu have the largest number of Asians, while Daly City, California, and Honolulu are Asian-majority cities. Some smaller cities in California such as Monterey Park (the first city in America that reached an Asian majority in 1990 and remained an Asian-majority city in 2000) have also reached Asian-majority status.

Traditional urban enclaves such as Chinatown, Little Tokyo, Manila-town, Koreatown, Little Phnom Penh, and Thaitown continue to thrive or have recently emerged in gateway cities. However, they no longer serve as primary centers of initial settlement for the recently arrived since many new immigrants, especially the affluent and highly skilled, bypass the inner city altogether and settle in the suburbs immediately after their arrival. For example, as of 2000, only 8 percent of the Chinese in San Francisco and 12 percent of the Chinese in New York live in inner-city Chinatowns. Similarly, only 13 percent of Vietnamese in Orange County, California, live in Little Saigon, a mere 14 percent of Koreans in Los Angeles live in Korea-town, and only 27 percent of Cambodians in Los Angeles live in Little Phnom Penh. The majority of the Asian American population has spread to the outer areas or suburbs in traditional gateway cities as well as in new urban centers of Asian settlement across the country.

A DEMOGRAPHIC PROFILE OF THE NEW SECOND GENERATION6

The new second generation refers to the children of post-1965 immigrants. The emerging literature on the new second generation, however, has covered not only U.S.-born children—the *true* second generation—but also foreign born children who arrived in the United States before adolescence (Gans, 1992; Portes, 1995; Rumbaut and Cornelius, 1995). The latter group is also known as the "one-and-a-half generation" (the 1.5 generation), a term coined by Rubén Rumbaut to characterize the children who straddle the old and the new worlds but are fully part of neither (Firmat, 1994; Rumbaut, 1991). Although scholars define the new second generation in different ways, they generally agree that there are significant differences among children of three cohorts—the first, the 1.5, and the second generations. These differences emerge most prominently during their physical and psychological developmental stages with respect to their socialization processes in the family, the school, the society at large, and their orientation toward their parents' homeland.

As Table 1.2 shows, the Asian American population is young. Except for the Chinese and Japanese, all other groups have relatively high proportions of children and young adults, compared with the generation U.S. population; approximately 25 percent of the Asian population is under the age of 17, 10 percent between the ages of 17 and 24, and 65 percent over the age of 24. Among members of the second generation (the U.S.-born with at least one foreign-born parent), the average age is even lower, especially if we focus on the new immigrant groups. For instance, the 0–17 age cohort accounts for 70 to 89 percent of all second-generation Asian Indians, Koreans, Vietnamese, and other Asians based on estimates of the 2000 Current Population Survey data. This finding confirms once again that the new second generation is very young and just coming of age. The Japanese are the exception, evincing a more mature age distribution, even compared to the overall U.S. population.

Children: The 0–17 Age Cohort

Table 1.3 provides a description of Asian American children between the ages of 0 and 17 by national origin based on the 1990 U.S. Census. Unlike a century ago, there is not much difference in the gender ratio across the national-origin groups, except for the Koreans, who had a higher proportion of females. The majority of the children of Asian ancestries belong to the "new" second generation (which includes the U.S.-born children of immigrant parentage and the foreign-born children who were brought here at preschool

Table 1.2 Asian American Population by Age Cohort and Generation: 2000*

	Total			Second Generation		
	Under 17	17–24	25 and over	Under 17	17–24	25 and over
Chinese	21.3	8.8	69.9	45.3	9.9	44.8
Filipino	27.6	9.8	62.6	63.6	12.9	13.5
Japanese	17.2	7.5	75.3	22.8	6.5	70.7
Asian Indian	26.6	11.8	63.6	70.4	14.5	15.1
Korean	29.9	9.9	60.2	78.9	10.1	11.0
Vietnamese	28.3	10.2	61.5	88.5	8.3	3.2
Other Asian	41.9	10.9	47.2	87.1	4.8	8.1
Total	2,276,600	826,900	5,263,631	1,732,764	272,766	723,704

*Percentages were weighted.
Source: U.S. Current Population Survey: 1994–2000

Table 1.3 Selected Characteristics of Asian American Children Aged 0–17 by National Origin*

	Chinese	Filipino	Japanese	Indian	Korean	Vietnamese	Other Southeast Asian
Gender							
Female (%)	48.2	48.3	49.5	49.9	53.3	48.3	48.4
Generation							
Second or later generation (%)	84.0	86.6	90.1	87.0	85.1	79.1	79.8
1.5 Generation (%)	12.7	10.9	8.2	10.6	11.8	17.0	17.5
First Generation (%)	3.3	2.5	1.7	2.4	3.1	3.9	2.7
Language use (aged 5 and over)							
English monolingual (%)	23.1	64.3	65.0	37.2	40.2	9.8	4.2
Fluent bilingual (%)	45.5	25.7	16.0	48.3	39.3	46.2	33.7
Limited bilingual (%)	21.7	7.1	9.6	10.1	12.9	28.7	34.1
No English (%)	9.7	2.9	9.4	4.4	7.6	15.3	28.0
Non-English spoken at home (%)	76.9	35.7	35.0	62.8	59.8	90.2	95.8
Living in linguistic isolation (%)	36.3	9.0	19.2	11.7	31.0	46.2	63.9
Household characteristics							
Married-couple household (%)	92.0	88.1	90.7	94.0	91.5	81.4	84.3
Single parent household** (%)	8.0	12.0	9.3	6.0	8.5	18.5	15.7
Average number of persons in household	4.7	5.0	4.1	46.0	4.3	5.5	6.9
Residence in California State (%)	46.0	53.4	35.4	20.7	28.6	50.0	51.4
Family economic status							
Living below poverty level (%)	13.2	5.1	4.4	8.3	10.4	3.2	51.9
Median household income (in 1989 $)	$45,014	$49,524	$55,332	$51,300	$43,050	$30,000	$19,388
Per capita income (in 1989 $)	$12,605	$11,580	$15,827	$14,965	$12,489	$7,042	$3,827
Home ownership (%)	71.9	68.5	65.0	71.9	65.9	47.2	19.9
Schooling (aged 5 and over)							
Public school (%)	75.1	66.9	70.2	72.3	70.5	77.4	78.0
Parochial or other private school (%)	13.6	14.7	19.1	15.3	14.7	6.9	2.2
Not attending school (%)	11.3	18.4	10.7	10.7	14.8	15.7	19.8
High school dropout*** (%)	2.4	4.1	3.5	2.9	4.5	4.2	6.5
Total N	17,350	15,487	7,179	10,375	11,344	8,634	8,451

*Including only children aged 0–17 living in family households. Percentages were unweighted.
** Including single female-headed and single male-headed households.
*** Among those aged 16 and 17 who were not currently enrolled in school and did not have high school diplomas.
Source: U.S. Census of Population and Housing, 1990 (5%-PUMS)

age), especially the 0–17 age cohort, 79–90 percent of whom are second generation.[7] More than 17 percent of Vietnamese and other Southeast Asian children, compared to less than 13 percent of other Asian American children, are members of the 1.5 generation. Across all national-origin groups, only a small fraction arrived as adolescents, who belong to the first generation. And because of historical circumstances, only the Japanese had a noticeable third or later generation (children of U.S.-born parents).

Language ability varies across national-origin groups. English monolinguals (those who speak English only) are most common among Filipinos and Japanese (around 65 percent) but least common (less than 10 percent) among Vietnamese and other Southeast Asians. All other groups, except for Filipinos and Japanese, are well represented by fluent bilinguals (those who speak both English and their parental native language fluently), ranging from 34 percent for other Southeast Asians to 48 percent for Indians. Chinese, Vietnamese, and other Southeast Asians show a much higher proportion of limited bilinguals (fluent in one language but not the other) than other groups. Among limited bilinguals, differences emerge among the ethnic groups. For instance, Chinese children tend to lack proficiency in their parental native language, while Southeast Asian children tend to lack proficiency in English. Vietnamese and other Southeast Asian children also have a much higher proportion of those with no English at all compared to other Asian ethnic groups. Except for the Filipinos and Japanese, the majority of Asian American children speak a language other than English at home. Other Southeast Asian children are the most likely to live in linguistic isolation, that is, in neighborhoods where English is not the dominant language. By contrast, Filipino and Indian children tend to be more residentially dispersed, often living in English-dominant neighborhoods.

The residential concentration in California is remarkable; over a third of Asian American children live in California, except for Indians and Koreans whose proportions are lower but still quite sizable. In terms of family structure, most Asian American children live in married-couple households. The exceptions are the Filipinos, Vietnamese, and other Southeast Asians who show a much higher proportion living in single-parent households. In addition, the children of these three groups tend to live in larger households.

Family economic status varies across national-origin groups, but most troubling is the high poverty rates among Vietnamese (32 percent) and other Southeast Asian children (52 percent). These figures are not only high relative to other Asian ethnic groups but also compared to the general U.S. population, whose poverty rate is about 10 percent. In other words, Vietnamese and Southeast Asian children are three and five times as likely to live in poverty as the overall U.S. population. Other Southeast

Asian children, in particular, are the most economically disadvantaged, whether measured by median household income, per capita income, or homeownership.[8]

The diverse family economic positions of Asians have significant implications for the second generation. Although the parent generation may move to America to seek a better life and brighter future for their children, now as in the past, younger generations may either realize those hopes or become disillusioned by them. For much of American popular history, we have heard success stories of immigrant children fulfilling their parents' dreams, but the past may no longer provide a reliable guide to the direction of today's second generation. The new second generation faces distinct challenges that may make it more difficult to become upwardly mobile. For instance, the lower class backgrounds of immigrant families mean residence in poor neighborhoods, attendance in lower quality schools, and exposure to adversarial urban subcultures, all of which limit their life chances.

School occupies a central part of a child's life. Among school-aged Asian American children, the majority (over 70 percent) attend public schools, and between 14 and 19 percent of them attend parochial or private schools, except for the Vietnamese and other Southeast Asians. Filipino and other Southeast Asian children show higher nonattendance rates—a potential problem area that may lead to dropping out of high school. Although dropout rates are fairly low among teenagers between the ages of 16 and 17 of different national-origin groups, these rates may be higher if we take into account those who are over 17 years of age.

Young Adults: The 18 to 24 Age Cohort

Table 1.4 provides a description of Asian American young adults age 18 to 24 by national origin based on the 1990 U.S. Census. As shown, the gender ratio in this cohort is nearly balanced, except for the Vietnamese who have a lower proportion of females. Although most Asian American young adults remain unmarried, other Southeast Asians have a particularly high rate of marriage, at 25 percent, indicating a tendency for this group to marry at relatively younger ages. Among the young adults, the proportions in the second or later generations are substantially lower compared to the younger age cohort—an indication that the new second generation is just coming of age, except for Japanese Americans.[9] For example, only 3 percent of other Southeast Asians and 7 percent of Vietnamese young adults belong to the second or later generations, compared with 70 percent of Japanese,

Table 1.4 Selected Characteristics of Asian American Children Aged 18–24 by National Origin*

	Chinese	Filipino	Japanese	Indian	Korean	Vietnamese	Other Southeast Asian
Gender							
Female (%)	50.3	49.6	50.3	48.0	51.7	44.3	50.3
Marital status							
Currently married (%)	7.5	13.6	7.3	17.3	9.9	10.1	25.2
Generation							
Second or later generation (%)	37.2	49.7	71.3	30.8	33.2	7.3	2.6
1.5 Generation (%)	23.4	19.0	3.2	22.6	33.3	47.0	46.2
First Generation (%)	39.4	31.3	25.5	46.6	33.5	45.7	51.2
Language use (aged 5 and over)							
English monolingual (%)	19.1	45.7	63.7	25.5	26.4	8.9	2.8
Fluent bilingual (%)	44.5	38.4	16.0	55.5	45.0	42.4	38.7
Limited bilingual (%)	26.4	13.2	11.5	14.1	18.0	33.1	37.9
No English (%)	10.0	2.7	8.8	4.9	10.6	15.6	20.6
Non-English spoken at home (%)	80.9	54.3	36.3	74.5	93.7	91.1	97.2
Living in linguistic isolation (%)	25.7	5.5	10.3	9.7	18.8	32.5	45.7
Household characteristics							
Married-couple household (%)	55.2	62.6	46.2	59.9	57.1	54.7	69.8
Non-family household (%)	28.3	18.1	40.5	28.1	27.9	16.1	5.7
Average number of persons in household	3.4	4.0	2.3	3.2	3.0	4.4	5.7
Residence in California State (%)	44.9	52.5	38.5	21.1	34.6	46.1	43.2
Family economic status							
Living below poverty level (%)	21.9	5.1	4.4	8.3	10.4	3.2	51.9
Median household income (in 1989 $)	$30,360	$48,855	$37,739	$35,800	$30,050	$32,400	$25,505
Per capita income (in 1989 $)	$11,403	$12,951	$16,182	$13,350	$12,397	$8,856	$5,702
Home ownership (%)	53.5	59.3	56.9	52.1	50.0	44.3	28.1
Schooling							
College enrollment (%)	47.8	35.6	48.9	47.9	42.6	36.9	19.2
High school dropout** (%)	5.4	8.1	3.4	6.1	4.4	13.1	23.7
Labor force participation							
In labor force (%)	54.0	71.8	58.1	57.7	51.5	56.2	51.6
In managerial/professional occupations							
Male	19.4	9.8	16.2	23.5	14.4	9.5	5.3
Female	22.4	13.6	18.6	19.7	15.7	13.7	8.6
Total N	8,726	8,080	3,814	4,030	4,343	4,271	2,222

* Including all young adults aged 18-24. Percentages were unweighted.
** Among those aged 18 and 24 who were not currently enrolled in school and did not have high school diplomas.

confirming the fact that Vietnamese and other Southeast Asians are the newest arrivals, while Japanese are a much more established group. The 1.5 generation and the first generation are both well represented for all groups, except for the Japanese.[10]

With regard to language ability, fluent bilinguals represent the modal category for all groups except for the Japanese. Again, the two refugee groups appear to be more disadvantaged than others since they show the highest percentages in the limited-bilingual and no-English categories. Parental native language is still the dominant language spoken at home for this age cohort except for the Japanese. However, compared to the child population, young adults are much less likely to live in linguistically isolated environments, providing some indication of residential mobility and linguistic assimilation.

Although young adults also concentrate in California, the family situation for this age cohort is quite different from that of the younger cohort. Most notably, young adults are less likely than children to live in married-couple families and more likely to live in nonfamily households (living alone or with other unrelated individuals). Household size is also smaller for this age cohort than for the younger cohort. The family economic status of the young adults appears to be more disadvantaged than that of the younger cohort, as indicated in higher poverty rates, lower median household income and per capita income, and lower rates of homeownership for all national-origin groups. However, these indicators point to the opposite directions for the two refugee groups, demonstrating that young adults among the Vietnamese and other Southeast Asians are relatively better off than their counterparts in the younger age cohort.

Like the younger cohort, young adults are doing relative well in school. Except for the two refugee groups, they attend college in disproportionate numbers and show fairly low rates of dropping out of high school. However, the dropout rates for the Vietnamese (13 percent) and other Southeast Asians (24 percent) are significantly higher. Across national-origin groups, labor force participation rates among young adults are relatively low, except for the Filipinos.[11] While rates of labor force participation may be relatively low, they suggest that a sizable number of these young adults may still be in college. In fact, as shown in Table 1.4, 36 to 49 percent of these young people are enrolled in college, except for other Southeast Asians whose college attendance rate is extremely low.[12]

With regard to occupational attainment, young Asian American workers appear to encounter some obstacles. Despite their unusually high educational attainment, both young men and women are underrepresented in managerial and professional occupations, compared with 25 percent for men and 28 percent for women in the general American labor force. Whether this gap is due to a lack of work experience, discrimination in the labor market, or some other factors is an important area of research that deserves further investigation.

What Contributes to Success or Failure?

Educational success is an important prerequisite to occupational achievement in adulthood, though not a guarantee of it. In today's labor market, a high school diploma can barely secure a job that pays a decent family wage, and those without a diploma face even more limited prospects. Thus, high school dropout rates are reliable indicators for one's life chances because they have serious consequences for the labor market prospects of today's younger generation. Existing research has shown that the length of U.S. residence indicated by immigrant generations, parental native language usage, family economic status, and family structure are among some of the most significant determinants of school adaptation among the children of immigrants (Portes and Rumbaut, 1996, 2001). We have seen that dropout rates vary across different groups of Asian American adolescents despite their generally high levels of educational achievement. However, a closer examination of the census data for the 1990s reveals some troubling findings that deserve attention.

First, there is a significant generational effect; the longer the time in the United States, the lower the risk of dropping out of school. The Koreans are an exception: first-generation Koreans fare significantly better than the 1.5 or later generations with regard to schooling. Second, there is a significant language effect; that is, adolescents who speak no English or who are limited bilinguals (lack proficiency in either English or parental native language) are at a higher risk of dropping out of school. However, fluent bilinguals fare better than English monolinguals, suggesting that bilingualism holds advantages. Third, poverty increases the risk of dropping out of school among Filipinos, Indians, Vietnamese, and other Southeast Asians but does not similarly affect Chinese, Japanese, and Koreans. Finally, living in single-parent families significantly increases the probability of dropping out of high school among the Filipinos, and to a lesser extent among Indians and Koreans, but does not have the same effect on Chinese, Japanese, Vietnamese, and other Southeast Asians.

College attendance is another important indicator of future success, since many well-paying jobs require an education far beyond high school. Except for other Southeast Asians, Asian American young adults seem to follow the normative path to social mobility taken by other Americans— attending college. These young people attend college at a rate comparable to, and in some cases higher than, the same age cohort in the general U.S. population. Again, we observe mixed results with respect to the effects of generation, language, family economic status, and family structure on college attendance. For most groups, members of the second or later generation attend college in larger proportions than their first-generation coethnic counterparts. Among Japanese, however, the college attendance rate of the second or later generation was more than 10 percentage points *lower* than that of the first generation, a phenomenon that may be overshadowed by an unusually high proportion of foreign rather than immigrant students among first-generation Japanese. With respect to language, the general pattern indicates that fluent bilinguals show the highest rate of college attendance rates. This is the case for all Asian ethnic groups except for Filipinos. Again family economic status and family structure do not appear to affect college attendance for Asian American young adults of any national-origin group.

Overall, the lack of significant effects of some of the key predictors, which are generally believed to influence immigrant schooling, indicates that immigrant status, language, and class factors alone cannot explain the variance in high school dropout rates across national-origin groups. Something else is going on that may be linked to the neighborhoods, or ethnic communities, in which these young people live. For example, the strong effect of fluent bilingualism may link immigrant children to their family and the ethnic community. Current research shows that bilingualism can facilitate constructive communication between children and parents in immigrant families, and can help immigrant children tap into social capital resources generated in interlocking social relations in ethnic communities (Bankston and Zhou, 1995). These resources, in turn, can be used to compensate for the disadvantages associated with immigrant status, language difficulties, and low socioeconomic status (Gibson, 1989; Zhou and Bankston, 1998). Unfortunately, census data do not provide information about the norms, values, and patterns of social relations of ethnic groups. Therefore, it is necessary to look more closely at specific groups with other sources of data, especially qualitative field research.

In summary, compared with the general U.S. population, Asian American children tend to do better in school regardless of their immigrant status, language usage, and family situation. Their academic achievement appears to carry them beyond secondary education and enables them to gain entry into college in large numbers. Indeed, the nation's best public high schools, colleges, and universities have seen rapid increases in the Asian American enrollment in their freshman classes. The current situation of this coming-of-age generation seems to reinforce the image of Asian American youth as the model minority.

A simple pass of the census data, however, shows clear inconsistencies with this portrait, reminding us that "Asian" is a heterogeneous category that includes diverse national-origin groups. For instance, while Chinese, Japanese, Indians, and Koreans show lower than average high school dropout rates, Southeast Asians are dropping out in disproportionate numbers. Second, some key factors, which are usually considered to be determinants of school performance for children, such as length of U.S. residence since immigration, language usage, and family's socioeconomic status, have different effects across groups, suggesting possible interactions between these key factors and group characteristics. Third, despite high levels of educational achievement, young Asian American workers are confronting barriers in the labor market. It is not clear whether education alone can translate into proportionate occupational returns. It appears that Asian Americans must overeducate themselves to gain entry into the labor market, and that even a good education may not necessarily guarantee comparable occupational achievement.

CONCLUSION

The demographic profile of Asian American children and young adults is designed to provide some background information on which we can come to understand the processes of Asian American youth culture, identity, and ethnicity. Two important facts about Asian American youth stand out. First and foremost, the majority of Asian American youth belongs to the 1.5 and second generations, growing up in immigrant families, and are just coming of age at the turn of the twenty-first century. Second, like their parental generation, Asian American youth are vastly diverse in national origins, socioeconomic status, and settlement patterns.

The diversity in national origins, coupled with the intimate association with immigrants or, for some, with a homeland, suggests that the processes through which U.S.-born or U.S.-raised Asian American youth establish themselves in American society must be vastly different. The diverse socioeconomic backgrounds among the 1.5 and second generations suggests that pathways to social mobility will not take on a straight line or be unidirectional. Although many children of immigrants may continue the traditional bottom-up route to social mobility, a significant number will bypass the bottom starting line and move directly into mainstream American society, and still a sizable number will be trapped in poverty with dim prospects for upward mobility. In addition, the coming-of-age generation will no doubt display enormously different worldviews, political orientations, cultural expressions, and behavioral practices.

The residential settlement patterns among Asian American youth are also diverse. The rapid suburbanization of some Asian American families and the settlement of others in inner-city ghettos suggest a duality in patterns of integration. For those who reside in suburban communities, many Asian American children grow up speaking only English and attend schools with predominantly white peers. But owing to the development of "ethnoburbs"—suburban ethnic communities—a large number of middle-class children attend Asian or other nonwhite dominant schools, become fluent bilinguals, and constantly interact with things "Asian" or distinctly ethnic, including food, music, and customs.[13] In contrast, those who reside in inner-city underprivileged neighborhoods are even more likely than in the past to come into contact with native groups who are trapped in the underclass or with other nonwhite immigrant groups. Along with their low-income, minority peers, these Asian American youth may adopt an oppositional stance, resist assimilation into the mainstream, and consequently face greater risks of downward mobility.

Perhaps most importantly, the culture and society in which today's Asian American youth grow up are more open than ever before and certainly more tolerant of cultural diversity than a century ago. In particular, in the area of education, opportunities have become increasingly available for Asian Americans and other minorities. Many Asian Americans have indeed taken advantage of these opportunities, gaining entrance to the nation's most prestigious colleges and universities, despite a prevailing anti-intellectual streak and growing "oppositional culture" among American youth. Although Asian American youth are successfully integrating into their host society, because of the continuously high volume of immigration and the globalized economic and geopolitical relations between the United States and Asian countries, U.S.-born and U.S.-raised Asians must still battle the stereotypes of "forever foreigners" or enemy suspects. These are the same stereotypes experienced by Japanese Americans during World War II, the Chinese during the 1950s, and, most recently, South Asians after September 11. This new paradoxical context defines the world that confronts young Asian Americans today. That encounter is likely to involve one of two scenarios: the child either succeeds in school and moves ahead, or falls behind the modest, often low status of the parents' generation. Herbert Gans (1992) refers to the second scenario as "second-generation decline."

Understanding the diverse experiences of Asian American youth promises to shed light on the conditions that influence the prospects for the much larger second-generation population in the United States. In the long journey to becoming American, the progress of immigrants depends not only on intragroup characteristics but also heavily on the social structure of the host society and that of the immigrant group. In contrast to their immigrant parents, Asian American children—like all other immigrant children in America—are unlikely to think of their parents' home country as a place to which they might return, nor will they use it as a point of reference by which to assess their progress in the new land. Rather, their expectations will be governed by the same standards to which other Americans aspire, and it is by those standards that young Asian Americans will judge themselves and be judged by others. While these young people launch a quest for social and economic progress to take them well beyond the lower levels of their immigrant parents, it is not clear whether they will succeed in their quest. In the answer to that question lies the future of Asian America, and it is also the issue with which future research should be concerned.

Notes

1. Based on estimates from the 1998–2002 Current Population Survey of the U.S. Bureau of the Census.
2. As of 1990, the third generation (the children of U.S.-born parentage) represented barely 10 percent of the Asian American child population. Japanese American children were an exception: 54.3 percent of them are members of the third or higher generation, compared with 9.2 percent of Chinese, 10.7 percent of Filipinos, 1.2 percent of Indians, 2.8 percent of Koreans, 1.2 percent of Vietnamese, and 5.3 percent of other Asians.
3. As of 1930, 41 percent of Chinese were U.S. born, but 20 percent were under 14 years of age.
4. Not including immigrants from Iran, Israel, and Turkey.
5. As detailed in the 1990 Census, more than 60 percent of immigrants (aged 25 years or older) from India and Taiwan reported having attained college degrees, three times the proportion of average Americans; but less than 5 percent of those from Cambodia and Laos so reported. Among the employed workers (aged 16 years or older), about 45 percent of immigrants from India and Taiwan had managerial or professional occupations, more than twice the proportion of average American workers; but less than 5 percent of those from Laos and only about 10 percent of those from Cambodia so reported. Furthermore, immigrants from India, the Philippines, and Taiwan reported a median household income of about or above $45,000, compared to $30,000 for average American households; those from Cambodia and highland Laos (where Hmong live) reported a median household income below $20,000. Poverty rates for Asian immigrants ranged from a low of 7 percent for Filipinos, Indians, and Japanese to a high of over 60 percent for Hmong and 42 percent for Cambodians, compared to about 10 percent for average American families.
6. This section is based primarily on my previously published work (see Zhou, 1999). The descriptive statistics are derived from the the the 5-percent Public Use Microdata Sample (PUMS) of the 1990 U.S. Census. The sample for the 0–17 cohort was limited to children who were living with their parents or guardians in family households. The high school dropout rates in this analysis are therefore somewhat more conservative than those found in the full U.S. census.
7. I classify three generational categories as follows: the second generation or second plus generation, which includes all U.S. born as well as the foreign born arriving in the United States before age 5; the 1.5 generation, which includes all the foreign born arriving in the United States between 6 and 12 years of age; and the first generation, which includes all foreign-born adolescents arriving in the United States after their thirteenth birthdays. Foreign-born children who arrived at very young ages are included in the second generation because these children share many linguistic, cultural, and developmental experiences similar to the U.S. born. The foreign-born proportion of this age cohort was 30 percent for the Chinese, 29 percent for the Filipinos, 24 percent for the Japanese, 33 percent for the Indians, 56 percent for the Koreans, 48 percent for the Vietnamese, and 55 percent for other Southeast Asians.
8. In the United States, median family income was $30,000 in 1989 dollars, and the home-ownership rate was 64 percent in 1990.

9. The second generation is broadly defined to include the foreign born who arrived before age 5.
10. The foreign-born proportion of this young adult age cohort was 69 percent for the Chinese, 64 percent for the Filipinos, 34 percent for the Japanese, 83 percent for the Indians, 86 percent for the Koreans, 97 percent for the Vietnamese, and 99 percent for other Southeast Asians.
11. This is true for both men and women. The rates for all working-aged Americans 16 and over were 74 percent for men and 57 percent for women.
12. Among those who were in the labor force, levels of educational attainment are even higher, ranging from a high of 68 percent for Indian men to a low of 30 percent for other Southeast Asian men, and from a high of 72 percent for Japanese women to a low of 31 percent for other Southeast Asian women, compared with 45 percent for all Americans aged 16 and over.
13. "Ethnoburb" is a term developed by Wei Li (1988) to refer to suburban ethnic clustering of diverse groups in which no single racial ethnic group dominates. Monterey Park in Los Angeles is a typical ethnoburb.

CHAPTER 3

Intermarriage and Multiracial Identification:

The Asian American Experience and Implications for Changing Color Lines[1]

Jennifer Lee and Frank D. Bean

The 2000 U.S. Census was the first census that allowed Americans to select "one or more races" to indicate their racial identification, reflecting the view that race is no longer conceived of as a bounded category. In 2000, 6.8 million people, or 2.4 percent of the U.S. population (i.e., one in every forty Americans), identified themselves as multiracial. Although one in forty may not appear to be a substantial fraction, by the year 2050, this ratio could soar to one in five (Farley, 2001; Smith and Edmonston, 1997). Asian Americans, however, have a much higher rate of multiracial identification compared to other groups, with 12.4 percent claiming a multiracial background, a figure that is rapidly rising. By the year 2050, sociologists project that 35 percent of Asian Americans could claim a multiracial background (Smith and Edmonston, 1997). If this projection proves accurate, more than one in every three Asian Americans could claim a multiracial background in just a few decades. This level of substantial growth in the Asian multiracial population could mostly result from today's high rates of Asian intermarriage, which at present involve more than one out of every four Asians, and more than one out of every two native born Asians, being married to someone of a different race, most commonly someone white.

Coinciding with the rise in intermarriage has been the growth of a new immigrant stream from Latin America and Asia (see Chapter 1). Today, immigrants and their children total almost 66 million persons and account for approximately 23 percent of the U.S. population. The increase in immigration from non-European countries over the past three and half decades has converted the United States from a largely white and black society into one that is composed of several racial and ethnic groups (Bean and Stevens, 2003; Waldinger and Lee, 2001). Trends in intermarriage and immigration over the past 35 years, along with the landmark change in thTabe census allowing Americans to report themselves as belonging to more than one racial group, reflect a significant weakening of the previously strong boundaries among racial groups (Lee and Bean, 2003). Combining data from the U.S. Census and Current Population Surveys, we examine the patterns of intermarriage, multiracial identification, and immigration and explore the implications of these findings for the future of Asian American identities and America's changing color lines.

THE RISE OF INTERMARRIAGE

The growth of the multiracial population is a result both of the rise in intermarriage between whites and nonwhites and of peoples' increased willingness to report their multiracial backgrounds. Intermarriage between whites and nonwhites has risen dramatically since the 1967 Supreme Court ruling of *Loving v. Commonwealth of Virginia,* which overturned state laws prohibiting interracial marriage and sex. As recently as 1967, interracial marriage was illegal in 16 states, but today about 13 percent of American marriages involve partners of different races. Within a 30-year period alone between 1960 and 1990, the rate of intermarriage between whites and nonwhites increased tenfold, from 150,000 in 1960 to 1.6 million in 1990 (Jacoby, 2001; Waters, 1999). If we go back even further to 1880, the rates of intermarriage among Asians and Latinos in this country were close to zero, but now, more than a quarter of all Asians and Latinos marry someone of a different racial background, mostly whites. These intermarriage rates are even higher among younger, native-born Asians and Latinos, and are likely to increase in future generations.

The change in intermarriage rates is significant because sociologists conceive of intermarriage between whites and nonwhites as a measure of decreasing social distance between groups, declining racial prejudice, and changing racial boundaries (Davis, 1941; Gilbertson et al., 1996; Gordon, 1964; Kalmijn, 1993; Lee and Fernandez, 1998; Lieberson and Waters, 1988; Merton, 1941). Moreover, the differences in the intermarriage rates between whites and various nonwhite groups provide some indication of the groups' social proximity to whites. In addition, these differences provide a measure of where the white-nonwhite boundary is breaking down most rapidly.

As Table 3.1 shows, more than one-quarter of all married Asians and Latinos—30.9 and 29.3 percent, respectively—have a partner of different racial background.[2] An even more striking finding is that two-thirds of young, native-born Asians and two-fifths of young, native-born Latinos

Table 3.1 Rates of Exogamy among Marriages Containing at Least One Member of the Racial/Ethnic Group in the United States, 1990 and 2000

United States	Total	White	Black	Asian	Latino	Other
1990	4.4	4.7	8.4	31.5	32.5	74.8
2000	6.4	7.0	12.6	30.9	29.3	70.7

Source: IPUMS, 2003

marry someone of a different race, and the majority of them marry whites (Qian, 1997). The rate of intermarriage among Asians and Latinos is yet more remarkable when we compare them to the intermarriage rate of blacks; only 12.6 percent of married blacks have a spouse of a different race. Hence, although more than one out of every four married Asians and Latinos has a partner of a different racial background, the comparable figure for blacks is only one in eight.

Not only is intermarriage more common among Asians and Latinos than among blacks, but the rate at which Asians intermarry with whites is also much higher. Among intermarried Asians, 86.8 percent marry whites, 7.6 percent marry Hispanics, and 4.8 percent marry blacks. Among intermarried Latinos, 90.0 percent marry whites, 5.3 percent blacks, and 3.0 percent Asians. Intermarried blacks are also more likely to marry whites, at 69.1 percent, but this figure is far lower than the figures for intermarried Asians and Latinos. Nearly one-fifth of intermarried blacks, or 20.7 percent, marry Hispanics, and 7.2 percent marry Asians. Hence, both Asians and Latinos are considerably more likely to marry whites as are blacks.

THE MULTIRACIAL MOVEMENT

The rise in intermarriage marriage over the past few decades has resulted in the growth of the multiracial population in the United States. This population became highly visible especially when, for the first time in the nation's history, the 2000 Census allowed Americans to select "one or more races" to indicate their racial identification. The way the U.S. Census measures racial identification, brought about by a small but highly influential multiracial movement, provides a new reflection of changing racial boundaries (DaCosta, 2000; Farley, 2001; Hirschman et al., 2000; Waters, 2000; Williams, 2001).

The multiracial movement was composed most prominently of advocates from groups such as the Association for Multiethnic Americans (AMEA) and Project RACE (Reclassify All Children Equally). In 1993, these groups criticized the standards of the Office of Management and Budget's (OMB) Statistical Policy Directive Number 15, which asks individuals to mark their "race" on the census. Advocates argued that it was an affront to force them and/or their children into a monoracial category. They elaborated that forced monoracial identification is not only inaccurate because it denies the existence of interracial marriages but also ultimately discriminatory.

A year later, in 1994, the OMB declared that racial categories in Statistical Policy Directive Number 15 were of decreasing value and so the agency considered an alternate strategy—the option to identify with as many races as respondents wished. Hence, the racial options on the 2000 Census included "White," "Black," "Asian," "Native Hawaiian or Other Pacific Islander," "American Indian and Alaska Native," and "Other." While "Latino" or "Hispanic" was not a racial category on the 2000 Census, OMB's directive mandated two distinct questions regarding a person's racial/ethnic background: one about race and a second about whether a person is "Spanish/Hispanic/Latino." Since someone who self-designates as "Spanish/Hispanic/Latino" can be of any race, the census asks both questions in order to identify the Latino population in the United States.

Although the spokespeople for the multiracial movement wanted a separate "multiracial" category and were not entirely satisfied with this option, they conceded that it was an improvement over forced monoracial identification. On October 30, 1997, OMB announced its final decision that, starting with the 2000 Census and extending to all federal data systems by the year 2003, all persons would have the option to identify with two or more races.

AMERICA'S MULTIRACIAL POPULATION

As noted above, 2.4 percent of the U.S. population identified itself as multiracial in 2000. Although this figure may not appear large, a recent National Academy of Science study noted that, because of high levels of intermarriage, the multiracial population could rise to 21 percent by the year 2050, with as many as 35 percent of Asians and 45 percent of Hispanics possibly claiming a multiracial background (Smith and Edmonston, 1997). Moreover, the multiracial population is young and twice as likely as other groups to be under the age of 18, demonstrating that the multiracial population is likely to continue to grow in future years. Of the multiracial population, 93 percent reported exactly two races, 6 percent reported three races, and only 1 percent reported four or more races.

Although most individuals who reported a multiracial identification reported only two races, multiracially identified individuals are not evenly distributed across all racial groups. As Table 3.2 illustrates, the groups

Table 3.2 Multiracial Identification by Census Racial Categories

	Racial Identification[2] (millions)	Multiracial Identification[1] (millions)	Percent Multiracial
White	216.5	5.1	2.3
Black	36.2	1.5	4.2
Asian	11.7	1.4	12.4
Other	18.4	3.0	16.4
American Indian and Alaska Native	3.9	1.4	36.4
Native Hawaiian or Other Pacific Islander	0.7	0.3	44.8

Source: U.S. Census 2000.
[1]Racial/ethnic group totals do not sum to the total U.S. population because multiracial persons are counted here in more than one group.
[2]Multiracial persons are counted for each race category mentioned.

with a high percentage of multiracial persons as a percentage of the total group include "Native Hawaiian or Other Pacific Islander (45 percent)," "American Indian and Alaska Native (36 percent)," "Other (16 percent)," and "Asian (12 percent)." The groups with the lowest proportion of persons who claim a multiracial background are "Whites" and "Blacks." However, because whites account for 77 percent of the total U.S. population, most individuals who report a multiracial identity also claim a white background. More specifically, the 5.1 million whites who claim a multiracial background account for only 2.3 percent of the total white population. Like whites, the proportion of blacks who claim a multiracial background is also quite small, accounting for only 4.2 percent of the total black population.

These figures stand in sharp contrast to those among American Indian/Alaska Natives and Native Hawaiian or Other Pacific Islanders who have the highest percentage of multiracials as a proportion of their populations at 36.4 and 44.8 percent, respectively. Asians and Latinos are in between with significantly higher rates of multiracial reporting than blacks and whites at 12.4 and 16.4 percent, respectively. In sum, when we compare Asians and Latinos to whites and blacks, we see that Asians have much higher rates of multiracial reporting as a total percentage of their populations compared to Latinos.

If we examine the rates of black–white, Asian–white, and Latino–white multiracial combinations as a percentage of the total black, Asian, and Latino populations, we find these figures equal 1.9, 7.0, and 4.9 percent, respectively. That is, among Asians, the Asian-white multiracial combination is about *three-and-a-half times* more likely to occur, and among Latinos, the Latino-white combination is *more than two-and-a-half times* more likely to occur, as the black-white combination among blacks. Why black-white multiracials are far less likely to identify multiracially compared to their Asian-white and Latino-white counterparts is especially puzzling when we consider that the U.S. Census Bureau estimates that at least three-quarters of the black population in the United States is ancestrally multiracial (Spencer, 1997). In other words, while at least 75 percent of black Americans have some white ancestry and thus could claim a multiracial identity on this basis, just over 4 percent choose to do so.

The tendency of black Americans not to report multiracial identifications undoubtedly derives from the legacy of slavery, including lasting discrimination and the legal and *de facto* invocation of the "one-drop rule" of hypodescent, by which all persons with any trace of black ancestry were labeled racially black. As Davis (1991) argues, the one-drop rule was once used to justify slavery and was later used to support Jim Crow segregation. The one-drop rule applies in no other country and for no other racial or ethnic group, thereby limiting the identity choices and options for multiracial blacks only. For example, the one-drop rule has not been similarly imposed on Asians, Latinos, or American Indians. Recent sociological studies reveal that about 50 percent of American Indian/white and Asian/white intermarried couples report a white racial identity for their children (Eschbach, 1995; Saenz et al., 1995; Xie and Goyette, 1997). In a study of multiracial Hispanic students, the authors find that only 44 percent choose a Hispanic identity (Stephan and Stephan, 1989). Hence, unlike the traditional "one-drop rule" that has historically imposed a black racial identity on black Americans, multiracial Asians, Latinos, and American Indians appear to have much more leeway to choose among different racial options, including multiracial and white identities. Historically, multiracial blacks were denied similar options, a constraint that seems to have lasting consequences, even today.

In addition, because a significant proportion of Latinos and Asians in the United States are either immigrants or the children of immigrants, their understanding of race, racial boundaries, and the black-white color divide is shaped by a different set of circumstances from those of African Americans. Most importantly, what sets Latinos and Asians apart from African Americans is that their experiences are not rooted in the same historical legacy of slavery with its systematic and persistent patterns of legal and institutional discrimination and inequality by which the tenacious black-white divide was born and cemented. The unique history and experience of black Americans in this country make the black-white racial gap qualitatively and quantitatively different from the Latino-white or Asian-white racial divides. For these reasons, racial/ethnic boundaries appear more fluid for the newest immigrants than for native-born blacks, providing multiracial Asians and Latinos more racial options than their multiracial black counterparts.

We also need to consider that race is a social and cultural construction rather than a biological category, which means that race is not primordial, rooted in biology, or fixed. Social scientists have even documented the processes by which racial categories have undergone reconceptualization throughout our nation's history (Gans, 1999; Gerstle, 1999; Omi and Winant, 1994; Waters, 1990, 1999). For instance, when the Irish, Italians, and Jews first arrived in the United States in the nineteenth century, they were considered racially distinct from and inferior to Anglo-Americans. In essence, they were *not* considered white. However, they successfully achieved whiteness by deliberately and forcefully distinguishing themselves from African Americans (Alba, 1985, 1990; Brodkin, 1998; Foner, 2000; Ignatiev, 1995; Roediger, 1991). Today, few would contest the claim that Irish, Italians, and Jews are white.

Race and racial boundaries have changed for other groups as well, including Asians. For example, the Chinese in Mississippi changed their racial status from almost black to almost white. Loewen (1988) details how the Mississippi Chinese achieved near-white status by attaining economic parity with whites, emulating their cultural and social practices, and distancing themselves from African Americans and the Chinese who married blacks. The change in racial classification among ethnic groups from nonwhite to white or almost white illustrates that race is a social rather than biological category that has expanded over time to incorporate new immigrant groups. As the historian Gary Gerstle (1999: 289) explains, whiteness as a category "has survived by stretching its boundaries to include Americans—the Irish, eastern and southern Europeans—who had been deemed nonwhite. Contemporary evidence suggests that the boundaries are again being stretched as Latinos and Asians pursue whiteness much as the Irish, Italians, and Poles did before them."

Given the change in racial boundaries over time, it is likely that the boundaries may stretch once again to include newer groups. For instance, some sociologists argue that Asians are the next in line to become white, and whether this hypothesis is correct will depend on a number of factors such as their rate of intermarriage, multiracial identification, continued immigration from Asia, and economic and political incorporation. Considering that more than half of native born Asians intermarry today and that the children of these unions have the option to identify as "white," Asians may indeed be on the path to whiteness. That many Asian ethnic groups have median household incomes above the national average also bodes favorably for this alternative. However, continued immigration from Asia and the racial stereotypes they face as "forever foreign" ensure that this process will be neither inevitable nor smooth. Moreover, as Zhou's chapter in this volume shows, "Asian" is a vastly heterogeneous category that masks differences in ethnicity and social and economic status. Hence, whether Asians—or at least some Asian ethnic groups—are the next in line to become white still remains to be seen.

THE GEOGRAPHY OF THE MULTIRACIAL IDENTITIES

Although differences in multiracial reporting across racial groups are readily apparent, it is also noteworthy that rates of multiracial identification are not uniform across the country. For instance, 40 percent of all those who report a multiracial identification reside in the West, a region of the country that has demonstrated substantially more tolerance for racial/ethnic diversity than other parts of the country (Baldassare, 2000; Godfrey, 1988). As Table 3.3 indicates, California leads as the state with the highest number of multiracial persons and is the only state with a multiracial population that exceeds one million. The multiracial population accounts for 4.7 percent of California's population, or one in every twenty-one Californians, about twice the national average. Like the figures for the nation as a whole, the multiracial population in California is young. As of 2000, 7.3 percent of Californians under the age of 18 were identified as multiracial. California's multiracial population appears to be growing rapidly, although we now have only indirect evidence of this growth. To help put this change into perspective, the number of multiracial children born each year in California already exceeds the number of black children born.

Like California, other states with high immigrant populations, and consequently high levels of racial/ethnic diversity, evince larger multiracial populations. In fact, 64 percent, or nearly two-thirds of those who are multiracially identified, reside in just ten states—California, New York, Texas, Florida, Hawaii, Illinois, New Jersey, Washington, Michigan, and Ohio—all of which have relatively high immigrant populations. In essence, states that have higher levels of racial/ethnic diversity (as reflected in the percentage of the population that is *not* non-Hispanic white or non-Hispanic black), boast much larger multiracial populations than states that are less racially diverse. We refer to these states as the country's "new diversity states."

On the opposite end of the diversity spectrum are states like West Virginia and Maine that have low racial minority populations, and thereby exhibit very low levels of multiracial reporting. States such as Mississippi, Alabama, South Carolina, and Louisiana, however, have relatively large black populations yet evince low levels of multiracial reporting. In these southern states, the traditional dividing line between blacks and whites and the historically constraining "one-drop rule" of hypodescent appear to hinder multiracial identification, leading persons

Table 3.3 State Summaries: Most and Least Multiracial States

Rank	State	Number of Multiracial Persons	Multiracial Population (percent)
1	Hawaii	259,343	21.4
2	Alaska	34,146	5.4
3	California	1,607,646	4.7
4	Oklahoma	155,985	4.5
5	Nevada	76,428	3.8
6	New Mexico	66,327	3.6
7	Washington	213,519	3.6
8	New York	590,182	3.1
9	Oregon	104,745	3.1
10	Arizona	146,526	2.9
.			
.			
.			
42	Tennessee	63,109	1.1
43	Iowa	31,778	1.1
44	Louisiana	48,265	1.1
45	New Hampshire	13,214	1.1
46	Kentucky	42,443	1.1
47	South Carolina	39,950	1.0
48	Alabama	44,179	1.0
49	Maine	12,647	1.0
50	West Virginia	15,788	0.9
51	Mississippi	20,021	0.7

Source: U.S. Census 2000

* Percent not non-Hispanic White or non-Hispanic Black.

to identify monoracially as either white or black rather than adopting a multiracial identity (Davis, 1991; Farley, 2001; Lee and Bean 2004).

The geography of multiracial reporting clearly indicates that the rate of multiracial identification varies widely across the country, with the highest levels in states that exhibit the greatest racial/ethnic diversity brought about by the arrival of new immigrants to these areas. Hence, although national patterns in intermarriage and multiracial identification indicate a loosening of racial boundaries, particularly for Asians and Latinos, these shifts appear to be taking place more rapidly in certain parts of the country. Areas of the country that have lower levels of immigration and consequently less racial/ethnic diversity demonstrate the tenacity of the black-white divide. Hence, although some parts of the country like the West may exhibit the softening of racial/ethnic boundaries, especially between blacks and nonblacks, other areas such as the South prove that the traditional black-white color line endures.

THE EMERGENCE OF A BLACK/NONBLACK DIVIDE

The Census Bureau's decision to allow Americans to "mark one or more races" to identify themselves is a landmark change in the way the U.S. government collects data on race, reflecting the growth of intermarriages and multiracial births. Perhaps even more importantly, it gives official status and recognition to persons who see their backgrounds as having involved racial mixing—an acknowledgment that speaks volumes about how far the country has come since the days when the one-drop rule enjoyed legal legitimacy. Moreover, such changes may mean that old racial divides are beginning to fade and race may no longer be conceived as rigidly as it was in the past.

What do current trends and patterns in immigration, intermarriage, and multiracial identification tell us about the changing nature of race and racial divides? It appears that increases in intermarriage and the growth of the multiracial population reflect a blending of races and the shifting of color lines. Because intermarriage and multiracial identification indicate a reduction in social distance and racial prejudice, these phenomena provide evidence of loosening racial boundaries. At first glance, these patterns offer an optimistic portrait, especially considering that interracial marriage was illegal in 16 states as recently as 1967, and today, about 13 percent of American marriages involve persons from different racial backgrounds. Judging from the past, it appears that as a nation, we have come a long way.

Upon closer examination, however, we find that patterns of intermarriage and multiracial identification are not equally distributed across all racial/ethnic groups. Not only are Latinos and Asians more likely to inter-marry than blacks, but they are also more likely to report a multiracial identification. In other words, of the three groups, blacks are the least likely to intermarry and the least likely to claim a multiracial identifica-tion. The different rates of Asian, Latino, and black intermarriage and multiracial reporting suggest that while racial boundaries may be fading, they are not eroding at the same pace for all groups.

The crucial consideration here is how we interpret the intermarriage and multiracial identification findings for Asians and Latinos. If we consider Asians and Latinos as racialized minorities (that is, as persons whose race or ethnicity constitutes a basis for substantial discrimination), and thus as persons falling closer to blacks than whites along some scale of social disad-vantage, the high levels of multiracial identification in these groups suggest that racial prejudice and boundaries might be fading for all nonwhite groups. In other words, if these groups are disadvantaged because of their race or ethnicity, but conditions appear to be improving for them, then this suggests the optimistic conclusion that conditions might be improving for all nonwhite groups. If, on the other hand, we consider Asians and Latinos as new immigrant groups whose disadvantage derives from their not yet having had time to join the economic mainstream, but who soon will, then their high levels of intermarriage and multiracial reporting signal that their experience may be different from that of blacks. Furthermore, it suggests that their situations do not necessarily mean that similar improve-ments can be expected among blacks.

This distinction is critical because it helps us to differentiate whether America's color lines are shifting for all racial/ethnic minorities, or whether they are fading mostly in the cases of nonblack immigrant groups. Based on the patterns of intermarriage and multiracial identification we have described, the color line appears to be less rigid for Asians and Latinos than for blacks. In their cases, Asians and Latinos have high rates of inter-marriage and multiracial reporting because they have not been treated like blacks to begin with and because the weakening of racial boundaries that has occurred has not been as fully extended to blacks. Although the color line may be shifting for blacks, this change is occurring more slowly, conse-quently leaving Asians and Latinos closer to whites than blacks are to whites. As a result, we may be witnessing the emergence of a black-nonblack divide that places Latinos and Asians closer to whites than to blacks. If much of America's racial history to date has revolved around who was white and who was not, it is critical that the next phase does not revolve around the issue of who is black and who is not.

The emergence of a black-nonblack divide in a context where diversity is increasing and racial/ethnic boundaries are diminishing represents a good news–bad news outcome for America. That a white-nonwhite color line does not seem to be emerging is the good news. But that newer nonwhite immigrant groups appear to be jumping ahead of African Americans in a hierarchy divided by race is the bad news. Based on immigration, intermarriage, and multiracial identification, it appears that Asians and Latinos are closer to whites than blacks are to whites and consequently may be participants in a new color line that continues to separate blacks from other groups. Thus, America's new color line may consist of a racial/ethnic divide that places many blacks in disadvantaged positions relatively similar to those perpetuated by the traditional black-white divide.

CONCLUSION

Over the past few decades, the rate of intermarriage between whites and nonwhites increased tenfold, and its increase went hand in hand with the growth in the multiracial population. Recognizing the growth of America's multiracial population, the 2000 U.S. Census allowed Americans the option to mark more than one race to identify themselves and their children. Coinciding with rising intermarriage between whites and nonwhites over the past 35 years was a new immigrant stream from Latin America and Asia, creating a nation that has moved from a largely black and white society to one that is more racially and ethnically diverse. Changes brought about by increasing immigration, intermarriage, and multiracial identification beg the question of how relevant the traditional black-white color line is for understanding today's racially diverse cast. If the black-white color line no longer characterizes America's multiethnic society, where will the line be drawn in the twenty-first century?

The trends in intermarriage and patterns of multiracial identification signal that the color line is shifting more readily to accommodate newer immigrant groups such as Latinos and Asians. And while the color line is also shifting for blacks, this shift is occurring much more slowly, demonstrating the tenacity of the black-white divide. Where do Asians and Latinos fit in this divide? At this time, the changing pace of the shifting color lines for these groups points to the emergence of a black-nonblack divide that places Asians and Latinos closer to whites than blacks are to whites. This change is most evident in areas with high concentrations of immigrants, high levels of racial/ethnic diversity, and high levels of multiracial reporting.

Notes

1. We would like to thank the Russell Sage Foundation and the Center for Immigration, Population and Public Policy at the University of California-Irvine for generous research support on which this chapter is based. This chapter was completed while Jennifer Lee was a fellow at the Center for Advanced Study in the Behavioral Sciences with financial support provided by the Willam and Flora Hewlett Foundation, Grant #2000–5633 and while Frank D. Bean was a Visiting Scholar at the Russell Sage Foundation. For invaluable research assistance, we thank Jeanne Batalova and Sabeen Sandhu.
2. For present purposes, we refer to Latinos as if they were an official "racial" group, although government data allows persons indicating that they are Latino to report themselves as belonging to any racial group.

PART II
Historical Patterns of Cultural Practices among Asian American Youth

CHAPTER **4**

Rizal Day Queen Contests, Filipino Nationalism, and Femininity[1]

Arleen de Vera

As night fell over San Francisco, the mood was joyous as friends, dressed in their best, gathered together on this Saturday night, December 28, 1929, and greeted one another in the lobby of the Native Sons Auditorium. While hundreds of Filipinos thronged about, above them elegant chandeliers glowed, catching the glints of crystal and marble, and the richness of velvet and evening dress. Suddenly an expectant hush fell over the crowd, and a thousand necks craned to see as a slight, pale young woman—a slip of a girl, resplendent in her tiara and Filipina finery—walked slowly through, then turned to face the crowd. Solemn, yet with face flushed and eyes sparkling, she took her vow, repeating the words uttered by San Francisco Mayor Rolph: "I promise to try to make everyone happy, my subjects and their friends, and to follow the example of her who bore before me this Great Crown. I swear to work for the cause of my country and my people."[2] As the echoes of her words died away, the crowd went wild. To the thunderous sound of applause and shouts and whistles, Estelita de la Peña was crowned "Miss Philippines," the 1929 Joint Pacific Coast Rizal Day Queen, to reign over the crowd.

This chapter examines the relationship between Rizal Day queen contests and nationalist and gendered discourses. Analyses of ethnic queen contests fall into two distinct groups. One group sees them as an expression of resistance against a society that devalues nondominant ideals of beauty and fashion (Lieu, 2000; Lim, 1998; Wu, 1997). The second argues that contests have no redeeming qualities and contends that they only replicate gender roles that enforce patriarchal domination, and in the process, naturalize power relations and constructs such as "race," "community," and "nation" (Banet-Weiser, 1999; Banner, 1983; Bonus, 2000; Cohen et al., 1996; Yung, 1995).

These views, however, overlook the contradictions and complexities of the contests. From the 1910s and into the period of Filipino exclusion, nationalists advertised the contests as a safe, respectable haven that allowed them to socialize with other Filipinos. They also utilized these events to portray Filipinos as unified, orderly, and capable of self-government; that is, they presented "the best" of the Filipino community before the American public and thereby achieved Philippine independence. Although nationalists insisted that these contests affirmed displays of an authentic, modern, Philippine national culture, their forms relied heavily on nostalgia and hybridity (Chatterjee, 1993; Lowe, 1996; Said, 1994). Furthermore, by commercializing the queen candidates through fundraising dances, nationalists undermined their own aims of female virtue, modesty, and "traditional" femininity, even while much of the funds went toward independence work and community activities (Ave, 1956). Most importantly, these events were opportunities for candidates to "contest" nationalist ideals of gender.

Queen contests imparted nationalist discourses of idealized femininity and self-restraint by combining performativity with visual culture. In making the queens figures of spectacle, nationalists forced comparisons between the queens' idealized Filipina femininity and those of everyday life. By promulgating these ideals of femininity and by promoting the queens as glamorous and yet properly "Filipina," these discourses amounted to a process of constructing gender identity, by which the queen candidates were observed and compared and were to be emulated by other young women and girls. This was how lessons of femininity were imparted—by intensifying the differences and allowing community members to become, as Barbara Kirshenblatt-Gimblett (1991) reminds us, spectators of themselves (Butler, 1990).

This process also had larger implications. In making the queens figures of spectacle, nationalists made visible the gap they saw between the idealized vision of what they aspired for the community and what the community actually was. By promoting queens as embodiments of Filipina "virtue," nationalists hoped to keep Filipina women in line and also reform Filipino men. This comparison, then, was also extended to Filipino men who, properly inspired by these virtuous women, would set themselves back onto the right path and lead a sober, orderly, and stable life—one in line with nationalist ideals. Queen contests were therefore part of a larger discursive strategy to fulfill nationalist fantasies of a unified community. These attempts at surveillance and discipline, however, were not entirely successful. Candidates critiqued aspects of dominant leadership, engaged in small acts of defiance or recalcitrance, expressed their own desires for self-fashioning and display, and used their physicality to put forth different styles of deportment (Blanc-Szanton, 1990; Butler, 1990; Foucault, 1981; Kirsheblatt-Gimblett, 1991; Parker et al., 1992). Their challenges remind us that women were not only products but also producers of signification.

To make the connections between gendered discourses, visual culture, and performativity, this chapter looks first at Rizal Day celebrations and their significance to the community. It then moves to an analysis of the queen contests and the ideals of femininity they promoted. The chapter ends with a discussion of the ways candidates became aware of and negotiated nationalist forms of discipline.

RIZAL, RIZAL DAY CELEBRATIONS, AND FILIPINOS IN THE UNITED STATES

Among Filipinos in the United States, Rizal Day was celebrated to honor the Philippines's national hero José Rizal. Rizal, a Spanish-Chinese-Filipino mestizo, was a medical doctor, social reformer, and author of two novels that critiqued Spanish colonial rule in the Philippines. Accused by Spanish authorities of inciting and initiating the Philippine Revolution against Spain, Rizal was executed on December 30, 1896. Later, with the transition to American colonial rule, the anniversary of his death was officially declared a holiday.

For Filipino migrants in the 1910s, Rizal Day celebrations were austere and somber affairs, featuring speeches on the then-current state of U.S.-Philippine relations and recitations of José Rizal's poem "My Last Farewell," followed by a formal dinner or refreshments. In keeping with the serious tone, local city officials and university administrators were invited as a way to develop ties with potential patrons. In organizing these events, nationalist leaders had two goals: to keep the issue of Philippine independence before the American public; and to further its cause by demonstrating the Filipinos' leadership and self-government capabilities. They pursued the second goal by displaying their level of unity, cooperation, and sense of order—the very qualities specified as the prerequisites to independence (Lawcock, 1975). For nationalists, Rizal Day was a patriotic reminder, a time to renew the bonds of community and demonstrate their state of progress.

By the 1920s, however, these simple Rizal Day celebrations gave way to more elaborate affairs. Although the speeches and recitations remained, the scope of events at the larger celebrations grew to include queen contests, banquets, and dancing. Usually, the formal speeches, recitations, and coronations were held in the evening at a hotel, while a parade kicked off festivities during the day.[3] Organizers of the Pacific Coast Joint Rizal Day celebrations also staged debates over the prospects and merits of independence and sponsored resolutions in its favor.[4]

In addition to these political aims, Rizal Day had other functions. At the celebrations, one could meet friends, exchange news, and socialize, without fear of discrimination or police reprisals. As one organizer recalled: "These social events were important to the Filipino Community, a necessity. . . . We weren't welcomed into many public places. . . . These were even more important for all these single men who were alone because there were hardly any women that came with them from the Philippines" (Cordova, 1983; Hemminger, 1980). Nationalists also saw them as a safe alternative to vice—activities for which Filipinos had been criticized—and as an opportunity to interact with the few available Filipina women.[5] Leaders therefore encouraged full participation and opened attendance to all. This policy proved fortuitous, as the funds raised were staggering. The winner of the 1929 Joint Pacific Coast Rizal Day queen contest brought in over $6,100 herself. The next year, the queen contest netted a total of $21,000.[6] Given the multiple social and political purposes, the Rizal Day events were wildly popular.

These changes were in line with changes in the community. The initial migrants to the United States were government students drawn mostly from the Tagalog and Visayan regions of the Philippines (Foronda, 1976). Called pensionados for the government moneys they received, the students were from elite backgrounds, educated, fluent in English, and sent to U.S. colleges and universities across the country (Chan, 1991; Cordova, 1989; Takaki, 1989). Other arrivals were former enlisted men with the Navy who had taken their discharges and remained in the United States (McWilliams, 1951; Takaki, 1998). Joining the few pensionados on the mainland in the 1920s were thousands of other migrants from less wealthy and educated backgrounds than the pensionados. Many of these young men, mostly Tagalogs, hoped to attend school while working. The majority became labor contractors and business owners, with only a few becoming professionals (Melendy, 1977).

By 1930, the community had changed dramatically. From a population of about 400 in 1910 composed of elite pensionados, Tagalogs, and Visayans, 20 years later, the predominant group was the Ilocano laborer group with similar aims. Overall, the community was overwhelmingly young, single, and male. Most had few years of formal education and spoke little Spanish or English (Mariano, 1933; Melendy, 1977). There were by then 45,208 Filipinos in the United States: mostly male, Ilocano, working class, and concentrated in California (Foronda, 1976; Mariano, 1933; Takaki, 1998).

Of the Filipino population in 1930, the census showed that only 2,940 were female, resulting in a ratio of 14 men to every Filipina woman. Moreover, due to the restriction on female migration, there was a marked difference in nativity; while the men were overwhelmingly foreign born, the majority of the women were born in the United States, most often in California or Hawaii.[7]

During the 1930s, hostility toward Filipinos grew more widespread, especially in California; consequently, nationalists increasingly turned to Philippine hero José Rizal, his writings, and his life for direction. "Rizal's writings," wrote one observer, "are widely known; his aspirations for Philippine freedom, his idealism and spirit, permeate far the ranks of educated nationalists, providing them with an ideology."[8] Many drew inspiration from his example of sacrifice under adversity and commitment to a cause. As nationalists viewed them, Rizal Day celebrations became an even more crucial means toward unity for a community uncertain of its future.

QUEENS AND FEMININITY

Just as Rizal was a symbol of unity on whom all could agree, the selection of a Rizal Day queen was a way to build communal unity. Some campaigns deliberately picked members from the different regional groups as a way to resolve differences. The manager of Estelita de la Peña's 1929 crown, for instance, made sure to appoint Tagalogs, Visayans, and Ilocanos to her strategy team, not only to forestall any tensions but also to create a strong working relationship and example of unity. Members were kept busy with the serious pace of the campaign. In its last month, de la Peña's team fanned out across the state, targeting the labor camps where Filipino workers resided and organized personal visits, including "speeches, dances, box socials, and songs." Where they could not visit, they "resorted to radiograms, telegrams, newspaper articles, [and] handbills."[9] As they sought to garner support for de la Peña, these appearances, visits, radio programs, and writings were also occasions to discuss what characteristics made the ideal Filipina woman. Nationalists used them not only to encourage interaction but also to establish common ground among migrants, regardless of class or regional background, by emphasizing their goals of unity, cooperation, and self-government. In this way, choosing a representative queen was also an opportunity to unite the community.

With the onset of tensions over exclusion and race riots, Rizal Day celebrations were also used to promote nationalist visions of an idealized community and to present the best in the Filipino. Nationalists believed that virtuous women, as represented by the queens, would inspire Filipino men to turn away from the temptations of vice and indolence and go back onto the straight path—one defined by nationalists as "Westernized" and "modern." This gendered association of high moral standards, virtue, and inspiration was common. Leaders emphasized the value of virtuous women as moral guardians to men. "What more natural than that women should inspire men to do great deeds!" wrote one (Blanc-Szanton, 1990; Lagiuo, 1931). However, this was a reciprocal relationship. For the inspiration they provided men, women needed protecting since they were considered vulnerable, weak, and incapable of exercising independent judgment. Women "can go astray; and we can go astray with them. It is for us to show fortitude; to husband our moral strength to save them and to save ourselves" (Laguio, 1931). As embodiments of virtue, queen candidates had a special role to play, one of "greatest importance" to the community, whose influence went far beyond their small numbers.[10] This was part of a larger discursive strategy. Although nationalists argued that they venerated Filipina womanhood, in reality, these ideals were about forcing women to remain within defined, "traditional," and idealized gender roles.

There were few Filipinas in the United States to begin with since gender conventions specified strict supervision and chaperoning of single women. Declared an officer with the Filipino Students' Christian Movement in America: "[I]t is inconceivable for a Filipino girl to leave the parental home without the company of either of their parents, any of the relatives, or trusted friends. It is a Filipino custom to have a girl chaperoned when she goes out, especially if she goes to a foreign country."[11] Without a chaperone, young women were unprotected and their virtue was put into question.[12] In the Philippines, there were fears that American culture had produced a "modern Filipino woman" who was "too alien in her own native land" (Enloe, 1989; Laguio, 1931).

CANDIDATES AND CONTESTS

The early Rizal Day queen contests were simple affairs, and not beauty contests per se (Banet-Weiser, 1999; Banner, 1983; Cohen et al., 1996). After the candidates canvassed for support, voting took place at an official tabulation dance held shortly before the coronation at which all candidates had to appear. There, those wishing to vote purchased a ballot (to be placed into the appropriate box for each candidate) or put in cash, with each dollar constituting one vote. Sometimes, candidates danced with all attendees; at other dances, in order to dance with a candidate one had first to purchase a ballot.[13] For both the small, local contests and the large ones, there were no judges, no talent sections, and no interviews to determine a candidate's poise and charm. Instead, the candidate with the most votes was declared the queen.

For small-scale celebrations, the sponsoring organization took nominations of local women who lived near or in the area. Often they were the daughters, sisters, or wards of local labor contractors, farm laborers, or small business owners. Once the young women were approved, they were then formally announced and fielded as candidates. For the larger organizations such as the Filipino fraternal societies, which held joint competitions, Filipina women from around the state competed with each other, each sponsored by a local lodge, for the title of "Miss Philippines." Given the small number of Filipina women, it was common for candidates to run in one contest after another. Thus, candidates for both the large and the local contests were familiar to the selectors, and their reputations already well known.

The queens who were chosen fit the idealized image of a Filipina woman, and education and English fluency represented one criterion of the image.[14] Nationalists wished to have as queen a representative who would not only present "the best" of Filipino unity and Philippine independence but also one who would be at ease in audiences composed of Filipinos and Euro-Americans, and could charm local government officials, as well as presidents of local Filipino organizations and grand officials of the fraternities. The most important criteria, however, were those associated with deportment and behavior. Among the qualities voters listed were modesty, gentleness, gratitude, and filial piety.[15] Especially admired were candidates who compared favorably with women "back home." The ideal Filipino woman, declared one, "is the paragon of modesty par excellence."[16] Noted another: "Mary reminds me of the conservatism of our girls way back home. And it is good conservatism. She is neither too conservative nor too radical in her ways of dressing, speaking, and acting. She is just natural. She is the Filipina, showing the virtue of the Filipina.... She is gentle and quiet."[17]

Notably, foremost among these qualities was tradition. In comparing candidates, voters said that a young woman's sense of tradition was what made her fit to be queen. "To my way of thinking," explained a labor contractor, "Filipino traits, habits and customs, must be carefully guarded and preserved against the encroachments of foreign fashions. Confirmed in my belief as I am, I feel certain that the election of Miss Losada as Queen of Rizal Day in San Francisco is one means of expressing our nation's ideals, for which Dr. Rizal labored and died; for Miss Losada manifests the true spirit of the Filipina unspoiled by foreign influences." Her election, he added, would raise the status of Filipinos in America, for it would send a message to "the people of America and the people of the Philippines that the Filipinos on the West Coast of the United States hold their traditions above every other consideration."[18] Candidates therefore tended to fit a middle-class, "traditional" ideal in line with nationalist visions. Criteria such as physical appearance and beauty mattered less.

These roles and qualities were not just amorphous ideals but were enacted over the course of the campaigns. Interviews became opportunities for candidates to discuss their patriotism. Completing community projects, bringing together and creating unity among Filipinos on the West Coast, and advancing the standing of Filipinos in California were cited as their reasons for running in the pageant.[19] One former Rizal Day beauty queen saw her participation not as a test of her popularity, but rather as a "duty," whereby "our people" gained a better understanding of the conditions facing Filipinos in California and those at home.[20]

As candidates sought to garner support, each commitment they agreed to—personal appearances, speeches, dances, even the radiograms—became an occasion to carry out or perform these gendered ideals (Butler, 1990). The events offered audiences numerous opportunities to observe candidates. For the large, joint contests, campaigning up and down the state was commonplace, with the tabulation dances starting six months before the coronation.[21] The local lodge sponsoring the candidate threw a dance; if a candidate had widespread support, other lodges also sponsored dances. Over the course of the months-long campaign, candidates distinguished themselves by their qualities: who was gracious enough to remember to thank her supporters and parents at each tabulation dance; and who reacted with modesty and not too much pride at the news that she had pulled in the top number of votes.

THE CORONATION OF THE QUEEN

Adding to the spectacle of the contests was the atmosphere of excitement and pleasure at these dances. It was here that elements of the visual and the aural came together and were embodied in movement. Entering the room, one's gaze was drawn to the candidates' booths, each with a prominent display of the candidate's picture and an official box into which all ballots were to be placed. With the start of the dance came the official announcement and introduction of the candidates to the audience. There, gazing at the queens and listening to their remarks, each became a judge, observing, listening, and comparing those who were running. For some, being part of the crowd was excitement enough; they were content to gaze at the queens and to stand back and watch, wearing their best clothing. Others pushed forward to cast a ballot, either purchasing a ticket or a dance with a candidate. On the dance floor, candidates and voters danced as couples, and as they whirled about, their movements timed to the music, their work and school lives seemed far removed. Spectators became participants, and vice versa. Even the counting of the ballots added to the suspense. The spectacle of the dances—their use of conventions of looking and comparison, and performativity—made these idealized images of femininity "real." All these activities helped break the feelings of isolation and monotony on the farms and in the cities.

The box social, which was another way to collect votes, also added to the drama of the affair. Toward the end of the tabulation dance, the dancing stopped, and an auctioneer took bids from the audience on a succession of wrapped boxes. Inside each was a small gift, often a scarf or a pair of nylons. The highest bid won the privilege of both giving away a wrapped gift and having a dance with a favored candidate.[22] The larger the bids, the higher the chances, and the more the funds raised. Bids approached hundreds of dollars and were added to a candidate's vote count.[23] At the end of the dance, the new tallies for all the candidates were announced. One community leader noted how the box socials were a crowd favorite, explaining: "there is the sound of the dance music; there is the hollering of the auctioneer; there is the yelling of the crowd; there is the applause.... To some people, this phase of the dance is nerve-wracking; to some, it gives thrills and excitement."[24] The competition and rivalry within the crowd for their candidates only heightened the excitement.

All these events led to the highlight of the Rizal Day celebration: the coronation of the queen and her court. The pageantry of the presentation attracted thousands.[25] Organizers saved these festivities for last, holding them in the evening at a hotel or large auditorium; they were the final cap on the series of events for the celebration. There, the long-awaited announcement of the runners-up and winner finally came. One by one, each candidate was presented and awarded her prize, her hard work acknowledged, until the queen was announced. For the queen, there were special ceremonies. First, she was crowned, and a sash was placed across her front, displaying her title of "Miss Philippines." Then, in front of the crowd, she took her vow, pledging to devote herself to further the cause of the Philippines and the Filipinos. For the rest of the evening, the queen, her attendants, and their supporters celebrated and danced their last dance. The spectacle of these events—the announcement of the winners, presentation of the candidates, ceremonies to crown the queen, and use of visual culture and performativity—made these ideal qualities "real."

Although the contests made the "ideal Filipina" appear real, outside of the contests, elites reminded queens that they were representatives of the community. With their crown came a special duty to further the cause of their people and their country. As virtuous women, elites said, queens had the power to inspire Filipino men to remain on the straight path. Declared the president of the Filipino Community of Vallejo: "In your present stellar role in Filipino society, you are in a position to do a tremendous amount of good for our people," adding "[w]ith your victory is a social responsibility."[26] Along these lines, queens took up community issues and provided moral direction, but always within the gendered terms of the virtuous woman. For instance, a former queen, chosen as the main speaker for the 1939 Rizal Day in Salinas, used her stature and visibility to urge the community to stay away from vice. Alluding to the district attorney's recent crackdown on gambling dens, Ramona Losada focused her speech on the impact of these "social ills" within the community. While she admonished "otherwise" talented and capable Filipinos to try again to follow the straight path, to avoid temptation and reach their potential, she softened her criticism, speaking "with love, with understanding, with compassion."[27] In their endeavors to raise the standing of the Filipino, women were the inspiration, and men were the leaders and doers. Women's moral character, their willingness to sacrifice time and effort in their devotion to duty, were examples for the larger community to emulate. In turn, the community could best meet these standards with their own acts of sacrifice and devotion to duty.

GOSSIP, DISCIPLINE, AND TRADITION

This sense of duty to the community had yet another side. Although nationalists liked to depict beauty queens as honored and venerated, the queens and candidates became aware that they were under scrutiny. Part of this was their visible and conspicuous role. Entering a contest entailed a kind of debut into Filipino society, wherein candidates were feted and talked about incessantly, almost as celebrities. Candidates themselves were well aware that for every achievement that was celebrated, their every move was scrutinized. Their very deportment during the months-long campaign was picked apart and gossiped over, in the newspapers and at the contests (Almirol, 1982; Cannell, 1999; Meñez, 1976). A former queen candidate noted that one "hurt that the Filipina is likely to suffer is unjust talk. From the minute she becomes known in the community, her every step is measured and judged—her faults are exaggerated, her good points mocked. No matter how sweet she may be, no matter what good aims and thoughts she entertains in her mind, there is always something wrong, or so it seems to those who always find something to criticize. Constructive criticism is a beneficial thing, but it should never be used to the extent that it hurts."[28]

Through scrutiny and gossip, candidates became used to "being seen" in public and learned to comport themselves according to the traditional values venerated by nationalists. Scrutiny and gossip were therefore a means of surveillance and discipline, forms of special pressures the queens had to endure. Part of this increased scrutiny also had to do with their idealized image. Presented by nationalists as leisured and glittering in their finery and crowns, the queens seemed far removed from the daily lives of most Filipina women and young girls. This was especially true from the 1920s into the Great Depression, when finances were tight, and when many labored in the fields and within their families to make ends meet. For example, Teresa Romero Jamero, who had grown up in the Central Valley in California, recalled her mother "working so hard in the kitchen. She not only did the cooking for camp and family, she also worked in the fields."[29] Similarly, Rosario Modelo Maglinte recalled her duties growing up in her hometown of Isleton: "I would get up at five o'clock in the morning, being the oldest girl I have to help my mother do the dishes after she send out the first load of chocolate linugaw [a dessert] and her homemade buns out to the cutters. I learned how to work in the fields.... I worked in the field until I graduated from high school."[30] Concordia Duhaylongsod, also of Isleton, also described a childhood of work in the fields with her family: "The camps, they have bunk houses where the family stay . . . but it was terrible. In this big wooden box houses, the families would be put in one and the singles in another. And one community kitchen. Cold. No heat."[31] Gossip arose in this perceived distance between the glamorous lives of the queens and the mundane workday lives of most women—even though, ironically, those lives could be, and often were, lived by the same person.

To preserve this distance, and to try to forestall any controversy, candidates were chaperoned, often by managers. The role of the managers—who could be parents, relatives, or family friends—was especially crucial. Managers planned and oversaw their candidates' campaigns. This was particularly true for the larger campaigns in which serious candidates were forced to canvass for votes up and down the state, and in far-flung communities in which they might have had no ties. The manager played the role of go-betweens who set up the contacts and personal appearances, introduced the candidate to officials, and lauded her fitness as a queen. This saved candidates the embarrassment of taking on these duties themselves and, moreover, helped them maintain the appearance of modesty. Having a manager also enlarged a potential queen's circle of contacts and networks in the community, and increased her chances of winning. Moreover, by conducting a successful campaign, a manager could also expand his own network and raise his standing in the community.

At every step, a chaperone protected the candidate, guided her safety, and vouched for her virtue. Like scrutiny and gossip, chaperoning, too, was a form of surveillance and discipline—another means through which candidates became used to "being seen" in public and learned to comport themselves. In fact, chaperoning did not prevent gossip, for chaperoning and gossip were flip sides of the same coin. Both gossip and chaperoning were attempts to make candidates, as objects of surveillance, into "disciplined" bodies. Although nationalists argued that they venerated Filipina womanhood, in reality, queen contests, as noted earlier, were a means of "disciplining" women to remain within defined, "traditional," and idealized gender roles. There was a basic and gendered unease with women's relationship to Westernization. Whereas men were to be Westernized, women had to remain "traditional."

Candidates were aware that they were to provide the community with positive role models and virtuous women as inspirational examples. To run in a contest was a necessary sacrifice to the community in order to better its status. As one candidate wrote: "She sacrifices her youth, which is the most beautiful period in one's life, to accomplish *the duty* that is every Filipino girl's; that is, to contribute the feminine roles which even today Filipino society lacks."[32] This was a sacrifice most candidates were willing to make, as she saw it: "And the Filipino girl is always proud to do it— always generous in giving herself to her people that they may learn to esteem the fellowship and companionship of girls of their own blood and from their own country."[33]

Not all candidates accepted this responsibility without protest. Some used the language of reciprocity to plead for less pressure, and left implicit was a criticism of dominant leadership. Because the contests were ever searching for new candidates, very young women, some as young as 14, were put up as candidates as soon as they were considered eligible.[34] One ruefully recalled the pressure to grow up fast, saying that as a queen candidate, she, too, "was taken away from baby dresses to evening gowns— playgrounds to dances—playmates to admirers." Generally, at such young ages, she felt that candidates were ill prepared to deal with the responsibility and the attention. "Here in this distant country, when a Pinay is as young as 12 or 13, she makes her debut in Filipino community. She is immediately swamped with admirers. An innocent unknown child, who should be out in the streets playing with youngsters of her own age, is shoved into a world of glamour and sophistication."[35]

Contestants sometimes expressed their own desires for self-fashioning and display, and used their physicality to show different styles of deportment. Rather than demure, acquiescent, and obedient figures of femininity, some candidates chose nonverbal means of communication, dancing with abandonment. Their movements were intended to shock and transmit a message of boldness. According to critics, this was nothing better than "insidious sexual mischief," for when they dance, "all its implied meaning smack in your astonished face, as it were." That they were doing so while wearing the formal mestiza dress, considered a symbol of Philippine national culture, was even more brazen. "The ancestors of these girls," declared one, "must turn in their graves across 7000 miles."[36]

For all the unease with Filipina women's problematic relationship to "tradition," certain features of the contests themselves undermined nationalist visions and authority. For one, in light of the time commitments, organizations offered incentives such as grand prizes in cash or gifts.[37] The most elaborate were those offered by the Salinas Rizal Day Queen contests, co-sponsored by local Filipino organizations and the *Philippines Mail* newspaper. Rather than grand prizes, one year each contestant garnering over 160,000 votes received "a free round-trip tourist cabin ticket to the Philippines and $150 for traveling expenses. Those with over 100,000 votes were promised a "free, round-trip tourist cabin ticket to Honolulu" and $100 in expenses. Votes were a penny each. Another option was a portion of the proceeds, or "forty per cent (40 percent)" of the money they collected through ticket sales.[38] Instead of encouraging sincere commitment to a cause and transforming relations in the community, these incentives seemed to violate the emphasis on modesty and patriotism.

The dances and box socials themselves constituted a second such feature. Asking participants to purchase a ballot or bid for dances, if anything, only forced a form of crass materialism on both the queens and their admirers that was at odds with the intent to transform behavior. Some felt that the events with the succession of dances—where at each one, candidates were swamped with so many suitors, so many partners asking for dances, and were the sought-after results of competitive bids, repeated over and over— had grown unseemly. One critic deplored them: "Filipina women are so few that their companionship is given on an auction basis. The highest bidder gets it in a materialistic country like the United States. This seems to be but a logical course. What is an affront in the Philippines is here taken as a social 'must'—and what a must!"[39] The sight of up to 200 men, all eager to dance with 10 to 15 young women, was a spectacle in itself.[40]

CONCLUSION

Queen contests remained a fixture of Filipino community events even after World War II. After the Philippines gained independence in 1946, the Rizal Days gave way to Philippine Independence Days, and queens were a part of these celebrations (Ave, 1956). In providing a powerful symbol of a feminine, middle-class ideal, featuring the spectacle and pageantry of the presentation of a queen and her court, the Rizal Days represented a nationalist attempt at reform as an alternative to vice and were part of a sophisticated discursive strategy to fulfill the nationalist fantasies of a unified community.

These attempts, however, were not entirely successful. Candidates critiqued aspects of dominant leadership, engaged in small acts of defiance or recalcitrance, expressed their own desires for self-fashioning and display, and used their physicality to exhibit different styles of deportment. In the process, these contests also affirmed such attributes and roles as the inspirational and virtuous queen, roles so celebrated by nationalists that also constituted forms of surveillance and control over women's bodies.

Notes

1. I wish to thank Valerie Matsumoto, Michael Salman, Don Nakanishi, Peggy Pascoe, Connie Chen, Jasamin Rostam, Catherine Komisaruk, Shirley Jennifer Lim, and Richard Lindstrom for their comments and critiques of earlier versions of this chapter.
2. *San Francisco Chronicle*, October 23, 1929, p. 9; *San Francisco Chronicle*, December 4, 1929, p. 6; *Philippines Free Press*, January 1931, pp. 4, 25.
3. James Earl Wood Papers, Folder 1:18, "Rizal and Rizal Day," p. 2, Bancroft Library, University of California, Berkeley, hereafter referred to as James Earl Wood Papers.
4. *Philippines Free Press*, February 11, 1933, pp. 48–49.
5. For diversion, one Filipino described driving with his friends all the way from Stockton to Sacramento "just for a dance"—a distance of some 50 miles. James Earl Wood Papers, Folder 2:5, "The Social Life of a Filipino," p. 4. It is beyond the scope of this chapter to present an in-depth treatment of the question of relationships between Filipino men and Euro-American women. See also Maram, 1996.
6. *San Francisco Chronicle*, December 4, 1929, p. 6; James Earl Wood Papers, Notes, Folder 1:18, p. 1.
7. See James Earl Wood Papers, Set B, Field Notes; Louis Bloch, *Facts about Filipino Immigration into California*, San Francisco: California State Printing Office, 1930, California Department of Industrial Relations, Special Bulletin No. 3.
8. James Earl Wood Papers, Field Notes, Folder "Materials Relating to Filipino Labor in California, Wages, Hours, etc."
9. *Philippines Free Press*, January 3, 1931, p. 25.
10. James Earl Wood Papers, Notes, Folder 1:18, p. 1.
11. Manuel A. Adeva, "Filipino Students in the United States," *The Mid-Pacific Magazine* 14 (August 1932), p. 121.
12. So rare was it to find a Filipina woman who would come from the Philippines alone that such journeys made the papers; see the *Philippines Mail*, October 9, 1933, p. 3, for an example.
13. *Philippines Free Press*, January 3, 1931, p. 25. In the use of ballots as a means of voting, these contests were similar to the pre–World War II Nisei Week queen contests among Japanese Americans in Los Angeles. See Kurashige, 2002 for detail.
14. *Philippines Mail*, August 5, 1935, p. 2.
15. These qualities of modesty and self-sacrifice call to mind the idealized vision of Filipina womanhood as offered by José Rizal in his novel, *Noli Me Tangere*, in the character of Maria Clara (Rizal, 1997, pp. 393, 398).
16. Cecilio Lopez, "In Praise of Women," *Philippines Mail*, December 28, 1938, p. 2.
17. Mary de Guzman was a candidate in 1935. See *Philippines Mail*, August 5, 1935, p. 2.
18. *Philippines Free Press*, December 28, 1929, p. 15.
19. *Philippines Mail*, September 2, 1935, p. 1; July 27, 1936, p. 1. Rick Bonus finds similar examples in his study of beauty pageants in San Diego, California, in the 1990s (Bonus, 2000: 92--127).
20. *Philippines Mail*, September 25, 1933, p. 4.
21. *San Francisco Chronicle*, June 24, 1934, p. A4.
22. Personal communication with Darlene and Phil Ventura, and Sam Balucas, Filipino American National Historical Society, Los Angeles, California, April 18, 1999. See *Philippines Mail*, March 10, 1942, p. 2, for a reference to "the social box hour" at a dance held in Watsonville.

23. James Earl Wood Papers, Folder 1:18, "Rizal and Rizal Day," p. 2; *Philippines Mail*, December 22, 1941, pp. 4, 6.
24. *Philippines Mail*, May 27, 1941, p. 1.
25. The 1930 contest had 1,000 spectators. The 1931 Pacific Coast Joint Rizal Day drew 2,000 to its queen contest. *Philippines Free Press*, December 12, 1931, p. 109; *Philippines Free Press*, January 1931, pp. 4, 25; *San Francisco Chronicle*, October 23, 1929, p. 9; *San Francisco Chronicle*, December 4, 1929, p. 6; *San Francisco Chronicle*, December 7, 1931, p. 7.
26. *Philippines Mail*, December 22, 1941, p. 1.
27. *Philippines Mail*, January 1, 1939, p. 1.
28. *Philippines Mail*, August 13, 1934, p. 5.
29. See Cordova, 1983, p. 153.
30. *Philippine Review*, November 1992, p. 5.
31. *Philippine Review*, November 1992, p. 5.
32. *Phillipines Mail*, August 13, 1934, p. 5, emphasis mine.
33. *Phillipines Mail*, August 13, 1934, p. 5.
34. *Phillipines Mail*, June 16, 1941, p. 2.
35. *Phillipines Mail*, August 13, 1934, p. 5.
36. Manuel Abella, "An Estimate of Women," *Phillipines Mail*, December 4, 1942, p. 2.
37. *Phillipines Mail*, March 4, 1935, p. 1. It offered prizes to the top three finishers: $500 for first prize, along with a wristwatch; $300 for second, along with a set of fountain pens; and $200 for third prize.
38. *Phillipines Mail*, May 27, 1941, p. 1.
39. Manuel Abella, "An Estimate of Women," *Phillipines Mail*, September 30, 1942, p. 2.
40. James Earl Wood Papers, Folder 2:5, "The Social Life of a Filipino," p. 4.

CHAPTER 5

Nisei Daughters' Courtship and Romance in Los Angeles before World War II

Valerie J. Matsumoto

INTRODUCTION

In 1940, Lily Tanaka, a 15-year-old Japanese American girl, poked fun at the contours of "A Modern Romance" in a breezy poem:

> He tooted the horn
> And he did shout
> "Hurry!" and Alice
> Did run out.
> She jumped in the car
> And slammed the door shut
> The engine lurched forward
> With a loud sput, sput.
> They went to a movie
> Then for a ride,
> They parked, and he said,
> "Please be my bride."
> She said "Yes!"
> Followed by a kiss
> The moon was shining
> And oh what bliss! ... [1]

By the eve of World War II, many urban Nisei (second-generation) women and men were enjoying mainstream practices of dating and courtship that differed dramatically from the arranged matches of their immigrant parents.

The "date," as described by Lily Tanaka, had become a familiar scenario for city youth who were more likely than their rural peers to have leisure time and parental sanction for such activities.

In the late 1920s and through the difficult years of the Great Depression, Nisei daughters in Los Angeles's Little Tokyo practiced the latest dance steps, planned club socials, and tried to balance dreams of romantic love and companionate marriage with filial duty and racial inequities. At times, like their Mexican American and Chinese American sisters, they struggled to negotiate between powerful mainstream notions of modernity and romance, on one hand, and the feminine ideals inculcated by parents reared in Meiji-era Japan on the other.[2] As Vicki Ruíz (1992) skillfully delineates, the multiple pressures nonwhite women faced within the family, the ethnic community, and the larger society complicated their participation in popular culture. As the Nisei endeavored to integrate popular and parental values, they introduced a range of gender-role issues into the Japanese American community. The tensions between competing notions of womanhood emerged most prominently in the discourse over romance, courtship, and marriage.

Women played energetic roles in pre–World War II Japanese American communities of the West Coast, where the majority of Issei (first-generation) immigrants had settled. The largest of these enclaves was Little Tokyo in Los Angeles. The English-language sections of the Los Angeles Japanese American newspapers vividly revealed the variety of Nisei women's involvement in urban ethnic youth culture. The Nisei-edited English sections of the *Kashu Mainichi* (Japan-California Daily News) and the *Rafu Shimpo* (Los Angeles Japanese Newspaper) provided a forum to discuss topics relevant to the second generation, including lively debates over women's roles.

In the early twentieth century, debates over gender-role shifts— embodied by the emergence of the "New Woman"—arose within both ethnic communities and the larger society. My research on Japanese American women—like Judy Yung's (1995) and Vicki Ruíz's (1998) findings about Chinese American women and Mexican American women—revealed that a considerable number bobbed their hair and rebelled against parentally prescribed gender-role strictures. While remaining steadfast contributors to the family economy, they also hoped to choose their own spouses, enjoyed mainstream entertainment, and organized a variety of Nisei girls' and women's clubs. Their synthesis of interwar notions of "modern" femininity was, of course, complicated by the racial discrimination they faced from the larger society and by their ethnic community's views regarding appropriate female behavior. Nowhere was the tension between the differing sets of expectations more evident than in the urban setting of Little Tokyo.

Little Tokyo in Los Angeles grew rapidly in the two decades before World War II and served as a major cultural hub for the Issei and Nisei in southern California. Japantowns emerged in San Francisco, Seattle, Sacramento, Tacoma, and Salt Lake City, but Los Angeles boasted the largest of the enclaves. In 1910, the Census Bureau recorded 8,641 Japanese Americans living in Los Angeles County, and by 1930 the number swelled to 35,000, half of whom were American-born Nisei. The majority of the Issei and Nisei resided in the area known as "Lil' Tokio," clustered around First and San Pedro streets, not far from City Hall. They ran shops and restaurants, and worked at the heart of the produce business, which was then located in the City Market on Ninth and San Pedro streets. The prospect of living in this bustling, vigorous community thrilled Nisei newcomer Mary Korenaga, who initially viewed California—and Los Angeles more specifically—as "the land of opportunity and fortune, the land of eternal sunshine and flower, and the land where the eyes of the Nisei are focused." To Korenaga and many of her peers, city life glittered with the allure of modernity and excitement.

In contrast to Japanese American farm women, whose lives Evelyn Nakano Glenn (1986: 55) characterizes as having retained "traditional peasant values," urban Nisei daughters had more comfortable, less arduous childhoods. Like their rural cousins, they helped out both at home and in the family business, but they were more likely to have free time and greater access to commercialized leisure. As Mei Nakano (1990: 120) suggests, the prewar period could be "a heady time for urban Nisei females, filled with the scent of gardenias, and the excitement of romance and dating." Certainly the packed social calendars of the *Kashu Mainichi* and the *Rafu Shimpo* reflected their engagement in a range of cultural, recreational, and social service activities within the ethnic community. This chapter provides a glimpse into the world of pre–World War II young Nisei women and examines how they defined, shaped, and sustained urban ethnic culture on their own terms, while also maintaining ties to their parents and the Japanese American community.

COURTSHIP AND ROMANCE

Urban Nisei women's notions of socializing and romance took shape at a time when courtship in the United States had largely moved from the private to the public sphere and dating had become widespread (Bailey, 1988/1989). Movies, magazines, radio shows, and songs influenced the dreams and expectations of youth across the country, including the second-generation Japanese Americans. As a second-generation columnist stated, so engrained was the ideal of romance that the notion of arranged marriage was unthinkable to many of those Nisei "who have sat with their mouth open during tense romantic scenes on the screen; those who are addicted to true confession magazines and motion picture periodicals; those who have pored over the Freudian Gospel or attempted to read the precepts of companionate marriage; those who go romantically [gallivanting] on automobile joy-rides; and those who believe that 'love is everywhere ... its music fills the air.' "[3]

At the same time, Nisei daughters were acutely aware that within the tightly knit immigrant community, female behavior and family reputation were closely linked and carefully scrutinized. Moreover, the practices of Nisei courtship—and the eligibility of potential partners—were affected by the structure of prewar race relations on the West Coast. Given all of these factors, a great deal of Nisei romantic socializing and courtship occurred (or at least began) within the monitored setting of youth-club activities and in the context of young women's extensive peer networks.

Dating

It is difficult to ascertain how many of the urban Nisei went on dates in the 1920s. The younger boys and girls often attended dances and socials in the company of a same-sex group, arriving and leaving together. The older Nisei were more likely to have the parental approval and financial wherewithal for heterosexual-couple social activities. Those second-generation women who did go on dates were very conscious about avoiding any potential blot on their reputation and, by extension, that of their family. However, the *Rafu Shimpo* reportage of the 1920s suggests that city life and access to automobiles gave some of them opportunities to conduct their flirtation and courtship away from the watchful eyes of parents or club advisers. In 1926, the *Rafu Shimpo* published a serialized poem, "The Evolution of a Flapper," apparently written by a contributor to the newspaper. The love-struck flapper and her sheik [young man] took advantage of automobility to go on a date in a popular seaside community:

> One dreamy night
> Her sheikie took her
> Out to Venice near the bay
> And there they danced
> And there they flirted
> Beneath the moon's soft ray

Their idyll was derailed by a car accident on their way home in "the wee small hours" of the next morning. When they reached the flapper's home, her boyfriend went with her, "The wrath of her folks to allay/For from experience/He well knew/That she'd have the deuce to pay."[4]

The car became a critical vehicle for heterosexual romance, as a number of Julia Suski's one-panel comics in the *Rafu Shimpo* reflected: below one picture of a stylized Asian-looking woman with a blasé expression was the caption, "Gertie sez: I would have enjoyed the ride last night if we had found a parking place."[5] The next week's panel echoed the same theme. Although the captions may have originated outside the ethnic community, the sentiments they expressed were familiar to the second generation. The concern of Issei parents and older Nisei indicates that these practices were not confined to mainstream youth or newspaper wit. In 1927, one columnist commented that dances often led to problematic consequences such as "surreptitious dates, the ride back home . . . and a score of other complications." He cited the ire of parents over a previous dance and the despair of the chaperone and sponsors of the event. As an aid to the Japanese YWCA and other organizations trying to figure out how to "make their entertainments foolproof," he wryly suggested that all girls be transported to dances in one large truck, that all persons involved wear thick armor lined with asbestos, and that all girls be muzzled to prevent conversation.[6] His "solutions" hint at the heat of youthful passion, the opportunities afforded by intimate car rides, and a sense of inevitability about both. His emphasis on the containment of young women conveys the sexual double standard and also, perhaps, the active role some Nisei *shebas* [young women] played in romantic socializing.[7]

Courtship practices provided much fodder for the newspaper. Julia Suski's drawings, which appeared regularly from 1926 through 1928, were coupled with sly humor regarding kissing, the romantic foibles of women and men, and the customs of dating.[8] One journalist in 1929 addressed a mild admonition to readers, writing, "All our pleasures become vices when taken in excessive amounts. Eating, petting, sports, study, play, and work—should we indulge too far in them, they may all become evil habits."[9] That this advocacy of moderation in pleasure included "petting"—which ranked second behind "eating"—suggested that the urban Nisei had been influenced by the dating practices of middle-class mainstream youth.

The collegiate development of "rating" potential dates had also percolated into the Japanese American community via the Nisei who attended local universities. In the competitive system of "dating and rating," a trend since the 1920s, popularity was the measure of success (Bailey, 1988/1989: 26–27). A 1931 Nisei college gossip column teasingly asked one "exuberant" and "entertaining" young man who had been a hit at a dance, "Gee, Vic, how do ya rate?" A less popular fellow, referred to as "non-rate Ned," glumly wished he was "cute, or a good dancer, or a club president." The female columnist also predicted of another man, modest and unassuming, "now that he's made Phi Beta Kappa he ought to become a real hi rater."[10] The "collegiate vernacular" terms of "rate and don't rate" had become so common that, as a *Rafu Shimpo* editorial in the same issue mentioned, Little Tokyo had adopted them to distinguish between its "better half" and "lesser half."[11] The editor's concerns about the frivolity of the lesser half— "practicing dance steps and learning late song hits"—were evidently shared by first- and second-generation elders.

The elders' worries about the behavior of Nisei sons and daughters— particularly daughters—prompted the hosting of numerous social hygiene and health education speakers at girls' club meetings and church gatherings. For example, in 1933, Mrs. Olds, a "noted lecturer on social hygiene," gave a talk at the International Institute on sex education, accompanied by an illustrative movie, for high school girls.[12] Sometimes teachers were invited to provide instruction, as when the Loha Tohelas gathered in 1937 to hear a Jefferson High School teacher give a talk on "Personal Hygiene" and "Boy and Girl Relations."[13] Sometimes the lecturers were female medical authorities like Dr. Nadine Kavinoky, who spoke to two YWCA clubs and showed a film, "Beginning of Life."[14] The impact of these efforts on second-generation girls is unclear, but the caption of a 1926 Julia Suski drawing hinted at sly rebuttal. Beneath the image of three glamorous Asian American women was a dialogue:

> LOU-LIA: Some terrible things can be caught from kissing.
> DORITA: I believe it. You ought to see the poor fish our Aggie caught.[15]

What Aggie caught from kissing was not a "social disease," but a lackluster suitor. Though aware of social disease, urban Nisei girls may have been more concerned about the suitor. Despite their adoption of the fashions and some of the pastimes of the flapper, Nisei women—along with their peers and elders—set limits on the carefree sensuality associated with the New Woman. Japanese American girls, like their Mexican American and Chinese American sisters, were under pressure to maintain a chaste reputation within the tightly knit immigrant community and thus were subject to greater surveillance than their brothers; premarital sexual intercourse was a line that few crossed in the prewar period.

By the mid-1930s, the components of a Nisei date had become well established: The young man would drive to the woman's family home to pick her up.[16] Then perhaps they would go to see the latest movie at the Carthay Music Box, or join their friends at a Nisei club dance, or go to one of the public ballrooms of the Southland. Afterward, they would repair to a cafe for refreshments, for which the male was expected to pay.

Indeed, Nisei dating practices mirrored those of the middle-class mainstream, with men usually bearing the expense of the evening. Columnist Ayako Noguchi may have addressed the secret fears of a number of men when she ran a satirical poem under the heading "Scrambled Brains":

> I took her to a night club,
> I took her to a show,
> I took her almost every place
> A boy and girl could go.
> I took her to the dances,
> I took her out to tea,
> Then suddenly I realized
> That she'd been taking me.[17]

From time to time, especially during the Depression era, a few male columnists like John Fujii grumbled about the unfairness of the cost. Fujii reported that a group of second-generation men were appalled at "the extravagance of their sisters," lamenting that the Nisei women, "though aware of the financial plight of the men, heartlessly want to go to this place and that place—to buy this and that. The men usually shoulder the burden and—as one fellow puts it—we get very little out of it."[18] Fujii advocated the virtues of going "50–50," with men and women sharing the costs of dates, but it seemed that this seldom happened. In 1938, columnist Bean Takeda detailed male expenditures to meet what he felt were urban girls' expectations: "High-powered cars, costly corsages, too many dances, redundant 'pig-stand' treats, and even expensive nightclubs."[19] Despite the issue of expense, which varied according to the age of the Nisei involved and the venue of entertainment, second-generation recreation and courtship showed no signs of slackening.

Dances

Dances, whether the Nisei attended them with groups of friends or as couples on dates, constituted an important—and perhaps *the* most important—arena of socializing and romance for the urban second generation. Like their mainstream peers in high school and college, the second generation viewed dancing as a respectable recreation and one that was a requisite for popularity (Fass, 1977: 300–301). Dances became a staple activity for the Nisei youth clubs. As Nellie Nimura stated, "There are two kinds of second generation young people: those who dance and those who don't dance. But there seems to be only one kind of organization: the kind that gives dances. They say every organization must sponsor a dance in order to keep up its membership."[20]

Dances also provided some opportunities for interethnic and interracial socializing. As writer Joe Oyama observed in 1936, "Los Angeles dances are more cosmopolitan than San Francisco, Sacramento, San Jose, Fresno, Salinas, or Berkeley dances. Here you will always see a handful of Caucasians dancing with Japanese girls or the other way around." The diversity of participants reflected that of southern California's population:

> Sometimes a tall handsome Mexican will drag a petite Nipponese maiden to some high school club dance. Beautiful blonde Russian girls come with husky Japanese boys. Koreans are numerous— with only a sprinkling of Chinese.

"Once in a blue moon," according to Oyama, African American men might "appear in the middle of the floor in the stag line." He reported, "There is little prejudice, in fact no prejudice at all against these other races 'intruding', for the Nisei boys are too busy cutting each other's throats."[21] However, mixed couples were not welcome at all public venues, as Oyama described five years later: "four of us, including one Caucasian American fellow, went to a certain ballroom in Ocean Park. We had heard before that mixed dancing (Whites with Orientals) was not allowed." The rumors were confirmed when one of the Nisei women and her European American escort "stormed out of the ballroom explaining that they had been insulted." One aspect of the incident that most angered the Nisei woman was that, at the time, "a Nisei couple was standing behind her giving her a very disdainful and reproachful look."[22] Oyama's observations reflected the range of opinions among the urban Japanese Americans regarding the boundaries of acceptable interracial socializing. His writing also reflected how the Nisei, like other racial-ethnic youth in the West, had to navigate a terrain in which the boundaries might vary in rigidity or malleability, depending on circumstances. Although some casual interracial dating did occur, most of the Nisei—mindful of the strong preferences of the Japanese American community as well as the legal restrictions of the larger society—searched for a romantic partner within their own ethnic group.

The polished floor, enveloping music, and happy throng at the dance provided a setting conducive to courtship. Nimura sniffed, "Somebody better establish a matrimonial bureau so that choosing a life time companion may be facilitated instead of going to ballrooms to look for them."[23] Other Nisei viewed this process less critically. Mary Oyama [Joe's sister] describes the entrancing ambience of the dance in a 1934 poem, "On Wings of Song, Young and Foolish":

> Syncopated beat, lightly gliding feet,
> The clarinet hums, the banjo strums,
> The violins call, the saxes wail;
> What a dance, what a melody—
> What a chance for grand whoopee![24]

Basking in his partner's warm glance and sweet perfume, the male dancer feels, "A mad desire to crush you tight/burns me up," The woman in his arms, similarly aswoon, thinks,

> Oh gee, I adore you, dear,
> So manly, so tall, so near!
> When you hold me like that—
> Ooh, chills chase up my spine!

As the band played the "Naughty Waltz," "their" song, it was clearly a night for romance. Writer Y. Kawagishi also delineated the enchantment of dance in a short story about a Nisei freshman's first such foray. Bashful and inept, Tom Suzuki was thrilled to be partnered with Alice Sato, "the best dancer in the hall." Thanks to Alice's skillful maneuvering, "Tom's sensations were floating in the air. The fragrance of the perfume intoxicated him, and the touch of Alice's body almost numbed his senses. He felt Alice's stray hair tickle his throat, but even that was bliss to him."[25] So great were Alice's skill and tact that he was euphorically unaware of stepping on her feet and being out of step with the music.

The "small beautiful Alice," graceful in dance and social relations, charming and sought after by boys, possessed the attributes to which urban Nisei girls aspired. In the same year, 1936, advice columnist "Miss Etiquette" advised those who would "like to be the 'belle of the ball'" that "[I]t's a rare gift to dance divinely, but it is both possible and essential to dance well." It is no wonder that Nisei girls spent so much time practicing their footwork at their club meetings and at home with friends. According to Miss Etiquette, additional sources of social capital were to be cultivated: "A girl must not only must dance well, be rather beautiful and fairly intelligent, but must also be unafraid and look as though she were having a good time even though she isn't." She assured them that the psychological effects would be "really astonishing."[26] These efforts at self-transformation were in large part motivated by the Nisei girl's hope of finding the male partner with whom she could "waltz away, all tho'ts of day" and "together make this dream to last for years."[27]

Yearning for Romantic Love

The young Nisei women's preoccupation with romantic love reflected the influence of popular literature, songs, and movies. As Lucille Morimoto wrote,

> To-night
> I want to feel your nearness,
> To hear your husky voice fade into a whisper,
> To me they will be like the sweetness of honey,
> The cool breeze on my feverish face.[28]

Margaret Uchiyamada also yearned and burned in cinematic style, as she lamented in a 1933 verse:

> There's a reason why I cry at night
> And writhe with pain in my heart,
> While I curse the intervening miles
> That relentlessly keep us apart.
> I know that it's foolish to lie here and dream.
> And wipe eyes that will not be dry,
> But memories are all that I have left
> Since the night we kissed good-bye.[29]

An outpouring of prewar poetry and short stories reflected Nisei women's romantic desires, disappointments, and dreams.

Yet even while attesting to the popularity of heterosexual romantic ideals, one Los Angeles columnist, "Mme. Yamato Nadeshiko," deplored their impact. Her diatribe also underscored the effectiveness of mainstream media as a vehicle for these rosy notions. She felt that "seeing too many movies" and "reading too many novels" had caused Nisei women to harbor unrealistic dreams of "tall stalwart sons of men, bronzed by desert's noonday heat and whipped by bitter rain and hail. Hearts of gold, strength of steel, romantic Romeos." She warned women not to wait for a "Sir Galahad" but to recognize the "everyday heroes [who] exist all about us."[30] Another columnist who identified herself as "a deb" similarly mused, "The trouble with us is—we build too many air castles. And we pick on a man, the dream of our 'teens as the 'one and only'—who not only seems sincere, but can do no wrong. But that's being over romantic and over idealized. Sort of dangerous, don't you think?" She advised her peers "to be hardboiled towards love" because "we're just bound to undergo some of its misfortunes."[31] Her admonition transmitted not only caution about, but also an expectation of, romantic love.

What did the urban Nisei women expect of their Nisei Galahads and Romeos? A 1938 *Rafu Shimpo* article presented a lengthy list of qualities that local Japanese American co-eds hoped to find in a "dream spouse." According to the reporter, the boys had better be well-groomed, sophisticated, manly or athletic, fluent in Japanese and English, loyal, sensible, sincere, considerate, cheerful, generous, tolerant, responsible, and good-looking. At this point in the litany, the writer warned, "Fellows, you're not perfect yet. You've also got to have ambition, be financially secure, or earning a salary of at least $150 a month, have a terrific I.Q., be a one-woman man, faithful, and have the same interests."[32] In addition to cosmopolitan bilingualism, they also incorporated the Japanese considerations of educational background and family heritage. Whether or not the co-eds truly expected to locate a paragon with all of these qualities, their collegiate wish-list reflected the strong influence of mainstream middle-class values along with criteria important to their parents.

And what did the Nisei campus men hope for in their dream girl? A 1931 account of a "bull session" among Japanese American men at UCLA revealed that, like their female counterparts, they had been influenced by mainstream ideals. According to the columnist,

> Perhaps most of the girls would like for a husband with the strength of a Samson, the sex appeal of Casanova, the wisdom of Socrates, and the personality of a Mussolini. Usually they want too much. *The same is true of the boys.* They want a Clara Bow, a Cleopatra, and a Portia all rolled into one [emphasis mine].

He concluded in the same vein as Mme. Yamato Nadeshiko: "But we're mortals and we must get to accept humans with their weaknesses and faults."[33] A prudently anonymous poem of 1939 expressed both Hollywood dreams and pragmatism with regard to the "Nisei Girl":

> Madeleine Carrol is a glamourous [sic] blonde
> And of her pictures I'm very fond; ...
> . . .
> Then it would be hard in partin'
> With a girl like Mary Martin.
> And Linda Darnell isn't bad
> But, of course, she can't be had.
> Yet, the NISEI GIRL I'd rather squeeze
> 'Cause she has curves below her knees.[34]

Jesting aside, for a range of reasons, the vast majority of Nisei searched within their own ethnic peer group for husbands and wives. Like their mothers and most U.S. women, Nisei women expected a future that centered around marriage and family. In contrast to Issei women, however, Nisei women expected their marital relations to be based on romantic attraction and individual choice—the hallmarks of mainstream ideals—as well as duty. Unlike their parents, they considered happiness "the first and last object of any marriage," and dreamed of finding true love.[35] To this end, in 1940 the *Rafu Shimpo* offered "hints which may help you win your man" and "romance tests" to help girls determine if what they felt was love or just infatuation.[36]

Given these values and hopes, it is not surprising that second-generation women increasingly challenged the practice of arranged marriage in favor of "love marriage." As Evelyn Nakano Glenn (1986: 57) explains, "With the loosening of traditional family controls, the urban Nisei had moved toward the ideal of 'free marriage' by the mid 1930s."[37] The sense that women were more likely than men to suffer in such matches prompted Wilfred Y. Horiuchi to relate the story of a "sweet girl" who "never said 'no' to her parents"; she gave up the man she loved, accepted the marriage they arranged, and then ended up at age 31 a strapped breadwinner with five children, married to a penniless "old crate" of 50. The columnist asked, "Ah, is marriage for men alone to enjoy? Have women no right to happiness?"[38] Nisei women, who had less veto power over the choice of marital partners than Nisei men, wrote frequently to Nisei advice columnist "Deirdre" to rail against arranged matches.[39] Extensive and heated dialogues among readers often raged for weeks in the popular San Francisco newspaper column. In a 1934 article in the *Kashu Mainichi*, Mary Korenaga passionately decried such unions, rhetorically asking if Nisei should allow themselves to "become a breeding machine to which we are forced by the third party merely for the purpose of keeping the world populated? Are we to lose emotions which we have harbored merely to become a human mechanism on the order of the common ant?" "No!!" she declared, "A thousand times, No!"[40] The priority Korenaga placed on individual choice and romantic love mirrors the Nisei's embrace of mainstream ideals of companionate marriage.

It is impossible to know exactly how many of the prewar Nisei marriages were arranged and how many were romantic unions. The newspapers rarely released this information as they did in the case of the 1928 engagement of a young woman from San Luis Obispo: "The young couple shyly confessed that it was a love match."[41] Yet even in this case, the announcement included the names of *baishakunin* (official matchmakers). As the *Rafu Shimpo* announced in 1937, it was also unusual to read that the betrothal of Yaye Tokuyama and journalist Noboru "Brownie" Furutani "was arranged in traditional Japanese manner."[42] The prominence of one of the six *baishakunin,* Sei Fujii—publisher of the *Kashu Mainichi*—may have prompted the inclusion of this detail. Although an increasing number of urban Nisei were finding their own spouses, *baishakunin*—usually older married couples—were routinely mentioned in the last lines of prewar wedding announcements. This may have reflected the second generation's accommodation of their Issei parents by adopting the conventional Japanese forms rather than the full practice.[43] In 1936, a forum of northern California Nisei men and women agreed that they preferred romantic love to arranged marriage, and said that in most cases "we who fall in love and desire to marry some one of our own choice will ask our parents to provide *baishakunin* and thus give formal approval to our romantic union."[44] In the same year, a Los Angeles Nisei columnist also reported that the second generation "prefer to have *baishakunins* perform the minor duties and leave the matter of selection to the individual."[45] More research is needed to discern how *baishakunin* adapted their roles and customs to fit the new circumstances of life in America.

Ironically, the dominant society not only broadened but also constrained Nisei marital choices, which were made within the framework established by state codification of racial discrimination and embodied in the antimiscegenation laws that Peggy Pascoe (1991, 1996, and 1999) examines. Like their mothers, Nisei women retained values of duty and obligation and expected to marry men of their own racial-ethnic group. This stemmed not only from the strong preference within the Japanese American community but also from the stronger opposition to interracial unions from the dominant society. In 1880, California's antimiscegenation law was amended to include Asians. The marriage of a white person to a "Negro, mulatto, Mongolian or Malay" was illegal until the overturn of the law in 1948. By the 1930s, fourteen states—including Arizona, California, Idaho, Montana, Nebraska, Nevada, Oregon, Utah, and Wyoming—had antimiscegenation laws aimed at Asian immigrants and their children.[46] When the author of "Nisei Girl" wrote that actress Linda Darnell "could not be had," Japanese American readers understood that her unattainability stemmed from both status and race. Like other social and economic arenas, in the arena of marital choice, the Nisei remained highly conscious of the boundaries of race, status, and gender.

The few interethnic and interracial marriages that did occur garnered attention in the Japanese American press. Publicized Asian-interracial matches on the East Coast—where antimiscegenation laws did not target Asians—often involved educated elite European Americans and Japanese Americans in university settings. On the West Coast, intermarriages were more likely to occur between Japanese American women and Chinese or Filipino American men. Given the dearth of women in the Filipino immigrant community, a number of Filipino men—often living and working in proximity to Japanese American enclaves—turned their attention to Nisei daughters. As Arleen De Vera (1999) and Eiichiro Azuma (1992) document, rural Issei disapproved of such matches. In the 1930 case of Felix Tapia and Alice Saiki, who had met in the Stockton pool hall of Alice's father, a starry-eyed elopement ended in anguish: Alice returned to her parents' home for what was to have been a short stay and was never seen again by her distraught husband, who believed her parents had sent her to Japan (De Vera, 1999). Some of the urban Nisei adopted a more tolerant tone regarding intermarriage. In 1933 journalist Larry Tajiri critiqued the stigmatization of interracial unions and the acute pressures such couples faced from "the attitude of the community as a whole."[47] Given the disapproval of the immigrant community and the legal restrictions of the dominant society, the number of interracial unions was small. As Kay Nishida observed in 1935, "On the Pacific Coast there have been a number of international marriages lately in which scions of the samurai joined their nuptial destinies with Chinese, Caucasians, and Mexicans. But they are, as a whole, rarities." Nishida predicted with foresight, "Among the future third and fourth generation people, this should not be so."[48] However, in the prewar years, deterred by ethnic community preferences and external legal sanctions, few Nisei pursued such matches.

By 1936, Nisei expectations of marriage bore the imprint of both Japanese and middle-class mainstream ideals, as well as the heavy stamp of the Great Depression. T. Roku Sugahara, a Los Angeles columnist, stated that "the average Nisei" wished to "have an understanding of equality in dealing and sharing all matters that affect them both" in their marriage and that they believed "both husband and wife should work in the first years, if necessary."[49] After attending a northern California Nisei discussion on "Marriage and the Home," Kimi Kanazawa reported that although women and men valued the "comradeship relation" between spouses, they held differing views with regard to wage-paid work for wives: "The second generation man, like his father, is still seeking the somewhat antiquated ideal of a wife who cooks, sews, stays in the home, does not earn money outside, and is generally docile (this last was merely implied)." The male ideal was to establish himself independently without financial support from his wife or relatives. Women, on the other hand, expressed willingness "to struggle together with their husbands and work with them." However, Kanazawa wrote, "without becoming gold-diggers," they also wanted "reasonable assurance that their future husbands have the ability to succeed."[50] Both Kanazawa and Sugahara noted that the Japanese American family was changing. Sugahara felt that the Nisei marriage rested on a middle ground—a "tough spot"—"just strange enough to the native Japanese to be criticized and just a bit too timid to be the real American romance."[51] Kanazawa concluded that the Nisei wished to retain some Japanese culture in their homes, and were "taking parts of both American and Japanese cultures to fit our own situation." Her expectation was that the second-generation family, "while retaining the old culture, will grow to be more and more like the American type."[52]

CONCLUSION

Girls and young women played dynamic roles in creating and sustaining a lively urban Nisei world from the Jazz Age through the Great Depression. Under the watchful eyes of the immigrant community, and well aware of the restrictions they faced within the broader society, they experimented with cultural forms of socializing and courtship, introducing popular mainstream elements into the ethnic enclave while retaining certain aspects of their parents' customs. This messy, exuberant, and variable process of synthesis is visible in their socializing and courtship, ideals of romantic love, and expectations of marriage. After they weathered the long winter of wartime internment, Nisei women's shared practices and dreams continued to shape and color Japanese American family and community life.

Notes

1. Lily Tanaka, "A Modern Romance," *Rafu Shimpo*, February 25, 1940, p.14. Reprinted with permission. The poem ended with the quick demise of the hasty marriage.
2. The Meiji era began in 1968 with the overthrow of the Tokugawa Shogunate and the restoration of imperial rule, and ended with the death of the Meiji emperor in 1912. See Niiya, 1993 (p. 230) for detail.
3. See T. Roku Sugahara, "So This Is Leap Year," *Kashu Mainichi*, June 28, 1936.
4. *Rafu Shimpo*, April 18 and 25, 1926. Reprinted with permission. The "Venice" referred to in the poem is a seaside community in southern California. The Venice Pier was a popular amusement site in the 1920s.
5. *Rafu Shimpo*, October 8, 1928.
6. *Rafu Shimpo*, October 15, 1927. The columnist, "Katy," was male.
7. *Shebas* was a slang term used in the late 1920s that referred to young women (and "sheiks" to young men), and was inspired by the romantic images of early movie stars such as Theda Bara and Rudolph Valentino.
8. Some of the captions were credited to published sources, often college publications; others were uncredited; still others that referred to events within the Japanese American community were clearly generated by Suski or the newspaper staff. Suski depicted both white and Asian/American-looking women and men.
9. *Rafu Shimpo*, December 9, 1929; Paula Fass (1977: 264) describes "petting" as encompassing "a broad range of potentially erotic contacts, from a casual kiss to more intimate caresses and physical fondling"; Nisei columnist Wilfred Horiuchi in 1931 wrote in defense of petting, citing European American educators and leaders on the subject. See *Rafu Shimpo*, November 8, 1931.

10. *Rafu Shimpo*, January 12, 1931.
11. *Rafu Shimpo*, January 12, 1931.
12. *Kashu Mainichi*, July 31, 1933. Mrs. Olds was the bilingual daughter of one of the founders of Tokyo Doshisha University; she was also giving talks for Issei parents.
11. *Rafu Shimpo*, April 16 1937.
12. *Rafu Shimpo*, November 29 1937. The two groups were the Debutantes and the Alpha Beta Club.
13. *Rafu Shimpo*, August 1, 1926. Reprinted with permission.
14. Boys lacking access to a car cringed at the prospect of having to ask a girl to travel by streetcar. *Rafu Shimpo*, holiday issue, December 24, 1936, p. 20. Male writer Kay Tateishi's short story shows that the "date" had become routine enough to be lampooned.
15. See "La Hash Exclusive," *Rafu Shimpo*, December 5, 1937. Reprinted with permission.
16. See "Hodge Podge" column, *Rafu Shimpo*, December 16, 1933. The Nisei man's complaint also perhaps reflects the boundaries of permissible premarital sexual behavior among the second generation.
17. *Rafu Shimpo*, November 6, 1938.
18. See "With Apologies to Will Rogers,"*Rafu Shimpo*, January 19, 1931.
19. *Kashu Mainichi*, May 3, 1936. The "stag line" referred to the line of men without female partners.
20. *Kashu Mainichi*, holiday issue, January 1, 1941. Oyama argued that the Nisei should not seek to avoid such racial discrimination but should face it squarely and fight it.
21. *Kashu Mainichi*, holiday issue, January 1, 1941.
22. *Kashu Mainichi*, January 21, 1934.
23. *Kashu Mainichi*, January 1, 1936.
24. *Rafu Shimpo*, October 18, 1936.
25. See Oyama, "On Wings of Song, Young and Foolish," *Kashu Mainichi*, January 21, 1934.
26. From "Three Thoughts," *Kashu Mainichi*, May 22, 1932.
27. From "Heartache," *Kashu Mainichi*, August 26, 1933.
28. *Kashu Mainichi*, July 10, 1932.
29. From "Feminine Interest," *Kashu Mainichi*, October 6, 1935.
30. *Rafu Shimpo*, holiday issue, December 23, 1938, p.22.
31. *Rafu Shimpo*, January 19, 1931. From "Brewin Typs" column by "RUS."
32. *Rafu Shimpo*, December 10, 1939. Reprinted with permission.
33. *Kashu Mainichi*, January 21, 1934. See "Editorials."
34. *Rafu Shimpo*, January 7, 21, and 28, 1940; February 25, 1940.
35. In the *Rafu Shimpo* of January 1, 1930, a Nisei man wrote approvingly of "companionate marriage"; other men described an ideal wife as being domestic, good-looking, having sterling character, and serving as an inspiration to them. The one woman who responded said an ideal husband would be intellectual, healthy, frank, and have good character.
36. *Rafu Shimpo*, November 22, 1931. Given the disparity in age, the match he described was probably between a Nisei woman and an Issei man. Horiuchi wrote a series of essays critiquing various aspects of the arranged marriage and urging the second generation to make their own decisions. He cited U.S. and European authorities such as Sherwood Eddy, Havelock Ellis, and Judge Lindsay to support his case.
37. For more on the "I'm Telling You Deirdre" column, see Matsumoto (1994).
38. *Kashu Mainichi*, March 4, 1934.
39. *Rafu Shimpo*, August 6, 1928. Kofuji Eto, the daughter of a wealthy Issei agricultural landowner, was engaged to T. Fukunaga, a businessman and secretary of the Pismo Pea Growers Association.
40. *Rafu Shimpo*, April 22, 1937.
41. It is also possible that the role of the *baishakunin* had shifted in the United States to involve potential mediation between newlyweds and in-laws, in the event difficulties arose.
42. See Kimi Yanazawa, "The Nisei Come of Age," *Kashu Mainichi*, May 24, 1936.
43. See Sugahara, "So This Is Leap Year..."
44. Peggy Pascoe's insightful work on antimiscegenation law is especially useful (see Pascoe 1991, 1996, and 1999); for a detailed discussion of antimiscegenation laws and their application to Asian Americans, see Osumi, 1982.
45. See "Village Vagaries," *Kashu Mainichi*, September 17, 1933.
46. *Rafu Shimpo*, January 6, 1935. Nishida appears to have been male.

47. Sugahara, "So This Is Leap Year...."
48. See "The Nisei Come of Age."
49. Sugahara, "So This Is Leap Year...."
50. Kanazawa, "The Nisei Come of Age."
51. See Kanazawa, "The Nisei Come of Age."
52. See Kanazawa, "The Nisei Come of Age."
53. See Kanazawa, "The Nisei Come of Age."

CHAPTER 6

Hell's a Poppin':

Asian American Women's Youth Consumer Culture

Shirley Jennifer Lim

Preparing pretty party sandwiches is an easily acquired art and one that shows off, to a very good advantage, the cooking prowess of a clever hostess ... [They include] avocado-pineapple sandwiches, raisin-peanut butter pinwheel sandwiches, celery seed breadsticks, cervelat (sausage) flash bars, cream cheese-jelly cube sandwiches, deviled ham-peanut butter star sandwiches.

"The Feminine Scene"[1]

Although the cartridge cases and sailor caps are basically alike, they don't look anything alike after the girls have worked on them for a while. For instance, they think a girl is a schmoe if she doesn't scribble all kinds of things on her case—such as the names of her favorite fella, songs, clubs, etc., No two purses look alike after all this scrawling! With the caps, it's the same story.

"Teen Age Fads"[2]

As the above magazine excerpts illustrate, in the middle of the twentieth century, young Asian American women were the quintessential gendered subjects who were affected by and also helped to shape Asian American youth culture. This chapter focuses on the postwar production of Asian American gendered public culture. Asian American ethnic presses such as *Scene*, the *Philippines Star Press*, and the *Chinese Press*, along with youth organizations such as Chi Alpha Delta, provide touchstones through which we may view the growth of Asian American youth culture during the post–World War II golden age of American consumption.³ During this time, Asian American youth became central to their communities. Indeed, becoming Asian American was a key step in claiming a place in the American nation and necessary to the rise of the Asian American movement.

Displaying Asian American cultural citizenship entailed participating in mainstream practices so that communities could show modernity, progress, and fitness for acceptance into the American polity. And while club activities, magazines, and community events could have easily been marked as male, the extent to which they were gendered female is particularly striking. In other words, none of the cultural sites under consideration had to be gendered female, but that they were suggests a particular kind of logic. Asian American communities demonstrated their fitness to be Americans by using cultural practices such as food, fashion, fun, and beauty. Through visual markers, young women could display ethnicity, race, and nation, which vacillated between "American" and "Asian" traits and sometimes resulted in hybridity.

THE EMERGENCE OF ASIAN AMERICAN WOMEN IN PUBLIC CULTURE

Four key historical developments propelled the symbolic significance of Asian American women's public culture: (1) the growth of gendered consumer culture; (2) the rise of "teen" as a demographic and marketing category; (3) Asian American demographics; (4) and changing U.S. race relations. First, changing American economics during World War II and the ensuing postwar consumer boom encouraged tremendous growth in the consumption of manufactured goods, creating a veritable "golden age" in consumer culture. During the industrial age of production, items such as clothing and food slowly shifted outside the home, but it was not until the post–World War II era that the consumption of manufactured goods increased for all Americans (May, 1988). In the postwar era, American prosperity, accompanied by the middle-class norm of female domesticity, accelerated the distinctly gendered nature of consumer consumption. Consequently, women's control over the private sphere of the home extended into the public realm of consumer culture.

Second, although "youth culture" has had distinctive forms and practices since the turn of the twentieth century, its commodification, nationalization, and pervasiveness exploded in the post–World War II era. In fact, the very word "teenager" entered popular usage during the 1940s (Palladino, 1996). Full employment and growing prosperity allowed families to support youth activities, and, as a consequence, "teen" culture—as a generational cohort, cultural phenomenon, and marketing category—

arose during this era (Austin and Willard, 1998a). For all youth, participation in the social life of American teen culture enabled them to distinguish their generation from that of their parents. Magazines founded in the postwar era such as *Seventeen* and *Scene* facilitated the commodification of American gendered youth culture.

Third, although the large numbers of births known as the baby boom affected all Americans, Asian Americans' unique demographic patterns set the stage for the growth of Asian American female youth culture in particular. Historically, Chinese American sex ratios had been heavily skewed toward the male as a result of nineteenth-century male migration and American immigration exclusion laws such as the Page Law, which excluded Chinese women (Hirata, 1979). In the postwar era, however, rising Chinese American birthrates leveled the sex ratios. For example, in 1940, only 20,115 out of a total of 77,504 Chinese Americans were women, but by 1960, the female population had grown more than fivefold reaching 101,743 out of 237,292 Chinese Americans (Yung, 1995). Owing to the historically higher numbers of female immigrants to the United States, Japanese Americans had more even sex ratios. For example, in California in 1940 there were 28,216 female Nisei (second-generation Japanese Americans) out of 60,148 Nisei, and a total of 93,717 Japanese Americans (Kurashige, 2002; Matsumoto, 1994; Yoo, 2000). The postwar era also saw a growing Filipino American youth population (Cordova, 1983; Posadas, 1999). Hence, not only did the Asian American population grow during this period, but its female population soared to even out the previously unbalanced gender ratio.

Fourth, in the postwar era, American race relations shifted profoundly, particularly for Asian Americans. Although all Asian ethnic groups had to prove their Americanness, the specific postwar political challenges were different for each group. For Japanese Americans, this meant overcoming the distrust caused by their abrupt uprooting, forced internment, and eventual resettlement into alternative geographic locales across the United States. For Chinese Americans, the major hurdle was proving they were not communists like the Chinese in the People's Republic of China. For Filipino Americans, the challenge rested in redefining themselves as people with a distinct national origin and identity who were no longer colonized subjects. All Americans faced the burden of defining themselves as Americans during the postwar era, but Asian Americans felt the predicament most heavily. They faced the challenge of having to embrace and define themselves by the liberal ideals of patriotism, egalitarianism, democracy, and freedom.

The twentieth-century racial distinction between immigrant and citizen exacerbated the postwar political climate for all Asian Americans.

Throughout the nineteenth and twentieth centuries, the legal category of foreigner (as opposed to American citizen) had been built around Asian Americans (Yu, 2001). Since it was impossible for most Asian-ethnic Americans to pass as white, they could appear most American by participating in mainstream cultural activities. And because they wished to appear American, Asian Americans remained cautious about demonstrating ethnic pride. Their cautious efforts eventually allowed Asian American communities to secure a measure of mainstream societal acceptance. However, this did not mean that Asian American women abandoned all things Asian. Rather, they melded Asian-ethnic and American traits, forged a hybridity, and thereby paved the way for Asian American youth to construct a distinctively Asian American identity that did not conflict with an American one.

DEFINING FEMININITY FOR AMERICAN WOMEN

What was new about postwar consumer culture was the extent to which all young American women turned to peers and magazines as arbiters of taste and style rather than relying on advice from their mothers. In postwar displays of cultural citizenship, Asian American women found numerous occasions to display peer-driven and nationally circulating "modern" and Western fashion and food choices. Consumer culture centered on the accumulation and display of goods, fashion, beauty, and food, becoming an integral part of the American female identity. Domesticity was the primary means through which middle-class African American and European American culture was gendered. For Asian Americans, although domesticity—house, home, family—was certainly emphasized, Asian American middle-class culture was more strongly marked by a class-inflected femininity that was single, fashionable, and in the public sphere. Yet for Asian American women, consumer culture was not only gendered, it was ethnicized. Asian American women frequently found themselves situated between Western and Asian social practices and thus deployed hybridity to create a distinctive Asian American culture. In short, Asian American women both appropriated and transformed aesthetic standards of white middle-class femininity and, in the process, redefined the meaning of femininity.

THE DIFFUSION OF CULTURE THROUGH MAGAZINES

A close examination of *Scene*, a leading Asian American magazine published in the postwar era, shows how the political need to prove Asian American cultural citizenship in the aftermath of the war compelled the display of wholesome, gendered all-American youth culture. Produced in Chicago from 1949 to 1953, *Scene* magazine provides a marvelous glimpse into the creation of gendered youth culture that initially focused on Japanese Americans but later depicted Asian Americans more generally. That *Scene* was not an explicitly youth or female magazine makes its emphasis on female and youth cultures especially notable. Modeled after *Life* magazine, *Scene* included features on international politics, Japanese-language feature articles, and Japanese advertisements. Yet *Scene* editors almost always placed young women of Asian descent on its cover and focused largely on women and youth activities. Accompanying the articles in *Scene* were pictures that indirectly promoted consumer culture by displaying well-dressed women in its pages, conveying the message that knowledge of appropriate class-inflected clothing and makeup was crucial for social success. Through features on food and fashion, *Scene* instilled in its readers the desire to buy the most appropriate products and display appropriate Asian American cultural citizenship (Anderson, 1983; Scanlon, 1995).

Division of labor is a key arena through which society reflects gender differentiation, and according to *Scene* magazine, holding a wage-paying job was the man's work, while cooking remained in the woman's domain. In *Scene*'s September 1949 issue, the monthly column entitled the "Feminine Scene" showed readers—ostensibly female ones—how to prepare party sandwiches. The article explained: "Preparing pretty party sandwiches is an easily acquired art and one that shows off, to a very good advantage, the cooking prowess of a clever hostess." The story profiled a number of different sandwich combinations shaped into various forms, including "avocado-pineapple sandwiches, raisin-peanut butter pinwheel sandwiches, celery seed breadsticks, cervelat (sausage) flash bars, cream cheese-jelly cube sandwiches, deviled ham-peanut butter star sandwiches." Of particular note is that while the article highlights domestic labor, all this preparation was for entertaining others rather than for serving the nuclear family. *Scene* was not alone in advising youth on the how-to of entertaining guests; *Seventeen* magazine published food columns three times a month in which the editors explained socially critical knowledge such as how to put together double-decker sandwiches that could be served when bringing "the gang" home after the movies (Palladino, 1996). At a time when entertaining was no longer reserved for the affluent, magazines such as *Scene* and *Seventeen* provided virtual blueprints of the craft of properly entertaining guests in one's home.

Scene's sandwich article underscored the importance of "American" food products—goods that changed due to the political economy. As the list of sandwiches shows, one effect of World War II was the introduction and immediate popularity of preserved-meat sandwiches—nowhere does the column include any ideas for fresh turkey or roast beef sandwiches. Moreover, the inclusion of warm-climate ingredients such as avocados and pineapples was a result of the growing population in, and awareness of, California and Hawaii and the improved U.S. food distribution networks and advertising which made such ingredients familiar, affordable, and desirable to the American middle class. The differing shapes of the sandwiches such as pinwheels, stars, and cubes reflected an interest in further developing domestic skills through innovative and clever presentation.

ASIAN AMERICAN SORORITIES, FOOD, AND FASHION

Founded in 1928 at the University of California, Los Angeles, Chi Alpha Delta was the first Japanese American and Asian American sorority in the United States. Asian American sororities were to become so popular that by 1959, another sorority, Theta Kappa Phi, had been founded on the same campus. Chi Alpha Delta attracted membership of approximately 60 sorors each year, and by 1960 the predominantly Japanese American sorority had attracted other Asian ethnic women as members. Through food and fashion, the women of Chi Alpha Delta carved a gendered, ethnicized, and generational identity that vacillated between Asian-ethnic and distinctively American. For example, the women of Chi Alpha Delta prepared and served "international" foods on a regular basis. For a social with Sigma Phi Omega, the University of Southern California Asian American sorority, the menu was American with a Mexican entree: tamales, dill pickles, salad, rolls, punch, sherbert, cookies, and coffee.[4] Magazines like *Scene* normalized "American" food for parties and provided daughters of immigrant women a venue to pick up on the knowledge of choosing, preparing, and presenting such foods.

Alongside food, fashion was another key marker of generational identity, and so the women of Chi Alpha Delta used fashion and fashion shows to promote the sorority and attract new members. The local Los Angeles Lanz clothing store would not only provide free loaner clothes for sorority fashion shows, but would also arrange for clothing fittings and accessories, develop the program of appearance, and either host it or type out comments for the sorority's choice of speakers. Chi Alpha Delta's 1959 fashion show, for instance, used Lanz clothing and sorority-member models. To make the event professional, the sorors rented a ramp from the Hollywood Dance Studio and hired Mrs. Merijane Yokoe, who had hosted similar events at the annual Japanese American festival known as Nisei Week, as their announcer. Chi Alpha Delta also wrote to local Los Angeles–area Japanese American newspapers such as the *Kashu Mainichi* and the *Rafu Shimpo* for advanced publicity for the event.[5]

Holding a fashion show had both positive and negative ramifications. Some of the sorors believed that the Lanz line was too costly and out of reach for most women, and hence found it illogical to hold a fashion extravaganza that featured clothing that many could not afford. Sensitivity to the price of the clothing belied any notion of a universal availability of commodity culture. It is poignant to note here how consumer culture marginalized working-class women and even those with barely a toehold in the middle class. However, the fashion show pointed to the desires and aspirations of young women as opposed to the reality of what they could afford. Using the Lanz name and fashions would undoubtedly appeal to the under-graduate female or "co-ed" population and thus heighten Chi Alpha Delta's prestige.

Although anyone could adopt Western clothes and show American cultural citizenship through clothing purchases, the reality was that the fashion industry designed clothes mainly for the figures of women of Northern and Western European extraction. Many Asian American women therefore had difficulty finding clothes that fit them. Even though 75 percent of the female population was 5'4" and under, most dress manufacturers made clothes for taller women. *Scene* magazine addressed petite clothing needs in the July 1950 issue:

> Even in these days of tall willowy models and matching dress creations, the petite milady is not entirely forgotten. Dresses and suits just as smart and exciting as those worn by her taller sisters can be found in stores which are devoted exclusively to dresses for the petite figure, such as Chicago's Pint-Size Shop which furnished the dresses on this page. You need not encounter the familiar "Please go to the Junior Miss Section" brushoffs.[6]

Instead of being at the mercy of fashions from the teenage clothing section, petite women could find age-appropriate clothing at stores such as the Pint-Size Shop.

Fashion also became an emblem in redefining the postcolonial Filipina American woman. The *Philippine Star Press* published columns such as "Salinas Tid-Bits" by Trudy and Glo and "As I Was Saying" by editor-in-chief Elizabeth Aquino Campbell. In these venues, the Filipina American authors would relay "news, gossip, and juicy tales" to the far-flung commu-nity of women who avidly read the columns. Newspaper chat and gossip columns written by women for women enabled a critical examination of the postcolonial Filipina American image in the United States. In the post–World War II era of increasing middle-class prosperity, Philippines independence, desegregation, gender conventions, and ethnic identity were debated, and behavioral norms formed through these venues.

In "Salinas Tid-Bits," for example, Trudy and Glo reported on the Filipino

American social scene in which fashions of young women played a prominent role. These columns are striking for their intimacy and friendliness,
and readers felt drawn into the community and could identify with the
concerns. For example, the columnists described various community
members' Easter fashions in loving detail. Trudy and Glo's description of
a Filipina American's Easter outfit represents the level of detail they provided
their readers. They recounted Riz Raymundo's clothing as, "very elegant,
very feminine look of spring fashion in a gray suit of Fortman's wool. It
was very outspoken in compliments to her figure. Her hat was that New
Look of black shiny straw with a black satin ribbon with net encircling the
hat. All her accessories were of black felt. Her shoes were of black suede
trimmed with gold."7 That particular feature continued with four additional descriptions of other young women's Easter ensembles of equal detail
and length. Such depictions of "modern" "New Look" clothing—a reference to Christian Dior's contemporary Parisian fashions—contrasts with
the hybrid Filipina and Western clothing that women wore in events such
as the Fourth of July queen contests (Lim, 2003).

PERFORMING ETHNICITY AND HYBRIDITY

While attuning themselves to mainstream societal practices, Asian American
women also created hybrid practices. Highly Americanized public culture
was in tension with the affirmation and display of ethnic solidarity and
history, and thus the degree to which the young women exhibited American
versus Asian traits fluctuated. At certain times, Asian American women
felt compelled to dress in mainstream American fashions, and at others, they
invoked the fashions of Asia. Hybridity—melding and showing both Asian
and American cultural traits—became a viable and acceptable solution
for Asian American women. As Lisa Lowe explains, hybridity "does not
suggest the assimilation of Asian or immigrant practices to dominant
forms, but instead marks the history of survival within relationships of
unequal power and domination" (Lowe, 1996). Hybridity was an attempt
to include Asia within the definition of American cultural citizenship.
Through their gendered and hybrid practices, Asian American women
created distinctly Asian American forms of culture.For example, young
women enthusiastically customized army surplus items to make the accessories their own.

> Although the cartridge cases and sailor caps are basically alike,
> they don't look anything alike after the girls have worked on them
> for a while. For instance, they think a girl is a schmoe if she doesn't
> scribble all kinds of things on her case—such as the names of her

favorite fella, songs, clubs, etc. No two purses look alike after all this scrawling! With the caps, it's the same story.[8]

Note the teenage slang such as "schmoe" and "fella," the use of which allowed the young women to enter into mainstream youth culture. Yet, as the women inscribed the names of their favorite men, clubs, and such on their hats and purses, these items took on Asian American characteristics. The naming of affiliation renders the artifacts as distinct from mainstream ones.

In a different variation of hybridity, Anna May Wong popularized supposedly Chinese beauty customs for presumably European American audiences. Well after her cinematic heyday in 1947, Chinese American actress Anna May Wong worked as a spokesmodel for Lentheric's Shanghai perfume. Born in Los Angeles's Chinatown, Wong's 57 films crowned her as the most important Asian American film actress of the twentieth century, which in turn added to her immense marketability. As part of the publicity campaign, Wong gave lectures on "Chinese Beauty Customs" in places such as New York's Plaza Hotel and Stern's Department store (Leong, 1999). During an era that displayed an interest in women of Asian descent and beauty, Wong spoke about how Chinese women cared for their hair and their makeup, offering the following "Chinese" beauty tips:

To beautify the eyes, spend half an hour or so a day watching goldfish swim.
To beautify the hands, try rolling a walnut in the palm of each hand daily as regular exercise.
To beautify the feet, practice concentrated toe wiggling.
And to tighten the skin of the face, instead of using all kinds of cream, try covering it with a mask of egg-white.[9]

Although these tips were not particularly Chinese, they were marketed as such. Anna May Wong's national beauty tour marks the beginning of the feminization of Asian women.

In another instance of hybridity, the "Feminine Scene" column in *Scene* magazine profiled not only Western foods but also Japanese food, indicating an increased level of comfort with Japanese culture. For example, in May of 1952, three years after the party-sandwich column, the magazine touted the versatility of sushi for parties: "Issei housewives and hostesses—and many of their Nisei daughters—never worry over what to prepare for that buffet or picnic. They immediately set about making some kind of sushi."[10] For Nisei daughters who did not know how to make sushi, the article explained the ingredients, preparation steps, and final presentation. The focus on Japanese food was particularly significant since it signaled that *Scene*'s editors and writers had become more flexible about the ideals of assimilation and Americanization; showing ethnic affiliating with food would not jeopardize Japanese Americans' efforts to gain social acceptance. The food profile coincided with stories on the kimono as appropriate and fashionable wear for women, further illustrating the larger currents of change in the social climate. America's fascination with Asia as part of America's de facto empire also signaled a desire to master Asian culture, and Asian Americans capitalized on this resurgence to make cultural gains of their own.

Similarly, the experiences of Chi Alpha Delta reflected the fluidity of racialized cultural citizenship. Throughout the 1950s, the members of Chi Alpha Delta continually debated how they should present themselves to the UCLA community. They used cultural markers that varied between Japanese, American, and those that merged the two (Ruiz, 1998). For example, during a 1950 campus fundraiser, they decreed that they would all wear kimonos and sell gardenias.[11] Two years later, they decided they would sell flowers again but would not wear kimonos. The young women of Chi Alpha Delta were fully aware that they had to "test" the waters of acceptability when performing cultural citizenship.

For Chi Alpha Delta members, events labeled "cultural" emphasized Japanese themes, and those referred to as "social" stressed more Americanized ones. In 1957, the Chi Alpha Deltas held their first cultural program that featured Japanese practices such as flower arranging and the martial arts of judo and karate.[12] Grossing $795, the event was an enormous success, prompting the sorority to discuss a second cultural program in 1960.[13] If one were to infer by name alone, any European American sorority could have hosted many of Chi Alpha Delta's social events between 1951 and 1960. For instance, the Chi's picked the theme, "Hell's a Poppin" for a 1951 winter dance, and in 1958, the theme was Sadie Hawkins, an American tradition in which gender roles are reversed, and women, instead of men, choose partners at the dance. In 1960, they organized a swim party with the Sigma Phi Omega sorority of the University of Southern California. Although these events may appear to be little more than mimicry of the social events organized by the European American sororities, upon closer examination, ethnic traits and hybridity become readily apparent. For example, rather than a typical American band, Chi Alpha Delta hired Joe Sakai's presumably Japanese American seven-piece band and held a party with a Chinese American sorority. This hybridity meant that Asian American culture formed in response to ethnic community imperatives within the broader trends of American society.

CONCLUSION

Although Asian American youth culture had been flourishing in ethnic enclaves since the 1930s, it began to emerge beyond the enclaves and into the American mainstream during the post–World War II era. Perhaps most intriguing about this emergence is that young Asian American women, in particular, represented the Asian American consumer. Exercising cultural citizenship in an attempt to claim a place in the American nation, Asian American female youth continually fluctuated between public displays of assimilation into white, middle-class America and Asian ethnic pride, and sometimes managed to forge a sense of cultural hybridity. These negotiations were crucial to the formation of an Asian American identity and would later form one of the bases for the Asian American movement (Wei, 1993). As is the case with most grassroots political and social movements, the Asian American movement required its participants to identify as a group with common interests before acting as a politicized entity.

While narratives of domesticity were the hallmark of African American and European American middle-class womanhood, most significant for Asian Americans was the performance of cultural citizenship through class-inflected ideals of femininity. Ethnic magazines such as *Scene* and The *Philippine Star Press* became instrumental media for disseminating middle-class American and Asian American values, tastes, and aesthetics. However, although consumer culture helped to increase the visibility of Asian American women, it came at the cost of class. Young, modern, middle-class women won the visibility stakes, but others remained at the margins.

Today, Asian American youth culture proliferates. Although *Scene* magazine no longer exists, *A, Face, Yolk,* and numerous other magazines engage the rapidly growing Asian American youth population. Chi Alpha Delta and Theta Kappa Phi continue to flourish and have been joined by numerous other Asian American sororities and fraternities across the country. No longer a predominantly Japanese American sorority, Chi Alpha Delta enjoys strong Chinese American, Filipina American, and Korean American membership. As the Asian American population becomes increasingly more diverse with respect to ethnicity, class, and immigration experience, one of the challenges that Asian American youth face today is not only how they will define themselves vis-à-vis white Americans but how they will build a culture and a community among themselves.

Notes

1. *Scene*, September 1949, p. 28.
2. *Nisei Vue*, Chicago, September 1949, p. 31.
3. Examples of periodicals with news about youth culture include *Scene* (Chicago); *Philippines Star Press* (Los Angeles); *Chinese Press* (San Francisco).

4. Chi Alpha Delta Archives, University Archives, UCLA, 1950–1951.
5. Chi Alpha Delta Archive, University Archives, UCLA, 1959.
6. *Scene*, July 1950, p. 44.
7. *Philippine Star Press*, April 9, 1948, p. 5.
8. *Nisei Vue*, Chicago, September 1949, p. 31.
9. *Chinese Digest*, December 21, 1948, p. 3.
9. *Chinese Digest*, December 21, 1948, p. 3.
10. *Scene,* May 1952, p. 52.
11. Chi Alpha Delta Archive, University Archives, UCLA, March 19, 1950.
12. Chi Alpha Delta Archive, University Archives, UCLA, September 1957.
13. Chi Alpha Delta Archive, University Archives, UCLA, February 1960.

CHAPTER 7

Shifting Ethnic Identity and Consciousness:

U.S.-Born Chinese American Youth in the 1930s and 1950s

Gloria Heyung Chun

The 1930s and 1950s are two historically significant periods for U.S.-born and -raised children of Chinese immigrants. Prior to World War II, the Chinese in America were a largely ignored and forgotten people. Legally excluded and racially segregated from the larger society, the majority of Chinese were confined to life in inner-city Chinatowns. Children were forced to attend "Oriental" schools designated for Chinese pupils, and the few who attended white schools were prevented from participating in extracurricular activities with white students. Chinese youth were also barred from public swimming pools, recreational facilities, and social clubs, so those who desired to play sports, dance, or debate had to form clubs of their own (Lam, 1987).[1] During this period, legal restrictions forbade the marriage between Chinese and whites, and social boundaries kept Chinese out of white social and recreational institutions such as restaurants, cafés, and hotels.

Given the legal and social exclusion from white American society, the children of Chinese immigrants looked to China as their surrogate homeland and considered "*returning* to China" or "going *back* to China" as a solution to blatant racial discrimination, legal exclusion, and blocked employment opportunities. Validating and embracing Chinese culture became a viable and enabling act of self-assertion in subverting the negative stereotypes of Chinese in America. However, when China turned communist in 1949, Chinese Americans severed all ties to China, publicly disavowed communism, and actively sought integration into mainstream society in their quest to fight racial hostility and become American.

Chinese exclusion prior to World War II and the repressive politics of anticommunism of the 1950s shaped how U.S.-born Chinese American youth negotiated their identity in this tumultuous political period. Unlike their European counterparts who could change their last names and lose their accents to blend into American society, second-generation Chinese did not have this option. Their physical appearance and ancestral relationship to China marked them as identifiably different, an image firmly etched in the mind-sets of most white Americans. Contrary to the widely held assimilationist perspective—which suggests that the second generation eagerly adopted and emulated the norms and values of mainstream American society, and in turn, was accepted by it—the experiences of U.S.-born Chinese illustrates that the process of assimilation was far from smooth. This chapter analyzes some of the most significant events that took place during the 1930s and 1950s, and examines how Chinese Americans negotiated their identities given the structural and historical constraints of the time.[2]

"GO FURTHER WEST ... TO CHINA": CHINESE AMERICA IDENTITY UNDER LEGAL EXCLUSION

Residential Life in Chinatown

The 1882 Chinese Exclusion Act and intense racism against the Chinese in the decades that followed resulted in severe economic and residential segregation, a highly unbalanced gender ratio, and a distorted development of the Chinese immigrant community. Because laws restricted the migration of Chinese women and family reunification, earlier Chinatowns were predominantly bachelor societies that consisted mostly of men. For example, in 1900, a full 97 percent of the Chinese population was male. In 1930, the male population declined to 80 percent, and in 1940, to 73 percent. As the gender ratio slowly began to level off, the proportion of U.S.-born children (including "paper sons") of Chinese merchants and laborers who had settled in Chinatowns grew.[3] By 1930, more than 40 percent of the ethnic Chinese population was U.S. born, and by 1940 that proportion rose to 51 percent. Disproportionately young, one out of every five U.S.-born Chinese was under the age of 14.

Even though second-generation Chinese were U.S. born, they, like their immigrant parents and other "bachelor" Chinese laborers, suffered from blatant legal and social exclusion that mirrored the status of African Americans in the South. By illustration, Thomas Chinn (1993: 54), who grew up in San Francisco's Chinatown during the 1930s, recalled, "We were 'ghettoized' within just these few square blocks. We were not allowed to come out and mingle with other people outside of our community. We were too strange and were even discriminated against physically."[4] Demeaning popular stereotypes abound of "the sleepy celestial enveloped in mists of opium fumes," "the long-fingered Mandarins chasing sing-song girls at chop suey shops," and the "yellow peril."

The living conditions of Chinatown's residents in the 1930s were bleak. The youth likened their situation to those trapped in crowded, dilapidated tenements, with two-foot wide hallways and no windows (Lum, 1935). A survey of 119 Chinatown families who received relief aid showed that, on average, there were 2.2 persons to a room, only 40 families with private kitchens, and 25 with private bathing facilities (Lum, 1935). David Gan's memories of the harsh living conditions of Apartment #301 in San Francisco's Chinatown offer a vivid account:

> It had two rooms and a closet-sized kitchen with a window facing other apartments. George and I slept on a sofa bed. Ma and Pa slept in the bedroom with Virginia, Norman and Hank, I think. The dimly lit and narrow hallway had brown linoleum and I rode my tricycle at times. There was no bathroom. Each floor had a communal bathroom, consisting of a tub and a toilet, shared by four or five apartments' tenants.[5]

Rodney Chow, a U.S.-born Chinese youth from Los Angeles, recalls that his family was so poor that they slept on floors. There was no furniture but a few wooden stools and a table in Rodney's apartment, and his family often had soda crackers and water with an occasional boiled head of lettuce with soy sauce for supper.[6] By 1935, more than 350 families in San Francisco's Chinatown received assistance from the San Francisco Relief Administration, demonstrating that these living conditions were not atypical (Lum, 1935).

Economic Exclusion in the United States and Economic Opportunities in China

Life in Chinatown in the 1930s was dreary, and residential segregation, stark, but even more daunting was the economic exclusion of Chinese from the mainstream American labor market. Barred from securing employment in the primary labor market, U.S.-born Chinese were forced to work in menial positions and confined to the walls of their enclaves. Even those who were highly educated found themselves with few employment options outside of Chinatown. A survey of Chinese high school students showed that the overwhelming majority of Chinese youth aspired to pursue careers in engineering and teaching (the two most popular professions), while less than 1 percent expressed a desire to follow the vocational footsteps of their fathers (Shih, 1937: 59). However, few were able to realize their professional dreams. For instance, of the 28 U.S.-born Chinese who graduated from the University of California in 1936 and earned degrees in engineering, economics, architecture, optometry, pharmacy, and commerce, few found jobs in the fields in which they were trained because most firms simply refused to hire Chinese Americans. [7] Sam Lee, who headed the Asian branch of the California State Employment Service, stated, "The only Chinese ever to obtain a doctor's degree in architecture at Berkeley is glad to work in a barbecue stand." Lee also knew of an electrical engineer who worked as a shopkeeper in Chinatown, and a young man with a master's degree in journalism who worked as a chauffeur for a rich woman (Hanser, 1940). In yet another case, a mechanical engineer worked as a draftsman in a steel mill for nine years without being promoted (Wang, 1936).

Unable to secure employment commensurate with their education, most second-generation Chinese had little choice but to take jobs that offered "no future worthy of their skills," carrying trays, washing dishes, cutting meat, ironing clothes, drying fish, and selling Chinese herbs (White, 1941). Many worked in their parents' businesses, and some opened small businesses of their own. According to the Oriental Division of the United States Employment Service in San Francisco, of the 5,000 young Chinese in San Francisco, over 90 percent were placed in positions in the service industry, mainly in the culinary trades (Shih, 1937; White 1941). Having grown up in Chinatown but educated in American public schools, second-generation Chinese knew all too well that to work as a cook, a restaurateur, a laundryman, or a waiter involved long, physically demanding hours, with little pay, and even less room for mobility. Most importantly, these jobs did not utilize the skills that they had acquired in high school and college.

Most employers refused to hire Chinese Americans, and legal restrictions also worked to formally exclude them from professional occupations. For example, California enacted laws against the employment of Chinese in fields such as law, medicine, financial administration, dentistry, veterinary science, liquor store ownership, architecture, engineering, and realty, among others. Although other forms of employment discrimination may not have targeted Chinese Americans specifically, they were exclusionary nonetheless. For instance, some jobs required union membership, a stipulation that automatically precluded Chinese and other ethnic minorities since they were barred from joining unions. Moreover, the seniority system sanctioned the practice of hiring Chinese last and firing them first, making them readily dispensable (Wong, 1982). The dearth of employment opportunities was all the more severe given that America was in the throes of the Great Depression.

Given the bleak economic circumstances combined with the pervasive employment discrimination in America's labor market, many young Chinese American men left for China—a haven that symbolized a racism-free life. The exclusion of Chinese from America's primary labor market undoubtedly "pushed" some U.S.-born Chinese to China, but certain factors in China also "pulled" them there. War-torn China in the 1930s advertised its need for American-trained workers, especially in engineering, and the Chinese government granted money, land, and machinery to those who were trained in the United States and willing to return.[8] The campaign was effective and attracted about 20 percent of U.S.-born Chinese to China in the 1930s, and by the middle of the decade, some Chinese Americans had successfully established fruitful careers.[9] *Chinese Digest* published a report in 1937 containing an extensive list of names of those who returned to China as well as their occupations, most of which fell in the categories of engineering, medicine, teaching, and research.[10]

The Great Debate of the 1930s— "Does My Future Lie in China or America?"

Given their legal exclusion, negative stereotypical depictions, and ties to China, U.S.-born Chinese became all the more eager to define who they were and what it meant to be Chinese American. A national debate on the future of U.S.-born Chinese in the 1930s set the grounds for doing just that. The Ging Hawk Club—a women's social club based in New York—sponsored a national essay competition in 1936 titled "Does My Future Lie in China or America?" Robert Dunn's (1936) essay "In America Lies My Future" won the first prize, and Kaye Hong's (1936) essay "Go West to China" came in second. *Chinese Digest* published the two prize-winning essays and turned this friendly writing contest into a heated national debate. Behind the authors' political and ideological claims lay certain assumptions about how they perceived their ethnic and national identities. From the ensuing debate, two opposing views emerged—one expressing allegiance to America and advocating for a future in the United States, and the other, allegiance to and in China. Although Dunn advocated for the former position and Hong, the latter, both made strong and positive assertions about what it meant to be Chinese in America. In part, the deeply diverging views reflected their different experiences of growing up American.

Robert Dunn grew up in Roxbury, Massachusetts, and was an undergraduate at Harvard University at the time of the national debate. Although he did not grow up in a large Chinese community, he claimed that his upbringing was very Chinese. By his own assertion, Dunn was "radical" and "unconventional" by virtue of the fact that he chose America over China.

In doing so, he broke away from the parental generation, whose members encouraged loyalty and service to China. Dunn (1936: 3) stated, "Ever since I can remember, I have been taught by my parents, by my Chinese friends, and by my teacher in Chinese schools, that I must be patriotic to China." By his own admission, his parents wondered how it was possible for their son to be loyal to America, a country where "the Chinese are mocked at, trodden upon, disrespected, and even spit upon." They also believed that any Chinese who desired a future in such a country was simply "losing face." His parents' opinions notwithstanding, Dunn decided to make a future for himself in America. The crucial factor for Dunn was his love for what he called "American" values and principles, which stood in striking contrast to "Chinese" ways and thought. He felt that he had learned "to live by Christian ideals, by liberal attitudes, and by an optimistic outlook on life." Dunn (1936: 3) embraced these principles as the very fabric of America and looked to his future in America as he wrote:

> I owe much pride and gratitude to America for the principles of liberty and equality which it upholds for the protection of its government ... and for its schools and institutions in which I have participated. Without them, I certainly could not be what I am now.

While acknowledging the existence of discrimination, Dunn believed that Chinese Americans could nonetheless succeed in America. "The color line," he wrote, "does not entirely prevent the U.S.-born Chinese from getting jobs. . . . It cannot be said, therefore, that it is impossible for Chinese American youths to obtain remunerative positions in either China or America." His experience at Harvard University showed that being Chinese actually worked in his favor at times since white students gave him "more respect" because he was Chinese. "Whatever I do in school and college in the way of extra-curricular activities or of attaining high grades, I am given much more credit and popularity than an American would receive, if he did the same things," asserted Dunn (1936: 3). Hence, he argued, "being a Chinese among American friends," was "a sort of advantage." Critics, such as the members of the Chinese Students' Club at Stanford University, charged that Dunn failed to acknowledge the pervasiveness of racism and its damaging effects on Chinese Americans. They fired back, "Can racial prejudice disappear in America in a few years? When you [Dunn] fail to take cognizance of these facts in your essay, you cannot blame us for accusing you of lack of information."[11]

By contrast, Kaye Hong, the second prize-winner, grew up in San Francisco's Chinatown and attended the University of Washington in Seattle.

Hong fully recognized and admitted that his patriotism toward China was shaped by his awareness of racism against the Chinese in America, and he found the ideals propounded by American Christian democracy, which Dunn embraced, "hypocritical." Hong (1936: 3) pointed out that the principle of "equal opportunity" did not apply to the Chinese by claiming, "I have learned to acknowledge that the better jobs are not available to me and that the advancement of my career is consequently limited in this fair land." He discovered that the cry to "make the world safe for democracy" left him "coldly unresponsive" and that his identity with America was of a "different hue and texture"—one "built on the mound of shame." Hong also added, "The ridicule heaped upon the Chinese race has long fermented within my soul."

Hong's patriotism toward China was unquestionably a product of his upbringing in Chinatown, a place founded on a long history of white racism. Having grown up in San Francisco's Chinatown, he was constantly reminded of racial injustice and could not walk away unscathed by the long and virulent legacy of racism against the Chinese. By contrast, having been raised in rural Massachusetts and safely removed from the history of the anti-Chinese movement, Dunn was more optimistic about his prospects in America.

Whether they felt greater loyalty to America or to China, Dunn and Hong shared some deep-rooted similarities; they could not escape the fact that they felt more Chinese than American. Identifying with Chinese culture had more to do with feelings that emerged from their marginalized status in America than with any expertise, familiarity, or education in classical Chinese art, history, or literature. Both wanted to be freed from the shadow of the "ancient glories" of the Chinese cultural past, as Hong (1936: 3) stated: "We, the younger generation, have nothing to be proud of except the time-worn accomplishments of our ancient ancestors." Similarly for Dunn (1936: 3), his parents' constant harping that he "should be proud of China's four thousand years of glorious and continuous history" left him "unmoved." Both Dunn and Hong knew that regardless of China's glorious past, in the present, China was seen by the United States as a weakling nation, economically destitute, socially backward, and politically impotent. They were convinced that they—Chinese living in America—would be more respected if modern-day China were stronger.

Those who might achieve this end had two options. Dunn's solution was to stay in America and become a goodwill "ambassador" in America: "Serve China by building up a good impression of the Chinese among Americans, by spreading good-will and clearing up misunderstandings, by interesting the Americans in the Chinese through personal contacts" (Dunn, 1936: 14). In contrast, Hong thought that a better method would be to physically build up China with hammer and nail. "Then and only then," claimed Hong, "can the present generation of Chinese really save their faces" (Hong, 1936: 13). Ironically, Dunn and Hong encountered opposite fates. Hong, who advocated "go further west to China," remained in the United States, and when I last spoke to him, he was a retired businessman living in San Francisco. When asked why he did not made the journey to China, he responded, "It was actually harder to find a good position in China, unless you had connections. Although in my heart, I wanted to serve China, practical circumstances—such as meeting my wife, getting married, and starting a family—led me to stay in America working at whatever odd jobs I could find to support my family."[12]

It was Dunn who went to China for a while after working with the Chinese United Nations delegation to help frame the UN Constitution. Fortunately for Dunn, he had connections to high officials in China who offered him a position he found "hard to pass up." Much to his surprise, his stay in China was "pleasant." He made friends with the Chinese whose values and ways of thinking were similar to those in the West, and he married a woman born and raised in China. When asked why he went to China, he replied that although he is "bi-cultural," he has always considered himself "first and foremost a Chinese." After the communist takeover of China, he came back to the United States with his wife and took up residence in Maryland.[13]

IDENTITY SHIFTS UNDER THE POLITICS OF ANTICOMMUNISM IN THE 1950S

Under legal exclusion, the majority of second- and third-generation Chinese Americans coming of age in the 1930s considered the possibility of a happy life in America as "just a dream."[14] They openly embraced the idea of "Go further West . . . to China" and enthusiastically identified themselves with China. This was evidenced in the language that they used to talk about China. For example, they used the phrase "return to China" or "going back" even though they had never been there. Denying America, their birthplace, they adopted China as their surrogate homeland and envisioned themselves as "pioneers of a new frontier." In the 1950s, however, drastic internal changes in China and U.S.-China relations brought about a sudden and complete turnaround in the orientation of U.S.-born Chinese.

The Politics of Anticommunism and Challenging Chinese American Identity

In 1949, the Chinese Communist Party led by Mao Tse-dong defeated the Nationalist Party led by Chiang Kai-Shek and established the People's

Republic of China (PRC). Consequently, Chiang's government of the Republic of China (ROC) retreated to Taiwan. The United States and the West severed diplomatic and all other relations with the PRC and supported Chiang's ROC government. In turn, China closed itself off to most of the outside world. The "loss" of China to communism came as a severe blow for all Americans and became particularly consequential for Chinese Americans. Given the history of anti-Chinese and anti-Asian movements on the West Coast, Japanese internment during World War II, and the American public hysteria about the communist threat, the Chinese American community exercised extra caution in its relations with white America. Chinese Americans publicly disavowed communism and promoted integration into American society as the twin strategies to thwart hostility and pledge allegiance to the United States.

In America, communism had always been associated with foreigners and immigrants (Polenberg, 1980). The communist takeover of China renewed the deep-seated images of the "Chinese menace," "yellow peril," and "forever foreigners" in the American mind-set. President Truman addressed the communist threat with the mission to defend "the worldwide menace of communist imperialism" and called for the fight for "freedom," while the evangelist Billy Graham invoked religious imagery by depicting communism as the "anti-Christ" and the "satanic religion." Chinese Americans—who had been historically viewed as foreigners and heathens and whose ancestral homeland had turned communist—"naturally" became the usual suspects.

In the early 1950s, the growing suspicion that every Chinese was a potential communist heightened concern over Chinese immigration and the resulting danger of communist infiltration. In response to these fears, the McCarran Internal Security Act of 1950 granted the U.S. attorney general the authority to detain or deport any persons suspected of espionage or sabotage, and whose actions might compromise national security. The act also denied immigrants the right to become naturalized and voting citizens (Takaki, 1989). The U.S. government's campaign to curb illegal immigration made every Chinese American a potential suspect. Right-wing leaders within the Chinese American community (who were backed by Taiwan) accepted the intervention by the federal government and collaborated with the Federal Bureau of Investigation (FBI) to root out potential communist foes and sympathizers. They also encouraged Chinese American "informants" to report to the government anyone suspected of communist affiliation. During the repressive era of anticommunist politics, any connections (even informal family ties to mainland China) were viewed as treacherous (Nee and Nee, 1986; Yu, 1992; Zhao, 2002).

The repressive politics of the 1950s not only raised a high level of anxiety among U.S.-born Chinese but also created the fear of a possible internment. Given what Japanese Americans had endured during World War II, Chinese Americans understood that citizenship was no guarantee against the infringement of civil rights. An editorial in *Chinese Press* reminded the reader that for no apparent reason other than the "crime of ancestry," the Japanese had been "swept out of their homes and locked in concentration camps." In addition, the editorial noted the increasing incidents of brutality against Chinese Americans in San Francisco, signaling that physical violence was a real threat. However, the editorial ended with a plea, "Despite these faint signs of intolerance which occasionally arises with uncomfortable swiftness in this country, ... Chinatown, USA, faces the future with the basic hope ... [that] this country will not let hysteria or prejudice flame uncontrolled again."[15]

Reflecting upon the events of the early 1950s brought home a clear message: the Chinese American community must continue their "goodwill public relations," and make all efforts "to maintain close contacts with Caucasian groups." Furthermore, Chinese Americans must be "on constant alert" so as to dispel any misunderstandings and unwarranted suspicions against them.[16] Given the rampant fear and intolerance of communism combined with the association of communism with China (and by extension, Chinese Americans), U.S.-born Chinese felt their best course of action was to renounce China, vow loyalty to the United States, and hope to be accepted by white Americans.

"Go out of Chinatown ... to Become Still Better Americans"

"Today the doors are closed," warned Rose Hum Lee (1950: 4), a prominent sociologist who frequently wrote for the English-language newspaper *Chinese Press*. Lee (1950: 4) pressed Chinese Americans to "learn to adjust themselves to the society here as never before" and to become "a more integral part of the American society." In order to demonstrate their loyalty to America, many Chinese Americans renounced their Chinese citizenship in favor of an American one. To further prove their commitment, a group of young community leaders from the Chinese YMCA and YWCA and local churches in San Francisco drafted a list of tenets to be adapted as the official position of all patriotic Chinese in America. Some Chinese Americans went so far as to post them on their doors and storefronts.

> We Chinese-American citizens pledge our loyalty to the United States.
>   We support the nationalist government of free China and her great leader, President Chiang Kai-Shek.
>   We support the United Nations charter and the efforts made by the

United Nations troops who are fighting for a united, free and independent Korea.

The Chinese communists are the stooges of Soviet Russia. Those who are invading Korea are the Chinese communists, not the Chinese, peace-loving people of free China.[17]

To appease their non-Chinese neighbors, some promoted the view that communism was antithetical to the character and thinking of the Chinese people. For instance, Shavey Lee, the unofficial mayor of New York's Chinatown, proclaimed, "Let me emphasize that the Chinese people on the whole—and that means 99 percent of them—whether in China, America, or any other place in the world, are NOT Communists."[18]

Among the U.S. born, there was a movement toward assimilation and integration into mainstream American society. A new term "American-Chinese" came into vogue to signal an identity shift. According to the sociologist Rose Hum Lee (1960), while "Chinese-American" had been used for several decades, it connoted the "descendants of a racial and cultural group" and carried "an over-manifestation of loyalty to the Chinese group." Thus, in Lee's opinion, "Chinese-American" would lead to "criticism and questions regarding their place in the American society." In contrast, the new term, "American-Chinese," would express primary allegiance to America and would lead to a better chance of becoming more fully "transformed into a homogeneous part of the majority society's core culture" (Lee 1960: 113).

Trained at the University of Chicago, Lee was a student of the renowned sociologist Robert Park and was strongly influenced by his theory of assimilation. Lee's personal history was one of successful assimilation. She was born into a wealthy merchant family in 1904 in Butte, Montana, the second oldest of four girls and three boys. Along with her siblings, Lee achieved honors throughout her high school years. After a brief period of living in Canton, China, with her husband, she got a divorce and returned to the United States with the goal of continuing her education. Lee put herself through college and was among the first group of Asian Americans trained at the University of Chicago, eventually earning a doctoral degree in sociology. After conducting ethnographic research on the Chinese American community, Lee concluded that the surest path to assimilation was the complete eradication of foreignness; by fully adopting the values and norms of the dominant society, one could hope to blend in and become indistinguishable from the larger society (Lee, 1949). She urged her fellow Chinese Americans to do everything possible to move out of Chinatown and melt into the American mainstream. Lee's assimilationist position resonated with the U.S. born who had grown up in the shadows of "Red China" and the repressive political climate of the 1950s.

However, a move toward integration presupposed a move out of China-town. Immediately following World War II, the majority of the Chinese lived in Chinatowns because of residential restrictions and racial preju-dice, but in 1947, restrictive housing codes were lifted and upwardly mobile Chinese Americans began their move out of ethnic enclaves and into the suburbs. In San Francisco, those with financial means (the merchant fami-lies, the well-educated U.S. born in white-collar professions, and Chinese exchange students who were stranded in the United States) began to purchase homes in the outer areas such as Oakland, Richmond, and Berkeley (Polenberg, 1980). Like the Japanese Nisei (second generation) who opted to disperse rather than return to their former ethnic enclaves during the post-internment years, many Chinese Americans elected to move to the suburbs, hoping to blend in with white Americans.

As the more affluent Chinese moved out of the enclaves and into the suburbs, Chinatown became home to the elderly, the new immigrants, and the poor. Those who moved out were referred to as "avenue kids" since they lived on wide, nicely kept streets lined with trees and single-family homes as opposed to the crowded streets and graffiti-marked tenement buildings in Chinatown. They were also labeled as "bananas" ("yellow" on the outside but "white" on the inside) since most avenue kids spoke only English, were socialized exclusively with white Americans, attended schools that were predominantly white, and adopted white, middle-class values.[19] For the avenue kids, Chinatown represented a dark, bygone era, as illus-trated in Jin Goodwin's award-winning high school essay titled, "Come out of Chinatown," in which she expressed the stark difference in attitude between the first and second generation:

> Since our parents and grandparents were hounded into the depths of degradation by fear and intolerance, many younger Chinese have grown up fearing the white man, and allowed themselves to be beaten into feeling inferior—so much so, that the majority of them cringe and creep back further into the black depths of China-town, afraid to come out and prove that they can be a desirable element in American society. (Goodwin, 1950: 6)

As they became acculturated, the avenue kids viewed life in Chinatown in increasingly negative, if not pathological, terms. Chinatown "is much more narrow-minded, inquisitive, and gossipy," complained a newly trans-planted suburbanite, adding that the air in the suburbs was "much healthier and better." Many suburban Chinese American youth agreed with Rose Lee Hum's assessment that Chinatown would soon disappear and, conse-quently, wanted nothing to do with what they felt would soon become a thing of the past.

Education as the Route to Achieving the American Dream

Upwardly mobile Chinese Americans in the 1950s believed that education would move them ahead in society, a belief strongly supported by the Chinese American community. However, recognizing that some fields presented more barriers than others, the *Chinese Press* urged Chinese American youth to practice caution in their choice of majors and urged them to judiciously avoid the arts and literary fields. Chinese youth were encouraged to pursue fields that had fewer entry barriers into the mainstream labor market such as mathematics and the natural sciences. In an effort to reward those who had attained distinction in their academic and professional fields, the *Chinese Press* regularly showcased the high-achievers. The academic and professional success of some U.S.-born Chinese American youth impressed the American public who soon concluded that far from posing a threat to the American way of life, Chinese Americans were the model minority. Although the term *model minority* was not explicitly invoked until the late 1960s, the image of the hardworking, high-achieving, well-disciplined Chinese American youth first came into vogue in the 1950s.[20] The model minority image, however, hid the bleak reality of the extreme unemployment, delinquency, and rampant gang activity among Chinatown's youth.

If the U.S.-born Chinese appeared to tenaciously and uncritically grip onto the American dream—that everyone, regardless of race, can make it in America—it was perhaps because they realized the precariousness of their status in America in the middle of the twentieth century. They felt that they had no choice but to be grateful for their fate in America, for somewhere in the back of their minds lurked the less sanguine possibility of being cast away, locked up, and interned as disloyal Americans. Their loyalist stance toward America was in large part a result of fear. Under the repressive politics of anticommunism and assimilationist thinking (particularly after China turned communist in 1949), all discussions about going "west to China" ceased. The U.S. government and American public more generally considered any links to ancestral China as treacherous, and anything Chinese, as un-American. In this political climate, Chinese American youth felt they had no choice but to distance themselves from Chinatown and their ethnic heritage in order to prove that they were unquestionably 100 percent American.

CONCLUSION

In the period prior to World War II, Chinatowns were segregated, institutionally complete neighborhoods equipped with Chinese restaurants,

"Oriental" schools, herb shops, opera houses, and ethnic institutions. Other than the tourists who would periodically visit the "exotic" enclaves, Chinatown's residents had little day-to-day contact with other Americans and were barred from participating in the American culture. During this period, U.S.-born Chinese youth identified primarily as Chinese and felt little desire to assimilate and become American. However, it would be a mistake to consider this wholly their choice; that Chinese Americans identified more strongly as Chinese was largely a result of their experiences with social, economic, and political marginalization from mainstream, white society, as reflected in Kaye Hong's 1936 essay. Even as some protested their parents' imposition of traditional Chinese conventions, few U.S.-born Chinese in the 1930s felt American. Although many had adopted the norms of white Americans, only a few believed that full assimilation into its socio-cultural matrix was possible.

The post–World War II era provided a vastly different context for identity formation among Chinese American youth. The fall of China to communism not only posed potential threats to American security but also created real challenges for Chinese Americans. The repressive political climate of anticommunism in the 1950s led to a denunciation of anything associated with communism, including Chinese in America who were immediately suspected of being communist sympathizers. The growing anti-Chinese sentiment, fear of violence, and possible internment left Chinese Americans with little choice but to pursue integration into the white, American mainstream. U.S.-born Chinese renounced their Chinese citizenship, vocally adopted American ideals, moved out of Chinatowns, and shed their cultural heritage in order to adopt an unequivocal American identity. Again, however, their decision to embrace an American identity was not simply a matter of choice.

Although U.S.-born Chinese youth adopted vastly different identities before and after World War II, their identity choices could hardly be considered voluntary or optional. Chinese Americans did not have the luxury to ponder the true essence of their identities—who they were, what they thought, and what they felt. Rather, in both periods, they were bound by social, economic, legal, and geopolitical constraints that forced them to assume two radically different ethnic options: self-asserting Chinese in the 1930s, and self-hating, sycophantic worshipers of white America in the 1950s. Chinese American writer Frank Chin saw such identity formation as distorted and equated the so-called identity crisis of the U.S.-born Chinese youth as nothing more than the manifestation of "white supremacist" thinking. Chin (1991: 19) poignantly lamented, "when they ... pondered the burning question, 'Does my future lie in China or America?' they asked the same question again and again ... without once confronting the white supremacist phoniness of the question."

Since the 1960s, Chinese American youth (along with their Asian American brothers and sisters) began to develop a vocabulary and language with which to discuss what it means to be American of Chinese or Asian decent. As part of the language, there exists—as if to testify to the reality of a distinctive Chinese American culture—a rich repository of familiar themes, motifs, and recurring references to the history of U.S.-born generations dating back to more than half a century. The shift in identity and consciousness offers far-reaching lessons for the U.S.-born generation of Asian Americans today—the distinctiveness of ethnicity, which defies explanation by the conventional theory of assimilation. The lived experiences of Chinese Americans reveal as much about the history of America as they explain how Chinese Americans were shaped by it. Social and economic exclusion on the basis of racial and ancestral traits forced the U.S. born to change their guise through the eras and vicissitudes of America's historical contexts. In the process, Chinese American youth have learned that identity—far from something that can be preserved and placed apart—is continually made and unmade depending upon the context.

Notes

1. For a more in-depth discussion of the social isolation of U.S.-born Chinese, see the introductory chapter in Shih (1937) and Lam (1987: 119–137, "*The Chinese Digest*, 1935–1940, in Chinese Historical Society of America").

2. This chapter draws heavily on my doctoral dissertation research and public work (Chun, 1993, 2000). Primary data came from oral histories conducted by myself and pulled from various archives at the Hoover Institute in Stanford, the Bancroft Library and the Asian American Studies Library at the University of California, Berkeley, and the Asian American Studies Reading Room at the University of California, Los Angeles. Secondary data included English language newspapers, written by and for U.S.-born or -raised Chinese Americans, such as *Chinese Digest* and *Chinese Press*, and memoirs, family histories, journals, autobiographies, and novels. I examined fiction not merely for its literary themes and motifs but also for its sociological context.

3. "Paper sons" referred to the foreign-born children whose parents had U.S. citizenship and claimed their sons' births in China when they visited China.

4. Thomas Chinn was one of the chief editors of the *Chinese Press*, a major conduit for U.S.-born generations and an invaluable resource for researching this time period. The paper was established in 1934 and folded in 1940. As the first truly Chinese-American newspaper in the English language, it served as a crucial venue for young Chinese Americans to voice their concerns as second generation, Chinese Americans. The articles mirrored their responses to and reflections on a variety of issues and concerns such as the Japanese invasion of China, the economic depression, their exclusion from the mainstream job market, the preservation of Chinatown against foreign entrepreneurial and cultural encroachments, and their involvement in the Chinese section of the 1939 World's Fair. Contents included happenings in China, Chinese art and tradition, news about San Francisco Chinatown as well as other Chinese American communities, and, occasionally, cultural and social essays on Chinese American life.

5. David Gan, "A Letter to the Gan Family," in an unpublished manuscript, History of the Gan Family, edited by Helen Gan and John Aston, San Francisco, 1991.

6. Interview with Rodney H. Chow by Emma Louie on January 24, 1978, in Los Angeles as part of the Southern California Chinese American Oral History Project sponsored by the Asian American Studies Center, University of California, Los Angeles, and Chinese Historical Society of Southern California. Vol. II, Interview number 27.

7. University of California, Berkeley, *Student Registry, 1935–36*, the Bancroft Library at the University of California, Berkeley.

8. Far East, "Engineers Needed in China," *Chinese Digest*, January 10, 1936, p. 2; Editorial, "Chinese Abroad as Ambassadors." *Chinese Digest*, August 21, 1936, p. 8.

9. In a telephone interview with Ben Tong conducted by the author in October 1989, Tong reported that an estimated 20 percent of U.S.-born Chinese went to China during this period, basing his observation on his interviews with San Francisco's Chinese Americans; see also Chinn (1989), p. 134.

10. "An Interview with Dr. Charles R. Shepherd upon his Return from China," by Lim P. Lee. *Chinese Digest*, February 11, 1937, p. 11.

11. Firecrackers, *Chinese Digest*, July 3, 1936, pp. 5, 14.

12. Interview with Kaye Hong by the author, San Francisco, February 1990.

13. Interview with Robert Dunn by the author, February 1990.

14. Firecrackers, *Chinese Digest*, July 3, 1936, p. 5.

15. Editorial, "Cathay, U.S.A.," *Chinese Press*, June 22, 1951, p. 4.

16. Editorial, "The Year Ahead," *Chinese Press*, December 28, 1951, p. 4.

17. Editorial, "Cathay, U.S.A.," *Chinese Press*, June 22, 1951, p. 4.

18. "Will China Stay Red?" *Chinese Press*, September 8, 1950, p. 4.

19. Chinese American folklore collection: Sayings file, at the American folklore archives at the University of California, Berkeley.

20. "No Chinese American Juvenile Delinquency," *America*, 93, July 6, 1955, p. 402; "Our Amazing Chinese Kids," *Coronet*, 39, December 1955, pp. 31–36; "Why No Chinese American Delinquents," Maybe It's Traditional Respect for Parents," *Saturday Evening Post*, 227, April 30, 1955, p. 12; "Americans without a Delinquent Problem," *Look*, 22, April 29, 1958, 22, pp. 75–81; "Chinatown Offers Us a Lesson," *New York Times Magazine*, October 6, 1957, p. 49ff.

PART **III**
Emerging Youth Cultural Forms
and Practices

CHAPTER 8

Instant Karma:

The Commercialization of Asian Indian Culture[1]

Sabeen Sandhu

India's economy has prospered during the last five years. It is now recognized as a global player in the information technology industry, developing and exporting software as well as software professionals (Ganguly, 2000). However, India has another fast growing export—culture. The nation's economic prosperity coupled with cable television has created a market for designer wear; tight skirts, cocktail dresses, and designer suits are "in," while traditional saris are "out." However, this is not the case in the United States; Asian Indian fashion, film, food, music, and spirituality have found a momentary niche in American popular culture. After *Vanity Fair* magazine featured *mehndi* adorning actress Liv Tyler on the cover of its April 1997 issue, just about everything Asian Indian became popular—*mehndi* (temporary henna tattoos), *bhindis* (decorative body art applied to the forehead), *beedis* (cigarettes wrapped in flavored leaves), sari-inspired clothing, and yoga became part of popular culture. Mira Nair's latest film, *Monsoon Wedding*, is an immense hit with the American public. When asked why a "homemade, Bollywood"-style film resonates and appeals to moviegoers internationally, Nair succinctly stated, "It's chic to be Indian" (Rose, 2002).[2]

Fashion, fitness, music, and spiritual industries have picked up on this trend; it is chic for Westerners to wear *mehndi*, adorn a *bhindi*, smoke a *beedi*, wear saris, sample a Hindi song, and practice yoga. Journalists and scholars of popular culture debate over whether the commercialization and mainstreaming of Asian Indian culture demystifies or exploits it (Batra and Wilde, 1999; Christopher, 1998; Malhotra-Singh, 1999; Mehta, 1979).

Some charge the Asian Indian community in the United States with apathy and suggest that they do little to raise awareness about defining authentic Asian Indian culture. For example, one journalist explains and then asks,

> It doesn't need to be intelligent. It doesn't need to be accurate. Since we're not exactly playing cultural police, they can distort and market the hell out of us.... Content we are, then to allow the easily digestible—Mira Nair blockbusters, Starbucks redundant Chai Tea, halva sticks—to represent us rather than gift away copies of Arundhati Roy and Shyam Selvadurai, inform Flaunt magazine that "chat" is hardly the "snack food of India," invite some friends over for a showing of "Brothers In Trouble," or having a Bhupen Khakar on the wall of our offices to incite and enlighten. (Malhotra-Singh, 1999: 39)

Journalists and scholars not only explore and debate what authentic Asian Indian culture is, but also who can claim it. However, when perusing the latest fashion magazines, it is clear that Asian Indians are largely absent from the commercialization and mainstreaming of their culture. How this trend affects ethnic identity formation among Asian Indian youth in the United States is a question that has largely been ignored. This multimethod study aims to fill this void by drawing on two sources of data: (1) 30 in-depth, semistructured interviews with female Asian Indian youth in the San Francisco Bay area; and (2) a content analysis of mainstream fashion magazines, including *Vanity Fair, Vogue, Seventeen, Jane,* and *InStyle Magazine,* from 1997 to 2002.

The San Francisco Bay area is home to a sizable population of Asian Indian immigrants, second only to New York, and the participants in this sample capture the regional and cultural diversity of India.[3] Using a snowball sampling technique, I selected 30 1.5- and second-generation Asian Indian youth between the ages of 16 and 25.[4] Half of the participants were between the ages of 16 and 21, and the other half were between the ages of 22 and 25. All of the participants were female since the commercialization and mainstreaming of Asian Indian culture is largely a gendered trend. I conducted the interviews between June and September of 2002 and asked the participants a series of closed- and open-ended questions about their backgrounds, ethnic identification, cultural practices, and views on the commercialization of Asian Indian culture.[5] How this group identified itself ethnically provides a glimpse of Asian Indian ethnic identity in the United States. Portes and MacLeod (1996) explain that while the second generation may lack the cultural viewpoint of their immigrant parents, they are still exposed to it as well as to mainstream symbols. Hence, how they ethnically identify is a contest between old and new ethnic labels.

The content analysis focuses on *Vanity Fair, Vogue, Seventeen, Jane,* and *InStyle* magazines because they are widely distributed and popular among women between the ages of 16 and 25. Although the magazines were selected for the purposes of analyzing the images of Asian Indian culture, the participants in the study are familiar with their contents. Although the content analysis captures the commercialization and popularity of Asian Indian culture, the data from interviews reveal how this impacts the ethnic identity formation of Asian Indian youth.

More specifically, this study examines the images of Asian Indian culture in the American mainstream and assesses its impact on the ethnic identity formation of Asian Indian youth. For the American mainstream, *mehndi* is temporary, *bhindis* can be taken off, the smoke of *beedis* quickly dissipates, and yoga can be a half-hour workout after work, but is this the case for Asian Indian youth? How do Asian Indian youth form their ethnic identities when their traditions are commercialized into mainstream trends from which Asian Indians are largely missing? Although Asian Indians are largely absent from these trends, they bear meaning for Asian Indian youth and weigh on their ethnic identities. The commercialization and mainstreaming of Asian Indian culture pits trends against tradition, production against consumption, assurance against ambivalence, and what is temporary against what is permanent. In essence, the ethnic identities of Asian Indian youth are not symbolic, but concrete and consequential. Unlike the instant karma worn and discarded by other Americans, karma is not instant for Asian Indian youth.

FROM FOREIGN TO FASHIONABLE: FASHION, FITNESS, MUSIC, AND SPIRITUALITY

The sudden popularity of Asian Indian culture can be traced to Herb Ritts's 1997 *Vanity Fair* cover featuring *mehndi* adorning actress Liv Tyler. Celebrities such as Demi Moore, Mira Sorvino, Gwen Stefani, and Madonna soon picked up on this fashion trend, and *mehndi* evolved from a Hindu marriage ritual to a temporary henna tattoo. Sumita Batra, henna tattoo artist to the stars, describes Madonna as *mehndi*'s most high-profile admirer. Batra hennaed Madonna's hands and feet for the "Frozen" music video from the *Ray of Light* album. When the music video was released, Madonna went on a global publicity tour wearing temporary henna tattoos on her hands and feet and catapulted this trend to global popularity. When asked to comment on her recent interest in Asian Indian culture, Madonna explained, "When Sumita hennas my hands and feet, I am transported to another time and place. A world of magic, passion and romance" (Batra, 1999: 9).

Bhindis, often described as "forehead dots" in the United States, are traditionally red and are worn by female worshippers at Hindu religious ceremonies. However, like *mehndi, bhindis* evolved from a religious symbol to decorative body art. Batra (1999: 51) describes *bhindis* as the must-have accessory of the West: "*Bhindis* can be worn for fun at the weekend and easily peeled off before you return to the office on Monday morning, showing how Eastern influences can provide a temporary Indianess way of making the boldest fashion statement without too much effort or commitment." *Bhindis*, too, were popularized by highly visible entertainers and models, including Madonna, Gwen Stefani, Helena Christensen, Naomi Campbell, Cindy Crawford, and Mary J. Blige.

Along with temporary henna tattoos and other body art, traditional Indian clothing influenced American fashion and was also popular among celebrities. For example, the June 1999 issue of *InStyle* Magazine featured Indian-inspired fashions in *Style File*—its regular fashion report. The article featured half of a fuchsia-colored traditional Indian wedding outfit, a skirt, paired with a white cotton tank top. Titled "Indian Summer," the article states:

> Talk about global village. The traditional dress of India is influencing fashion in a big way. The result: easy, soft, summer clothes—flowing skirts, charming camisoles and exotic sandals—made with beautiful rich sari trims, swirling prints, intricate embroidery and charka symbols. Add a few jangling bangles and you've got yourself some instant karma. (Arbetter, 1999: 79)

Like *mehndi* and *bhindis*, the meaning of traditional Indian clothing changes once it becomes commercialized and part of mainstream fashion; wedding attire becomes everyday wear, and Americans gain "instant karma" by appropriating or consuming these fashion trends. Maybelline Cosmetics adopted the same phrase for its 1999 *Cosmic Edge* makeup line, promising consumers, "beauty Nirvana for the face and body—instant karma: body shimmer, Zen gems, tattoos too" (Maybelline Cosmetics, 1999: 4).

The recent hype and popularity of yoga also captures the Western intrigue of Asian Indian culture and the desire for "instant karma" and "nirvana now." In India, yoga is an *ayureveda*—an all-encompassing spiritual practice that is more than two thousand years old. However, in the United States it is marketed as a physical activity that is all the rage in health clubs across the nation. A recent USNews.com article describes yoga as a full-blown fitness craze and reports that since the mid-1990s, the percentage of health clubs offering yoga classes has doubled and the number of yoga practitioners has grown from six to twelve million (Kleiner, 2002: 1). When asked to comment on the popularity of yoga in the United States, a second-generation yoga instructor explains,

I think yoga is growing because it's a needed form today, you know, of kind of dropping into oneself—self-realization. There's a reason why yoga is big—we need it. We need yoga. And yet it's hyped up in a different direction as a pure exercise form. It's not just a physical form, but spiritual as well. In the West it's physical, physical, physical. And the yogis in India understand this and stress that the West is all about the body. It's through the body that they will eventually learn their spirituality. In my opinion, there needs to be a stronger connection with the spiritual benefits of yoga. This is what I try to instill in the students in my classes.[6]

Her explanation of the physical focus that yoga takes on in the United States is evident in its commercialization and mainstreaming—yoga is in vogue.

The August 2002 issue of *Vogue* Magazine covers yoga in "VogueView," its monthly feature on runway fashions. With a hint of sarcasm, Arakas (2002: 148) remarks that nothing is left sacred in her feature on the marketing of yoga gear:

Sure, a wandering ascetic in ancient India practicing the meditative exercises that would one day become what the twenty-first century calls yoga might have gotten away with wearing a loincloth while practicing his various poses. But today he would have to do a lot better than that in order to detach his mind from the external world. Today, if he was not wearing at least a pair of formfitting yoga-specific shorts, then surely the class would be disrupted with snickers, or worse. And if he were a she, then she would perhaps be taking the whole withdrawal-from-the-physical world thing a little too far if she did not consider, for example, the new line of mind-and-body Lotus-print briefs and tanks tops by Adidas or, at the very least, the Mei, also by Adidas, which was a yoga shoe featured in a Yohji Yamamoto show.

Hence like *mehndi, bhindis,* and traditional clothing, the commercialization and mainstreaming of yoga changes its traditional meaning; yoga evolves from an all-encompassing philosophy to a fashionable workout. In fact, yoga not only creates a market for fitness wear but is also a marketing tool for vodka. Absolut Vodka's recent advertisement capitalizes on the popularity of yoga—an inverted bottle of Absolut Vodka is positioned upon a yoga mat followed by the text, "ABSOLUT YOGA." When asked her opinion regarding this advertisement, an Asian Indian yoga instructor replied, "That ad isn't yoga's fault. Advertisers and fashion designers make money off of what's popular, and right now that's what yoga is."[7]

Similarly, hip-hop producers have picked up on the popularity of Asian Indian culture by sampling traditional Hindi songs. For example, DJ Quick sampled a classic Hindi song by Lata Mangeshkar for the R&B single "Addictive" by Truth Hurts. The single reached number five on Billboard's Hot R&B/Hip-Hop singles chart. In a recent interview with a reporter at India-West, DJ Quick explained how he got the idea to sample this traditional Hindi song. He recalls, "I was watching one of the Indian cable TV shows, like I always do, and this song came on. I didn't know what the song was. But it had so much magic, it was so soulful, that I just hit the 'record' button on my VCR and taped it" (Tsering, 2002: C1-C2). This R&B hit initially appealed to the majority of the Asian Indian youth in the sample. However, after the release of the music video and failure of DJ Quick to pay royalties to the Indian music label that owns the rights to the song, the participants expressed offense to the song.[8]

Eric Sermon and Redman followed DJ Quick's lead and also sampled a traditional Hindi song in "React," their latest hip-hop release. Although participants in the sample stated that the sampling of the Hindi song makes no sense when paired with the hip-hop lyrics, they appreciated that Eric Sermon and Redman admitted that they do not understand what they sampled. After their hip-hop hit plays the Hindi sample, a woman singing about suicide, Redman states, "whatever she said, then I'm that." Hence, these two examples, like *mehndi, bhindis*, traditional Indian clothing, and yoga, take on different meaning in this commercialized and mainstream form.

Although once regarded as foreign, these facets of Asian Indian culture are now fashionable in commercial and mainstream form. In this transition from foreign to fashionable, Asian Indians were removed from their culture, customs, and traditions. The American mainstream consumes Asian Indian culture to achieve instant karma; however, this is not the case for Asian Indian youth. When Asian Indian youth practice these fashion trends, they are no longer regarded as fashionable. Rather, they take on a different meaning, evoke tradition, and affect the identities of Asian Indian youth.

ETHNIC IDENTITY AMONG ASIAN INDIAN YOUTH

For Asian Indian youth, instant karma is not an option. Indeed, elements of their ethnic identities, too, are symbolic, but the way in which others ethnically identify them and the situational nature of their identities reveal that they are concrete and consequential. Asian Indian youth balance stereotypes with traditions and negotiate between the Indian and American cultures to form their ethnic identities. The interviews reveal that Asian Indian youth are ambivalent about the commercialization and main-streaming of their culture because Asian Indians are missing from this trend. However, they strongly assert an Asian Indian ethnic identity.[9] Ethnic identity among Asian Indian youth is not simply symbolic (Gans, 1979; Waters, 1990), ascribed (Nagel, 1994; Waters, 1999), or situational (Hall, 1995; Okamura, 1981), but rather, a combination of these facets.

Mistaken Identity

Participants in the study were asked whether people inquire or comment on their ethnic background and to describe the last time that such comment was made. The data from the study reveal that all Asian Indian youth confront ethnicity on a daily basis. For example, one participant, a 21-year-old college student, explained that complete strangers seem intrigued about her ethnicity. She elaborates, "It was just three days ago—it was a Saturday—I was actually in a club, in the restroom, and somebody stopped me and asked, 'Oh, what ethnicity are you?' and it was because they thought that I was half black. And so I told them no and that I was full Asian Indian. I get African American a lot. I think it's the hair ... I don't know; it's black looking hair. Or I got this *Punjabi* man talking to me in Spanish and I was like, 'I'm Punjabi.' People, even Indian people sometimes, have a hard time picking out Indians."[10]

Another participant explained that people usually think that she is Mexican or Latin American. When asked to describe the last time someone asked or commented on her ethnic background, she explained, "That actually happened today. I was at the grocery store and a man approached me and asked if I knew how to speak Spanish and if I was Mexican. I get that a lot. People rarely get it right, unless they are Indian. It's usually only Indian people who ask whether I'm Indian."[11]

When asked whether people comment or ask about her ethnic background, a 21-year-old college student expressed the same thing—mistaken identity:

> People always think I'm Mexican at first. I don't like that; obviously I don't want to be classified as something I'm not. You know, most people don't know us 'cause they just confuse us with other people—Mexicans, Latinos, Afghans, or something. I just say I'm Indian. And the first thing everyone says is, "Oh, you're Indian? But you have such light hair and light skin?" As if everyone from India is dark. They have a stereotypical idea of who's Indian and don't seem to recognize that I am.[12]

Another participant, a 16-year-old high school student, also commented that the American mainstream has a stereotypical idea of Asian Indians. In her experience most people who inquired about her ethnicity were men interested in dating her:

> Well, a lot of people don't know if I'm Indian or if I'm like Arabic, or they even think that I'm Pakistani. I don't really have a problem with it, but it's usually guys. Like last week some guy approached me and was talking to me. At first when he started talking to me, he asked my name, then what race I was. I told him that I was Indian and then he made some stupid comment about belly dancing.[13]

These cases reveal that non-Asian Indians have difficulty differentiating Asian Indians from other ethnic groups.

Mistaken identity is not only reserved for ethnic identities but also spills over into ethnic culture. For example, an 18-year-old respondent who works in her parents' Asian Indian clothing store explained that the people have a difficult time differentiating between Arabs and Indians. Noticing an increase in Latin American customers who purchased traditional Indian clothing and jewelry, she asked them about their interest in Indian clothing and jewelry. The Latin American customers explained that there was a new *telenovella* about an Arab family on the Spanish television channel, and the clothes were all the rage in the Latin American community. They explained that belly dancing was a big part of this *telenovella* and wanted to purchase belly chains also.

These examples illustrate that Asian Indian youth react to these mistaken identifications by asserting an Asian Indian ethnic identity. They try to keep their ethnic identity as simple as possible to avoid mistaken identifications. The reason few participants identified as Indian American was to avoid being confused with Native Americans. A 22-year-old aspiring model and actress explains, "It usually tends to confuse people when I identify as Indian American, which is why I say East Indian or Asian Indian. I find this really annoying, but what can you do. It's not my fault that Christopher Columbus messed up."[14]

Trends against Traditions

For the American mainstream, temporary henna tattoos, body art, Asian Indian-inspired clothing, yoga, and sampled traditional Hindi songs are simply fashion trends, but this is not the case for Asian Indian youth. Although they, too, may be picking up and following fashion trends, non-

Asian Indians ascribe meaning and tradition to it. For instance, when I asked an 18-year-old respondent why she got her nose pierced, she responded as follows,

> I just wanted to get it. I think it looks pretty. But, I guess it kind of has to do with being Indian, or both.... This story makes me laugh. Back when I was in high school some of girls asked me, "Why isn't your nose pierced? Aren't you Indian? You're supposed to like have your nose pierced." I was like no—you don't have to just cause you're Indian. Not all Indian people have their noses pierced. In fact my parents weren't even cool with it. I had to tell them I got it to show that I'm Indian, but they were worried that I looked like a hippie and thought it didn't look professional.[15]

Another participant, a 16-year-old high school student, expressed the same idea when asked why she got her nose pierced, "I wanted it ever since I was really little. And finally, about two months ago, I convinced my parents to let me get it. They didn't want me to get it, but I used the excuse that I'm Indian. I might look more Indian now, but I wouldn't say I feel more Indian. People ask me if I got it for some Indian thing, but I say no, I got it to get it, not for some Indian reason."[16]

Although Asian Indian youth may simply be following fashion trends; these trends evoke tradition. For non-Asian Indians, *mehndi*, *bhindis*, traditional Indian clothing, yoga, and traditional Hindi songs are trendy, but even though Asian Indian youth pick up on these symbolic forms of ethnicity, the American mainstream ascribe meaning and tradition to them.[17] Asian Indian youth largely affirm an Asian Indian identity. Despite being missing from the commercialization and mainstreaming of their culture, mistaken ethnic identification, and stereotypes about Asian Indian culture, they identify as Asian Indian in response to these trends.

Conclusion: The Fine Line between Foreign and Fashionable

Mehndi, *bhindis*, traditional Indian clothing, yoga, and traditional Hindi songs are all the rage in the United States. Now commercialized, these Asian Indian traditions are marketed to the American mainstream as temporary henna tattoos, body art, sari-inspired clothing, a half-hour workout, and a sampled song in a hip-hop hit. These traditions have become trends that exist in a more palatable form that is acceptable to Americans. For Asian Indian youth, however, these trends retain their traditional meaning regardless of how they may view them. One participant's description of her experience at an audition for an independent film about the commercialization and mainstreaming of Asian Indian culture illustrates the ambivalence that Asian Indian youth feel about the commercialization and mainstreaming of Asian Indian culture:

> I actually auditioned for a movie, and it was about a woman who could not deal with her white friends wearing *bhindis*. They really don't know what it means, but do I even know what it means? I think the tension is that it's one thing for them to show interest and appreciation, but it's a whole other story when people are telling me how to be Indian.[18]

But as the data from this study reveal, it is not really Asian Indian culture that is being commercialized and marketed to the American mainstream—Indian people are blatantly missing from this trend.

A photograph from Batra and Wilde's (1999: 42) book sums it up best. Like the commercialization and mainstreaming of Asian Indian culture, this image offers a clear view of an Asian Indian woman's hennaed hand extending into the foreground, while a blurry image of her face and body disappears into the background. Hence, the consumption of Asian Indian culture does not necessarily mean that it is accepted. And a participant in the study points this out—"It's one thing when an American person wears a *bhindi* and stuff, but when my mom does it people stare and whisper. In general, when people wear it for a religious statement they get stared at, but for a fashion statement it's okay."[19]

I concluded each interview by asking the participants whether the images of Asian Indian culture in the mainstream impacted how they ethnically self-identified and how others defined them. This participant's response was representative of the sample:

> This is just a fashion trend. It may be "in" to be Indian right now, but when it goes out of fashion, I'll still be Indian. Indian fashions are "in," but that doesn't mean the culture is accepted. Take turbans for example and the backlash against Sikhs after September 11. People still have stereotypes about Indians—they own 7–11 convenient stores, motels, are software engineers in the Silicon Valley, beauty queens, sex experts because of the *Kama Sutra*, or just thought to be submissive and pretty.[20]

Hence, a fine line exists between what is fashionable and what is foreign, and social consumption does not necessarily mean social acceptance. Asian Indian culture may be in vogue this year, but in the past Chinese culture was all the rage (Hua, 2000), and who knows which culture is next in line to be commercialized, popularized, and mainstreamed? Although this study focuses on the relationship between the commercialization and mainstreaming of Asian Indian culture and ethnic identity formation among Asian Indian youth, future research can reveal whether the findings may be generalizeable to other racial/ethnic minorities and immigrant youth.

Notes

1. I thank Professor Jennifer Lee for academic training, encouragement, and mentoring. For comments and suggestions, I thank Professors Herb Green, Matt L. Huffman, and Min Zhou. I also thank the Asian Indian youth who participated in the study for sharing their experiences.
2. India's film industry is concentrated in Bombay and is named after Hollywood—*Bollywood*. *Bollywood* produces more feature-length films than any other country in the world and holds the 1990 and 1994 Guinness World Records at 948 and 754, respectfully.
3. Data from the 2000 U.S. Census reveals that the San Francisco Bay area is home to 1.6 million Asian Indians.
4. According to Portes and Rumbaut's (2001: 23) definition, 1.5-generation immigrants are foreign-born but arrived in the United States before the age of 12; hence, they are not quite first-generation immigrants nor are they second-generation immigrants. This study includes 1.5-generation Asian Indian youth in the sample because they arrived in the United States during childhood, are socialized by mainstream American values, and share experiences that are similar to second-generation immigrants.
5. I pretested the questionnaire on five participants who had similar characteristics to the sample, which increased the validity and reliability of the interview instrument. I used an audiotape recorder to accurately capture information from the participants. I transcribed the interviews verbatim using ethnographic software that facilitates the analysis and coding of the data.
6. Personal Interview, July 2002.
7. Personal Interview, July 2002.
8. Several participants in the study expressed offense to the music video for Truth Hurt's single, "Addictive." Although a traditional Hindi song is sampled in this hip-hop hit and Truth Hurts and her dancers are wearing sari-inspired clothing and Asian Indian jewelry, no Asian Indians appear in the video and the dancers are belly dancing, a Middle Eastern cultural dance.
9. All but two participants ethnically self-identified as Asian Indian. The two participants who did not identify as Asian Indian chose the hyphenated, Asian Indian–American ethnic identity.
10. Personal Interview, June 2002.
11. Personal Interview, June 2002.
12. Personal Interview, July 2002.
13. Personal Interview, July 2002.
14. Personal Interview, August 2002.
15. Personal Interview, September 2002.
16. Personal Interview, August 2002.
17. Cultures in India vary according to region. *Mehndi, bhindis,* sari-inspired clothing, and yoga are not prevalent in every region and culture in India. This sample of Asian Indian youth is representative of India's regional and cultural diversity. Yet, because the American mainstream defines what it means to be Asian Indian through these trends, reducing it to temporary henna tattoos, body art, sari-inspired clothing, yoga, or a sampled song, the identities of Asian Indian youth are essentialized.
18. Personal Interview, August 2002.
19. Personal Interview, July 2002.
20. Personal Interview, September 2002.

CHAPTER 9

Transnational Cultural Practices of Chinese Immigrant Youth and Parachute Kids[1]

Christy Chiang-Hom

Growing up in America is challenging for all children of foreign-born parentage, for these children must straddle their parents' worldview and that of the larger American society. Children of foreign-born parents must often negotiate the competing, and often conflictual, demands from home, society, and peer groups. For foreign-born youth who arrive in the United States as teenagers, the challenge of growing up takes on a different twist. Unlike those born or raised in the United States—who have no personal experience with, or little memory of, the ancestral homeland—foreign-born youth who arrive in their teens have been uprooted from the familiarity of their ancestral homeland and placed in an alien culture.

Before immigrating, foreign-born adolescents spent the majority of their formative years in a different culture, were schooled in a different language, established peer groups, and were immersed in a different youth culture than that of the United States (Zhou, 2003b). In their homeland, they were the masters of their own culture—defining what was *in*, cool, and trendy. However, their status changed when they moved to the United States, where they often would find themselves categorized and ridiculed as racialized minorities and FOBs by their U.S.-born peers, including their acculturated coethnics.[2] Although all foreign-born youth experience difficulties growing up in an immigrant family while adapting to mainstream American society, those who arrive in their teens must deal with a unique set of issues that are even more vexing, more intense, more demanding, yet less understood.

This chapter examines the adjustment of foreign-born adolescents of

Chinese ancestry, including the subgroup of foreign-born youth known as *parachute kids,* youth who initially came to attend school in the United States without their parents.[3] For analytical purposes, the term *foreign born* is used to refer to those who came to the United States *after* the age of 12, the term *immigrant* for those who immigrated to the United States *with* their parents, and the term *parachute* for those who live in the United States *without* their parents. The term *U.S. born* broadly includes not only those who were born in the United States but also those who immigrated to the United States before the age of five.[4] This chapter highlights the distinct patterns of academic, psychological, and social adjustment of Chinese immigrant and parachute youth compared to their U.S.-born or -raised coethnic peers. The chapter also examines how immigrant and parachute youth forge a positive identity and create their own cultural and social space in their quest to adjust to their new host society.[5]

FOREIGN-BORN ADOLESCENTS IN ASIAN IMMIGRANT COMMUNITIES

Parachute Kids

Included among the population of foreign-born youth is a subgroup, popularly known as "parachute kids"—youth who come to the United States to attend middle or high schools by themselves, while their parents remain overseas.[6] They gain entry into the United States on foreign exchange student visas, tourist visas, and, for some, immigrant visas (green cards). Although some Americans may regard leaving one's parents to attend school in a foreign country as highly unusual, risky, and perhaps even harsh, Asian parents who send their children abroad feel that their reasons for doing so are important enough to outweigh the reservations and potential risks.

The parents of parachute kids choose to remain in Asia while their children live in the United States for a variety of reasons, the main one being financial. Developing markets and economies in Asia offer Asian parents more lucrative business opportunities than the economy in the United States. Lack of English fluency, familiarity with American business practices, and professional connections also deter Asian parents from moving abroad. Some parents must also remain in Asia to fulfill family obligations, such as looking after the elderly or the family business.

Meanwhile, Asian children are sent to study and live in the United States for a number of reasons. Nearly half are sent to America in search of a "golden opportunity." Both parachute kids and their parents believe that the United States is a better place to live and offers more opportunities to succeed than their native country. Furthermore, they feel that an English-based education is a practical and valuable asset in an increasingly global economy (Zhou, 1998). Thus, "parachuting" to America is considered an investment that will have a predictable future payoff that outweighs the difficulties and challenges for both parents and their children.

Second, approximately a quarter of parachute kids are sent to America—"the land of the free"—in search of a safe haven or an escape from the environmental, political, educational, or family situations in their countries of origin. For example, the heavy pollution and poor air quality of many Asian countries are particularly problematic for children who suffer from asthma, so living in the United States offers a far healthier alternative. Parents also send their children to the United States because they worry about the political instability in their homelands, such as the escalating tension between Taiwan and China and the return of Hong Kong to China. Still others send their children to the United States as a means of evading the mandatory military service in their country (Zhou, 1998). In some cases, parents send their children abroad as a solution to a difficult or problematic family circumstance such as divorce, the death of a parent, or parents who are busy traveling and managing their transnational businesses.

Third, parachute kids are sent to America in order to "circumvent" the rigorous academic programs and intense competition in their countries of origin.[7] The extremely competitive junior high and high school exams make it prohibitive for all youth in Asia to attend college or even high school, even if they would like to do so. Hence, approximately 15 percent of parachute kids come to the United States to seek a second shot at college, high school, or a fresh start altogether. Typically, these youth had poor academic records in their homeland and were at risk for failing (or actually failed) the high school entrance exam. Others associated with the "wrong crowd," and so their parents sent them to America with the hope that they would disassociate from their old friends and find new, positive peer groups. The parachute kids who come under these circumstances often do not take the opportunity for a second chance for granted; rather, most make a concerted effort to work hard and do well in school because they understand the consequences of failing to do so.

The overwhelming proportion of parachute kids come to the United States for instrumental and practical reasons, but 15 percent come in search of an adventure, viewing America as the "land of excitement and intrigue." Unlike the other cases, these youth often propose the idea of parachuting to their parents because they are eager to learn about a new culture and language. As a result, this group of parachute kids tends to have a more optimistic outlook about exploring a new country, even if this means that they must leave their parents behind. Rather than feeling forced to come to the United States alone, they view it as an invaluable learning experience that will help them become more well-rounded, better informed, and more cosmopolitan individuals.

Parachute versus Immigrant Adolescents

Although parachute kids face many of the same challenges as immigrant youth in adjusting to their new host society, they differ from their immigrant peers in several significant respects. First, parachute kids live in the United States without their parents and must adapt to a new living arrangement on their own. Their guardians, especially relatives, are frequently overly protective and place strict constraints on the parachute kids, imposing limits on the time they spend with friends outside of school, talking on the phone, or watching television. Some parachute kids are faced with having to do chores for the first time in their lives and/or living with frugal guardians who limit their access to food, household items (e.g., blankets, towels), and energy (heat, electricity). Others stay with paid caretakers (known as "homestays"), whom their parents may have never met in person, while some live with other parachute kids, underaged siblings, or simply alone. In my study, 36 percent of the parachute kids live with a relative (including 6 percent with a grandparent), 30 percent live with a homestay, 5 percent with siblings only, 5 percent with friends of the family, 4 percent with a cousin, and 3 percent completely alone.

The second difference between parachute kids and immigrant children is that parachute kids shoulder enormous day-to-day responsibilities from which other youth, including immigrant youth, are shielded. In their parents' absence, many parachute kids have to manage their routines and needs on their own, including looking after younger siblings, paying bills, cooking, and cleaning. Third, they must mediate their relationships with their guardians or other caretakers and deal with different levels of bureaucracy, all while trying to excel in school. Fourth, parachute kids often bear the brunt of criticism from school officials and the public, who generally perceive them as maladjusted aliens who inundate public schools at the expense of American taxpayers. Similarly, some school administrators, community leaders, and reporters portray their parents as "bad" and "neglectful" for allowing their children to come to this country on their own.

Clearly, parachute kids must take on a great deal of responsibility that frequently forces them to grow up quickly, and possibly prematurely. Research studies have found that such premature transitions into adulthood are often linked to negative outcomes such as increased rates of substance use, delinquency, and feelings of stress and confusion (Grant and Compas,

1995; Krohn et al., 1997). The media and community have also depicted parachute kids as severely maladjusted and distressed, with a tendency to abuse illegal substances and become involved with gangs (Chao, 1997; Hamilton, 1993a, 1993b; Kasindorf, 1999; *Los Angeles Times*, 1993). Although some media reports highlight the major struggles and obstacles that parachute kids routinely face, the media is often biased in its coverage. Rather than surveying a range of parachute kids, reporters often choose to focus on the most sensational and extreme cases—the severely maladjusted and distressed or the extremely successful.

THE ACADEMIC, PSYCHOLOGICAL, AND SOCIAL ADJUSTMENT OF IMMIGRANT AND PARACHUTE YOUTH

Uprooting is a particularly stressful experience resulting in significant changes in social status, orientation, relationship, and lifestyle. Thus, some researchers argue that foreign-born youth who arrive at older ages are at greater risk for psychological and social maladjustment (Sodowsky and Lai, 1997). Other researchers have found that stressful experiences due to immigration are generally associated with poorer adaptation, lower levels of life satisfaction, lower school engagement and academic performance, and higher rates of behavioral disorders (Padilla et al., 1985; Rotherham-Borus, 1993; Rutter et al., 1974; Thomas, 1995; Ying, 1995; Ying and Liese, 1991). Given that foreign-born youth suffer the loss of familiar sights, sounds, language, and customs of their homeland, their majority status, as well as the emotional support of their family and friends, many believe that many immigrant and parachute youth have difficulty adjusting to their new host culture. To make matters worse, immigrant youth often lack adequate English-language proficiency, familiarity with American customs in school, and, for the first time, suffer from prejudice and discrimination based on race and national origin.

However, recent research challenges the conventional perception that foreign-born youth suffer from adjustment problems, and suggests that foreign-born youth may be better adjusted academically, psychologically, and socially when compared with their U.S.-born or -raised coethnic peers. In fact, researchers consistently find that foreign-born youth have higher academic achievement, and fewer psychosomatic problems, and are less likely to engage in violence or delinquency (such as drugs, alcohol, and sex) than U.S.-born adolescents of the same ethnicity and demographic background (Fuligni, 1998; Harris, 1999; Kao and Tienda, 1995; Rumbaut, 1997a; Steinberg, 1996). In addition, foreign-born youth have similar or lower levels of depressive feelings and psychological distress than U.S.-born adolescents (Harris, 1997; Steinberg, 1996). My research on Chinese immigrant youth confirms these recent findings (Hom, 2002). Foreign-born Chinese youth seem to be relatively well adjusted academically, psychologically, and socially when compared to U.S.-born Chinese adolescents, despite the numerous challenges, stresses, and discontinuities previously described. Academically, foreign-born Chinese youth, including parachute kids, have similar grades and class attendance as U.S.-born Chinese youth. Although foreign-born youth have slightly lower grades than their U.S.-born coethnic peers, foreign-born youth still earn a grade point average (GPA) of 3.25, which is remarkable considering that they take classes in a *second* language. Their U.S.-born Chinese adolescent counterparts earn a higher GPA of 3.50, but the difference is less astounding when we take into account that they take classes in their *native* English language. The similarity in academic performance and attendance—particularly between parachute and immigrant adolescents—implies that parachute kids are motivated to do well in school; they attend class and do the necessary work, even though their parents cannot physically monitor them. Parachute kids may actually work harder in school since they have generally been in the United States for a shorter period of time and arrived at a later age than other immigrant youth, which places them at a greater disadvantage in terms of learning English and mastering coursework.

Psychologically, foreign-born Chinese youth have similar rates of depression and loneliness compared to their U.S.-born coethnic peers, and parachute kids have similar rates of depression and loneliness as other immigrant Chinese adolescents who live with their parents. Furthermore, parachute kids' scores on established measures of depression suggest that they are not more depressed than the average adolescent in the United States or the average adolescent in Asia.[8] Given the early transition into adulthood and the tremendous responsibilities that parachute kids must bear, it may come as a surprise that they do not exhibit higher levels of depressive symptoms. However, most parachute kids are able to adjust to life in the United States without significant problems or distress. One reason may be selection bias—parachute kids who attend schools in the United States by themselves are qualitatively different from those who remain in their homeland or those who immigrate with parents. Parents who send their children to the United States unaccompanied are likely to take their child's temperament, cognitive skills, maturity level, and coping abilities into account, and consequently are unlikely to send off those deemed immature, irresponsible, inflexible, or unable to handle the separation. Hence, the parachute kids who come to the United States without their parents may be more assertive, self-confident, open to new experiences and people, and more independently minded compared to those who do not make the journey. Another possibility is that those who actually move and live in the United States for an extended period of time simply learn to be responsible and become resilient.

Socially, both foreign-born and U.S.-born Chinese youth engage in few delinquent and antisocial behaviors (such as smoking, drinking, vandalizing, shoplifting, and lying to their parents about where they have been and with whom, and individual or gang fighting) compared to their non-Asian peers. The findings in my study reveal that both foreign-born and U.S.-born adolescents have similar rates of truancy, vandalism, and individual physical fighting, but compared to foreign-born youth, U.S.-born Chinese youth have higher rates of shoplifting. Among foreign-born Chinese adolescents, parachute kids have a greater tendency to lie to their parents/guardian about where or whom they had been with and also participate in more gang fights than immigrant adolescents. Moreover, parachute kids are more likely to smoke more cigarettes and drink more alcohol than both immigrant and U.S.-born Chinese adolescents. By comparison, Chinese immigrant youth have the lowest rates of substance use. Although parachute kids tend to be more sexually active than their immigrant counterparts as a whole, it is only the parachute male youth who are more sexually active than their immigrant counterparts. Parachute females are not more sexually active than immigrant girls; both groups of foreign-born females have low rates of sexual activity.

Although the majority of parachute kids do not engage in any maladaptive behaviors, those who do so engage in these behaviors at a higher rate than immigrant or U.S.-born adolescents who participate in the same behaviors. For example, 79 percent of parachute kids, 75 percent of immigrant youth, and 94 percent of U.S.-born youth have never had sex. But among the sexually active participants, parachute kids report being the most active, with 19.5 percent of parachute kids having had sexual intercourse more than twice, compared to only 2 percent of immigrant adolescents and 6 percent of U.S.-born adolescents. Similarly, the majority of parachute kids (91 percent) have never participated in a group or gang fight (compared to 95 percent of immigrant youth and 91 percent of U.S.-born youth), but parachute kids are the only youth who report having been in three or more gang fights. Neither immigrant nor U.S.-born adolescents report having been in more than two gang fights.

The lack of parental or adult supervision may be one reason parachute kids participate in more experimental and antisocial behaviors than other Chinese American adolescents. Their parents are simply not physically present to effectively monitor their use of money and free time, or their physical state. Because parachute kids are free from their parents' supervision, they are less fearful about smelling of smoke and coming home intoxicated. In short, without parents to keep close tabs on their social activities, parachute kids are not held as accountable as other immigrant and U.S.-born youth who live with their parents. Not only do they have more freedom, parachute kids often have more income at their disposal compared to adolescents who live with their parents because they regularly receive large sums of money from their parents who are overseas to cover their living, food, and school expenses. On average, the parachute kids in my study report receiving approximately $600 a month from their parents, while their immigrant peers report receiving approximately $200 a month. In addition, parachute kids report spending approximately $62 a week (excluding the payment of bills), whereas their immigrant peers report spending approximately $38 (39 percent less) a week. And without their parents physically there to monitor their whereabouts, parachute kids are less likely to be caught lying about how they spend their time or money since there is no way for parents to verify the information.

One of the most crucial consequences of migrating solo is that parachute kids spend a considerable amount of time hanging out with friends compared to other immigrant adolescents who live with their families. As a result, parachute adolescents may rely on their peers for a sense of family and belonging, and may therefore be more loyal and protective of their friends, especially if their friendship network consists primarily of other parachute kids. In some cases, parachute kids who lack a sense of belonging may be more inclined to turn to gangs for a sense of family. For example, past research on Southeast Asian adolescents found that some turned to gangs to gain a sense of brotherhood, fellowship, and family, and also engaged in delinquent behaviors as a consequence (Ima and Nidorf, 1998; see also Chapters 13 and 14 in this volume). However, the majority of the parachute kinds in my study tend to associate with other foreign-born youth who value education and have respect for their elders, including parents, guardians, and teachers. Consequently, these positive peer groups help keep each other accountable, focused, and dutiful.

It is important to emphasize here that parachute kids are not more sexually active, do not lie to their parents or guardians more frequently, and do not participate in more gang fights compared to U.S.-born Chinese adolescents, and compared to immigrant Chinese youth who live with their parents. Also, the majority of parachute adolescents do not smoke or drink alcohol. Similarly, most parachute youth are not sexually active. Overall, parachute kids appear to be adapting to their life in the United States just as well as immigrant youth who live with their parents. Moreover, both types of foreign-born adolescents do not appear to be more distressed or maladjusted than U.S.-born Chinese adolescents.

TRANSPLANTATION: BRAVING ROUGH TERRAIN AND GROWING UP IN A NEW CONTEXT

Foreign-born Chinese youth and their U.S.-born counterparts share important similarities—most notably, foreign-born parents who want their children to succeed. Their parents are foreign-born and immigrated to the United States as adults, but were reared in traditional Chinese cultural beliefs, norms, and behavioral patterns. Their parents expect them to excel in school, achieve success in the workplace, and supersede their socioeconomic status. However, unlike U.S.-born or -raised Chinese adolescents, foreign-born youth arrive in the United States in their teens. While their parents may have similar expectations, the two groups of youth are remarkably dissimilar in some fundamental ways that lead them to navigate their host society from different frames of reference.

Prior research shows that the immigrant, or foreign-born, status offers a variety of protective factors that shield foreign-born adolescents from downward mobility. A densely knit coethnic support network, a heightened sense of ethnic solidarity and pride, combined with a clear sense of duty and obligation to their families, provide some of the building blocks for success among foreign-born youth (Fuligni, 1998; Harker, 2001). Together, these protective factors—or what Bourdieu (1977) referred to as *cultural capital*—reduce the likelihood of academic failure, depression, delinquency, and antisocial or risky behaviors.

Three primary findings of this study explain why foreign-born Chinese youth have adapted relatively well academically, psychologically, and socially. First, foreign-born youth actively rebuild their networks of social support to include those who understand the complexities and hardships of adjusting to a new culture at a later age. Not surprisingly, most often, these networks include other immigrant youth who share similar experiences. Second, foreign-born youth consciously develop in-group solidarity in order to assuage the negative effects of prejudice, discrimination, and rejection from U.S.-born peers. Rather than internalizing some of the negative stereotypes that U.S.-born youth hold of them, immigrant youth strongly adhere to the belief in the superiority of their culture, which, in turn, allows them to rebuff prejudice and succeed in the face of adversity. Finally, foreign-born Chinese youth generally adjust well to their new culture because they maintain both ethnic and transnational cultural practices. In doing so, they not only generate meaningful leisure activities, but they also re-create a space for themselves that allows them to extol a sense of ethnic pride.

Rebuilding Networks: Ethnic Insulation as a Coping Strategy

For decades, research in social psychology has consistently shown that people form relationships based on similarity of characteristics and physical proximity, and this is certainly the case among foreign-born Chinese youth. Foreign-born Chinese youth often befriend other foreign-born youth rather than U.S.-born Chinese, Asian, or white youth because they share similar backgrounds, experiences, and an appreciation for a culture other than the American one (Shih, 1998). They have an instant connection with those who speak their language, experienced similar childhoods, share similar beliefs and values, observe the same norms and customs, and follow the same popular culture from their homeland such as music, movies, and books. Perhaps most important, foreign-born youth share the same disorienting effect and sense of loss associated with transplanting to a new place. These shared experiences provide them with a common frame of reference.

Just as instrumental for building a tight social support network is shared language. For example, despite having studied English for an average of three years prior to moving to the United States, the foreign-born participants in my study report that they had a difficult time speaking and expressing their thoughts in English when they first arrived. Currently, less than 10 percent of the foreign-born participants in my survey report that they prefer to speak in English over their native language, even though 18 percent prefer to read things printed in English and 39 percent prefer to write in English. In other words, despite being able to read and write in English, a large number of foreign-born adolescents still prefer to speak in their native language. Although a common foreign language can facilitate communication and network formation, it can also function as a mechanism of exclusion. Not only are non-coethnics unable to join such networks, but foreign-born youth also exclude themselves from actively attempting to partake in other social support systems. In short, the use and reliance on a foreign language constrains foreign-born youth from extending their networks to include U.S.-born and -raised coethnics, or peers of other racial and ethnic groups with whom they attend school and live nearby.

Foreign-born Chinese youth are also likely to befriend other foreign-born because of sheer proximity; they are more likely to come into contact with other foreign-born youth than with either U.S.-born coethnic or non-coethnic youth. Almost all Chinese immigrant and parachute youth enroll in English Language Development (ELD) courses when they first enter the American school system. Thus, the first students they meet and are likely to befriend are other foreign-born youth. Moreover, immigrant families and parachute kids tend to reside in neighborhoods that have large immigrant populations and therefore are likely to meet other foreign-born adolescents in their community grocery stores, cafés, restaurants, churches or temples, SAT and TOEFL[9] prep courses, and ethnic language schools. For instance, 41 percent of the foreign-born participants in the present study attend a Chinese church or temple, 25 percent receive private tutoring (which is often conducted in a group setting), 17 percent attend a test preparation course (typically run by Chinese entrepreneurs), and 15 percent attend a Chinese-language school.

Having a social circle or network comprised of other immigrant youth serves as a positive adaptive strategy in a number of ways (Ying, 1995). First, the ethnic social networks provide foreign-born youth with practical assistance and resources such as information about school policies, community resources, navigating bureaucratic procedures, and translation. Second, the ethnic networks provide emotional support, empathy, and companionship. Foreign-born youth are likely to be comforted and encouraged when they hear that others have experienced the same struggles and were able to overcome similar obstacles. Moreover, forming relationships with coethnics who migrated in their later adolescent years also provides foreign-born youth with a sense of continuity and connection with one's culture of origin (Ying and Liese, 1991).

Unlike the media's portrayal of immigrant and parachute youth as isolated and maladjusted, the data for this study reveal that many actually have an advantage over their U.S.-born coethnic peers since they proactively construct tightly knit social networks. They successfully build a community on their own terms—one in which they are an integral part, are important, and in control. Even though immigrant and parachute youth face unique barriers since they must adjust to a new school environment in their teens, they are generally more satisfied with their school life than their U.S.-born counterparts. The data also indicate that foreign-born youth feel closer to their school friends, more a part of their school, and happier to be at their school than their U.S.-born coethnics. Their tendency to stay focused and engaged in school may be due to a confluence of needs and circumstances, such as an immediate need to overcome the language barrier, the lack of friends upon arrival, and the subsequent acquisition of a foreign-born friendship network.

In-Group Solidarity and Out-Group Derogation

Unlike their U.S.-born counterparts, foreign-born Chinese youth generally do not self-identify as American. They are acutely aware of their limited and accented English as well as their unfamiliarity with American youth culture and social norms. Many believe that most Americans will never consider them to be "American" because of their physical features and Asian accent. Moreover, most have personally experienced the brunt of prejudice and discrimination, having been mocked as "fobbish" and uncool. Others fear that acculturating to the American culture will make them less "Asian" and left without a distinctive identity altogether; they will be neither fully American nor Chinese. Whether they feel constrained in adopting an American identity or whether they choose to actively preserve their ethnic identity, foreign-born youth frequently polarize the differences between Asian and American culture. More specifically, they develop a unique ethnic solidarity that allows foreign-born Chinese youth to take pride in their ethnic identity and culture. Furthermore, the strong and cohesive sense of ethnic solidarity leads to in-group bias and out-group derogation. That is, immigrant and parachute youth view Chinese culture as having more positive qualities than American culture and American culture as having more negative qualities than Chinese culture. In short, they reverse the commonly held belief among Americans in the superiority of American culture and identity.

Although most American youth—including many second-generation adolescents—believe that American culture is more sophisticated and attractive, Chinese-born youth who arrive in their teens do not necessarily subscribe to this view. Indeed, they consider Asian culture and foreign-born youth to be more culturally sophisticated than American culture and their U.S.-born counterparts. For example, most of the participants interviewed for this study described Americans, in general, as rude, ignorant about other cultures, and superficial. They explained that it is difficult to be friends with Americans because they are only interested in befriending those who have something to offer them, such as help with homework. In addition, the foreign-born Chinese youth in my study had few positive things to say about American and U.S.-born Chinese teenagers. At best, they describe their U.S.-born Asian and white peers as being helpful but not thoughtful or encouraging.

The tendency for foreign-born youth to hold in-group biases and derogate out-groups serves as a useful adaptive strategy to minimize the impact of prejudice and discrimination. Although foreign-born Chinese youth admire America as a country and do not take the opportunity to study abroad for granted, they do not look up to American teenagers as role models. Because of the conscious ethnic solidarity that they develop among themselves, foreign-born Chinese adolescents are in a better mental state and position than their U.S.-born coethnic peers to counter adversity. Unlike some U.S.-born ethnic minorities, foreign-born Chinese have come to terms with and even accept the disadvantages associated with not being white. Compared to second-generation Chinese youth, they are less anxious about being accepted by Americans, less concerned with their inability to "fit in" with the cool crowd, less irritated by their treatment as foreigners, and less distressed by overt discrimination. Their strategy of in-group bias and out-group derogation prevents them from feeling helpless and gives them a sense of control over their own fate and their environment. Rather than internalizing rejection or inferiority, immigrant Chinese youth reverse the situation and actively reject mainstream American culture and their U.S.-born peers.

Ethnic Pride and Cultural Involvement

Rejection and discrimination by "Americans" and close association with other foreign-born coethnic peers, in turn, increase the sense of ethnic pride and commitment to Chinese culture among foreign-born Chinese youth. Although they spend part of their free time engaged in typical American youth activities—going to the mall, watching American movies, playing video games, and surfing on the Internet—foreign-born Chinese youth also spend a significant portion of their leisure time engaged in culturally distinct activities. For instance, they sing karaoke songs with Chinese lyrics, watch video movies and television programs produced in their homelands, listen to popular music originating from Taiwan, Hong Kong, and mainland China, read Chinese novels, magazines, and comics, and eat in Chinese cafés or restaurants. In particular, foreign-born youth spend considerably more time watching videos than their U.S.-born counterparts by a ratio of four to one. On average, foreign-born Chinese youth spend 12 hours a week watching videos, compared to only 3 hours among their U.S.-born coethnic peers, and most of the videos they watch are in their native language rather than in English.

Because of their relatively high levels of Chinese-language proficiency and ethnic cultural literacy, foreign-born Chinese youth can utilize various resources already available in the Chinese immigrant community much more effectively than their U.S.-born coethnic peers. For instance, most foreign-born youth turn to the Chinese newspaper for community news and resources. They locate homestays, tutors, test prep courses, seminars, and workshops all through the Chinese newspaper, a resource that most U.S.-born adolescents cannot access due to lack of Chinese literacy. Similarly, foreign-born youth tend to shop at Chinese music, book, and video stores, and eat at Asian cafés, places that enable them to keep up with Asian pop culture and provide them with access to Asian role models.

Continued participation in cultural activities and in ethnic institutions is another adaptive strategy for adjusting to life in the United States because it affords foreign-born Chinese youth the opportunity to participate in the popular youth culture in which they grew up, speak their native language, maintain their newly rebuilt networks, and routinely practice their cultural customs. By remaining actively engaged in ethnic cultural practices and institutions, foreign-born youth create a familiar space for themselves in a foreign land while simultaneously reaffirming a sense of ethnic pride, self-worth, and power and control over their new environment. Although they may not be familiar with American culture and may not speak English fluently, they do know a great deal about their own cultural heritage and language and use these cultural capital resources to navigate the uncharted territory in their new host country. Thus, by choosing to remain "Chinese" or "Asian," rather than trying to become "American," foreign-born Chinese youth actively distinguish and separate themselves from native-born Americans.

Moreover, unlike many of their U.S.-born coethnic peers, they struggle less with trying to straddle two cultures while gaining acceptance into the American mainstream. Instead, they remain critical of American culture and do not subscribe to the belief that becoming American is necessarily positive or the path to getting ahead. Foreign-born Chinese youth utilize a different strategy to cope with their immigrant and minority experiences in the United States. Instead of focusing on what they do not have, they focus on what they do have, such as coethnic support, empathy, companionship, and connection to their culture—a strategy that allows them to adjust to their new host society and enables them to carve a space for themselves in which they feel both comfortable and safe.

CONCLUSION

Despite the loss of majority status and changes in family relationships, friendships, and lifestyle, foreign-born Chinese youth are generally not at greater risk for academic, psychological, or social problems than their U.S.-born counterparts. Numerous factors affect an individual's ability to cope with the strains of immigrating and adjusting to a new culture, such as their personality, maturity level, motivation for moving to the United States, sense of familial obligation, and future goals. However, individual characteristics tell only part of the story. Just as critical are the social factors that facilitate the process of adjustment for foreign-born Chinese youth, such as their development of social support networks, involvement in ethnic institutions, and adoption of in-group bias and out-group derogation. Together, these strategies work to buffer the effects of discrimination that foreign-born youth experience due to their foreign-born status and/or Asian physical features.

One important caveat to note before concluding is that the lack of apparent maladjustment does not negate the stress associated with moving to a new country, halfway around the world, and having to learn an entirely new language and culture. Immigrant and parachute youth face enormous challenges, especially because they move to the United States during or after adolescence—a developmentally sensitive period during which all youth experience significant physical and emotional changes regardless of migration status. Parachute kids, in particular, must deal with even more stressful life events, such as an uncertainty about one's future country of residence and family separation during their formative years. This chapter suggests that the ability to cope with these challenges successfully depends largely on the determination, resiliency, and proactive efforts of foreign-born youth. Immigrant and parachute youth have managed to lend a sense of belonging and meaning to their transnational and bicultural encounters between East and West.

Notes

1. This chapter is drawn primarily from my doctoral dissertation. I would like to thank the Chiang Ching-Kuo Foundation for International Scholarly Exchange for funding my research. This research is partially based on data from the National Longitudinal Study of Adolescent Health, a project designed by J. Richard Udry (PI) and Peter Bearman, and funded by grant P01-HD31921 from the National Institute of Child Health and Human Development to the Carolina Population Center, University of North Carolina at Chapel Hill, with cooperative funding participation by the National Cancer Institute; the National Institute of Alcohol Abuse and Alcoholism; the National Institute on Deafness and Other Communication Disorders; the National Institute on Drug Abuse; the National Institute of General Medical Sciences; the National Institute of Mental Health; the National Institute of Nursing Research; the Office of AIDS Research, NIH; the Office of Behavior and Social Science Research, NIH; the Office of the Director, NIH; the Office of Research on Women's Health, NIH; the Office of Population Affairs, DHHS; the National Center for Health Statistics, Centers for Disease Control and Prevention, DHHS; the Office of Minority Health, Centers for Disease Control and Prevention, DHHS; the Office of Minority Health, Office of Public Health and Science, DHHS; the Office of the Assistant Secretary for Planning and Evaluation, DHHS; and the National Science Foundation. Persons interested in obtaining data files from the National Longitudinal Study of Adolescent Health should contact Add Health Project, Carolina Population Center, 123 West Franklin Street, Chapel Hill, NC 27516-2524 (email: addhealth@unc.edu).

2. FOB stands for "fresh off the boat." It is a derogatory slang used by highly acculturated 1.5- and second-generation Asian Americans to refer to those who are considered too *Asian* and unassimilated.

3. "Parachute kids" are underaged foreign students who are sent to live and study in the United States without their parents as early as in the first grade. Some of the parachute kids in the present study came on tourist or exchange student visas, while others came on immigrant visas (green cards) but were not accompanied by their parents because their parents delayed their immigration for work or other reasons. All parachute kids come with the hope of obtaining a good education in a less competitive and stressful educational system (Hom, 2002; Zhou, 1998).

4. Youth who belong to the 1.5 generation (children who immigrated between the ages of 5 and 12) will not be discussed.

5. This chapter is based primarily on two datasets. The first dataset is the LA survey—which I conducted with 232 foreign-born Chinese adolescents (105 immigrant youth, 127 parachute kids) from over 12 different schools in the greater Los Angeles area. The majority of the participants, however, were sampled through three schools (two high schools, one K-12) either through English Language Development (ELD) courses or by class period (Hom,

2002). The second dataset is a subset of the National Longitudinal Study of Adolescent Health (Add Health), a nationally representative study of adolescents from grades 7–12 in the United States (see Bearman, Jones, and Udry, 1997). Only information from the 287 participants (165 U.S. born, 116 immigrant, 6 parachute) who identified themselves as being solely of Chinese ancestry were used. Both datasets contain information that was collected through questionnaires and individual interviews that took place in the respondent's home. Interviews in the LA survey were approximately 60 minutes in length and conducted in Mandarin, Taiwanese, or English, depending on the respondent's language fluency and preference. Interviews from the Add Health study were approximately 90 minutes in length and conducted in English only. Both studies used questions from the Add Health study. The findings presented in this chapter are likely to apply to youth of other East Asian origins due to similarities in their cultural upbringing and postmigration experiences. The term *Chinese* is used broadly, with the caveat that foreign-born Chinese youth on the West Coast may have different experiences from their coethnic peers in other parts of the United States. Because of the long-standing settlement history of Chinese immigration and the continuous influx of contemporary Chinese immigrants to the West Coast, foreign-born Chinese youth in California are more likely to have peers and school personnel who speak their native language and have access to ethnic food, cultural and consumer products, and ethnic community resources such as churches, temples, and Chinese-language schools. Foreign-born Chinese youth on the West Coast are also more likely to encounter second- or even third-plus generation Chinese American adolescents who neither speak Chinese nor share the foreign-born's beliefs, values, and cultural practices.

6. Parachute kids can be as young as eight years old, but the majority are between ages 13 and 17. According to government and media reports, most parachute kids come from Taiwan, followed by Korea, Hong Kong, and China, then other Asian countries such as Indonesia, Malaysia, and the Philippines (see Hamilton, 1993a, 1993b; Hom, 2002; *Los Angeles Times*, 1993; Zhou 1998).

7. The American educational system has a reputation for being less stressful and less competitive than many educational systems in Asia. American students not only attend school for fewer hours each day but also for fewer days in a school year. More importantly, American students do not have competitive junior high or high school entrance exams like the students do in Asia. In addition, the United States offers more flexible methods of earning a college degree, such as first attending a two-year community college and then transferring into an accredited four-year college or university.

8. More specifically, Chinese parachute kids had similar ratings of depression as Chinese adolescents in Hong Kong.

9. Scholastic Aptitude Test and Test of English as a Foreign Language.

CHAPTER **10**

Reinventing the Wheel:

Import Car Racing in Southern California

Victoria Namkung

For years, street and organized racing catered almost exclusively to white males who drove American-made V-8 automobiles, and Asian Americans who drove import cars were excluded from mainstream car races. This scene changed in July 1990 when 500 Asian American street racers and import car enthusiasts drove their Hondas, Nissans, and Acuras to the Los Angeles County Raceway for an event called *Battle of the Imports*. This day marked the first organized presence of import car racing in southern California, the capital of automobiles and the breeding ground for car cultures. Frank Choi, the founder of *Battle of the Imports*, invited everyone he knew and asked them to spread the word, and in the end, drew an impressive crowd. Today, the import scene is so popular that *Battle of the Imports* attracts more than 20,000 people and is televised on ESPN2.

Import racing is an emerging youth cultural form reconstructed by Asian Americans as a proactive response to cultural exclusion. Distinct from cruising and hot rodding of the 1950s and 1960s, Chicano low riding, or Anglo muscle car traditions, import racing is much more than racing; it also entails customizing or modifying import subcompact vehicles and combining this with a youthful lifestyle. Participants "fix up" their Asian subcompacts and transform them into lighter, faster, louder, and visually fancier cars. The cars, however, are not only reserved for racing but are used in everyday life, reflecting the "show" aspect of the import car culture.

Since its debut in the early 1990s, import racing has soared in popularity in California, spreading as far south as San Diego and as far north as the San Francisco Bay area. Another regularly held event, *Hot Import*

Daze/Nights, boasts more than 15,000 attendees.[1] Asian Americans comprise between 50 and 60 percent of the crowd, based on estimates among import car industry workers and magazines such as *Auto Week*. However, personal years of observation suggest that these estimates are conservative at best.

The growing import racing scene has unquestionably changed the automotive industry and altered the dynamics of the vibrant car culture in southern California. Although import racing has propelled a historically invisible ethnic group onto center stage of the previously Anglo-dominated consumer market and culture, it has also become an important venue for socialization and identity formation among Asian American youth. This chapter examines the following questions: What are the distinct features of import racing, and why is it uniquely Asian American? How do young Asian Americans negotiate race and gender through participation in import racing? Is import racing a reaction to alienation from mainstream youth culture, or is it simply a new version of American consumer culture in which Asian American youth participate? Is it deviant, or is it a normal youth practice that merely aims to establish an identity? And finally, what are the implications of this emerging youth subculture for Asian American identity formation?

The data on which this study is based were collected over a two-year period between 1998 and 1999, and consist of four components: (1) in-depth face-to-face interviews with ten import racers whose ages range from 14 to 24 (eight males and two females) at four sites in southern California—*Battle of the Imports* in Palmdale, University of California, Los Angeles, University of California, Irvine, and University High School in Irvine; (2) informal conversations with numerous import racers, event organizers, and auto marketers, both Asian and non-Asian;[2] (3) participant observation in organized events;[3] and (4) media accounts—magazines and videos of actual racing. In this study, import car racers include not only those who race their cars but also those who attend racing-related events, as well as those who modify and fix up their cars. The study investigates the history and development of import racing as an Asian American socializing tradition, but given the limitations of the data, the study is not intended to provide a comprehensive analysis of the entire import car racing scene.

SOUTHERN CALIFORNIA'S CAR CULTURE AND IMPORT RACING

The car culture has always been a salient feature of southern California's imagery. Francis Ford Coppola's classic, *American Graffiti*, for example, depicts the days of hot rodding and drag racing in Los Angeles, and, today, MTV's hip-hop videos depict rap artists in "low rider" Chevys bouncing up and down with hydraulic systems. Cars are undoubtedly a driving force behind southern California's consumer culture. Since World War II, rapid suburbanization and the lack of accessible public transportation have rendered Angelenos dependent on the automobile, and with the proliferation of automobiles was born a car culture. The emergence of the car culture became evident in the 1950s and 1960s when hot rodding and drag racing dominated the scene, and drive-in movie theaters and drive-up restaurants sprouted across America's cities to cater to the culture. Cars have served a function far beyond transporting individuals from one locale to the next; they constitute a key component of popular culture based on consumerism and materialism. In contemporary America, cars affirm one's status, express a lifestyle, form an identity, and socialize youth.

Hot Rodding, Low Riding, and Muscle Car Racing

Although cars have played a large role in southern California's identity, this culture has been particularly salient for male youth. In the 1950s and 1960s, legal and illegal hot rodding and drag racing gained popularity among white teenagers in the San Fernando Valley. Teenagers would take a Ford or other American-manufactured cars and rebuild or modify them to increase their acceleration and speed. Even today, the hot-rodding culture remains very much a part of the popular car culture in America, thriving through car clubs, car shows, and magazines.

In the 1970s, a new movement entered the car scene—low riding. Originating in Mexican barrios in East Los Angeles, the low rider movement asserted a new cultural form with a strong Mexican flavor into the dominant Anglo car culture. Although Chicano low riding involves cruising and modification, unlike hot rodding, racing is not a central component of this culture. Low riding began as a hobby exclusively among Mexican American youth that entailed customizing cars, but today it boasts a multiracial cast that includes black and white youth. Since gaining popularity among American youth of different backgrounds, Chicano low riding is now an undisputed feature of the dominant car culture. It has become such a central feature of the American mainstream that the toy manufacturer Mattel launched a line of Hot Wheels based on low riders.[4] Moreover, there are numerous car shows and magazines devoted specifically to low riding, the recently held exhibition on Latino car culture at the Petersen Automobile Museum in Los Angeles being a prime example.

Contemporary Import Car Racing and *Battle of the Imports*

Like hot rodding and low riding, import car racing was born and developed in southern California and has since spread up the California coast to other parts of the country (Witzel and Bash, 1997). However, unlike hot rodding and low riding, Asian Americans were the innovators of this newest car trend, which emerged as a result of their exclusion from other forms of popular car culture. Until recently, Asian Americans were invisible in America's car culture, but as they came of age in the late 1980s and 1990s, Asian American youth prominently established their place in California's car racing scene.

Import car racing entails modifying and dressing up cars to drive faster, sound louder, and look fancier and flashier. Although some import car racers choose German or Italian cars, the vast majority drive Asian imported, compact cars such as Honda Civics and Nissan Sentras. Young racers typically receive their first cars from their parents as gifts but then spend their own money from part-time jobs to modify and dress up their cars, devoting as much as tens of thousands to "fix up" their "ride." Considering that the base price of cars is between $15,000 and $30,000, and that import car racers pour thousands more into their cars, it is not difficult to understand why middle- and upper-middle-class youth dominate this trend.

Style is an important element in the import car racing scene, so it is not only a question of how well the car runs but also how good the car looks. Import car racers lower their cars to the ground, and many plaster them with bright stickers across the front, down the hood, or on the side; the stickers serve as advertisement for various import car companies, often in Japanese writing. Racers often tint their windows and add parts such as giant spoilers and oversized wheels and rims, and the modifications do not stop there (see Figure 10.1). Import car racers also install top-of-the-line stereo systems, customized seats, and even dashboard consoles that feature video games. Hence, the visual appeal of the car is tremendously important. This is not to say, however, that performance is unimportant. On race day (Figure 10.2), racers remove seats in order to lighten their load and maximize speed.

The first import car racing event made its debut in July of 1990 at the Los Angeles County Raceway in Palmdale—a desert-like suburban city northeast of Los Angeles that serves as the main venue for import racers to practice legal racing. Organized by Frank Choi, *Battle of the Imports* aimed to unite racers from California for a legal car race and show. Over 500 young people (mostly Asian American) and about 50 cars participated in the first event, and since then *Battle of Imports* has become a biannual weekend extravaganza that draws as many as 20,000 racers and friends

Figure 10.1 The Wheels. Photograph by Victoria Namking.

Figure 10.2 Race Day. Photograph by Victoria Namking.

through word of mouth, the Internet, and import car-part sellers. Because of the popularity of import car racing, its founders have recently christened the Import Drag Racing Association (IDRA), which oversees many other racing organizations.

"Grudge Night" and the Import Lifestyle

Although *Battle of the Imports* is the biggest event in import racing, groups of Asian American racers also gather on Friday evenings for "Grudge Night," often in Palmdale but also in other places. Other enormously popular events include *Import Showoff* and *Hot Import Daze/Nights* in the Los Angeles area, which combine the display of cars with a nightclub ambiance that includes strobe lights, hip-hop and dance music, and other forms of live entertainment. The events are essentially a fusion of car show and night club—evidently a formula for success considering that they attract thousands of Asian American youth. In 1999, the social event *Hot Import Daze/Nights* was so packed that the organizers were forced to turn away 4,000 people. Racers and their friends hang out in various social groups, chat and laugh boisterously, and take pictures and videotapes of the night's events. Generally, alcohol and drugs are absent from the import car racing scene, although the party culture often extends to hotels after some events.

Certain racers like Adam Saruwatari have even achieved minor celebrity status.[5] Saruwatari can race his Mazda RX-7 "in the nines" (reaching speeds of more than 140 miles per hour) on a quarter-mile stretch in less than ten seconds. Although no one can rely on import racing as a full-time career, some events offer racing and show purses in the thousands, and Saruwatari often walks away with the most cash. Others in the same caliber of racing as Saruwatari are now sponsored by top corporations in the automotive industry and have teams of people fixing up their cars to get them ready for race or show time.

Participation in actual import racing begins as young as 16 years of age and even earlier for those whose friends or siblings are involved in the hobby. Racers and "racing crews" (groups of racers who are friends) are mostly 1.5- or second-generation Asian American males between the ages of 16 and 24 from suburban middle- and upper-middle-class families.[6] In Orange County, for example, the youth are predominantly Chinese, Korean, Vietnamese, and Japanese American. Although most youth modify or change their cars to look a certain way, only half may actually participate in races at professional tracks. Groups of crews often simply gather at deserted places like Oxnard (a farming community about 45 miles north of Los Angeles) to hold illegal races. As import racing increasingly gains in popularity, one finds a growing presence of African Americans, Latinos, and Euro-Americans, but the scene is largely dominated by Asian American male youth. These events also draw hundreds of young women who come to participate, hang out with friends, or work.

Import racing is an expensive and time-consuming hobby. Although some racers complain about the enormous monetary and time investment, others actually profit from the growing market demand by selling their fixed-up cars and reinvesting the money into new vehicles. Jason, a 24-year-old Filipino American college student and an import racer on his way out of the scene, estimates that he has spent over $9,000 in modifications over the last three years alone. Although his parents live in a middle-class neighborhood in Orange County, California, Jason has paid for his own costs through a series of part-time jobs that he has held over the years. Jason's 1992 Honda Accord LX is sharp-looking, with clear corner, bumper, and rear taillights, and a custom leather interior. He has also installed an HKS air filter, Nitrous Oxide, and Neuspeed Race Springs, and even reached the level of sponsorship from a well-known custom interior company.

Jason used to race and show his car frequently and with pride, but now, at the ripe old age of 24, he acknowledges that he is pushing the upper age limit for the hobby. Participants typically leave this hobby after graduating from college when they begin their first full-time, career-oriented job and live on their own. They calculate that the costs to maintain and fix up their vehicles are prohibitive when they become financially independent. So although former import car racers may own an import car like an Acura or a Nissan, they tend not to fix them up as they once did.

Accompanying the races and shows (which take place year-round in various parts of southern California) is a unique import lifestyle. Unlike mainstream car racing, import racers drive their dressed-up cars day-to-day, hang out in large groups, speak the same slang, listen to hip-hop, and don similar styles of dress and hairstyles. At races and shows, racing crews and friends often sport clothing that promotes their car club or sponsor. Capitalizing on this trend, vendors set up booths to sell car parts and lifestyle-related merchandise such as clothing and accessories.

The import racing identity has exploded, and today thousands of Internet web sites are dedicated to this culture. For example, the Internet service provider *America Online* features numerous chat rooms dedicated to "O.C. Racerz" and "Import Scene." Since import racers are typically high school or college students from middle- to upper-middle-class backgrounds with Internet access, promoters, vendors, and participants have found it easy to spread the culture far beyond the confines of southern California. Recognizing that their target audience is on-line, promoters of racing events utilize and rely on the Internet to access customers. There are also numerous publications dedicated to import racing such as *Import Tuner* and *Super Street*, available in local grocery stores in Orange County and Los Angeles, making the culture readily accessible to many of America's youth.

IDENTITY FORMATION VIA IMPORT RACING

Import racing has a unique Asian twist—racers are predominantly Asian American; cars and parts are mostly imported from Asia, and, most importantly, races and shows serve as a cultural space constructed and used by Asian American youth and young adults as a proactive response to the history of marginalization and exclusion. Import racing forges a distinct identity for Asian American youth that allows them to look and feel good, cool, and sexy.

Forging a Pan-Ethnic Community

A unique characteristic of the import racing identity is the formation of a pan-ethnic community. In the beginning, racing crews and other participants started in various ethnic groups, hanging out and racing separately by ethnicity. For example, Japanese Americans believed that they started the trend, while Filipino Americans claim that it originated in P (Pilipino)-Town. Groups were initially exclusively Chinese, Korean, or Vietnamese, but, with time, ethnic group boundaries faded and converged toward a collective pan-ethnic identity. Now, import racing has become one of the few places, aside from political alliances, where Asian Americans have come together as a group.

Over the years, an import racing identity and culture have emerged in which young Asian Americans hang out, date, and attend events in groups of two, four, or more. Crews help their friends prep for a race, and although some racing crews are coethnic, others are pan-ethnic and multiracial. Given its growing popularity, especially in southern California, import car racing has enormous crossover appeal and has attracted whites, blacks, Latinos, and women, who not only attend the events but also get behind the wheel. The crossover appeal has propelled import car racing into the mainstream in the world of automobile racing. The makers of popular import cars, parts, and even corporations like Anheuser-Busch sponsor racers and events in order to expand their markets. In some cases, the sponsorship has even extended to Asian American organizations.

Although group identity is often based on a set of boundaries that distinguish insiders from outsiders, import car racing transcends ethnicity, race, and gender. What matters is the legitimacy of the racer, fitting into the culture, or just being "cool." The erosion of boundaries fosters a sense of community and identity for those who participate in the culture. For example, Todd, a 20-year-old college student at UC Irvine and an import racer, describes how the hobby makes him feel "a part of something":

> It's like you feel you're a part of something exciting. The import market is growing so fast I can barely keep up. Before it was just a few cars on the road here and there, but now it's like all over the place. Even when you go to a club or a rave, the parking lot will be full of racers and they're just looking for a place to hang out and talk about cars and shit. Where I'm from, there aren't that many Asian kids, and most of them are really FOB-like. But here at UCI and in San Gabriel there's just so many Asian kids, we're bound to hang out together and hook up because of the car stuff.[7]

Although import racing is racially inclusive, Asian American males are the creators of and dominant forces behind this youth culture. Given the large Asian American population in southern California, especially in some local high schools and college campuses where the Asian American population now exceeds 50 percent, Asian American males will continue to have a strong hold on this cultural form.

Asserting Masculinity and Hyper-Heterosexuality

Social scientists generally agree that masculinity, like race, is a social rather than biological category (Kimmel, 1994; Messner, 1992). Import racing provides a cultural space for Asian American youth to form a pan-ethnic community and also allows Asian American males to construct and assert an unequivocally masculine, hyper-heterosexual identity. Historically, Asian American men have been depicted and stereotyped as weak, effeminate, nerdy, asexual, or sexually deviant. For example, Nayan Shah (2001) illustrates that the dominant white world viewed nineteenth-century Chinatowns as immoral bachelor societies of dissolute men with peculiar living arrangements, deviant sexualities, and vice habits that undermined American morality and family life. Sau-ling Wong's (1992) exploration of ethnicity and gender in Chinese immigrant literature finds that feminization and demasculization of Asian men goes far beyond the physical and becomes a part of a distorted ethnic identity imposed on all Asian Americans. Robert G. Lee (1999) argues that the entry of Chinese men into the domestic sphere as household servants in the nineteenth century created a threat to the existing patriarchal hierarchy of the family since it led to the possibility of immoral intimate relations between white women and the deviant "third sex." Although historical representations have depicted Asian American men as effeminate and sexually immoral, contemporary images are very different in this regard; Asian American men continue to be portrayed as asexual, nerdy, and forever foreign or "fresh off the boat" (FOB).

One of the appeals of import racing for Asian American male youth is that it directly challenges the negative stereotypes associated with Asian American males. Like other youth cultural forms such as African American hip-hop and Chicano low riding, import car racing is infused with masculinity and hypersexuality. As many of the interviewees observed, much of the import scene is fraught with "attitudes" and acts of demonstrating toughness. For instance, Jason recalls:

> I used to encounter a lot of inadvertent stares and revs (revving your car up like you want to race) from a lot of muscle cars whose drivers were usually young white males. In a way, it [import racing] has given a lot of youth a positive hobby to get involved in. For many Asian Americans, it has given them something to identify with much like during the 50s and 60s white teens had muscle cars.[8]

Illustrating the attitudinal aspect of import racing, Spencer Lee (1999) states: "[N]onracers themselves often get in the mix, with 'crews' fighting at shows. Turf and being 'hard' have become as much a part of the scene as the cars themselves." While tensions flare from time to time, they do not stem from differences in race or ethnicity, but rather from competition and racing, which is quickly settled behind the wheel. As the interviewees agree, it all comes down to what you can do inside the car.

In a recent issue of *Gidra*, published in Los Angeles, Naomi Iwasaki (1999) analyzed how Asian American males use import racing to counter their history of feminization. A cartoon that ran beside the article features an Asian American male smoking a cigarette, wearing baggy jeans, and leaning against an import car. Iwasaki refers to the insecurities or demasculization of the Asian American male as the Asian Male Complex and elaborates how males overcome it with their import cars. Iwasaki explains: the Asian American male who "turns into a motor-revving so loud it sets off my car alarm, is the same one that causes me to roll my eyes and throw up my arms in disgust at the lack of Asian men out there who are secure enough to not have to front off and prove how hard they are."

With thousands of Asian American males participating in this car culture, male dominance and sexual exploitation are problems that cannot be overlooked. Like other male-dominated sports such as football, boxing, or wrestling, import car racing places most females on the sidelines, often in sexually explicit and exploitative roles. For example, flyers and other promotional items display scantily clad women sprawled on cars to attract attention, and corporate sponsors like Budweiser and Toyo Tires hire women and sometimes "playmates" to dance and pose with cars and participants. Although some of the women are Asian American, most are Anglo. Other female attendees who are not hired by corporate sponsors also show up at events and pose in pictures. Most men may have no objections to the role of women in these events, but several Asian American males have voiced dismay about the behavior of some Asian American women. A former racer laments:

> Nowadays, I think that the import scene is becoming too polluted with bad attitude. If you go to *Import Showoff* or *Battle* all the dudes look like thugs or wannabees. The women who model for the cars, especially Asian women, exploit themselves in skimpy outfits spreading their legs so guys with video cameras can snap a few seconds of whack-off footage. It's so embarrassing when I saw that sort of crap, and it led me to get out of the scene.[9]

Import car racing is undeniably crossing over into the mainstream at a high speed, and, given its popularity, it may become a vehicle through which the image of Asian American males changes.

While Asian American males begin to transform their image through the import car culture, in the process, they are also alienating and exploiting their female counterparts.

HARD GIRLS AND HOOCHIES: ASIAN AMERICAN FEMALE PARTICIPATION

Asian Americans make up over half of the import car scene in southern California, and at least 90 percent of Asian American racers are male. Car clubs such as "Go Gyrl Racing" (Figure 10.3) include females who are serious about racing and showing their cars at events. Asian females typically fix up Asian compact import cars like Hondas, Nissans, Mitsubishis, Acuras, and Mazdas, the results of which are often referred to as "rice rockets" or "rice burners." Whether racing, showing their car, participating as a member of a crew, or just hanging out, Asian American females are becoming an increasingly visible and integral part of the scene. And while racing remains largely in the domain of Asian American males, females are slowly making inroads into the racing scene.

The gender element is particularly interesting because car cultures have historically exploited women. Caucasian women are pictured in car culture–related magazines, posters, and flyers, and a glance at *Lowrider* Magazine features Latina women in bikinis posing with various cars and drivers.[10] Asian women play a similar role as accessories, "import playmates," and sexualized and exploited objects in the import car culture. Bikini-clad Asian American women lie on hoods of cars in magazines, and some Asian American girls who attend racing events and car shows actually strip and pose for photographs with the cars on-site. Corporate sponsors also hire "import playmates" (who are often non-Asian) in order to attract attention at their booths during shows. Although females are just begin-

Figure 10.3 Go Gyrl Racing. Photograph by Victoria Namking.

ning to enter the race and show scene, the presence of "hoochies" (a pejorative term used to describe the women hired to decorate the sidelines and advertisements) presents an obstacle for Asian American females who are serious about participating in import car racing.

Many women also attend the events as fans who are interested in the sport and enjoy hanging out with friends. Like any sport, there are import groupies—typically groups of young, Asian American females who enjoy talking to, flirting with, and posing for the racers. The events serve as a meeting ground where young Asian American males and females can get together and "hook up." Many of the participants and spectators bring video and still cameras to record the evening's events. And while some of the females crave male attention, others attend the events just to watch, hang out with friends, and meet new people. From all visible evidence, the females appear to be in control of their actions.

For Stella, a 19-year-old Korean American female, the women who decorate the sidelines and magazine covers do not bother her, although she does notice the so-called hoochies who attend the events.

> Why would I care about the hoochies at the races? Sure, some of them are annoying, but they're really just like the Budweiser girls or something. Plus, they're only there because the corporate sponsors bring them in. When you're just out on the street racing or hanging out, they're not around. I just come to do my thing and I leave. Most of the guys treat me okay, but some of them try to stare you down or act hard, but they're just fronting.[11]

Although the sexualization of females exists within the import car culture, both men and women participate in these activities and representations by choice. Moreover, there are plenty of females who attend the races as spectators and participants who take no part of the sexual exploitation.

IMPORT RACING—A NORMAL OR DEVIANT SUBCULTURE?

Youth subcultures in any form tend to be treated as deviant from broader societal perspectives. However, import car racing is not a deviant subculture; rather, it is a celebration and affirmation of a positive identity, as well as a proactive strategy that challenges negative stereotyping. However positive, import car racing has often been perceived and misrepresented as a deviant subculture of "car gangs." Indeed, import car racers participate in "crews" or "posses" like other young gangs, and some crews have as many as 500 members. And like many of today's youth who have adopted the hip-hop culture and styles, they sport a "gangsta" image style of dress—baggy pants, sportswear, shaved heads, piercings, and gold chains and earrings. In addition, there are notable similarities between Asian youth gangs and participants of the import car culture. Both are masculine subcultural spaces focused on the formation of an empowering ethnic identity. Members of youth gangs and import car racers also sport similar styles of dress, such as Tommy Hilfiger or Nautica sportswear, and borrow elements from African American hip-hop culture. Finally, both have a connectedness to their ancestral homelands in Asia and a shared appreciation of Asian cultures and pride (Alsaybar, 1999). Albeit rare, unfortunately there have also been instances of gang-banging, fist fights, civil disturbance, illegal races, and even deaths associated with import racing. However isolated and infrequent, these negative instances have led some local law enforcement officials to regard import car racers as dangerous trouble-makers.

The loudness of import cars and visible markers such as large, bright stickers and car modifications make racers easy targets for local police and business owners who readily identify them as gang members and want them to be excluded or controlled. The Edwards Cinema movie theater in Alhambra, California, for example, posts a sign that reads, "No import cars allowed."[12] Some interviewees complained that local and state police often target import racers through racial profiling, especially in areas with high concentrations of Asian American youth such as Garden Grove and Irvine in southern California. Asian American drivers of import cars have been singled out for police harassment, ranging from illegal searches to civil rights violations. Some police departments have even taken photographs of the drivers to store in a "mug book" for future use. Over one hundred Asian Americans, predominantly male, but also some female, have been subjected to this illegal harassment.[13] The "Asian mug books" are based not only on race but also on the import style of the vehicle. As a former UC Irvine graduate bitterly explains, "Irvine sucked. UCI cops focused on ticketing lowered import cars. Other cities that I would cruise such as Old Town Pasadena had cops. Street races were dangerous too. There were numerous police busts."[14] The experiences of racial profiling are certainly not unique to Asian American youth; African American and Latino youth have been victims of racial profiling for years. As Robin Kelley (1994) states, "Even more common to the collective experience of young black residents of L.A.'s inner city was the police policy of identifying presumably suspicious characters on the basis of clothing styles."

Many import racers complain about police harassment and about the problems that arise from misunderstandings and misperceptions by the local community, especially during racing events when thousands of youth pour in from all over California. Frank Choi has seen this happen time and again during his biannual event, *Battle of the Imports*. He describes the type of harassment that import car racers face:

> Yeah, I mean we experience it with the local law enforcement up in Palmdale. It becomes really strict, pulling people over for stupid things like being too low, or having clear tail lights, or freaking hanging a stuffed animal from your rear view mirror, or something like that. I guess it all boils down to the fact that there's always a few bad apples that ruin the rest of the bunch.

He explains that the harassment often stems from police officers who mistake racers for gang members:

> They did that in Irvine, they did that in Garden Grove. It's probably because the local law enforcement of today's society views car clubs as gang members. And, you know that problem is in existence in Torrance, Palos Verdes, you know, everywhere. You know? And it's a shame. But it's similar to how it's perceived here in Palmdale.

Frank Choi adds that, while import car racing may be no different from other forms of legal racing, the fact that the racers have a distinctive look makes them easy targets for law enforcement officials:

> So that's why, you know, they're speeding on the streets, they do a little burn out here and there. You know it's like, it's no different than what's going on in this time period than it happened in the 1950s, when you guys had national events at other racetracks. Except these kids look different! You know, so they have their noses pierced, their tongues pierced, their lips and their bodies pierced, they have tattoos, their hair's a different color, their clothes look funny, but other than that it's the same thing. You know I think there is this huge generation gap between the older generation as business owners and this new generation, these Gen X'ers and Gen Y'ers that are actually consumers and users and patrons that are gonna come and make you money.

Understandably, import racers are frustrated that the media portrays them as gang members and that the local community mistakes them as such and misinterpret their intentions. The negative misrepresentations are difficult to erase, but individuals such as Frank Choi among others are committed to creating a safe, legal space in which import racers can participate. Although some may view import racing as deviant, it can be seen as a highly functional and surprisingly positive form of youth culture.

CONCLUSION

Unlike other Asian-derived forms of popular culture such as Japanese anime, kung-fu films, or Hello Kitty paraphernalia, import car racing is made in America and is unquestionably Asian American. Excluded from the V-8, Anglo-dominated muscle car culture of the 1970s and 1980s, Asian American youth decided to start their own races and shows with their own cars and on their own terms. With its inception in the early 1990s, import car racing has become the most distinctive identity among Asian Americans in southern California. It is a sport or hobby for some, but for many Asian American youth, particularly males, import car racing and its lifestyle have become a socializing tradition. Although import racing has no overt political agenda, it has some parallels with the African American hip-hop culture in the sense that both cultural forms provide a sense of identity, community, and empowerment.

For American youth, a car and driver's license are the first steps to freedom and independence, but cars represent more than a means of transportation. For Asian American youth, cars are a symbol of masculinity, individuality, ethnic pride, and an instrument for empowerment. Many Asian American youth may excel in academia, but they are often invisible in arenas such as sports, drama clubs, and leadership roles. Import racing has filled a void for Asian American youth by providing them with an avenue for extracurricular activities that is both productive and positive. The study reveals that import racing is not simply about drag racing or expensive wheels, but rather an opportunity for Asian American youth to form a collective pan-ethnic identity and reclaim their masculinity. As the first wave of import car racers departs the scene, the next generation is taking their place in unprecedented numbers. Given its popularity, import car racing will continue to thrive as a cultural form in southern California.

Mainstream culture is now beginning to embrace the import culture, and advertisers have come to recognize that import racers represent buying power with their disposable incomes to spend on clothes, cars, parts, and accessories. Print advertisements and television commercials have featured import racers and their vehicles, and even Hollywood wants in on the action. Director Rob Cohen's 2001 film *The Fast and the Furious,* which is set in California and stars Vin Diesel and Paul Walker, grossed $144,512,310 in the United States alone. The film is not an accurate depiction of the import racing culture, but it features many import cars. More importantly, the film's box office success proves that the subject of cars and racing is not only popular but also profitable. The 2003 sequel, *2 Fast 2 Furious,* which starred an even more racially diverse cast, grossed $127 million domestically, proving that it is a hugely successful franchise.

Frank Choi's creation of the first *Battle of the Imports* gave hundreds of Asian American youth a place to belong, although that may not have been Choi's original intent. The tens of thousands of teens and college students who attend import racing events on the weekends have found a place to be accepted. The culture has grown so rapidly and so furiously that it is practically the norm for Asian American youth to participate in the scene in one way or another. Today, import racing has spilled over into the mainstream to such an extent that people in southern California rarely even blink when they drive behind a fixed-up car on the freeway. The Asian American import car racing scene has hit the American cultural mainstream with high speed and shows no signs of slowing down.

Notes

1. Author's interview with *Battle of the Imports* founder Frank Choi and *Hot Import Daze/Nights* promotional director, Mike Munar, December 7, 1999. See also "Here to Stay," *SEMA News*, February 1998.
2. Most of my Asian American informants were male, and second or third plus generation.
3. I also attended two illegal street races in Oxnard, California, but only observed the way the racers interacted and competed with one another.
4. See "With Their Contributions to U.S. Culture, Latino Teens Are Finding Their Place in the Picture," in *Dallas Morning News*, September 21, 1999.
5. See "The Kid and the King," *Los Angeles Times*, November 24, 1999, and "In the Fast Lane: Adam Saruwatari," *Yolk Magazine* 5, no. 4 (Winter/Spring 1999).
6. See "A Turbocharged Obsession," *Los Angeles Times*, January 22, 1997, and "Asian Car Club Races into the New Year," *Los Angeles Times*, December 31, 1997. Both articles delve into the car club and racing crew aspects of the import racing scene.
7. Face-to-face interview with Todd conducted by author on September 6, 1999, in Irvine, California.
8. Face-to-face interview with Jason conducted by author on October 6, 1999, in San Francisco, California.
9. Face-to-face interview with Jason conducted by author on October 6, 1999, in San Francisco, California.
10. *Low Rider Magazine*, McMullen Argus Publishing, February 2000.
11. Face-to-face interview with Stella conducted by author on October 11, 1999, in Palmdale, California.
12. Based on the author's own observation in 1999. The sign is posted in several areas outside and inside the garage at the Edwards Movie Theater in Alhambra, California.
13. The information regarding mug books came from the author's conversation and research with Daniel Tseng, a librarian of UC Irvine who has done extensive research on the subject.
14. Face-to-face interview with Jason conducted by author on October 6, 1999, in San Francisco, California.

CHAPTER **11**

"No Lattés Here":

Asian American Youth and the Cyber Café Obsession[1]

Mary Yu Danico and Linda Trinh Võ

In urbanized suburbs—where there are limited alternative recreational spaces or activities for youth—cyber cafés attract elementary- to college-age Asian American youth. "PC rooms," "PC Bangs," "Internet Cafés," and "Cyber Cafés" have surfaced across the country, but southern California is home to the nation's largest cluster of these cafés. Located in mini malls or strip malls, cyber cafés have become the fastest-growing business in Asian ethnic enclaves, particularly among Koreans, Vietnamese, and Chinese. Using the latest in interactive technology and state-of-the-art computers, youth compete in computer games with individuals who sit beside them, or even in other cafés. Although these cafés offer an affordable and accessible form of entertainment, some critics argue that video games encourage violence and are addictive, referring to them as "on-line heroin." Our research, however, finds that cyber cafés not only provide Asian American youth with a social outlet but also offer a safe space where they can form bonds of friendship and reclaim their masculinity.

In southern California, recently enacted laws have restricted youths' freedom to drive, imposed curfews in some areas, and provided few accessible social outlets, leaving teenagers only limited options to establish their own leisure space.[2] Asian American youth—most of whom are immigrants, refugees, or the children of immigrants or refugees—have even fewer spaces to "kick back." In this chapter, we discuss the development of the cyber café culture in ethnic communities and explain why Asian American youth are drawn to these social outlets.[3] We examine the evolution of cyber cafés from places where youths play virtual games to alternative social outlets for them to hang out after school, into the night and on weekends, sometimes even luring them away from school. In particular, we focus on the activities that take place in cyber cafés and explore why Asian American youth, in particular, are drawn to the cyber community.

Although some sites are known to be hangouts for "deviant behavior" such as gang havens for drug dealing and other vices, for the purposes of this chapter, we focus on the economic, social, and cultural reasons that attract Asian American youth to cyber cafés. This research is based on ethnographic observation of cyber cafés and their surrounding areas, formal and informal interviews with cyber café owners, managers, and patrons, and focus groups with cyber café youth patrons.[4]

THE TRANSNATIONAL AND DOMESTIC DEVELOPMENT OF CYBER CAFÉS

Cyber cafés are part of the global Internet computer revolution and have become a profitable niche for ethnic entrepreneurs. Like other trendy Asian predecessors—such as Pokémon, karaoke, and anime—the cyber gaming industry is another imported "craze" from Asia. The cyber café phenomenon first surfaced in South Korea along with the term PC "Bang" (meaning "room" in Korean). Following the 1997 Asian financial crisis, which drastically devalued its currency, Korea turned to the Internet to help reinvigorate its fallen economy. Borrowing $57 billion from the International Monetary Fund, Korea set its sights on becoming technologically competitive with First World countries like the United States (Sullivan, 2001). Today, South Korea, with its 48.6 million population, leads the world in high-speed home access. Although many South Koreans have personal computers and therefore need not frequent cafés to play video games, the country boasts more than 20,000 cyber cafés that are dedicated to gaming.

Although high-speed home access is readily available in their homes, Koreans go to cafés to escape their notoriously tight living quarters and to meet, socialize, and play computer games with their friends (Graham, 2002). Gaming is serious business in South Korea; players compete in nationally televised tournaments, win cash prizes, are offered movie roles and product endorsements, and receive Hollywood-style celebrity status and treatment (Baker, 2000). Other Asian countries, such as Taiwan, Malaysia, the Philippines, and China, quickly followed suit, and café mania has now spread across Asia and beyond (Baguioro, 2002; *Bangkok Post*, 2001; Ni, 2002). By the late 1990s, PC Bangs made a trans-Pacific move to the United States, finding their way into predominantly Asian communities throughout the nation.

Cyber cafés are different from traditional Internet cafés where people drink coffee, check their e-mail, or browse the web. In the past, because of the high price of purchasing a computer and costly Internet connections, people flocked to these Internet cafés where computers were readily available for $7 to $14 an hour. In metropolitan areas like New York, San Francisco, and Honolulu, patrons of Internet cafés came to hang out, drink cappuccino, check their e-mail, and chat on-line. The cost to "hang out" in Internet cafés limited its access to the larger public, and, therefore, during the initial period of the Internet craze, middle- and upper-middle-class yuppies, or DINKs (couples with Double Income No Kids), were their primary patrons. By the mid-1990s, however, personal computers and Internet services became more accessible and affordable and, consequently, made them available to a much wider population. As a result, by 1998, Internet cafés in metropolitan cities like New York and San Francisco went bankrupt (Marriot, 1998). However, as Internet cafés disappeared from upscale neighborhoods, PC Bangs gained widespread popularity in urban, low-income Asian immigrant communities.

According to the web site, www.cybercafes.com, southern California alone is home to 395 cyber cafés. However, this list includes cafés that serve drinks and food, so it is difficult to determine exactly how many strictly offer game playing. These businesses—owned mainly by Vietnamese, Chinese-Vietnamese, or Koreans—have been noted for "spreading like viruses" throughout Orange and Los Angeles counties, with some owners operating businesses in multiple locations. Community groups estimate that there are more than twenty cyber cafés in Los Angeles's Koreatown, over ten in the West Los Angeles area, and many more have been sprouting up in the northern part of the San Fernando Valley and the eastern part of downtown in cities like Diamond Bar. Although most communities do not keep an accurate count of cyber cafés, Garden Grove, which is part of Little Saigon and home to 135,548 Vietnamese in Orange County,[5] has been keeping track of these businesses since 1998 (Song, 2001). In 2000, there were only two cafés, but two years later, there were about twenty, with additional clusters of cafés in surrounding cities such as Santa Ana and Westminster.[6]

Located in nondescript strip malls that dot southern California's commercial landscape, many cyber cafés are barely noticeable and tucked amid other businesses. For instance, having visited one cyber café in a strip mall that intersects Little Saigon and Orange County Koreatown, we found that it was located in a two-story mall amid dentist, real estate, insurance, and social service offices as well as an auto parts and paint store. Judging from the Korean and/or Vietnamese language signs, the businesses cater to a predominantly ethnic clientele. The strip mall also includes entertainment businesses such as a dance studio, a Vietnamese restaurant, and a Vietnamese café. In the second-story cyber café, Vietnamese and Korean teens sit quietly in clusters playing games in the airy and spacious room, surrounded by anime posters. Other cyber café sites we visited in Los Angeles and Orange counties were similarly intermixed with other ethnic businesses.

In these cafés, visible signs—like those marking parking regulations on the street—are posted listing rules such as no yelling and no cursing. In all the sites, glass windows may cover some sidewalls letting in natural light and allowing pedestrians to see the activities inside; however, large portions of the windows were covered to prevent glare on the computer screens. On average, the cafés have 40 to 70 cubicles, each with a state-of-the-art computer and a plush executive-style office chair. Just a few years ago, the price for playing on the computers was $5 an hour, but it has since dropped to only $2 or less owing to increased competition.

Depending on the location, some cyber cafés are racially diverse. For example, an owner of a cyber café in Orange County's Garden Grove area estimates that his business is one-third Vietnamese, one-third Korean, one-fourth Mexican, and the rest "American," meaning white. In these cafés, a range of languages is spoken with English, Korean, Vietnamese, and Chinese dialects. Some 1.5- and second-generation youth "code-switch," and combine English with an ethnic language, symbolizing generational as well as ethnic bonds that form in the cafés.

During our visits to various cyber cafés, we observed individuals with their headsets on, playing intently on their computers, while hip-hop music played in the background. Some youth sat in clusters, casually chatting and joking around with one another, and, in most cases, the employees are individuals who are gaming fans and play at the terminals when customers do not occupy them. Although they are called cafés, they are not coffeehouses in the traditional sense; the refreshments served in cyber cafés are typically cold drinks such as soda and a few snacks.

COUNTER-STRIKE AND THE INTERNET GAMING TECHNOLOGY

In the past, games were based on the concept of individual players against an "enemy." It was not until computer game makers began incorporating multiplayer network features into their products—which enabled gamers to compete with each other on a local area network or the global Internet—that youths began frequenting PC Bangs in groups and playing as teams. In a very competitive market, software companies must constantly advance their gaming technology to stay on top of the youth market.

Currently, the most popular video game is Counter-Strike, a multiplayer game that provides the experience of a "trained counterterrorist unit or terrorist unit"; one team plays the role of the terrorist, and the other, the counterterrorist team (the U.S. Special Force). In Counter-Strike, the players are assigned roles such as hostage rescue, assassination, or bomb diffusion.[7] To make things more interesting, each side has access to a different set of equipment such as "pistols, shotguns, assault rifles, sniper rifles, grenades, and demolition devices," and each team has varying access to these weapons. The appeal of the game is its simplicity since the basic skills to eliminate the enemy are easily mastered, yet the game is never the same twice. The players are also able to send each other e-mail messages, adding an edge to the competition. Counter-Strike (and other games like it) creates a venue for interactive computer play that allows gamers to play one other in the same cyber café through "LAN games," and even with other players at other locations through "net games."[8] Through these means of social exchange, players are able to virtually and simultaneously join antiterrorist or terrorist groups with individuals in the same cyber café, or even one that is nearby.

THE SOCIAL AND ECONOMIC REALITIES OF IMMIGRANT AND REFUGEE YOUTH

The cyber cafés that have sprouted up across the southern California region cluster in middle- and working-class neighborhoods in which immigrants and refugees reside. Although some immigrant and refugee families lead seemingly middle-class lives, family members often work long hours at multiple jobs to maintain a middle-class lifestyle. Still others struggle to live on meager incomes or depend on welfare services to make ends meet. The busy workday leaves parents with little time to closely monitor their children, which leaves latchkey immigrant or refugee children with hours of unsupervised time after school and on weekends. As a result, cyber cafés serve as quasi-after-school programs for many Asian American working-class male youth. Not surprisingly, the busiest time for the cyber cafés is after 3:00 in the afternoon, when school lets out. Capitalizing on the popularity, some cafés lure youth by promoting "happy hours" where they reduce costs even further between the hours of 3:00 and 5:00 P.M. Although many youths inform their parents that they are at the cyber cafés, others do not tell their parents their whereabouts and sometimes skip school to play. Some youths reported that as long as they were attending school and receiving decent grades, their parents did not question their activities or have any control over them.

Cyber cafés are popular not just because they serve as convenient after-school diversions for immigrant youth but because of the digital divide that separates those who can afford household technological advances (such as home computers and Internet access) from those who cannot. Children of working-class immigrant families who do not have the luxury of home computers turn to cyber cafés to fill this void; at a cost of $1.50 to $2.00 an hour, this form of entertainment is an affordable way to play the most technologically advanced games. Immigrant youth often use their allowance money or the money they earn from their minimum-wage jobs to play for hours at these cafés. For working-class youth who have few economic resources, cyber cafés provide an affordable means of entertainment that is a lot cheaper than going to the movies, eating out at fast-food restaurants, or even going to a mall. Spending hours at cafés is even more appealing when managers and owners provide discounts to repeat customers, which, in turn, keeps the youth coming back. Moreover, the vast landscape and the nonpedestrian friendly environment in southern California make it difficult for youth to navigate without a mode of transportation. Many youths who do not have cars or access to them must rely on public transportation, which is limited in these areas. Others get rides from family members and friends, while some ride their bikes to these sites. Hence, the proximity of the cafés to their homes makes them convenient.

Problems and pressures at home also make cyber cafés a welcome diversion for immigrant youth. Immigrant children of working-class parents often live in cramped, multigenerational households, and in some cases, with multiple families, so the cyber cafés provide a refuge for youth. Furthermore, children of immigrants often have adult responsibilities at home; they act as translators for their first-generation parents who have no or limited English-language ability and must therefore rely on their children to assist them with complicated medical, housing, or financial matters (Park, 2002).

Given the linguistic and cultural barriers between the two generations, parents and their 1.5- and second-generation children often have difficulty communicating and relating to one another. The barriers make it difficult for youth to confide in their parents about their daily struggles at school and at home (Zhou and Bankston, 1998). Consequently, these young adults feel disconnected from their parents and look for a second "family" with their peers. Ultimately, many find a second "home" at the cafés. Some youth even have computers of their own, but they frequent cyber cafés because they provide a sense of community and belonging that keeps them coming back for more. Anthropologist Tim Tangherlini, who has researched cyber cafés, elaborates, "It's a multiethnic community that really speaks to the alienation of a lot of the big cities.... It's a place where kids can come together and make connections instead of playing by themselves in their parents' homes" (quoted in Song, 2001).

In addition, because parents work long hours, immigrant youth must often fend for themselves and look after their younger siblings, which explains the presence of elementary school-aged children at cyber cafés. Asian American males often bring their siblings with them to the cafés when their parents saddle them with babysitting responsibilities. Females, by contrast, are expected to assume the gendered responsibilities of doing household chores and taking care of younger children. Compared to their male counterparts, females have less leeway and leisure time to spend on their own, which explains, in part, the smaller presence of females at these cafés. Although Asian American females may have more adult and house- hold responsibilities than males, both often complain that they do not have a childhood (Danico, 2004).

CYBER CAFÉS AS SAFE SOCIAL OUTLETS FOR YOUTH

Asian immigrant youth have difficulty locating safe social spaces where they can hang out and establish friendships while also forging a sense of community. Entertainment and social sites in ethnic communities often exclude youth who are under the age of 18 or 21. For instance, pool halls often cater to an older crowd, and ethnic cafés with hostesses and karaoke bars are expensive and serve alcohol, and therefore, exclude youth. And while extremely popular, the import car racing scene, which gathers infor- mally and periodically, is not easily accessible for those without cars or connections to people with cars (see Chapter 9 for more details). One Asian American youth summed up the situation explaining, "Parents do wonder when you come in at 3 or 4 in the morning. They're not too happy about it. There are a lot of 10- and 11-year-olds playing. They're not into sports anymore. Everything is so spread out in California. There are not a lot of things you can do since they cost money."

It is difficult for Asian American youth to just "hang out" in public urban spaces in groups without arousing suspicion from law enforcement offi- cials. Asian American high school and college-age youth in southern California often complain about profiling and harassment by police offi- cers who stop them because of the import cars they drive and the type of clothing they wear, automatically treating them as "gang" members. Given the difficulties of finding a space to just hang out, Asian American youth gravitate to cyber cafés because they provide a safe and comfortable space to socialize. A Vietnamese American male who attends community college full time and has been frequenting cyber cafés for a year and a half in Orange County explains their appeal: "There's nothing to do. I hate malls. I don't like going to parties because too many people get into fights there. I think that this cyber café is really safe and it keeps me out of trouble." His close friend, a Korean American male, who sat at the computer next to him, readily agrees that he feels safe in the café and that there is little for them to do otherwise. Another Vietnamese youth who attends a local state university explains that he comes in twice a week for a couple of hours as a way to kill time between or after classes.

Cyber cafés are also appealing for youth who hold similar interests in the subculture of video gaming. For instance, Keith, a 20-year-old, states:

> Even if you're sitting at home playing by yourself, it's not as fun playing with someone else. You can't say things like, "Oh my God, you just died!" or "Go get the last guy!" It's like renting versus seeing a movie at a theater. When you're alone you don't laugh at things. When everyone is laughing, you're laughing too.

Kevin, a 13-year-old, states, "When you play these games at home, the action lags. These computers here are much faster. This is a great place to hang out" (quoted in Graham, 2002). And James, a 19-year-old, says: "I guess it's a way of socializing through friendly battles."

Players, along with some parents, consider computer game rooms a safer alternative than hanging out on the streets. Although the games they play depict violent acts, in a number of these settings, there is a sense of camaraderie and bonding among the young patrons and employees who maintain a relaxed attitude. Lynn Ho, an 18-year-old female college student who works part-time at the cyber café in Garden Grove explains, "It's a good thing there's a place like this for kids. . . . Instead of sitting around doing drugs, they're here, safe, in their own little world" (quoted in Graham 2002). A 20-year-old Chinese American male we interviewed adds, "Initially, the idea of going to a PC game room was kinda lame, [I thought] who would want to go?" Then his roommate introduced him to Counter-Strike and he was basically hooked, remarking, "It's a fad, everyone wants to play." In our focus group, they agreed that "People want to belong [so they play]. Everyone wants to fit in."

Unlike ethnic pool halls or other ethnic leisure sites that are typically thought of as exclusively male domains, cyber cafés welcome women, although, as noted earlier, few females come. Cyber café owners, managers, and players all concur that female customers are rare, and, by some estimates, the male to female ratio is twenty to one. Our observation confirmed that young women come in far less frequently than males, and when they do, they often arrive in pairs, although this varies on the time and the cafés. Whereas most males come to play the computer games, the young women come mainly to use the Internet and check and send e-mail. However, a few play similar games to their male counterparts. In some cases, boyfriends or brothers introduce the young women to the games and often accompany them to the cafés. Males certainly respect the skills of good girl players, but the stereotype holds that only "unattractive" girls are serious players. According to one interviewee:

> There are girls who play and the ones who play are so good. There are ten guys and one girl and she beat everyone. Everyone looks over to see who the girl is and they're like, "Oh, we know why she's in here."

ASIAN AMERICAN MEN AND MASCULINITY

One late afternoon in Orange County's Koreatown, we visited a café where the patrons explained that, although camaraderie and having a place to go after school were the initial reasons for coming to the café, the games appealed to their "basic male instincts." In our focus groups, Asian American youth remarked that they were attracted to Counter-Strike because of the "guns and violence." For example, when asked what was appealing about Counter-Strike, a Korean American youth replied: "You're killing other people. Every time it's different. You have skills at certain things. When you first start, you have an adrenaline rush killing people, especially when you have your first kill." And as a Chinese American youth reiterated, "It's pretty much what guys are raised to, you see things on TV and the media, especially in the U.S.... Women play with Barbie, men play with guns, it's natural."

Cyber cafés have become a social and cultural outlet where young Asian American men can feel a sense of achievement and assert their masculinity in a society that often demasculinizes them. In a culture in which Asian American male youths see few positive images of themselves in the media, computer games are a safe means by which they can gain a sense of empowerment. In some cases, these youth may not excel at athletics or school; however, they are good at these games. They are not the "model minority" whiz kids, nor are they the trouble-making "gang bangers"—extreme stereotypical labels often ascribed to Asian American males. They struggle with school and realize that they are not living up to the educational expectations of their immigrant parents, who have made incredible sacrifices for them to have educational opportunities unavailable in their homeland. For instance, when asked about the most challenging aspect of his life, a Korean American male responded, "The most challenging thing is school. The fact that I go to a JC (junior college).... there's a pride factor. My girlfriend goes to Berkeley." This Korean American youth had internalized the parental pressure of getting into a "top" college, and his failure to do so had affected his sense of identity as an Asian American male, especially when he compared himself to his "smarter" girlfriend.

The youth we interviewed were also cognizant of the racialized and gendered constructions of Asian American males. In our focus groups, for example, participants identified themselves ethnically as Chinese American or Korean American or Asian American but not as "American." When we asked, "Why not just say you're American?" they seemed to concur with the statement made by one individual, "Because we look different." A Chinese American youth in his early twenties in one of our focus groups expressed his perception of Asian American men and women: "Asian women are more favored than Asian men in Hollywood. Asian men are known for stereotypes such as kung fu. . . . We have it better than my parents' time, but obviously, we're still a minority I guess."

When asked about his ethnic preferences in dating, he stated, "I'm open to dating Asian women as long as they're not the stereotypical 'Koreatown' girl, like they have to dress up every time you go out and wear a lot of make-up." He did not want to date a "stereotypical Koreatown girl," who could be read as a female who wanted a guy with a lot of money (not necessarily referring to a Korean American female). His aversion to dating stereotypical Koreatown girls, however, appeared more like a defensive reaction to his own class status. He also remarked with some disdain that it was easier for Asian women to date non-Asian men and explained, "My parents would want me to date Chinese." However, he added, "I wouldn't mind dating a white woman because it's not typical" and "You have more status [as an Asian male] if you date white women."

Like the other Asian American males in the study, this male recognized how racial, gender, class, and status dynamics played out in the "real world," and he also understood his position in it. Asian American male youth gravitate toward the cafés where they can hang out with others like them and act out their aggression though the video games. The violent computer games allow players to be judged by their gaming skills rather than their race, class, or status, and provide a way for young men to display their virtual masculine abilities. They may not be able to control their social environment or the direction of their real lives, but through their "virtual lives," they can acquire and maintain a sense of status and power.

JUST ENTERTAINMENT OR "ON-LINE HEROIN?"

Local governmental officials, police officers, teachers, and mental health specialists have expressed concern that computer games encourage youth violence and are addictive (Yi, 2002). They describe these games as "on-line heroin," they refer to cyber cafés as "virtual opium dens," and they portray the players as "video game junkies." Although some youth play only a few hours a week, others spend as many as 40 to 60 hours a week at cyber cafés. We found one player who attended a local community college and spent five hours daily playing computer games and even more on weekends. He was the exception, however, rather than the norm. Former players we interviewed spoke fondly of their game-playing days, stating that the cyber café obsession was a passing phase in their lives before they entered adulthood and found other forms of entertainment.

In the chat rooms for cyber café devotees, youth who regularly play these games were defensive about being characterized as violent and maladjusted. On the contrary, they argued that they could differentiate between the violence in the games and real life. Others stated that they did not understand the fuss over what they considered merely a game. Furthermore, they contended that the games allowed them to vent their aggression in an appropriate and safe venue. The games, however, can trigger explosive bursts of anger among their players. A Vietnamese American employee at one cyber café explained that "Some people get so mad that they want to go kill someone. I've seen people get really mad. I've gotten that way myself." Frustration and anger are commonplace, especially when one's character is "virtually" killed, but all the same, actual acts of violence in the cafés are rare. When violence does erupt near a café or is associated with players, it attracts much media attention, but the violence may be a manifestation of other social or personal problems, and it is not necessarily derived from the games themselves (Hicks, 2002; Rams, 2002).

For the most part, the objective of the games that youth play is "good" conquering "evil." Ironically, Counter-Strike, the most widely played game at the cafés, was popular before September 11. In many ways, it mirrors the current American political commitment of fighting terrorism, which partly explains its sustained popularity. This game reflects the media images of patriotic heroes—firefighters, police officers, FBI agents, SWAT units, and military personnel. However, it is a mistake to assume that the violence reflected in these games is any more graphic than the violence depicted on television. Even with the improved realism, the violence is visually inferior to the realistically violent images that kids can easily watch on nightly television dramas, the nightly news, or in Hollywood movies.

Interestingly, violent games have been readily available in arcades for decades, yet these social outlets have not received the same level of criticism as cyber cafés. Upscale gaming and entertainment centers—such as Dave and Busters, located in exclusive shopping centers in southern California that attract mainly white, middle- and upper-middle-class singles, couples, and families also have violent games, yet they have not been targeted and criticized in the same way.

CONCLUSION

Like all youth, Asian American youth seek alternative social outlets where they can hang out with others like them. For low-income Asian American teenagers who reside in southern California's urbanized suburbs, finding social outlets that are both accessible and affordable presents a challenge. They want a diversion from the boredom, stresses, and problems of everyday life but have limited economic resources to entertain themselves. Cyber cafés provide an affordable space for them to fill some of these needs and offer a venue for Asian American youth to channel their energies. The cafés also provide a space where young Asian American men can form bonds of friendship and reclaim their masculinity in a society in which they sometimes feel demasculinized and marginalized. The video games allow them to become someone who has skills and status, and give them an opportunity to demonstrate their gaming prowess. At the same time, the cyber community offers them an opportunity to participate in a network that encourages teamwork and alliances to defeat "an enemy" in their virtual lives. Cyber café players have created a growing youth subculture with their own language, rituals, and protocol on how to be an "engaged citizen" of this community.

On the negative side, some argue that these cafés are merely a breeding ground for violence. In light of the recent criticisms, café owners have opened their doors to families and community members to show them that their cafés are safe spaces. Some owners advertise their cafés as places where youth can do their homework and class projects, and so they have even added printers, scanners, and other equipment to accommodate these needs. With few after-school programs, organized activities, or youth centers in their communities that cater to the interests of high school or college age immigrant and refugee youths, cyber cafés provide an attractive option for them. The cyber café culture is likely to grow in popularity as long as technological gaming innovations continue, as long as officials allow the businesses to stay open, and, most importantly, as long as new generations of Asian American youths remain attracted to this form of leisure.

Notes

1. We thank Chiayu Chang, Nicole Chiu, Corey Chow, Irene Miyashiro, Kris Ruangchotvit, and Quan Tran for their excellent research assistance with this project.
2. The following new restrictions are for minors who apply after July 1, 1998, pass their driving test at the Department of Motor Vehicles, and are issued a provisional driver license: "During the first 6 months you are licensed to drive you must be accompanied by a driver 25 years of age or older if you drive between the hours of 12 a.m. and 5 a.m. or if you have passengers under the age of 20 in the car at any time. During the second 6 months, you must still be accompanied by a driver 25 years of age or older if you drive between the hours of 12 a.m. and 5 a.m., however, now you may have passengers under the age of 20 in the car without

supervision between the hours of 5 a.m. and midnight." See http://www.dmv.ca.gov/dl/dl_info.htm#FIRSTYEAR. In Orange County, the curfew is currently 10 p.m. for minors, with cyber cafés closing at midnight. However, new laws are shooting for an 8 p.m. curfew for minors. See http://www.time.com/time/nation/article/0,8599, 201866,00.html

3. This research is part of a larger study of Asian American in youths in Orange County, particularly at-risk youth and Asian American youth culture.

4. During the summer and fall of 2002, we conducted extensive field observations of four cyber cafés in Orange County, two in Pomona, two in Los Angeles Koreatown, and two in West Los Angeles. We conducted informal and formal interviews with owners, patrons, and workers at the ten cyber cafés. The interviews ranged from 30 minutes to 45 minutes. We also conducted two focus groups with three men in their early twenties. Each of the focus groups lasted about one and a half hours. Our research team thoroughly researched newspaper clippings, interview transcripts, journal articles, and the Internet for our sources. All the quotes in the chapters were from focus group discussions unless otherwise specified. We use pseudonyms to ensure anonymity.

5. U.S. Census of the Population 2000.

6. Little Saigon—located in the general area of Garden Grove, Santa Ana, and Westminster in southern California—is the largest Vietnamese community outside Vietnam.

7. Counter-Strike was created by the software companies Gearbox and Valve. See http://www.counter-strike.net/about.html

8. LAN games are those where patrons play with others playing in the same game room. Net games are games played with anyone logged on to a game around the world, although with the current technology, local connections are faster than international ones.

CHAPTER 12

Filipinotown and the DJ Scene:

Cultural Expression and Identity Affirmation of Filipino American Youth in Los Angeles

Lakandiwa M. de Leon

On August 2, 2002, over one hundred community leaders, city workers, war veterans, students, and residents of Filipino descent gathered in Los Angeles City Hall to witness the proclamation of a new neighborhood sign that read "Historic Filipinotown." The unveiling of this humble marker was a significant event for the long-standing Filipino community at the heart of this global metropolis.[1] Since the gentrification by a cluster of upscale offices, banks, and hotels in the 1960s, this ethnic community has experienced political wrangling and several major urban redevelopment cycles in its struggle for formal recognition. Although the Filipino American population is fairly geographically dispersed, Filipino Americans have often identified this Filipinotown at the heart of Los Angeles as the symbolic cultural center of their community.[2]

For Filipino Americans born or raised in the "City of Angels," the search for community takes on a markedly cultural dimension. Like many 1.5- and second-generation youth, Filipino Americans are often caught in a cultural limbo where they feel disconnected from the traditions of a homeland culture, yet not fully a part of mainstream American culture. Many Filipino youth grow up in ethnically mixed urban neighborhoods of predominantly white suburbs where they have little or no exposure to Filipino culture, language, or customs. Making matters worse is the lack of accurate representation in mainstream media and other institutions. Although Filipino Americans are the second largest Asian ancestry group in the United States and highly concentrated in southern California, they remain virtually invisible in American popular culture. Consequently, many Filipino youth often find themselves in a position where they feel "neither here nor there, peram-bulating between a culture that alienates them and a culture they know nothing about, or are ashamed of" (Gamalinda, 1998).

Out of the need for social acceptance and belonging, many Filipino American youth respond to this cultural limbo by gravitating to various urban subcultures, most notably the street gang culture. Filipino street gangs strongly emerged in LA's urban landscape in the early 1970s and still persist in today's Filipinotowns in the Los Angeles area. As gangs grew in popularity through the 1980s, they penetrated affluent suburban areas, carrying with them violence and battles over turf and identity (Alsaybar, 1999). Today, urban youth gangs remain a powerful force that continues to influence and shape the cultural practices of Filipino youth in Los Angeles.

Although gangs remain a prominent feature in the lives of some Filipino American youth, they have also found an important expressive voice through another powerful medium—hip-hop, a reality-based visual and sonic culture born on the inner-city streets of New York among African American and Latino neighborhoods in the early 1970s. Since its inception, hip-hop has captured the imagination of urban youth and has become a dynamic space for creativity and innovation for young people around the globe. As active participants in all aspects of hip-hop culture—DJing, graffiti-writing, break-dancing, and emceeing—young Filipino Americans have played a prominent role in its local and global development.

This chapter examines how gangs and hip-hop culture shape the experi-ence of Filipino American youth in Los Angeles. More specifically, the focus is on how pioneering Filipino DJs and club promoters moved Filipino American youth to a cultural space "beyond the block" through the DJ scene, thereby providing Filipino youth an opportunity to forge a collective iden-tity and build coalitions. By inspiring Filipino youth to envision new possi-bilities, the DJ scene and broader hip-hop culture provide role models who have created an original, distinct, and positive culture for Filipino American youth.[3] To better understand the physical and cultural context of Filipino American youth culture, the chapter first discusses the "cultural limbo" that young Filipino Americans face given their generational status and the unique colonial history of the Philippines. Second, the chapter traces the origins and development of the Filipino hip-hop scene, making connections between the gang culture and the rise of Filipino American DJ crews. Finally, the chapter examines some new and exciting avenues of Filipino expression that have emerged from these interrelated cultural forms.

CAUGHT IN CULTURAL LIMBO

The colonial history of U.S.–Philippine relations has had a powerful impact on the Filipino youth's identity formation in the United States. As a result of American colonization of the Philippines in the twentieth century, immigrants adopted the American lifestyle long before stepping foot into the United States. Filipino immigrants landed in the United States already possessing fluent English-language skills, having attended American-style schools, and having been exposed to American media and popular culture. The American presence in the Philippines is so strong that for at least one researcher, Eric Gamalinda (1998: 2), "in the Philippines, America is a presence as huge as God."

Although Filipino immigrants may be equipped with the necessary tools for rapid acculturation in their new host country, many are plagued by a colonial mentality—that is, "an attempt to conceal the native or indigenous, a manifestation of acute inferiority complex" (de Leon, 1995: A10). Many Filipino immigrants (especially those who came during the "brain-drain" era of the early 1970s) are acutely aware of the American racial system and its varied effects on different national-origin groups. Consequently, they consciously choose to suppress their Filipino ethnic identity and maintain an ambiguous Asian racial identity as a strategy for socioeconomic mobility and success (Pido, 1997). Moreover, parents often teach their children to feel proud of being "Americanized" and to try their best to "assimilate as though by birthright, blending into the landscape with little effort or recalcitrance" (Gamalinda, 1998: 3). Lacking the sense that they are entitled to equal rights in America, some Filipino Americans adopt an orientation of invisibility, rarely acknowledging their contributions or accomplishments in America, though numerous and significant. This attitude further perpetuates the invisibility of the Filipino American community and renders the community a "sleeping giant." And whether intended or unintended, first-generation Filipino parents often transfer this orientation to their American-born and -raised children. Hence, Filipino American youth not only have to search for a history and culture that is sometimes lost or kept from them, but they must also battle the mentalities that prevent them from embracing that heritage.

Making identity formation even more challenging is that a disproportionately large number of Filipino immigrants who are highly skilled and highly acculturated bypass ethnic enclaves and settle in America's suburbs. The suburbs provide safer streets and better schools, but geographic dispersal makes it more difficult for Filipino American youth to form a collective identity. As a result, the image of the homeland quickly vanishes, and the younger generation is often caught in a cultural limbo. The youth do not feel connected to the culture of their ancestral homeland, and at the same time they find themselves excluded from the culture and history of their host society. The historian Dawn Mabalon emphasizes this point when she asks, "How many of us really know our history? Or that our history is more than just a chronology of laws and immigration waves—

that it is a record of our hopes and dreams, cultural creations, and of our struggle for dignity, justice and self-determination?" Mabalon's questions hint at the Filipino youths' lack of knowledge of both the culture in the Philippines and their history in America. The personal insight expressed by Jack De Jesus (aka Kiwi), a 26-year-old emcee from Los Angeles, further illustrates this point:

> Whether they [Filipino American youth] are middle class, or grew up in the suburbs, what they see out there in the media or at institutions does not reflect their experience. And it doesn't give them a sense of dignity. I can say for my mom she moved to America, she found her sort of American dream, and she was set and ... even though there was shit that she experienced after she got her job, she still felt that I achieved this goal, and I feel dignified. But, for us growing up it's a little different ... because we had this whole other experience and we're just more aware of racism and just what it means.[4]

Although parents may push their children to adopt and embrace the American system, culture, and norms, Filipino American youth find themselves caught between their parents' immigrant dreams and the American realities of race and racism.

Youth subcultures arise at the intersection of the parent and mainstream cultures. Filipino American youth may draw upon many of the same forms of adaptation, negotiation, and resistance of the parent culture, but they do so in new and sometimes transformative ways (Clarke, 1976). Although in some instances, Filipino American youth may accept their parents' strategies of invisibility, their lived experiences in American society also inspire them to perform acts of resistance in their attempt to reconcile their history and present situation. As young people grapple with the ambiguity of their experiences, the new strategies of adaptation, negotiation, and resistance play themselves out through their affiliations, practices, and cultural production. "Digging in the crates" of the Filipino American experience and exposing unclaimed cultural spaces—such as those found in gangs and hip-hop—illuminate the ways in which the younger-generation Filipino Americans transcend cultural limbo.

"GANGS AND CREWS": THE REVIVAL OF FILIPINO AMERICAN YOUTH SUBCULTURE

> Yeah, hip-hop is large here, but we got a lot of gang influence, and I got caught up in that too, which wasn't that good, but I think

being more involved in hip-hop kinda saved me, kinda took me away from the trouble that I could'a got in.

DJ Clenzrock of the *Immortal Fader Fyters*[5]

Filipino involvement in Los Angeles street gangs dates back to the 1920s. *Satanas*, the largest and most feared Filipino street gang, did not emerge on the scene until the 1970s, however.[6] Founded in 1972 as a *barkada* (an indigenous male peer grouping emphasizing mutual caring, loyalty, and friendship) and a car club by young Filipinos residing in the Temple-Rampart district near present-day Historic Filipinotown, *Satanas* was and remains to this day largely Filipino; more than 90 percent of its members are Philippine-born (Alsaybar, 1999). Since *Satanas* and other Filipino American youth gangs at the time were largely composed of first-generation Filipino youth, they were founded on the ethos of "Pinoy pride" or "Pinoy power." Reinforcing racial pride was the animosity and intimidation they confronted from other gangs, particularly Latino gangs. Sharing the same neighborhoods with Latinos, many urban Filipino youth routinely dealt with racial slurs and suffered violent assaults in their fights over turf, which only strengthened their desire to adhere to their cultural heritage and reconstruct their identity. Based on the principles of the *barkada*, gang members often asserted their Filipino identity by speaking Tagalog and the street lingo of Manila; they adopted the names of places in the Philippines as names of their gangs. Moreover, they observed traditional festivities such as Christmas midnight mass, child baptisms, and other community events (Alsaybar, 1999).

Subsequently, these street gangs and their lifestyle became ingrained in much of the emerging Filipino American youth subculture. As Filipino families dispersed into the outlying suburbs of Carson, Cerritos, Long Beach, and West Covina in the 1980s, newer "suburban" gangs emerged. However, unlike the inner-city gangs like *Satanas*, suburban gangs are composed mainly of second-generation Filipinos who have grown up with more economic resources and in more desirable and protective social environments. Although they may not have experienced the harsh inner-city conditions of their urban counterparts, suburban gang members share a markedly similar reason for participation in gangs—identity construction. For instance, Mark Pulido explains:

By the 1980s, with the increase of Pilipino families moving into suburbs and having children, more gangs began to emerge out of the need for ethnic identification among these American-born Pilipino youth. The need for survival is not a crucial issue in these middle class communities but rather the need for ethnic identification and social support is the impetus for the formation of gangs in areas like Carson, Cerritos, and West Covina.[7]

Gangs are not a unique feature of youth culture, but DJ crews are new to the scene. Deeply influenced by the music and culture of African American hip-hop, Filipino American youth throughout Los Angeles have formed numerous DJ crews since the early 1980s.[8] From the inner city of Historic Filipinotown to the outlying suburbs of Carson, Cerritos, Long Beach, and West Covina, the DJ scene is a growing youth phenomenon among Filipino Americans, serving as an avenue to establish, express, and affirm a collective identity. DJ crews normally consist of several members who pool their resources, including equipment, records, and transportation to "spin" at various parties and events in their neighborhood. These crews help to create new identities through the adoption of DJ names and crew affiliations, and they also serve as "new kinds of families forged with intercultural bonds that, like the social formation of gangs, provide insulation and support in a complex and unyielding environment" (Rose, 1994: 41–47).

Interestingly, some Filipino gangs, such as *Pinoy Real* (PR) and *Mabuhay Pilipino* (MP), established themselves as DJ crews from the beginning, while other DJ crews in Los Angeles like *Majestics* have membership affiliation with gangs, illustrating the tangible connection between Filipino hip-hop culture and gangs. Although there are some similarities between gang culture and DJ crews, there are some distinct differences, too. Today's hip-hop crews adhere less to notions of "Pinoy pride" and instead choose to create an identity that is fun, exciting, and influenced by the culture of hip-hop. José Buktaw (aka DJ Dwenz), a member of *Majestics*, explains why gang and hip-hop cultures hold obvious appeal for young Filipino American men and women:

> They knew they didn't fit into the white culture, so they rejected it and embraced hip-hop because hip-hop was already embraced by gang culture. . . . Filipino youth, not knowing anything about their own history or themselves, took to something they could identify with more. So they embraced the whole Black, Chicano, underground hip-hop culture.[9]

Buktaw hints at the complicated racial dynamics at play in the lives of Filipino American youth growing up in inner-city and suburban Los Angeles. Like their parents, many Filipino American youth have a keen awareness of their separation from white "mainstream" culture. However, unlike their parents, they do not readily accept and adopt the assimilationist ideology; rather, they choose a different path of assimilation by embracing the made-in-America hip-hop culture. The process of assimilation is not toward white culture but rather toward hip-hop culture, which the media has depicted as a purely African American art form, especially in its most visible form, emceeing or rapping. In its formative stages, hip-hop was not merely a category of music that one could find at a local record store, but it was a style and a culture that one had to practice, represent, and live. While drawn to hip-hop, Filipino American youth have had no coethnic role models to emulate. Instead, they have had to adopt distinct African American cultural roles, as Jack De Jesus (aka Kiwi) recalls: "When I was in high school trying to come up as an emcee, there was *no* acting like a Filipino if you wanted to rap ... because you're putting your persona out there."[10]

De Jesus acknowledges the difficulty and intimidation associated with becoming a rapper since one could easily be dismissed based on appearance or be perceived as unauthentic, an important element in hip-hop's adherence to "reality." Because of the strict racial hierarchy within hip-hop, many Filipino American youth choose to pursue less visible roles that are not as closely scrutinized, and, more importantly, roles that are evaluated on the basis of skills and talent rather than race alone. Through years of exploration and practice, Filipino youth have carved niches for themselves as DJs, graffiti writers, and break-dancers without the fear of ridicule, rejection, or stigma.

"GOD DAMN THAT DJ MADE MY DAY": THE FILIPINO AMERICAN DJ CREW

> Jay's like King Midas as I was told/Everything that he touched turned to gold/He's the greatest of the greater get it straight/He's great/Playing fame cause his name is known in every state/His name is Jay/To see him play/Will make you say/God damn that DJ made my day
>
> Run-D.M.C., "Peter Piper" from *Raising Hell* (1986)

Beginning in the late 1970s, mobile DJ crews sprouted throughout the greater Los Angeles metropolitan area. One of the earliest and most widely recognized mobile DJ crews was *Spectrum*, founded by Jimmy Corpus, an American-born Filipino from the Temple-Rampart district in downtown Los Angeles. Filipino DJs were usually hired out for weddings, house parties, banquets, and other events in the larger Filipino American community throughout southern California. The demand for DJs grew as Filipino Americans came of age and gravitated toward hip-hop, which in turn provided Filipino DJs with a steady source of business that contributed to their success. As the anthropologist and gang ethnographer Bangele D. Alsaybar (1999: 127) explains, "partying is a way of life for Filipino American homeboys and homegirls. Through the gang and youth culture network, everyone seems to know when and where the next party will be held, especially on the weekends." This is especially true for suburban Filipino American gang members and crews who need not worry about turf wars, face less racial hostility, and have more free time and economic resources for leisure activities such as partying and fixing cars (see Chapter 9 in this volume for more details on car culture).

The growing relevance of hip-hop in young Filipinos' lives also contributed to the flurrying DJ scene. Nazareth Narza (aka DJ Rhettmatic), a former member of a crew from Cerritos called *Double Platinum,* recalls: "All of us mobile DJs were into hip-hop, at least a majority of them were. From here to Frisco, anyone who were Filipino and were DJs, were mobile DJs."[11] New DJ crews have appeared on the scene throughout southern California since the mid-1980s. Some of the most prominent include *Unique Techniques* from Carson, *Publique Image Musique, Double Platinum,* and *Ultra Dimensions* out of Cerritos, *Style DJs* from Long Beach, and *Majestics* based in the Temple-Rampart section of Los Angeles. These DJ crews are usually composed of a group of friends from the same high school and represent their respective neighborhoods at parties and social events. Isaiah Dacio (aka DJ Icy Ice) from Carson, a former member of *Spectrum,* remembered this practice: "I had one turntable, a friend had a mixer, another friend brought one turntable, and we'd just hook up at each other's house."[12] DJing skills are also acquired through similar collective practices as Jose Buktaw recounts: "I learned how to DJ off my homeboy Spider's beat up 1200 [Technics turntable] and a Radio Shack mixer that was falling apart. The thing to do was doubles, put it up top 45 rpm and do doubles, that was like the test of the Mixmaster."[13]

For many novice Filipino DJs, turntables at home or at a friend's house, combined with inexpensive equipment, provide the necessary elements to learn the trade. The success of a mobile DJ crew is based on its whole being greater than the sum of its parts, which is also essential to the *barkada* philosophy that promotes the collective over the individual. By pooling their resources, DJ crews can acquire more sophisticated equipment and play in larger venues, which ultimately allows them to "move the crowd" through a particular musical selection and mixing style. Between 1983 and 1988, *Spectrum,* largely through the entrepreneurial vision and leadership of its founder, Jimmy Corpus, earned the reputation for throwing the largest and liveliest dances in the Filipino scene at banquet halls, hotels, and bar and grill restaurants throughout Los Angeles. Corpus understood that in order to succeed he needed to recruit the best DJ crews from all over southern California to play at his dances:

> Jimmy DJ'd a little bit, but his talent was more in promotion. The biggest thing that he brought to our community was the fact that he had the vision to bring groups together and form our scene. He

would throw the biggest dances in Los Angeles. Back then, 600, 700 people were a lot of people, for a scene.... Going into '85, I was really young. I was learning about all this stuff ... Jimmy had that vision, he would bring together like, Long Beach, *Style*, and Carson, *Unique Technics* ... That's how our scene started, it started like that.[14]

The DJ scene grew rapidly following the *Spectrum* model, which tapped into the popularity of the different neighborhood crews and brought them together under a large umbrella group. This approach brought young Filipinos from all over the Los Angeles area together to interact and socialize. DJ crews not only helped promote the party scene, but they also created an important cultural space that became pivotal to the formation of a Filipino American youth culture, community, and identity.

As the Filipino DJ scene gained popularity and prominence, it soon crossed ethnic and racial boundaries. Corpus's *Spectrum* crew took advantage of working with other thriving hip-hop scenes beyond the Filipino community; he coordinated events with the largest African American promotion groups at the time, *Uncle Jam's Army* and *Ultrawave,* and expanded his efforts in the Asian scene by forming another umbrella group to handle parties under the name of *Island Magic,* which catered to Japanese Americans. In addition, another *Spectrum* DJ, Chris Flores, established extensive connections with the Latino hip-hop scene. By hiring famous Los Angeles DJs like *Jammin' Gemini,* one of the KDAY Mixmasters, and *General Lee* (another well-known African American DJ), *Spectrum* soon attracted larger multiethnic crowds, making this crew extremely popular and reputable throughout Los Angeles.[15] As Dacio claims, "throughout the whole L.A. area, wherever there was a party, [Corpus] was part of it."[16] Corpus's vision proved that coalition-building across ethnic, racial, and class lines was not only possible but could also provide a sense of commonality among all youth, regardless of background. For Filipino youth in particular, the proliferation of the DJ scene continues to be an important facet of their experience growing up American.

At about the same time that *Spectrum* secured its foothold in the party scene, a Cerritos crew called *Publique Image Musique* also began to gain popularity in the Filipino scene. The head of this crew, a young DJ from Cerritos named Ray Belling (aka DJ Curse) was elevated to legendary status among local youth through his innovative skills on the turntable. Nazareth Narza (aka DJ Rhettmatic) remarked:

Everyone was like "there's this kid named Raymond Belling, he's a Filipino kid!" ... the fact that he was Filipino and he was getting down. I mean, he was getting respect from the Black kids.... His name throughout Southern California was pretty big. I mean, he

was a legend ... in our generation, a lot of the middle school kids ...
all looked up to Curse.... It was so pathetic that his reputation even
went to Northern California.[17]

Belling's ability to "get down" by re-creating and improving the scratching
and cutting techniques found in songs like the classic jazz/hip-hop fusion
record of the 1980s, Herbie Hancock's *Rockit*, as well as manipulating or
"doing doubles" on classic recordings like Malcolm MacLaren's *Buffalo Girls*,
earned him the undying respect of his Filipino peers. Many Filipino DJs continue to mention him as an influential figure in the Los Angeles hip-hop scene.
Belling was also legendary for battling many of the top DJ crews at the time, a
skill that often had to do with how good one could "rock the crowd" through
musical selections and blends. As Ray Belling (aka DJ Curse) explains, there
were times when these battles arose spontaneously and got out of hand:

> I remember being in a party out in El Monte and we were spinning,
> and this guy was just talking a lot of shit. Yeah, we'll be DJing in a
> backyard, and people would just be sitting there getting mad at you,
> and we'd go, "Fuck you, we'll battle you right now, hundred bucks!
> Our boy could put up a hundred bucks! A hundred bucks right
> now!" Ended up beating them, take their money, fights would break
> out.[18]

Such battling among DJs was usually a nonviolent method of proving
one's self-worth. But as the gang scene expanded, at times fights and gang
violence marred Filipino parties and escalated in the latter half of the 1980s.

A UNITED KINGDOM: TRANSCENDING THE "DRY PERIOD"

> Murdering over stupid things/And now this music brings/
> Reasoning to kill one another/Over platinum things/Over a bouncy
> beat/Vision getting hazy gray/Know when to hold them/Fold
> them/And walk away
>
> > Bambu, "Gamble Life" from *Self-Untitled* (2002)

From 1987 to 1991, Filipino gang violence, especially in suburban areas
like Carson, Cerritos, and West Covina, reached critical proportions. Ray
Belling (DJ Curse) vividly recalls the upsurge of gang activity and the
trouble it caused at parties:

> We used to carry a gun underneath our DJ stand, just because it got
> so hectic ... that's when a lot of like Filipino gangs like STS (*Satanas*)

... or CPC would come, and CPC didn't get along with those people from West Covina, and West Covina didn't get along with these people. We used to DJ all their parties, so we always had to be real chill.... It was kinda wack, because you're friends with everybody from every group. That's the way we maintained it.[19]

Nazareth Narza (aka DJ Rhettmatic) described this period as a "dry spell" for the scene. Many Filipino American youth were forced to shut down dances at the time due to the fear of gang activity: "It got to a point where it was just a dry period. There wasn't even parties you could go to ... I mean, you had some good jams here and there, but it was kinda dry, it was getting too violent."[20]

Even non-Filipino promotion groups distanced themselves from the DJ scene because gang activity began to spiral out of control, especially after a young girl was shot at a gathering in Cerritos, caught in the crossfire of two rival gangs. Isaiah Dacio (aka Icy Ice) recalls: "After that happened, a lot of people, a lot of parents, wouldn't let their kids out ... and from there you had retaliation, since that was a rival gang shooting at rival gangs, so ... gangs really got bad and it just went on."[21]

The relationship between hip-hop and gang culture undoubtedly created problems for DJ crews and the party scene more generally. DJ crews unaffiliated with a particular gang learned to walk a fine line to stay out of trouble. Other DJs who were loosely affiliated with certain gangs were weary of doing parties in certain neighborhoods, especially given the risk of being outnumbered and overpowered by rivals.

Although problems of gang violence put the brakes on the party scene in some parts of downtown and suburban LA, other DJ crews formed in Orange County. As *Spectrum*'s reign began to decline in the early 1990s, another enterprising Filipino promoter, Tom Corpus (no relation to Jimmy Corpus), emerged on the map. Corpus took the initiative to revive the "party vibe" that was missing from the scene during the "dry period" of the late 1980s by mobilizing many of the original die-hard hip-hop crews such as *Double Platinum*, *Publique Image*, *Ultra Dimensions*, and *Majestics*. Together, these DJ crews began organizing dances in upscale suburban areas, such as Orange County and Huntington Beach, areas that were not paralyzed by gang activity. After several successful events, these DJ crews decided to expand their efforts into a new collective, known as the all-mighty *United Kingdom* (UK).

Debuting in 1991, at precisely the time when many DJ crews grew tired of the violence in the Filipino community, *United Kingdom* found a niche for themselves by promoting peace and positivity, as Isaiah Dacio (aka DJ Icy Ice) notes:

It was perfect timing . . . [United Kingdom] were promoting peace, positivity. At that time also, in the African American community, they were always like, "peace, power to the people" . . . Afrocentric, the medallions, and everything . . . so it came full circle again, and United Kingdom brought it up another level.[22]

In the early 1990s, *UK* grew rapidly and began to hold regular hip-hop events at large night clubs, such as *Club Spice* in Hollywood. Filipino DJs went "back to basics" by playing music that had been overlooked or forgotten. As Nazareth Narza (DJ Rhettmatic) recalls:

We brought back the party vibe of back in the days, of *Spectrum* and the whole *Publique Image* era, and . . . KDAY, cuz this was when KDAY just stopped!! We started playing hip-hop a lot more. We introduced back the old school. What we were listening to back then . . . in that dry spell . . . none of the kids were really listening to . . . y'know even if the crowd didn't know it, we introduced it, we taught them and made them like it. Whereas today it has to be on the radio for people to like it, here we broke anything.[23]

Returning to the old school drew a larger, more multiethnic crowd to Filipino hip-hop events. As Jose Buktaw (DJ Dwenz) recalls:

It was a time when the underground and the mainstream were pretty much merged because the attitudes of Filipinos back then were a little bit different. The hairstyles changed from the "pompadours and tails" to "steps," and people were experimenting with hair styles, clothing styles, and shoes. It was sort of a decline in the gang culture, because people got sick of fighting and shooting and all the hard looks . . . it also started to get more integrated back into the Black and Chicano hip-hop scene.[24]

In the early 1990s, the success of *UK* took the Los Angeles hip-hop scene by storm, but the positive vibe it created flourished for only a couple of years. At the tail end of 1992, Los Angeles-based artists such as Dr. Dre and Snoop Doggy Dogg ushered in the "G-funk" era (gangster-oriented hip-hop), and as DJ Dwendz says, "everybody became a gangster again." *UK* dissolved in 1993, and many of the original mobile DJ crews parted ways in the hopes of pursuing other projects. Most retreated to the underground once again, building their skills and searching for new styles.

Still *UK* brought many Filipino youth out of the "dry period" in the late 1980s and laid the foundation for a new and different form of Filipino American cultural expression. It ushered in a hip-hop scene that was infused with the principles of the "Afrocentric" or "T.R.I.B.E" (The Radical International Boogie Era) movement by promoting underground hip-hop artists such as the *X-clan, BDP, the Jungle Brothers, De La Soul,* and *A Tribe Called Quest.* The "Afrocentric" ethos espoused a return to cultural roots, a reexamination of American history, and a celebration of originality. Inspired by the messages of the music, Filipino American youth also sought out their cultural roots, developed their own cultural forms, and forged a sense of community. As Jose Buktaw of DJ Dwenz points out:

> Filipino youth developed their own culture and styles that were emulated by other people of color even though they don't get credit for it. They were dope dancers and DJs, especially in towards the later part of the '80s, during the tribal thing ... a lot of brothers and sisters started to look at themselves like, "what does it mean to be Filipino?"[25]

Hoping to transcend the problems associated with gang violence, innovative DJ crews formed broad coalitions and expanded the scene to include a larger youth population across diverse sections of the city. Alsaybar (1999: 129) emphasizes this point: "I credit the safer youth scene today to the efforts of leading Filipino American production crews in curbing violence on the dance floor; these DJs and promoters are virtual icons and significant role models to thousands of youths." Filipino DJs set the stage for young Filipinos to participate fully in hip-hop culture, and, more significantly, inspired them to imagine alternative possibilities as artists, promoters, and organizers.

LOOKING FORWARD: THE NEXT MOVEMENT

> We be the hopeless and innocent/the welfare recipient that can't afford rent/the street bum that spent half of his day bent/that's the outcome of growing up in this environment/we the gang-bangers living a life of violence/the battered women living a life of silence/getting beat even though she's six months pregnant/with her emotionally and physically scarred infant/we the single mother child asking where dad went/the bastards of an industry gone stagnant/we the voice of every inner city resident/in the trial against the government/we the evidence/objection overruled cause we're relevant/we represent the purest hip-hop elements/we the movement that remain resistant/fighting for the very freedom of our existence/ ... knowledge is the key ... so I think it's time you learn.
>
> Kiwi, "mama always said" from *the concrete ep* (1999)

In the years after *UK*, many of the former DJ crews contributed to advancing movements and trends in hip-hop culture. The formation of the *World Famous Beat Junkies* from Los Angeles, along with the now defunct San Francisco-based *Invisbl Skratch Piklz* ushered in a new genre of hip-hop known as *turntablism*, a term used to describe the complex soundscapes created from the manipulation of the turntable.[26] Beat Junkie DJs Curse, Rhettmatic, Babu, Icy Ice, Symphony, and others honed many of their innovative skills as a part of Filipino mobile crews and the Los Angeles hip-hop scene more generally.

Filipino Americans have also gained recognition as DJs on popular radio stations. For example, the original *Spectrum* DJ Icy Ice can be heard on 92.3 The Beat, and Long Beach *Style* DJ E-man is featured on Power 106. The presence of popular radio DJs provides Filipino youth with highly visible coethnic role models. Isaiah Dacio, aka DJ Icy Ice, also utilized the momentum built by UK to start his own promotion company, *Legend Entertainment*, which has dominated the night-club and college scene since the 1990s. In addition, Jose Buktaw, aka DJ Dwenz formerly of *Majestics*, established a widely popular underground hip-hop coalition called the *Foundation Funkollective*. This multiethnic, cross-generational collective continues to promote the concept of "edutainment" (based on KRS-ONE's brand of politically charged hip-hop) to youth of all ages; it has grown in size and stature over the years with chapters located as far as Pomona, Pacoima, and Long Beach. *Foundation*, as many simply refer to it, provides a consistent space for young people to learn about hip-hop culture and take part in an inclusive, multicultural environment. Recent Interscope recording artists, the *Black Eyed Peas*, and Filipino American producer *Poet Name Life* also have their roots in this scene.

In many ways, the visibility of the DJ culture in Los Angeles has also created fertile ground for new forms of cultural expression for Filipino American youth. Most recently, a new generation of artists, musicians, and organizers in Los Angeles is seeking to build on the foundations of past generations and bridging the gap between hip-hop culture and a progressive Filipino cultural ideology. For instance, the *Balagtasan Collective* combines the dynamism of hip-hop, spoken word, photography, muralism, and traditional Philippine poetic forms, such as the *Balagtasan*,[27] to organize and inspire a new generation of Filipino youth. Organizer Terry Valen (1999: 5), one of its founding members, describes *BC's* agenda as "ranging from personal and family struggles, to farmworker and bus-rider unions, to revolutionary movements in the Philippine countryside and globalization . . . taking cultural performance back into the heart of the struggles of Filipino communities . . . and to explore artistically the common grounds for political struggles at every level." Los Angeles-bred emcees *Kiwi* and

Bambu are members of this collective, and work to build a following on the West Coast with their politically charged lyrics and focus on Filipino issues. Firmly grounded in hip-hop, progressive politics, and cultural pride, Filipino cultural groups like the *Balagtasan Collective* strive to establish the linkage between the hip-hop scene, cultural awareness, and community activism.

CONCLUSION

Tracing the development of the Filipino hip-hop scene and highlighting the current movement of Filipino cultural expression allow us to understand how far the Filipino American community has come since the 1970s. Through the hyperbolic pathways of gangs and hip-hop that have transcended the geographic boundaries of Filipinotowns around Los Angeles, Filipino American youth have discovered innovative ways to name their experience in America by forming multiple and overlapping identities. In their struggle to reclaim history and fight racism, Filipino American youth have actively created and retold their own stories through writing, scratching, dancing, vocalizing, and organizing, and, in the process, they have skillfully carved out a space of their own.

Notes

1. The area, known as "Bunker Hill," has been a low-income Filipino neighborhood since the 1920s. Because of corporate redevelopment of downtown Los Angeles, most of the ethnic population was pushed out in the 1960s and resettled in the nearby Temple-Rampart district.
2. The officially recognized Historic Filipinotown is bordered by Hoover Street, the 101 Freeway, Glendale Boulevard, and Beverly Boulevard, also known as the Temple-Rampart district of Los Angeles.
3. My research was done primarily through face-to-face interviews with Filipino DJs involved with the hip-hop scene of the 1980s and 1990s. My interviewees were made up of six DJs and one emcee, all of whom were male and identified themselves as second-generation Filipino American. All of these contacts were made through referrals by people associated with the current hip-hop scene, using a snowball methodology. I also did much of my research through participant observation at open mic events, DJ sessions, concerts, and through audiovisual documentary work. I used a wide variety of mainstream and independent articles, found both in print and on the Internet, as well as musical recordings. The main body of research was done over a span of two years between 1997 and 1999, with a few followup interviews in October of 2002, in and around the greater Los Angeles area.
4. Face-to-face interview with Jack De Jesus (aka Kiwi), October 2002, De Jesus residence, Oakland, California.
5. Face-to-face interview with DJ Clenzrock, Burbank, California.
6. According to Alsaybar (1999), the Temple Street gang is one of the oldest street gangs, reportedly cofounded by Latino and Filipino youth in the late 1920s or early 1930s. There is also evidence of Black, Latino, and Filipino youth forming similar gang formations characterized by the wearing of "zoot suits" in the 1940s. Since the 1960s, street gangs have tended to be coethnic rather than multiracial.
7. Cited in "Youth Gangs and the Pilipino Community," *UCLA Pacific Ties*, June 1990, p. 13.
8. For other works that detail the history of hip-hop culture, see Cross (1993), Rose (1994), and Toop (1994).

particular, Little Saigon (the heart of Orange County's Vietnamese community that encompasses Garden Grove, Santa Ana, and Westminster) has witnessed a steady stream of Vietnamese immigrants. In fact, Little Saigon holds the largest concentration of Vietnamese outside of Vietnam. But along with its burgeoning population growth has been a rising concern about crime. For instance, polls conducted in 1981 indicated that 41 percent of Orange County's Vietnamese population believed that crime was a major concern, and in 1984, this figure jumped to 64 percent. In 1989, 41 percent of the respondents listed "crime and gangs" as the "worst problem they faced," and more than 87 percent felt that crime was a major concern. These figures are all the more stark when we consider that a 1989 countywide survey of the general population indicated that only 10 percent cited crime as their primary concern (Weikel, 1990). Moreover, a study of gangs in Little Saigon reveals that of the 404 Asian offenders in the sample, 352 are Vietnamese, and gang members account for 48 percent of all delinquency (Kent and Felkenes, 1998). Clearly, crime and gang involvement among Vietnamese youth is no small problem in Orange County, and, as a result, Orange County provides a strategic research site for the study of Vietnamese youth gangs.

This chapter is based on over 40 ethnographic interviews and a dozen-and-a-half life histories of Vietnamese gang youths from the Orange County area. We also draw upon in-depth interviews with prominent Vietnamese businessmen, teachers, community activists, social workers, police officers, and professionals, as well as non-Vietnamese law enforcement experts, real estate brokers, government officials, and social workers who are active in the Vietnamese community. In addition, we spent a great deal of time on the streets of Orange County, talking directly with Vietnamese youths and adults. Finally, we draw upon unedited videotapes of gang youths taken by student ethnographic filmmakers.[1]

THE TWO SIDES OF LITTLE SAIGON

Vietnamese refugees migrated to Little Saigon in two major waves, and the different historical and socioeconomic circumstances of the two waves have strongly influenced their adaptation to life in America. The "first wave" began in 1975, when news of the communist takeover of South Vietnam first spread through Saigon. Highly educated and hailing from upper- and upper-middle-class backgrounds, Vietnamese refugees in the first wave easily adapted to their new host country. Many arrived with English- or French-language skills, and nearly half held college degrees (Bach and Bach, 1980; Kelly, 1977; Liu, 1979; Marsh, 1980; Nguyen and Henkin 1984; Stein, 1979). Furthermore, most were young, urbanized, predominantly Catholic, and, most importantly, arrived with their families intact. The bundle of human capital advantages proved vital for their successful adaptation in the United States.

The story of the second wave of arrivals—the "boat people"—is less sanguine. Unlike their predecessors, the second wave of Vietnamese refugees did not have the resources to escape the fall of Saigon, and, consequently, were forced to endure communist rule. During the communist takeover, the government routinely confiscated businesses, sent parents to "re-education camps," and tortured and killed innocent civilians. Weary of these circumstances and hoping for a better life, many Vietnamese boarded slipshod boats in a desperate attempt to flee communist rule. The influx of boat people in America reached its peak in the early 1980s, with southern California as the primary destination.

Compared to the first immigrant wave, the second wave of refugees was far less prepared for life in America. The later arrivals were poorer, younger (over half were children or teenagers), less educated (often illiterate), less urbanized (many were rural farmers), and with few job skills useful in America's economy (Bach and Bach, 1980; Grant, 1979; Marsh, 1980; Nguyen and Henkin, 1984; Skinner, 1980; Zhou and Bankston, 1998). Moreover, many came without their families; relatives had either died en route to the United States or were simply too poor to pay for their own escape.

The difference between the two waves of Vietnamese migrants led to a polarized ethnic enclave in Little Saigon and represented the dichotomy of Orange County's population. For instance, in 1981, less than one-quarter of the second wave of Vietnamese arrivals were in the labor force, and of this group, only half had been able to secure employment. By contrast, Vietnamese immigrants who arrived between 1975 and 1977 demonstrated higher rates of labor force participation and lower rates of unemployment than the United States population overall (Office of Refugee Resettlement, 1988). Moreover, in 1982, only 25 percent of the first-wave arrivals lived in poverty, but among the second wave of refugees, the proportion reached a staggering 90 percent. In 1986, the average annual household income of first-wave refugees was over $17,000, but among the second wave, it was only $13,000 (Efron, 1989). And although the Vietnamese comprised only 5 percent of the total population in Orange County in 1989, 14 percent of the county's welfare assistance cases were Southeast Asian households, principally Vietnamese (Cooper, 1990).

The first wave of Vietnamese refugees soon achieved income parity with the general population of the United States, but the second wave fell far short. Noting similar conditions in many Southeast Asian communities across the country, William J. Wilson (1987: 36) writes that the "influx of immigrants from Southeast Asia ... has been associated with ... problems that have traditionally plagued inner-city black neighborhoods." Like the African American underclass, many second-wave Vietnamese refugees faced an economic predicament that offered only menial, part-time "dead-ends" with little opportunity for mobility and wealth (Bach and Bach, 1984; Brody, 1986; Gold and Kibria, 1989). This underprivileged segment of the Vietnamese population has been doubly marginalized, both within the larger Orange County community and within the ethnic enclave of Little Saigon.

THE APPEAL OF GANGS FOR VIETNAMESE YOUTH

The rise of Vietnamese youth gangs has gone hand in hand with the migration of the second wave of refugees into Little Saigon and their experience of double marginalization. All of our gang-involved informants are second-wave refugees whose families were disrupted by the migration experience to the United States, and, as a consequence, turned to gangs as an alternative source of social and psychological support. The yearning for family was perhaps the most important reason for joining gangs.

As prior studies repeatedly show, family disorganization through the process of migration has a devastating effect on children (Allen and Hiller, 1985; Kibria, 1993; Zhou and Bankston, 1998). Furthermore, changes in gender and parent-child roles that often result from family disruption, combined with cultural and language barriers, intensify intergenerational conflict and weaken the traditional mechanisms of social support and control. Within the traditional Vietnamese culture, the family is the locus of support and control, and the authority of the parents, or elders more generally, goes unquestioned. As parents immigrate to America, however, they find that their children not only question but also blatantly challenge their authority. As a Vietnamese youth openly declares, "I was tired of my dad beating me all the time man. Fuck that shit. This is America. He can't do that here." A key source of conflict is the clash between Eastern and Western norms. As a social worker explains:

> In Vietnam, your children appreciate you. You could be gone year-round, but your children still behave because they know that their parents are working for them. They are taught that by the Vietnamese culture. Here, it is not a cultural value in the United States. In fact, what the schools do in here is to interfere with the family by encouraging the children to question their parents.

Furthermore, the children of immigrants generally acculturate much more quickly than their parents, creating even more intergenerational friction. For instance, many Vietnamese American youth attain a high degree of English fluency, while their parents struggle to get by with only a few English phrases or words. This marked difference in English-language ability can easily undermine parental authority, as a social worker emphasizes:

> I've seen a lot of parents who are very ignorant of the American culture, or are illiterate even in the Vietnamese language. . . . They cannot control their children because they cannot speak a word of English. The children are the ones calling the shots, not the parents.

Making matters more difficult for immigrant youth is that their parents often work long hours, further contributing to the lack of communication between the two parties. As parents witness their children becoming ever more wayward, they become even more desperate to firmly assert their control. For example, one child was literally handcuffed to prevent him from running away, but the youth picked the lock and escaped. Other informants had their own stories of defiance: "They tell me to go to school, I say I ain't going to school. See, my dad, he know if he going to hit me, it ain't going to hurt me, 'cause I'm still going to go back and do the same thing."

Another Vietnamese youth explains how his mother is unable to keep him from running away. As he asserts, "My mom can't punish me. She knows nothing that works on me. She talks to cops to try to keep me at home, but it don't work. I just go far away." Language barriers for adults, combined with their heavy work schedules, preclude them from actively engaging in their children's process of growing up American. Social workers lament the weakness and absence of adult participation in PTA meetings and school functions. Parents' inability to monitor their children's activities also facilitates an attitudinal shift among already frustrated youth; freed from close supervision, many simply flout their parents' expectations without consequences.

The breakdown of the traditional family has affected females in unique respects. With increasing frequency, daughters are leaving the constraints of their families and choosing to run away and live on the streets. Several of our sources noted that girls in earlier gangs were "gang whores," but in recent years, more females have struck out on their own to form independent groups. Police officers, social agency representatives, and even male gang members agree that the rise of female runaways is a grave problem. A disapproving Vietnamese social worker described female gang members as follows:

Most of their parents are not here or they are disowned by their parents.... They are even worse than boys, because they have more needs for clothes and jewelry and they want to eat in a fancy restaurant, but they don't want to work for it.

The loosening of family control and the stressful problems at home push some Vietnamese youth out onto the streets, where street gangs provide a "surrogate" family for astray youth (Vigil, 1988). The family problems are also compounded by difficulties in school. The highly visible academic achievement of Vietnamese youth, as that of other Asian American minorities, is often attributed to the ethnic community's strong emphasis on education. Refugee parents often justify their long working hours by arguing that they must work hard and make sacrifices so that their children can attend college and have a chance at upward mobility. A Vietnamese parent states:

In the Vietnamese culture, we believe that the only way to maintain a high social status is through education. For a poor family, if you want to get out, the only way to get out is through education. So, in our culture, regardless of background, the bottom line is education. Education is key. Everybody talks about education.

However, for each Vietnamese student who adopts the value of education and, achieves success, there are many others who do not. For example, a study of Westminster High School reveals that while half of the straight-A students are Vietnamese, the Vietnamese dropout rate is twice that of the school average: 25 percent compared to 13 percent for the school as a whole. A similar pattern appears in the Garden Grove School District, where the Vietnamese dropout rate is double that of white students, at 16.8 versus 8.7 percent. In some high schools in Orange County, the dropout rate for Vietnamese students reaches as high as 30 percent (Bankston and Zhou, 1997).

Another problem that Vietnamese students encounter in schools is harassment from other youth, particularly from members of other ethnic youth gangs. Because of their smaller physical stature and obvious racial characteristics, Vietnamese youth are often the target of violence and scorn, and as a result, several of our respondents carry weapons to school for protection. For instance, a gang member recalls, "In 1982, 1983, when one white person jumped us, they had to fight the whole school because the Vietnamese stick together.... We just take care of ourselves at school. We like a family." Law enforcement officials stationed in Orange County's high schools report that they have confiscated knives, guns, and even semiautomatic, high-caliber weapons from Vietnamese students. At least one law enforcement expert posited a protection-based theory of gang formation, "That's what it started out as, and what happened was that the Asian kids were banding together for protection much like the Hispanic kids banded together, and that's basically how they started."

Although Vietnamese youth gangs originated as a means of protection from other ethnic gangs, today, they join gangs for a host of other reasons. Gang membership provides recognition and a sense of self-esteem that youth desperately seek. As a 15-year-old Vietnamese youth proclaims, "I'd die for it [my gang], that's how I feel, I feel tough. When I say I'm from the Santa Ana Boys, I feel good." Another youth states that he joined his gang because "I had nothing else to do and I wanted to be accepted and just to have attention." For many youth, gang membership is their way of achieving "success" and building self-esteem. A 20-year-old Vietnamese youth pointed out the difference between gang and school life:

> The majority of kids want a name. They want to be famous. They want people to know them. That's why most of the kids doing what they're doing.... In school, people don't know you. They just think you're a schoolboy.... We thought they were nerds, they didn't know much about reality.

In addition to family- and school-related difficulties, another source of pressure toward gang involvement is the discrimination the youths perceive from law enforcement officials. Informants complain that they have been unjustifiably harassed and even beaten by police on several occasions. As a 20-year-old explains:

> Sometimes when I drive a fixed-up car, they stop us for nothing. Just because we're young and Vietnamese. We're driving normally, like everybody else is, but they just pull us over. They be searching us, search the car, and we don't have anything. They treated us like shit.

Our observations confirm some of these complaints. For instance, some law enforcement officials casually use racial slurs, apparently not with conscious hostility, but nevertheless with utter disregard for the potential effect on ethnic minority youth. One of the authors also observed a police officer search a car that was in the vicinity of several youths being questioned, and only after searching the car did the officer ask if the car belonged to any of the youths. It did not; the group had just happened to congregate by the vehicle outside a nearby pool hall. From the perspective of Vietnamese youth, such treatment constitutes racist behavior on the part of law enforcement officers who are supposed to protect them.

HUC: A VIETNAMESE GANG MEMBER

The life history of Huc provides an illustrative example of the experiences that led this Vietnamese youth to join a gang. Huc was born during the Vietnam War and raised outside of Saigon in the aftermath of the war. Life was marked by fear and hatred of the communist government. His father, imprisoned in the government's "re-education camps," was absent during most of Huc's childhood. When Huc's father was finally released, he made plans to send his entire family to America, where he had heard there was freedom and the streets were literally paved with gold. Huc and his family boarded a dilapidated ship and escaped from Vietnam in 1979. However, the ship capsized, drowning his mother (who was pregnant at the time), all of his siblings, and his aunt. Such losses were not uncommon among Vietnamese "boat people;" as many as one-third of all Vietnamese refugees lost their lives in the sea during their attempt to escape (Grant, 1979).

Huc and his father survived and later reached the United States, both still numb from their loss and totally unprepared for their new life here. Like most second-wave refugees, they were poor, had very little education, and came from the countryside (Kelly, 1977; Nguyen and Henkin, 1984). Although Huc and his father once had a close relationship, after their refugee experience, his father became more distant, sullen, and withdrawn. Huc was eager to learn English and meet new friends, but his father preferred to stay only in the Vietnamese business district and was too embarrassed to learn English. By contrast, Huc began losing his fluency in Vietnamese, and, eventually, he and his father could barely communicate and found little in common. Huc's relationship with his father became even more strained when his father decided to remarry. Still haunted by nightmares of his mother's death, Huc resented his stepmother. Huc's father would beat him for disrespecting his stepmother, which only strengthened Huc's resentment and rebellious spirit. And because his father and stepmother worked long hours in menial jobs, he saw less and less of them.

Huc's experiences at school made matters even more difficult. The federal government dispersed Southeast Asian refugees across the county in an effort to alleviate antirefugee sentiment, and so Huc and his father were first assigned to a sponsoring family on the East Coast. Like thousands of other dispersed refugees, they quickly made plans to move to southern California, home to Little Saigon. Over the course of a year, they moved from city to city until they reached Los Angeles. Moving from one city to the next also meant that Huc changed schools with each move, and he was usually the only Vietnamese student in his class.

School was initially a demoralizing and confusing experience for Huc. He could not speak English at the time, and something seemingly so simple as asking the teacher to go to the bathroom became a major ordeal. Because he could not speak English, his father placed Huc in a class several grades below where he should have been for his age (a common practice among Vietnamese refugees). Thus, Huc's classmates were three or four years younger than he, and that in turn made it even more difficult for him to relate to his peers and adjust to school life. His years in the United States created a sense of ambivalence about his new identity as an "Americanized Vietnamese." As he explains, "You don't know what you are really ... the confusion about what you want to be, trying to convert yourself into American. You're stuck in between, you don't know where you supposed to belong. So alone ... you don't know who you are."

In junior high school, Chicano youth gangs regularly harassed Huc, and as a result he started to carry a knife for protection. He began to spend most of his time in and out of school, banding together with the other Vietnamese students to fight the Chicano gangs. As he spent more time fighting, Huc soon lost interest in school activities. Moreover, he enjoyed the popularity that he earned from fighting; he became known as a good fighter, and other Vietnamese students looked up to him. His core group of friends quickly became a cohesive unit. As he observes: "This is the only family I know. You grow in the gangs. You might start out with five or six friends, then suddenly you have twenty friends. It's a happy family." To support his lifestyle with his "family," Huc skipped school regularly and spent his time stealing cars and robbing homes of other Vietnamese refugees.

Huc's father never understood the extent of his gang activity because he was much too busy working to monitor him. Whenever he received a notice that Huc had been suspended from school for fighting, Huc had to translate the notice for him, and, not surprisingly, Huc did not translate the message correctly. Compounding matters was the unfamiliarity of Huc's father with the educational system and other institutions in America, as a result of which he was unable to help Huc with his homework or provide him with direction. Eventually, Huc ran away from home and spent his nights with his new family in motels, as they traveled from city to city on the West Coast.

Huc's belief in the American dream—where the streets are paved with gold—quickly vanished, and he grew increasingly cynical. As he saw his father toiling in menial jobs for minimal pay and no chance for mobility, Huc opted for the shortcut to the American dream. Gangs provided that shortcut, and offered him a new value system, which is now tattooed on his thigh: four "Ts," representing the Vietnamese words for love, prison, crime, and money.

GANG CHARACTERISTICS AND ACTIVITIES

Law enforcement officials estimate that there are 500 to 3000 Vietnamese gang members in Orange County, but even these broad estimates are highly speculative. Unlike the traditional ghetto and barrio gangs of other ethnic groups, most of these relatively new gangs do not adopt the formal trappings of group monikers, colors, symbols, or turf claims. Rather, many of our respondents characterize their association as not so much a "gang" but, rather, a loose collection of friends, amorphous and fluid in structure. Membership is determined almost arbitrarily; initiation rituals are absent. Such characteristics still prevail today, although Vietnamese youths are starting to copy black and Chicano gangs. Hand signs, clothing styles, gang names, and even graffiti are becoming more common among Little Saigon's groups (see Kent and Felkenes, 1998).

Social workers, community activists, and Vietnamese businessmen estimate that no more than 10 percent of the youth population is engaged in crime, but gang members assert that the figure is much higher. Vietnamese street gangs tend to commit different types of offenses from organized crime groups and other ethnic gangs. Unlike black and Chicano groups, they do not deal drugs, although some Vietnamese gang members do use them; they feel that the risk involved in dealing drugs is far too great compared to the potential gain. And unlike members of other ethnic gangs, Vietnamese gang members tend to downplay violence and "gang-banging" and instead opt for more profitable endeavors:

> We tried to stay low key because that's the best profile you know. If we have a problem, it takes a week to solve that problem and that's one week of business that we have to forego to deal with this problem. And what do we gain from it? We beat some people up, and you know we're losing money, so we didn't really go out and do that. We dealt with it when it was necessary, but we tried to concentrate on making that money.

More recently, however, several outbursts of violence have caught the media's attention, including a series of incidents at "cyber cafés" in the Little Saigon area (Leonard, 2002) and a major gang fight that erupted at a popular shopping mall (Welborn, 2002).

The primary emphasis remains on the "business of obtaining money"— most notably through auto theft and home invasion robberies. The concentration on materialistic crimes appears to go hand in hand with our informants' awareness of their impoverished backgrounds. For instance, some of the gang youths we interviewed felt they were a burden on their parents. One gang member notes: "I never asked my family for money, but I got out and I fuck around, and I need money, but I would never go to my mom for money, 'cause the money is for me." Others resented their families for not adequately providing for them. As another declares, "That's why I think my family is poor. They don't take care of me enough. I just want to go my own ... I just want my own money. I want to make my own money." The respondents stress that the quick scores made possible through criminal activities provide them with a high degree of independence that would have been impossible through traditional employment routes. As another gang member states,

> I didn't want my parents' money. I wanted my own money ... I feel like maybe they need the money. I always tried to get my own money.... So I got the job [as a hotel bellboy] to save money. But the money was too slow. I didn't have enough money. I wanted more money. So I quit ... with my homeboys, I could make $10,000 a day.

The one criminal activity that embodies the "quick score"—and distinguishes the criminal involvement of Vietnamese gang members more than anything—is the home invasion robbery. Gang members know that refugees are traditionally distrustful of financial institutions and therefore keep their savings within their homes, often in the form of gold (Song, 1992). Relying on inside information, gangs target a Vietnamese home and survey it for several days. After obtaining sufficient information, they invade the home and force the victims to reveal the hidden location of their savings and valuables. One common method is to employ "look-out" drivers equipped with cellular phones, so that in the rare event that police arrive at the scene, the look-outs can alert the robbers and distract the authorities.

Home invasion robberies are highly profitable. Our informants claim that they commonly steal about $20,000 from each venture, and police reports indicate losses of upwards of $100,000. Vietnamese gang members capitalize on their victims' reluctance to report the crimes to law enforcement since many fear physical retaliation and distrust law enforcement agencies. Many refugees still hold memories of corruption in Vietnam, where apprehended criminals could purchase their freedom from certain law enforcement officials. Unfamiliar with America's bail system, many new arrivals initially believed that gang members who were released from custody had bribed their way out of confinement. As a result, few Vietnamese trusted the police to protect them, and rather than risk payback for reporting the crime, most victims remained silent. Conversely, youth gangs are extremely reluctant to invade the homes of non-Vietnamese residents. In fact, with the exception of auto theft, Vietnamese-on-Anglo crime is extremely rare in Orange County. A Vietnamese gang member explains why they are reluctant to choose Anglo targets: "We believed that they [the victims] were scared of us and of the law. But we scared of whites, [of] any other race, 'cause they know a lot of law and they don't keep cash within their home." Another elaborates why coethnics are a better bet: "It's easier. Most of the Oriental, they don't go to the police unless they rich and stuff. Most of them [the victims] are on welfare and they make money on the side."

Police departments have improved their public image substantially by opening substations in Little Saigon, forming Asian Crime Units, and hiring police officers who are fluent in Vietnamese. Presently, few residents fear police corruption, but misgivings about the bail system remain strong. As a Vietnamese informant comments:

> You are not going to report the crime. You have to think about your family. I know the police are good guys, but they are not going to protect me. Within 72 hours, the criminal can be out on bail. So I'm not going to tell. . . . The robber will not only go after me if I do, but my children. So I am going to tell the police? No way!

This sentiment appears to be widespread; Orange County law enforcement officials estimate that 60 to 90 percent of home invasion robberies go unreported—a fact that, understandably, frustrates the police.

Gang members and law enforcement officers agree that an extensive "fence" network exists in the Vietnamese communities in both Los Angeles and Orange counties, giving gang members an easy means of converting their stolen items into cash. Informants maintain that pawn shops, gold shops, and jewelry stores often accept stolen items without asking questions, As they explain, "You sell to jewelry stores. . . . I would say the majority of jewelry stores have bought illegal stuff. They buy the goods because we sell it cheap." The profits are then split among the gang members, and spent on cars (some youths boasted that they purchased a new car each week), expensive "GQ"-like clothing, weapons, drugs, gambling, and bills for restaurants, cafés, and nightclubs.

When gang members acquire a substantial amount of cash, they will often rent a motel room where more than a dozen individuals of both sexes gather to eat, talk, listen to music, watch videotapes, drink beer, and use drugs into the early morning. According to some youths, sharing drugs as well as other material goods is important not only to reinforce interpersonal bonding but also to demonstrate the host's economic well-being.

Interestingly, participants in such motel room celebrations are by no means limited to gang youths; a few students or wage earners—friends of gang members—typically join in these parties despite having no involvement in other gang activities.

CONCLUSION

Like many of the immigrant groups discussed in this volume, the Vietnamese community in Orange County encountered various forces that disrupted their adjustment to life in America. The historical circumstances of their immigration and assimilation experiences posed uniquely severe challenges to these refugees of war. In Little Saigon, such circumstances resulted in a socioeconomic polarization that further complicated the adaptation processes of many arrivals, most especially the youths who came to America's shores as boat people.

The immigrant family was not strong enough to provide social support and exert control for many of these children as it did in Vietnam. For those who were fortunate enough to have relatives nearby, the strains of family poverty and cultural conflict engendered severe intergenerational problems that undermined healthy adolescent growth and self-identification. Racism and other adjustment issues in the educational context only fueled the sense of hopelessness and alienation that many Vietnamese American children already experienced. In the face of such obstacles and an inadequate support structure to fall back on, the gang serves as a surrogate family and a bastion of dependability and self-esteem. In the eyes of some Vietnamese youth, the gang holds appeal as a provider of affiliation, community, material well-being, protection, and guidance—for many, an all-too-scarce source of security and comfort in a strange, foreign land and an alternative means to the American dream. Like their African American and Chicano counterparts, Vietnamese youth join gangs in response to the multiple marginal situations they face: family poverty and bicultural stress, troubled school life, disruptive neighborhood environment, street peer socialization, and strained relations with law enforcement and other institutions (Vigil, 1988). Hence, it is crucial to understand gang subcultures in a broader perspective.

Note

1. We are indebted to Nicholas Rothenberg and Ahrin Mishan of the USC visual anthropology department's Graduate Studies in Ethnographic Film for providing us the opportunity to view their footage and for the insights they have shared with us in many informal discussions of their work. We also wish to thank the various officials who took time to speak with us, especially Detective Bill Johnson of the Garden Grove Police Department, who was particularly generous with his time. We are extremely grateful, of course, to the Vietnamese community and those members of it who are cited anonymously in the chapter.

CHAPTER 14

Lost in the Fray:

Cambodian American Youth in Providence, Rhode Island

Sody Lay

Rolling by my foes,
without any doubt that I
will smoke those fools.
As I lock and load my piece,
I think not of my enemies
And then without any doubt,
I squeeze. BANG! Bang! BANG!
I hear the sounds of blood, sweat, and tears.
Their kinfolks cursing at me as I speed away.
I heard the sounds before
They're the sounds that I ran away from during the War.
The same sounds made by the Khmer Rouge when
We were trying to escape. The sounds of gunfire.
Now I'm the Khmer Rouge per se,
Killing my own people as the Khmer Rouge had done
I reason "disrespect" while I know not of a term to justify my
action
As the Khmer Rouge had done, killing millions of our own
There is no just because the Khmer Rouge's actions and as mine
Undermines the given title "Cambodian."
So, I continue to wander as an outcast . . .

> "Gang-Banging in the U.S.A.: Where Are You from Fool?"
> by AK-187 published in *Proleung Khmer* 1997,
> a publication of UCLA United Cambodian Students

As this poem suggests, in order to understand today's Cambodian American youth and the many complicated issues with which they must cope, one must first understand the difficult background from which they have emerged. Their history does not simply begin in the poor neighborhoods of America where their families were transplanted during the influx of Southeast Asian refugees in the early 1980s. It dates back to the 1960s and 1970s, a time before many were even born, a time when the conflict in Vietnam began to spread into Cambodia, and violence on a massive scale hit the lives of their parents and grandparents like a catastrophic monsoon. One must understand the poem's reference to the Khmer Rouge and the Cambodian American's sense of displacement, the sense that he/she continues to "wander as an outcast," in order to understand the factors leading Cambodian American youth of today to join gangs.

Based on interviews with a half dozen Cambodian gang members currently residing in Providence, Rhode Island, and participant observation, this chapter examines the reasons behind the emergence and growth of Cambodian American youth gangs in the United States. The study has a twofold purpose. First, I detail how Cambodian American gangs initially emerged to protect refugee youth from harassment and victimization by other ethnic gangs and were later transformed into the more permanent, often violent, and dangerous form found today. Second, I illustrate how Cambodian American gangs may be viewed as a medium through which readers may also learn about other very basic issues with which many Cambodian American youth must contend, such as estrangement from parents and the difficulties associated with straddling two cultures and feeling a part of neither.

"THEY'RE THE SOUNDS THAT I RAN AWAY FROM DURING THE WAR"

The vast majority of Cambodians in America are refugees who have made this country their home for one primary reason: to escape the bloodshed and misery that engulfed their land of origin in the latter half of the twentieth century. Cambodians have had to continuously endure various degrees of conflict and violence over the past several decades. From the late 1960s to the early 1970s, they were victims of relentless American bombing. U.S. planes rained approximately a half million tons of explosives on Cambodia, the equivalent of twice that dropped on Japan during World War II, leading to the estimated death of over a half million people.

In April of 1975, the Cambodian communist group popularly known as the Khmer Rouge took over Cambodia and set up the Democratic Kampuchea regime, a regime whose principal policy was to force the country's entire population to work as slave labor in agricultural communes. In their paranoia, they executed tens of thousands of people whom they considered a threat to their power, including government officials and military personnel associated with the former regime, religious practitioners such as Buddhist monks and Muslim clerics, and anyone who was educated. They even executed individuals for simply wearing glasses because, to the Khmer Rouge, it suggested the person was tainted by education and Western influence. During the Democratic Kampuchea period, Cambodians worked from dawn until dusk seven days a week, barely surviving on the bowl of watery rice gruel they were given each day to eat. They did not have access to even the most basic of medical care, and many people needlessly died of easily curable ailments such as dysentery. Between April 1975 and January 1979, an estimated 1.7 million Cambodians, or approximately 25 percent of the population, died of disease, starvation, and execution.

The overthrow of the Democratic Kampuchea regime in 1979 by the Vietnamese People's Army curtailed the Khmer Rouge terror but also plunged the country into another decade of civil war. As the Khmer Rouge and Vietnamese-backed People's Republic of Kampuchea fought for control over the country, hundreds of thousands of Cambodians fled to refugee camps along the Thai–Cambodian border. Unable to return to their homeland because of the ongoing war, over 100,000 applied for and received refuge in the United States in the early 1980s. Today, well over 200,000 Cambodians reside in the United States, with the three largest communities being in Long Beach, California, Lowell, Massachusetts, and Seattle, Washington, respectively.

"WE WERE TRYING TO ESCAPE THE SOUNDS OF GUNFIRE"

One gang member described the birth and growth of Cambodian gangs in America succinctly by saying, "We used guns to defend ourselves and it got spread all around." The history of violence in Cambodia may have pushed Cambodians to America, but the elements indigenous to poor, urban America are what pushed Khmer youth toward gang formation and violence. The only neighborhoods where they could afford to settle were hostile environments that contain drugs, gangs, and violence. The brutality that Khmer parents fled Cambodia to escape was visited upon their children in American schools and on American streets. Lacking language proficiency and being the new immigrants in town, Cambodian children became the target of harassment by other students, most often those who were themselves poor minorities such as Latinos and African Americans. The level of mistreatment ranged from simple name-calling to physical assault and battery.

After having lived through the destruction of the Khmer Rouge and the lawlessness of the refugee camps, some Cambodian youth had little fear of violence and even less intention of remaining helpless victims of it in their new country. These youth banned together to protect themselves, responding to the physical violence perpetrated against them with violence of their own. The largest and most well known Cambodian gang in America began in such a manner. The Tiny Rascal Gang (commonly referred to simply as TRG) was founded in Long Beach, California—a city that is home to the largest Cambodian community outside of Cambodia itself. The initials TRG also represent the initials of its three founding members—three young Cambodian American men who created the gang in the early 1980s in response to being repeatedly victimized in school by some of their non-Cambodian classmates. In the case of Long Beach, most of the perpetrators of violence against Cambodians were Latino youth affiliated with gangs. The formation of Cambodian gangs such as TRG in Long Beach escalated the violence as Cambodian and Latino gangs have fought for supremacy of the city. It is a conflict that has lasted well over a decade and resulted in numerous casualties on both sides.

Although it was not their experience of violence in Cambodia but their experience of violence in their new homeland that provided the impetus for Cambodian refugee youth to create gangs, the Khmer Rouge experience undoubtedly influenced the manner in which they responded to their tormentors. Under the Khmer Rouge regime, authority figures could not be trusted, and brute force was the final solution to most conflicts. Even in the refugee camps, roaming bands of hoodlums and soldiers would terrorize the local population, robbing and beating them. Sometimes the very individuals who were supposed to be in charge of law and order were the ones leading the abuse. By the time Cambodians arrived in America, fear and mistrust of authority figures had already become inculcated in the minds of many, and they did not consider turning to school or police officials for protection. Compounding this problem was the inability of Cambodians to express themselves: most lacked even a rudimentary level of English-language proficiency. Hence, these youth responded to violence and intimidation committed against them in the only way they knew how—with violence and intimidation of their own.

The rise of Cambodian American youth gangs occurred throughout the 1980s, not only in Long Beach but in all major Cambodian communities throughout the United States. In cities such as Oakland, Stockton, Seattle, Chicago, Lowell, and Providence, Cambodian refugee youth took up arms to defend themselves. The gang structure provided the most convenient vehicle for institutionalizing their chosen means of protection. They have names as basic as Asian Boyz and Oriental Rascals and as creative as Exotic

Foreign Creation Coterie. They also now have affiliate gangs such as the pre-teen and teen-oriented Oriental Rascals Junior and the women-oriented School Bitches Chillin' and Lady Rascal Gang.

"KILLING MY OWN PEOPLE AS THE KHMER ROUGE HAD DONE"

Cambodian American gangs have long shifted their activities and goals, although they were originally created for protection. Members gradually embraced more and more of the gang lifestyle, picking up on the dress and attitude of the very people against whom they were trying to protect themselves (Latino and African American gangsters). They adopted other aspects of gang life as well, such as crime and senseless violence. Now, like other gangs, Cambodian American gang members engage in theft, robbery, and, to a lesser extent, petty drug sales. They also commonly engage in that other kind of "protection," the kind that honest shopkeepers in the community have to pay to receive from them.

Today, rather than receiving protection from gang membership, it seems that youth actually put themselves in more jeopardy by joining a gang. Unlike in the past, however, their safety is threatened mostly by other Cambodian or Southeast Asian gangs rather than Latinos or African Americans. In Providence, for example, territorial protection has become an important aspect of Cambodian American gang life. In contrast to organized crime, it is territorialism based more on machismo than on economics. Two weeks prior to my interview with him, Oak, as he is known to his friends on the street, was jumped by a group of other Cambodian American youth near his home. Asked what provoked the attack, he simply explained, "Around here it don't matter where you're from, it matters where you're at"—his way of saying he happened to be at the wrong place at the wrong time. Although on friendly turf, he was caught lounging outside by himself, vulnerable to an attack by youth who claim allegiance to a gang down the street.

Gang life in Providence, as in other places, is about rivalry and feuds. Even in Long Beach, Cambodian gangs have increasingly turned on each other as they compete for membership and prestige as the biggest and toughest. Their conflicts are a series of back and forth, and, as one gang member states, they are "always about retaliation." Often the conflict arises from something trivial like competition or jealousy between rival gang members over a girl. Sometimes the violence is even more senseless. Just weeks before my interview, a gun battle between TRG and Oriental Rascals left a 16-year-old gang member dead. Asked why he was gunned down, the reply was cavalier and curt: "for talkin' shit."

UNDERMINING THE GIVEN TITLE "CAMBODIAN"

Nature of Cambodian Gangs in America

Gangs are not a social organization indigenous to Cambodia. In fact, there is no direct translation in Khmer for the English word "gang."[1] Hence, as mentioned before, Cambodian gangs in America have patterned themselves after already existing African American and Latino gangs, acquiring from them clothing style, hand signs, and other conspicuous gang attributes. Cambodian youth gangs are generally very fluid in nature, with few rigid rules. As ethnic gangs, they are unique in that they do not display the ethnocentric attitude found in many other gangs. A trend common among Cambodian American gangs is to be accepting of ethnic and racial diversity within their ranks, and other youth may often become part of the gang the same way a new person is introduced to a circle of friends.

Looseness in gang structure has both positive and negative consequences. According to John Reis, a Crime Prevention Specialist for the Rhode Island Department of Attorney General, the informal nature of Cambodian American youth gangs make it possible for gang members to fairly easily leave their gang affiliations behind should they so desire. Moreover, the informal nature of gangs allows members to freely pursue activities such as education or employment without incurring the wrath of the gang unit. In Providence, many OGs (original gangsters) have been able to acquire steady employment and start families in the very neighborhoods they used to roam as teenagers. On the other hand, the downside of loose gang structure is that members tend to be more violent than their more organized counterpart. Without a formal leadership structure to issue commands and relegate antisocial behavior, members are more apt to engage in spontaneous acts of violence and crime. Because they need not answer to anyone, gang members are freer to commit crimes without having to justify their actions within a formal hierarchy.

Although there is usually little formal leadership structure, Cambodian gangs—like many mainstream gangs—do adhere to a loose hierarchical structure, with younger members given the title "juniors" and older members (usually those in their mid-twenties or so) being anointed with the title of OG. Junior members are known for their enthusiasm for violence, as they constantly seek to demonstrate their toughness and daring. Through their aggression against rival gangs, they act as the conservators of gang pride. The activities of OGs, on the other hand, shift from their youthful days of seeking danger and excitement to mostly just engaging in recreational drug use and alcohol consumption. Nevertheless, they are always prepared to retaliate if conflict should come their way. As one gang member put it, "OGs don't go lookin' for drama, they let the trouble come to them." When asked if he was still a gang member, an OG replied by lifting his shirt to reveal TRG tattooed in large gangster-style script across his back and proclaimed, "TRG for life." Yet, as mentioned earlier, many OGs, including the aforementioned, do move on, gaining steady employment and raising families.

The appearance of Cambodian youth gang members varies from region to region. In Long Beach, for instance, they tend to shave their heads bald; in Oakland, they grease up their hair and slick it back; and in Seattle, the trend is toward cornrows. Each gang also has its own personality and values. One gang may emphasize drinking and womanizing, while another, drug sales. The one common denominator of almost all Cambodian American gangs, however, is the acceptance of violence by members as an inevitable part of their lives.

The "Cambodian" in Cambodian American Gang Members

Although members have picked up the style of other gangs, many are still very much Cambodian in nature. Oak is part of a new generation of Cambodian American youth gang members. At age 16, he already has years of experience leading the gang life, having been involved with gangs since the age of 11 while residing in Oakland, Seattle, and now Providence. These days 11 is the standard age of initial membership, he informs me. His choice of dress is called "sagging," which consists of baggy pants that hang low and a loose-fitting shirt. When asked why he decided to choose the gang lifestyle, he initially had difficulty answering. After some thought, however, he offered that he was perhaps simply following in the footsteps of his uncles, members of a Cambodian gang in Oakland called the Asian Street Walkers. Growing up, he had admired them for their cool attitude and fearless demeanor.

Through our conversation, Oak also revealed that his father and mother separated when he was young, with his father taking a new wife. He nonchalantly remarks that sometimes his father beat him, but mostly he just neglected him in favor of his step-siblings. While rebellion against an abusive parent may have contributed to Oak's decision to join a gang, his family life is actually not typical of other Cambodian American youth who join gangs. Many gang members live peacefully at home with their parents, and, as a gesture that can only be construed as respect, often attempt to keep their gang affiliation hidden. According to John Reis, many parents are actually shocked when they learn that their children are involved in gangs.

The fact that many youth are even able to hide their gang affiliation from their parents perhaps reflects a more serious and pervasive problem within the Cambodian American community: the lack of communication between parents and children. Here, the aftermath of the Khmer Rouge tragedy continues to haunt individuals and families. Many Cambodian parents have difficulty coping with post-traumatic stress, recurring nightmares about the Khmer Rouge, and other mental health disorders such as feelings of exile, causing them to become depressed, irascible, and/or withdrawn. These mental health problems can make it difficult for parents to communicate with their children or even effectively perform their parental duties.

A difference between Cambodian and American culture with respect to parental interaction with children also contributes to estrangement between Cambodian American parents and their children. Cambodian culture does not generally promote overt displays of affection between parent and child in the manner children witness on American television. Cambodians view raising children to be proper as one of the most important of parental duties; hence, they tend to express their love and concern for their children through instruction in and admonishment of behavior. As a result, many Cambodian American children develop the perception that their parents do not love them and complain that their parents criticize them too much.

Finally, like many second-generation immigrant youth, Cambodian children become more quickly acculturated into their new environment and acquire a new value system that clashes with their parents' traditional Khmer notions of appropriate and inappropriate behavior. The children often also develop a preference for speaking English, further compounding the already difficult lines of communication between Cambodian parents and their Americanized children. This cultural and linguistic divide increasingly pulls and pushes parents and children apart, giving Cambodian youth yet another reason to search outside the immediate family for a social support network.

Although the estrangement between parent and child is not necessarily antagonistic in nature, it does leave a void within the child's life, a void that can be filled on a variety of levels by gangs. In a gang, Cambodian American youth find those who speak a common language, older gang members who may fill the role of surrogate parents, and camaraderie with individuals who share a common experience of estrangement from parents and society at large. Gang members as individuals share that sense of being outcasts, not quite fitting in within the context of a traditional Khmer family or American society in general. Within the gang unit, they find individual acceptance but still remain outcasts collectively, an undesirable entity in poor neighborhoods.

Acculturation into the new American context, however, does not mean that Cambodian youth have rid themselves of all ethnic traits and characteristics. Although they may have acquired many American values and characteristics, most Cambodian American youth who participate in gangs are still very much in touch with their Khmer roots on a fundamental level. Even beyond overt claims of Cambodian pride (one gang actually calls itself "Cambodian Pride"), gang members display cultural characteristics that set them apart from other ethnic gangs. Many still use formal Khmer titles of respect to refer to those older than themselves (one example of the proper behavior Cambodian parents try to instill in their children). For instance, despite his five years of life as a gang member, Oak still addresses his elders politely and properly in the Khmer tradition. Even during our conversations, he and other gang members respectfully refer to me as "*Pu*" (roughly meaning "uncle") or "*Bong*" (roughly meaning "older brother"). Many Cambodian American youth in gangs also consider themselves Buddhist, a religion they accept by virtue of their Khmer heritage more than anything. Hence, although gang members may seem far removed from their traditional Khmer heritage, outward symbols of their culture emerge within the gang system itself such as expressions of respect for parents and elders, the use of honorific titles, and the acceptance of Buddhism.

The "American" in Cambodian American Gang Members

Just as Cambodian American youth gang activities have shifted, so have the motives of members for joining gangs. Although the need for a surrogate family, sense of identity, and protection may still contribute to gang membership, today there are also a host of less convoluted reasons why youth decide to join gangs. The answers given by gang members themselves to the question of why they joined gangs included: "because it's cool"; "for the adrenaline rush"; "for the chicks"; and "to sell drugs and make money."

Even these seemingly superficial motives have as their foundation the unique position of the Cambodian as outcast in America. Cambodian American youth, like other youth, are interested in the opposite sex, recreation, and social acceptance. These are also the values promoted by popular television stations that appeal to teenagers and young adults such as MTV. Like other Americans, many Cambodian youth would like to own fashionable clothes, attend parties, and pursue romance; unlike other Americans, however, they do not always have a culturally acceptable or financially viable means with which to attain these desires. Many Cambodian families in America are either part of the working poor or recipients of government aid and hence cannot afford the exciting lifestyles promoted by television. Cambodian culture is also extremely restrictive with regard to premarital romance; dating is not permitted, and marriages are traditionally arranged. Moreover, social interaction with the opposite sex before marriage is frowned upon. Hence, Cambodian American parents often prohibit their children from participating in activities such as parties and dances, resulting in a buildup of frustration and indignation on the part of Cambodian American youth as they witness their Anglo American, Latino, and African American counterparts engaging in these social activities.

In contrast to restrictive cultural norms and financial hardship, gangs offer Cambodian American youth the allure of romance, money, and excitement. Gangs provide a vehicle through which these youth can participate to some degree in popular American youth culture such as dating and parties. In the middle of my conversation with Oak on the front porch of a friend's home, he cavalierly waves down a car and walks over to speak with the young woman driver. After a few minutes, he comes back with a satisfied grin on his face and phone number in hand. Asked how he knew the girl, he coolly says that he had never seen her before. He just waved her down and tried his luck. His boldness in flirting with women at the age of 16 demonstrates the advantages of gang culture over traditional Khmer culture. The freedom to associate romantically is an allure of gang life that many youth, both young men and young women, find too tempting to pass up.

The particular gang with which Oak is affiliated in Providence is known for its drinking, recreational drug use, and womanizing, activities also favored by fraternities at colleges and universities throughout America. Although many of today's youth may drink while under the age of 21, do drugs, and seek attention from members of the opposite sex, the means to achieving these ends are not easily or equally attainable for all youth. College youth—especially those from affluent and middle-class households—have the means to drink at fraternity parties, dabble in drugs, and engage in premarital sex; for many Cambodian youth, however, these recreational options are closed, because of both their culture and class. The important difference between gangs and fraternities, however, is the willingness of gang members to commit violent crimes to achieve these ends. And as with school rivalries played out on the football field or basketball court, rivalries between gangs are an avenue for members to express bravado and interject excitement into their lives, often resulting in violence, bloodshed, and even death. It appears that when you cannot afford to be cool like Jason Priestly or Luke Perry in *Beverly Hills 90210*, you can always fall back on being cool like Marlon Brando in *The Wild One*.

"SO, I CONTINUE TO WANDER AS AN OUTCAST …"

Cambodian youth in America are no different from any other youth in their desires. They feel a need for social acceptance and the weight of peer pressure. To fit in, they acquire the clothing styles, mannerisms, and values of their neighbors. At home, parental mental heath problems and linguistic and cultural divides leave Cambodian American youth in various degrees alienated from their parents. At school and on television, they are exposed to values and lifestyles that are in direct contrast to the cultural and economic realities within their homes. Given these conditions, the allure of gangs to Khmer youth in America makes sense. In gangs, one finds opportunities for companionship, protection, excitement, romance, money, a sense of identity, and, not least of all, acceptance.

Nevertheless, it would be a mistake to conclude that gang membership is inevitable for Cambodian American youth, even taking into account their particular background and migration experience. Although the poor neighborhoods in which many Cambodians reside provide an environment where the temptation to choose gang membership is all too readily available, joining a gang is still ultimately a conscious decision. Gang members fully recognize and accept this fact. That they should even attempt to hide their gang affiliations from their parents shows that they understand the undesirability of their choice. There are alternative means of acquiring companionship, protection, excitement, romance, money, identity, and acceptance—means that do not involve harm to others or invite the possibility of harm, imprisonment, and death to oneself.

Oak and other gang members are aware that they have had and continue to have options in the lifestyle they choose. In this awareness lies room for hope. Oak, for instance, asserts that he would like to make a change in his life. At 16 he sometimes feels weary of the gang lifestyle, although he still seems allured by its perks, as in the case of his brashly approaching the young woman in the car. He is aware that the gang life will lead him nowhere, and he expresses a desire to complete his high school education or work toward his GED. His mentor, an OG of approximately 30, has a wife and son and a well-paying job as a finisher at a local furniture company. His status within the gang appears to be that of semiretirement, with participation in gang life at this point mainly relegated to drinking and recreational drug use. Of course, his continued affiliation with a gang means that violence, although only intermittently now, is still a part of his life. Pointing to the porch of his home across the street, he declares matter-of-factly, "I'm gonna die on the front stoop there." Still, when asked if he wants his eight-year-old son to become a gang member when he grows up, he replies curtly and soberly, "No. He's a college boy."

Note

1. English–Khmer dictionaries inaccurately translate it as *Krom,* a word that carries neither the negative connotation nor denotation that is usually affiliated with youth gangs in America. *Krom* simply means "group or grouping" and may be used to refer to everything from commercial companies to government councils and bureaus. Even Cambodians in America with the most limited of English-speaking proficiency will simply use the English word "gang" to refer to gangs.

PART IV

Negotiating and Affirming Identity, Space, and Choice

CHAPTER **15**

Made in the U.S.A.:

Second-Generation Korean American Campus Evangelicals

Rebecca Y. Kim

At lunchtime, one need only walk into Berkeley's Sproul Plaza, that famed arena of leftist politics, to note the transformation: where a salvo of free speech and anti-war slogans could once be heard, mantras of religious recruitment now drown out all sounds of protest. Pamphlets promising salvation, karoke and full immersion baptism, all in the same night, are proffered eagerly by members of the Evangelical Formosan Church, the Asian American Christian Fellowship and the Chinese Graduate Christian Society.

—A scene from the Sproul Plaza at the University of California, Berkeley (Chang, 2000)

Whether studying the Bible at Berkeley, engaging in feverish prayer at Harvard, or singing "praise" at Yale, Asian American Christian fellowships have become a familiar sight at many of the top colleges and universities across the country. Today, there are more than 50 evangelical Christian groups at the University of California at Berkeley and the University of California at Los Angeles (UCLA) alone, and a full 80 percent of their members are Asian American (Busto, 1996; Chang, 2000; Hong, 2000). The same holds true at elite private universities like Harvard, Yale, and Stanford. At Harvard, for instance, Asian Americans constitute 70 percent of the Harvard Radcliffe Christian Fellowship, and given the popularity of evangelical Christian fellowships, one can easily spot students who proudly don tee shirts with phrases like "the Asian Awakening" (Chang, 2000: 1). At Yale, the Campus Crusade for Christ is now 90 percent Asian, which is astonishing considering that 20 years ago it was 100 percent white. And like Yale, Stanford's Intervarsity Christian Fellowship has become almost entirely Asian (Chang, 2000). From 1989 to 1999, the Asian American membership at Stanford's InterVarsity Christian Fellowship increased by 84 percent, compared to a 31 percent increase in its overall membership (Busto, 1996). The ten largest InterVarsity chapters with a high percentage of Asian Americans include Cornell, Northwestern, Rutgers, the University of Illinois-Chicago, Boston University, the University of Michigan, Emory, Washington University, Harvard, and the Massachusetts Institute of Technology.

Among the growing Asian American campus fellowships, second-generation Korean American fellowships are the most visible, particularly on the West and East coasts, where the Korean population is most concentrated. For example, UCLA boasts more than ten Korean American Christian fellowships. However, the growth of Korean American campus fellowships is not restricted to the coasts; virtually every top-ranking university and college across the country has at least one Korean American campus fellowship. Second-generation Korean American evangelicals and Christian fellowships not only embody, but also constitute, a major part of the surge of Asian American evangelicals on elite campuses in the United States.

The growth of ethnic Christian campus fellowships among second-generation Korean American and other Asian American college students challenges our conventional understanding of religion and ethnicity. It contests secularization theories that predict a decline, if not total disappearance, of religion with increased modernization and emphasis on scientific and rational thinking—characteristics that epitomize institutions of higher education (Berger, 1967; Wilson, 1982). The growth of ethnically centered Christian campus fellowships also challenges conventional assimilation theories that presume a decline in ethnic ties, especially as groups achieve socioeconomic mobility and gain entry into mainstream institutions (Alba and Nee, 1996; Gans, 1992; Gordon, 1964; Park, 1950).[1] Amid theories about secularization, religion, and assimilation, however, ethnic evangelical fellowships have sprouted up across the nation's elite college campuses. These new ethnic evangelical fellowships are not replicas of the ethnic churches frequented by their first-generation parents, nor are they mere reproductions of white evangelical Christian fellowships. Rather, second-generation Korean American Christian evangelical fellowships formed in response to their dissatisfaction with first-generation ethnic churches and their marginalization from white-dominant evangelical fellowships. Hence, they are a product of an "emergent ethnicity," created in the United States as a result of the interaction of second-generation Korean Americans with the ethnic community and their experience within the broader American society.

Through a focused study of second-generation Korean Americans, this chapter examines the growing number of Asian American campus evangelicals and their ethnic Christian fellowships. The study examines the factors that draw second-generation Korean American evangelicals to ethnic Christian campus ministries. Moreover, the study illustrates how the activities of Korean American evangelicals differ from those of the first generation and from those of other mainstream campus evangelicals. The data for the study was collected over the course of two years and includes intensive fieldwork in a variety of Korean American, multiethnic, and white-majority campus evangelical organizations; 100 face-to-face interviews; focus group meetings; and informal conversations with second-generation Korean Americans as well as members of other ethnic groups involved in campus evangelical organizations.[2]

GROWING OUT OF THE KOREAN IMMIGRANT CHURCH: THE EMERGENCE OF KOREAN AMERICAN CAMPUS EVANGELICALS

The "Silent Exodus"

Among the growing numbers of Asian American campus evangelicals, Korean Americans, most of whom are second or 1.5 generation, constitute the majority (Busto, 1996).[3] Their participation stems, in part, from the fact that second-generation Korean Americans are now attending colleges in large numbers, but demographics are only part of the story. It is also important to note that religious participation is notably higher among contemporary Korean immigrants than among other Asian ethnic groups in the United States, which predisposes the second generation to have stronger religious ties. For example, recent studies find that approximately 17 percent of Filipinos, 32 percent of Chinese, and 37 percent of Japanese in the United States regularly attend their respective ethnic religious centers. By contrast, over 70 percent of the Korean immigrants attend ethnic churches (Hurh and Kim, 1990; Min, 1992; Williams, 1988). Thus, the growth of second-generation Korean American evangelicals is partly a result of their parents' strong attachment to ethnic churches.

Although immigrant parental religious beliefs and practices profoundly influence their children, they do not guarantee that the second generation will follow suit, especially given the different sociocultural environment in which their children are raised. Young adult second-generation Korean Americans may retain some of their parents religious beliefs, but they have begun to leave their parents' ethnic churches in a movement dubbed the "silent exodus" (Pai et al., 1987). The mass exodus of the second generation from Korean immigrant churches is referred to as "silent" because much of it goes unnoticed by their parents, and "exodus" because the numbers are staggering; more than 80 percent of the second generation are said to have left their immigrant parents' ethnic churches (Kim and Kim, 1996). So pervasive is the "silent exodus" that a recent study of Korean American churches describes the "church of family members" as the "church of parents" (Song 1994). Second-generation Korean American youth leave their parents' churches and gravitate to ethnic campus ministries for more than religious reasons. These organizations provide the second generation with a physical site to develop a sense of identity and to create an ethnic or religious experience that is all of their own—one that is neither assimilative nor simply inherited from the first generation.[4]

Coming into Their Own: The Reaction against the First Generation

> We are kind of in limbo ... we are Korean but also American ... so we have to define our own culture in a lot of ways. If you grew up in an American church, you grew up in a certain social scene where that heritage is just there in terms of what is appropriate social behavior. You have something that is already established for you. Even with the first generation, they have their heritage and history ... but for second-generation Koreans ... we have to create on our own ... figure out everything on our own.

Second-generation Korean American campus evangelical organizations formed, in part, as a reaction against the flaws and pitfalls they witnessed emerge in their parents' immigrant churches. Much of this reaction comes from what the children of Korean immigrants describe as cultural and generational differences in religious participation between the first and second generation. Second-generation Korean Americans characterize the first-generation's religious participation as hierarchical, patriarchal, and static. By contrast, they describe their own as democratic, egalitarian, and dynamic. For instance, a second-generation Korean American pastor who has worked as liaison in the Korean church between the two generations describes the differences by pointing to the differing emphases placed on titles and hierarchy:

> The first generation is into distinctions, they are title-oriented ... for example, *gip san nim* [the Korean word for deacon] means servant, but the Korean interpretation of that is like a higher stage of being religious, more reverential, more honorific. But the second generation do not view it that way, once you are done serving, you discard the title, being a deacon is more functional.

Unlike their parents, the second generation are not preoccupied with titles and hierarchy, and tend to choose their religious leaders based on ability rather than age and status, as the pastor continues to elaborate,

> The first generation see authority by virtue of age. In our first-generation congregation, we have 200 members and 209 are deacons! That is over 100 percent! ... But with the second-gen[eration] ministry, we have about 150–200 English speaking second gen[eration] and we have three deacons and we do not appoint deacons according to age but by what they have done, which is more in line with American culture.

The pastor also explains that "American thinking is not so hierar-chical," and he alludes to the American cultural influence on the second generation. Reflecting on some of the intergenerational and cultural differences, several second-generation Korean Americans point out that they are more likely to call pastors or church staff members by their first names rather than by their religious titles. In addition, second-generation Korean American pastors and staff members appear "more approach-able" and more egalitarian than immigrant pastors and church leaders. As a Korean American college student explains, "The second-generation pastors are more approachable ... my pastor prefers that I just call him 'Joe.'"

Perhaps one of the starkest differences between ethnic immigrant churches and the evangelical fellowships on college campuses is the role of women. Whereas women are placed in subservient and subordinate posi-tions in the ethnic immigrant churches, they are full participants on the college campuses. According to a female student leader:

> How is the first and the second generation different? Definitely the role of the women. The first-generation church puts women in a very powerless position. They don't have a real voice in the church, and I don't think they are much regarded as part of the church, while the second gen[eration] tend to realize that women have to be recognized as definitely part of the church.

Other women, especially young women, feel stifled, limited, and pres-sured to assume traditional gender roles in immigrant churches. For instance, a young woman describes how the pastor at an immigrant church she used to attend responded to her excitement about pursuing an acad-emic career,

I was telling him all of the things I was excited about—my vision of being an academic, about my New Testament class, history courses in religion ... and I was starting to open up about studying abroad—and I was talking ... and then he grabbed my hand and said, "you know a woman's very highest calling is to be a mother. . . ." I listened, but I was so disappointed. The sad thing is that it is not so rare to hear things like that.

Another Korean American woman states that compared to the first generation, the second generation are far more egalitarian with regard to gender relationships,

First-generation churches think that if you want to be a good mom you have to stay home and take care of the kids, but the second gen[eration] are definitely more aware that we can't always choose that. Just because you work doesn't mean that you are a bad mother ... the second gen[eration] are less tradition-bound in that way.

Generational differences extend beyond social status and gender roles. Many children of Korean immigrants note that the first generation's religious participation is more static, antiquated, and inexpressive compared to their own. A college student explains the notable difference in worship styles:

When I sit in the regular Sunday worship with the adults [older immigrants] ... it is boring, not very exciting, but [the second generation] are more likely to hit people with something they are not expecting ... like throw in a skit, maybe even a movie, maybe a hip-hop dance, mix it up more ... it's just so much more fun and creative.

Another student similarly adds,

The first generation is very dry ... their worship services are very quiet, not a lot of emotions ... they just sit there, listen, and leave; and the speakers are first-gen[eration] Koreans, just stone-faced and straightforward. But for us there is a mix of emotion and rational thought and I think in that sense there are a lot of differences. We clap, we get lively, and we have drums in our praise ... not just an organ and singing hymns. We have guitar, bass, keyboard and all those different instruments; and the speakers are a lot of times more exciting.

Live music from drums, guitars, keyboard, and bass, along with music from Vineyard, Hosanna Music Groups, and Integrity (which are popular among contemporary evangelical Christians), provide a striking contrast to the quiet and solemn atmosphere and a single monotonous organ with "boring hymnals" in Korean immigrant churches. Having once attended a special "praise night" at a Korean American campus ministry—where a band of Korean American Christians led the night of singing Christian "praise" music—I felt like I was at a rock concert rather than a religious gathering. Except for the lyrics of the songs, the atmosphere and mood resembled that of a concert—the room was dimly lit, lights flashed only on stage, and the praise leader had an electric guitar strapped across his chest and sang loudly into the microphone. Accompanying the praise leader was a drummer, electric bass and keyboard players, all backed up by a superior sound system. The audience was energized and immersed in the scene, and one student turned to his neighbor and asked, "Don't they sound like Pearl Jam?" [5] Clearly, this style of worship is far more dynamic and contemporary than the subdued style of their immigrant parents. And perhaps most important, this style of worship is one that the second-generation has made their own.

In Search of Religious Authenticity

Second-generation Korean Americans react to the forms and practices of immigrant churches by creating and participating in their own religious organizations. Although the exit from the immigrant church stems, in part, from differences in opinion about status, gender roles, and worship styles, it also reflects the second generation's questions about the religious authenticity of their parents' churches. They charge that immigrant churches are not only factious but also not "biblical" or "religious" enough. Citing the frequent internal political battles and subsequent splitting off within immigrant churches as prime examples, many second-generation Korean Americans explain that the churches they had once attended with their parents have since divided. For example, a second-generation Korean American student recounts how several lay leaders physically fought with one another over a dispute regarding which pastor to hire:

> Korean churches, what are they known for? Splitting. They are all splitting, practically everyone here experienced it. . . . And it is one thing if they are splitting because they want to spread God's words in other places . . . but it is mostly political, like we don't like that pastor or you guys are not giving us respect . . . or money conflicts.

There is a running joke among Korean American Christians at Stanford and Berkeley: "Let's make like a Korean church and split." The punch line is that the most effective way to get students going and moving is to replicate the behavior of a Korean church—to split. The internal political squabbles and frequent splitting, combined with the preoccupation with status, make immigrant ethnic churches appear more akin to ethnic organizations than to religious institutions.

In addition, some second-generation Korean Americans believe that their parents are not very serious about Christianity and spreading the word of God. For example, although immigrant parents encourage their children to attend church, they often disapprove of them becoming "too religious," especially at the cost of one's career. According to a Korean American college student:

> It is like they dropped me off at Sunday school to pick up good values, but did not expect me to really take [my religion] seriously, so when I said I wanted to be a missionary to China, they were like whoa ... no way, you are going to med school.

Another Korean American student adds, "My Dad tells me go to church, but don't get too serious about it." Other Korean Americans similarly note that their parents are concerned that they are becoming "too involved" in campus ministry and neglecting their studies. From the perspective of the second generation, these parental concerns contradict the very tenets of the evangelical Christian faith which challenge individuals to be serious about their faith and put "Jesus first above all else."

Second-generation Korean Americans also note that their immigrant parents' churches are purposefully ethnically exclusive and too self-contained, which they feel contribute to the lack of religious authenticity. By illustration, a second-generation Korean American staff member who grew up in an immigrant church located in a Latino neighborhood describes the following scenario that captures the attitude about ethnic exclusion:

> One time these neighborhood Latino kids wanted to come out to our church ... and they came up to the courtyard [near a table full of after-church refreshments], and this old grandma Korean deaconess started yelling at the Latino kids, yelling at them that the donuts are not for them ... so I was like what is going on here? So I gave them the donuts and she gave me this dirty look. I took these kids to the elementary group [which is held in English], and they came every week after that. I mean they so wanted to hear God's words. If you don't want to affect the

community, what are you doing? The church should be a place where the whole neighborhood [is] affected ... otherwise, are they really doing God's work?

From the perspective of the second generation, the ethnic exclusivity in first-generation churches and their lack of involvement in local communities go against Jesus' command to "love one's neighbor," practice charity, and share the gospel "to all nations." Thus, second-generation Korean Americans find it difficult to accept first-generation churches as authentically religious organizations.

Many second-generation Korean Americans fail to understand that Korean immigrant churches in the United States are not established for purely "biblical" reasons in the first place. Instead, they are founded in large part because the Korean community needs a social institution that provides fellowship, maintains homeland traditions, provides social services, and sustains social positions. Pyong Gap Min (1992) argues that Korean immigrant churches seek to preserve Korean culture and identity while serving as the most pivotal social institution in the ethnic community for meeting the pressing needs of immigrants as they struggle to establish themselves in their new homeland. Thus, if there is much splitting and struggles over power, status, and positions, it is because there are so many lay leaders who are involved in immigrant churches. And there are so many lay leaders because immigrants cannot attain their pre-immigrant levels of status and respect in their new host society. Consequently, ethnic churches serve as the institutions in which immigrants can regain and reclaim their pre-immigrant status.

For example, consider a man who was an attorney in Korea and now owns and operates a liquor store in a poor, inner-city neighborhood. Although his new position offers little in the way of status or respect, he can regain some status by taking a leadership position at his ethnic church, where his educational and pre-immigrant occupational attainments are recognized. Making matters more difficult for the first generation are their language and cultural barriers, which, in turn, prevent them from reaching out to the broader, non-Korean community.

Like most immigrants, first-generation Koreans are most concerned about the future financial stability of their families and children, and, as a result, they tend to be more pragmatic than the second generation regarding their religious orientation and practices. Accordingly, they tend to push their children to focus on educational and professional achievements over purely religious pursuits, which are a focal point of intergenerational conflict that contributes to the emergence of second-generation campus evangelicals. Ironically, although Korean American campus evangelicals aim for greater religious authenticity and broader inclusiveness, they find themselves back where their parents started—ethnic exclusivity. A puzzled Korean American student remarks, "It is not like there is going to be a Korean section in heaven ... so I don't think it is right for us to all have our own separate thing."

ASSIMILATION OR ETHNICIZATION? THE THRIVING KOREAN AMERICAN CHRISTIAN FELLOWSHIPS

Korean Americans form campus ministries, in part, as a reaction against the gripes they hold regarding the first generation's religious practices. They claim to be more religious and Americanized, as well as more democratic, egalitarian, and dynamic, than those in immigrant churches. However, the fact that Korean American Christian fellowships thrive across the nation's major universities and colleges suggests that these second-generation religious organizations are becoming more ethnic (or more "Korean American") rather than simply resembling mainstream campus ministries. Why do second-generation Korean Americans prefer *Korean American* campus ministries over a variety of other multiethnic or white-dominant campus ministries to which they also have access? Moreover, what is "Korean American" about these Korean American campus ministries?

The Shared "Korean American" Experience

What brings second-generation Korean Americans together is their shared experience of growing up "Korean American." Second-generation Korean Americans choose Korean American campus ministries over others because they can be with coethnics with whom they share the *most* similar experiences of growing up in Korean immigrant families in America. A Korean American student reports:

> Most of us have first-generation parents. We know what goes on in a Korean house ... the parental pressure ... study, study, study ... marry a Korean ... don't talk back. So it is easier to get closer with other Koreans. They know where you are coming from. Even if you give someone the best explanation of Korean culture, it's not the same.

Among the shared familial experiences that Korean American students mention, the pressure to excel in school is not only the most common but also the most extreme:

Korean parents are like you have to do this, this, and this to be successful . . . you have to go to medical school or law school, and study, study, study. They think the best colleges are Harvard, Yale, Princeton. I am not saying white people don't stress education, but Koreans . . . they take it to another level.

In an extreme case, a Korean American student recounted how his mother wrote his college entrance essay and filled out an application for Harvard, even though she knew that her son did not want to apply:

My mom applied for me. She wrote my essays and everything . . . all grammatically incorrect. I even had to go to an interview [for Harvard applicants]. It lasted five minutes. I told her I didn't want to go there or apply, but she just wouldn't listen. She just did it for me.

Parental pressure does not end in high school but often extends into college, as suggested by several students who noted the difficulty they had with their parents when they announced that they wanted to major in the social sciences, such as psychology, sociology, or anthropology. They state that their parents consider a college degree in the social sciences a waste of time and money because they feel that such majors will not lead to financially lucrative careers. They pressure their children to major in the hard sciences, in medicine or law—fields they believe will lead to a more financially successful and secure future. As a result, the struggle over choosing a major is a stormy battle between immigrant parents and their U.S.-born and -raised children in the Korean immigrant family. For example, a student recalled how her brother severed his ties with his parents because they adamantly opposed his decision to be a cartoonist after graduating from Princeton. Though extreme, this case illustrates the type and degree of intergenerational and cultural conflict that second-generation Korean Americans face. Korean American students also share stories about the pressure to please their hard-working parents by succeeding educationally and professionally, while also struggling to develop an independent identity. Second-generation Korean Americans explain that fellow ethnics best understand their experiences of growing up in Korean immigrant households.

Being in a Korean American campus ministry (as opposed to being in a multiethnic or white-dominant campus ministry) provides coethnics with a sense of comfort associated with a shared ethnic origin and cultural upbringing. For instance, although most can no longer speak or read Korean, the second generation often sprinkle in Korean phrases when they speak and make jokes that evoke images that may be comical only to coethnics, as a leader of a Korean American campus ministry illustrates:

> Say like you are making a joke on your dad ... and like you are
> describing how your dad goes outside to wash his car wearing his
> dress socks in sandals and the *nan ning go* (a tank top that Korean
> males often wear), that is funny to a Korean American because
> there is a common understanding ... but with ... let's say ... a
> Caucasian, they wouldn't find it very funny.

In addition to being able to appreciate certain jokes and stories unique
to the experiences of second-generation Korean Americans, Korean Americans feel comfortable in ethnic campus ministries because they grew up
worshipping only with coethnics. A Korean American student explains:

> Why did I pick a Korean one? It is not that I am racist.... I grew
> up with white people, but I don't know. I grew up in the Korean
> church and the majority of my Korean friends are Christian while
> all of my white friends are Jewish. I never worshipped with white
> people, so I think that has a lot to do with it.

Another student adds that he did not feel as though he really "fit in" at
the white church:

> I just felt like I did not fit in at the white church, but I could have
> been over self-consciousness ... it was just a different environ-
> ment from what I was used to. I had white friends before ... hmm
> ... it is because church time is the time that I am used to being with
> Koreans, because that is what I grew up with.

Thus, what is "Korean" about Korean American campus ministries—
what makes worshipping with other Korean Americans most desirable are
the shared experience they have growing up in first-generation homes and
churches in America and the comfort of maintaining habitual religious
interactions with other coethnics.[6]

Ethnic/Racial Categorization and Marginalization

> What I liked best about visiting Korea was that I felt this big burden,
> weight, lifted off my shoulders because I did not have to think about
> race, being Korean ... you just felt lighter. In America, a significant
> part of your energy in everyday life is exerted thinking about race ...
> you don't have to deal with that if you are just with Koreans.

The formation of Korean American campus evangelical organizations
is the result of both push and pull factors. Although second-generation

Korean Americans may feel that they have the most in common with one another, their coethnic affinity and affiliation are only partially their choice; coethnic ties also reflect broader ethnic and racial categorizations in society. The desire to be with those who are most similar to them pulls Korean Americans into ethnic fellowships, but their sense of marginalization and the feeling that they do not quite fit into white-dominant fellowships also pushes them toward this direction. For example, a Korean American student who had considered joining a white majority campus ministry prior to joining the Korean American Christian fellowship recalls, "When I got there [the white-majority campus ministry] this guy told me, 'We are starting an Asian thing that you can go to.'" This Korean American student was encouraged to attend the Asian American Christian fellowship rather than the white-majority campus fellowship because he was categorized as different, nonwhite, and more specifically as "Asian."[7] Furthermore, Asian American campus fellowships often pass out flyers advertising their gatherings to students who "look Asian."

Many second-generation Korean Americans are also tired of having to "deal with" racial insensitivity, stereotypes, prejudice, or even simple misunderstandings that other ethnic and racial groups in the broader society might have about Koreans and about those who "look Asian." Hence, being with other Korean Americans is a way to cope with the problems associated with marginalized group status. For instance, a Korean American student states:

> If you are with other Korean Americans, you are not going to be faulted for being Korean or looking Asian. You don't have to hear people say, "Do you speak ching chong?" "Do you guys eat dog?" "Why are your eyes so small?"

A first-generation Korean pastor from a second-generation Korean American campus ministry similarly remarks that Korean Americans and Asian Americans are frustrated over being treated as "strangers" and not "real" Americans in the larger society.

> To the first-generation, the second-generation say, "we are American" and act elite; but to whites … they are still strangers. Very few are just like whites … I am not talking about their professional status, but talking about their heart and deeper level of consciousness. They are not white. Although Americans say they are multicultural, there are still differences [among] blacks, whites, Asians … you can't deny it.

In an ethnically homogeneous setting, Korean Americans do not have to feel like strangers, foreigners, or second-class citizens because of their ethnicity, cultural background, or phenotype. Several Korean American pastors and staff leaders pointed out that being in an ethnically or racially homogeneous religious setting means that Korean American and other Asian American students are not burdened or hampered by racial stereotypes. Hence, both push and pull factors lead Korean Americans to establish and join ethnic campus fellowships.

Finally, students and pastors report that because it is "still all white at the top," ethnic campus ministries provide opportunities for leadership and growth that Korean American students may not otherwise have in a white-dominant campus ministry. As a pastor notes, "When I went to the headquarters [of one of the largest campus ministries in the U.S.] ... do you know what? It is still all white at the top. So if Asians want to move up in power, they can't do it over there."

Similarly, a Korean American staff member of a Korean American majority Asian American campus ministry explains:

> We are separate because whites welcome Asians, but not into leadership positions and they don't realize that by being status quo, they discriminate and make it hard for Asians to move up ... they are used to having leadership ... so if Asians start their own separate organizations, they are more able to take on leadership positions.

Thus, being in an ethnically homogeneous Korean American campus fellowship helps second-generation Korean Americans to escape the marginalization they sometimes experience in school and in the larger society, and also affords them leadership opportunities within religious organizations.

CONCLUSION

This case study of Korean American evangelicals suggests that second-generation Korean Americans, and Asian Americans for that matter, do not enjoy as many "ethnic" options as the children of European immigrants and cannot simply practice symbolic ethnicity like white Americans do. For second-generation Korean Americans, ethnicity is neither primordial (inherited from the first generation) nor assimilative (holding little meaning or consequence). Instead, the growth of ethnic evangelical fellowships reflects an "emergent ethnicity" that is made and remade in America—a product of second-generation Korean Americans' continued interaction with their ethnic community and the broader American society.[8]

The experience that Korean Americans obtain in ethnic evangelical organizations may be part of the long process of "growing up American." As second-generation Korean Americans graduate from college and enter the "real world," they are less likely to have as many opportunities to regularly associate with coethnics. Whether their ethnically oriented religious practices will continue to persist remains to be seen. However, given the marginalization of ethnic minorities, there is reason to believe that separate ethnic associations will remain even after college. Facilitating the growth of ethnic associations after college is the fact that most Korean Americans reside in cities where coethnics concentrate. Moreover, coethnic friendships established in college tend to form the nucleus of close social networks afterward, which explains, in part, the growth of ethnically based voluntary associations in major professions such as law, medicine, business, and academia. As long as ethnic groups feel a sense of marginalization, ethnic associations will persist, and ethnic ties will remain strong.

Notes

1. Multicultural theories regarding the salience of ethnic group boundaries also fall short in explaining this social phenomenon because ethnicity is still viewed largely as a working-class phenomenon; ethnicity is expected to be salient for those who are residentially and occupationally segregated and dependent on ethnic institutions for support (Conzen et al., 1992; Yancey et al., 1976). Multicultural accounts of ethnic retention also fall short because they fail to articulate precisely what the later generations are retaining, that is, how ethnicity may change for the later generation. Theories of racial formation and continuing racism (Omi and Winant, 1994) are helpful for explaining the salience of racial boundaries; but they do not address how distinct ethnic boundaries within particular racial groups may remain significant for the later generations.
2. Data were collected between 1999 and 2001. My methods consist of four main components: (1) historical research on the growing number of Asian American evangelicals and their organizations, using resources available through the Internet and organizations' directories; (2) participant observation in five types of campus evangelical organizations at a large diverse university campus (one first-generation Korean American, two second-generation Korean American, two Asian American, one multiracial, and one white-majority campus ministries), with a focus on the two second-generation Korean American campus ministries; (3) 100 personal interviews with the students as well as directors, staff, and pastors involved in campus evangelical organizations (50 were conducted with second- and 1.5-generation Korean Americans in Korean American campus ministries, 25 with second-generation Korean Americans as well as non-Korean Americans involved in pan-Asian, multiracial, or white majority campus ministries, and the remaining 25 with the pastors and staff members of the various campus ministries); and (4) data gathered from various informal conversations, focused group interviews, and an e-mail survey that I sent out to 30 members of the Association of College and University Religious Affairs (ACURA) regarding the growth of Asian American campus evangelical organizations. I also benefited from attending the annual conference of ACURA and having conversations with chaplains, deans, and organizational coordinators on various university campuses across the United States, regarding the growth of Asian American campus evangelical organizations.
3. "*Christianity Today* reports that InterVarsity's seventeenth triennial conference on missions, 'Urbana '93,' noticed a fundamental change in the makeup of the delegates, with nearly two-fifths of the 17,000 or so attendees ethnic minorities. Asian Americans represented over 25 percent of the conferees, and Korean Americans accounted for 'for nearly one out of ten attendees'" (Busto, 1996, p. 137).

4. The two preconditions required for separate ethnic associations include desire for community and changes in ethnic density that makes separate ethnic associations more possible. Like other college students, second-generation Korean Americans come on to the college campus in search of community and belonging. In this situation, they also find themselves in a setting with a high concentration of coethnics. As an Asian American student responded to the question of why there are so many Asian American campus evangelical organizations, "Why? . . . because there are just so many of us!" Thus, the preconditions to the growth of separate ethnic Christian fellowships for Korean Americans and other Asian Americans are students' desire for community interacting with changes in ethnic density, which make separate ethnic associations more possible.

5. Pearl Jam is an American "grunge" rock'n roll band.

6. Growing up in ethnic Korean churches also increases the probability of coethnic ties. Those who attend ethnic Korean churches are more likely than others to have social ties and having information that would lead them to other Korean campus ministries rather than to other multiracial or white-majority campus ministries.

7. White students themselves do not attend Asian American campus ministries because they presume that they will be categorized as distinct and an "outsider." As a white student recalled, "I checked out campus ministries, but I was always the only white person there . . . and I felt like everyone looked at me like what are you doing here? I felt alienated."

8. The term *emergent ethnicity* was originally coined by Yancey et al. (1976). My use of the term is distinct from that of Yancey at al. in that it is used to capture the salience of ethnicity among the children of contemporary immigrants, who are not residentially/occupational segregated and who do not need to depend on ethnic institutions for social or economic support as much as their parents do.

CHAPTER 16

Performing Race, Negotiating Identity:

Asian American Professional Actors in Hollywood

Nancy Wang Yuen

In acting, you can be hired for looks alone (particularly when you don't have to speak), and be hired largely on account of your physical "type".... Moreover, you can be rejected purely on the same grounds—you're the wrong race, sex, age, or size—grounds which, in almost any other field, would send the hiring officer to court.

Robert Cohen (1990: 24)

The key is to be able to really know the vehicles that work well for you. And a lot of Asian actors, they just are bent on doing these archetypes. If you're gonna do an archetype, do YOUR archetype, at least it'll be just that much more genuine. Greatest performances can come from that. But if you try to pound yourself into a mold, which Hollywood continues try to do with Asian Americans ... I mean is there a reason why we're not getting anywhere as a whole? Of course. Because everyone's getting pounded into the mold as opposed to saying, "screw it, I'm just gonna make my own mold."

Scott, an Asian American actor[1]

Hollywood,[2] the most influential entertainment conglomerate in the world, relies on conventions such as formulaic plots and typed characters. Howard Becker (1982: 46) points out that art forms designed to reach the maximum number of people in a society, such as film and television, take advantage of conventions in an established way. One consistent convention employed by Hollywood is the manufacture of characters based on racial and gender stereotypes, resulting in the frequent misrepresentation of racial and ethnic minorities. Consequently, professional actors of racial minorities—who often have to embody these stereotypes in order to secure roles—bear the responsibility of developing characters beyond the assigned stereotypes. This case study explores how Asian American professional actors interpret and negotiate the types of roles available to them and how they maximize occupational opportunities while pursuing nontraditional roles in Hollywood.[3] Through extensive ethnographic fieldwork in a Los Angeles-based Asian American theater group, the study uncovers how Asian American actors consciously and proactively embody, challenge, and redefine racially delimited roles within and outside of Hollywood.[4]

HOLLYWOOD AS INSTITUTION OF RACIALIZATION: THE UNMARKED SITE OF WHITE PRIVILEGE

Conventions such as character types help facilitate the production process by providing writers, producers, directors, actors, and the audience with a common set of simplified physical and behavioral traits. Berg (2002: 42) describes the maintenance of stereotypes as a narrative tool within the Hollywood industry:

> As a purely industrial practice, then, stereotypes are maintained because of their valued narrative economy, which is related to their financial economy as well. Because they require little or no introduction or explanation, and because they are so quickly and completely comprehended as signs, stereotypes are an extremely cheap and cost-effective means of telling a movie story.

In Hollywood, however, the typing of "race" (and arguably gender) does not manifest uniformly among all character types. As a classification system based on perceived physical features or phenotypes such as skin color, hair texture, body forms, and cultural or behavioral characteristics, race is utilized in the United States mainly to characterize nonwhite characters (Cornell and Hartmann, 1998; Fenton, 1999). Omi and Winant (1994) describe U.S. society as racially structured from top to bottom within which institutions "racialize," or infuse with racial meaning, people and groups. Arguably, Hollywood is an institution that racializes selected groups, utilizing race as "the marked term to designate 'black' or 'people of color,' while 'white' remains the unmarked site of privilege" (Kondo, 1997: 6).

The most discernible manifestation of this "unmarked site of privilege" is the ability of white actors to cross racial boundaries and portray characters of other races, black, Latino, American Indian, Asian, and the like. Racial minority actors, in contrast, are almost never allowed to portray "white" characters. Through the use of cosmetics such as blackface or yellowface, white actors have performed nonwhite roles in often demeaning and stereotypical ways (Bogle, 1989; Eng, 1999; Lee, 1999, 2000; Wong, 1979).

This practice continues primarily because white male writers, producers, directors, and actors dominate in Hollywood. Whites make up nearly 80 percent of feature film writers, 70 percent of television writers, and the majority of the industry's directors, producers, and executives (Gray, 1995; Hunt, 2002; Writers Guild of America, 1998). White actors dominate the number of hires in film, television, and commercials, occupying three-quarters of all roles, compared to African Americans at 14 percent, Latinos at 5 percent, and Asian Americans at less than 3 percent (Screen Actor's Guild, 2000). Moreover, in "lead" roles, which serve as a marker of quality, there is an even greater discrepancy between whites and nonwhites, particularly Asian Americans. In film, television, and commercials, whites portray 77.4 percent of all lead roles compared to Asian American actors who portray only 1.7 percent (Screen Actor's Guild, 2000). For Asian Americans, access to primary roles in film and television is extremely limited. In prime time television shows, for example, more than 60 percent of white recurring characters and 58 percent of black recurring characters are lead characters, while over 75 percent of Asian American recurring characters are *secondary* characters (*Children Now*, 2002).

The lack of diversity among the producers, writers, casting directors, and actors has contributed to the perpetuation of limited, stereotypical, and typecast representations of racial minorities. In the case of Asian Americans, Hollywood creates one-dimensional Asian characters rather than roles that are sensitive to the character's individuality, skill, ethnicity, and national origin (place of birth). In an interview, Scott, a Chinese American actor in his early thirties, describes how Hollywood castings gloss over the diversity of Asian American actors:

> The market has not evolved to sophistication where you can define everything. Asian is just Asian.... So Asian American guys, they tend to be lumped in a big pack ... Lump, good-looking Asian okay, martial art Asian okay, character Asian alright, okay, here you go, there's your three.[5]

Furthermore, Hollywood racializes Asian characters by imbuing them with various stereotypes that essentialize particular physical and behavioral traits as racial or gendered. Stereotyping tends to occur where there are gross inequalities of power in which dominant cultures represent marginal or foreign groups in a manner that presents these characters as "othered"— that is, not only as different from people in the dominant culture but also as less than completely human or civilized (Hall, 1997; Moy, 1993). Ji, a second-generation Korean American female actor and one of the founders of Essential Theatre, elaborates on how Hollywood characterizes Asian Americans as anything but "normal":

> Asian American actors are asked to be either below the normal person—incomprehensible, kind of dumb, or they're character-ized as really bright. So whether you're below human, or super human—like with karate—you're never considered as a normal human being; or you're never like accepted as such or appreciated as such.... It's racism.... Most of the roles, I mean, I rarely get an interesting role where I play a woman that's flawed, or a housewife that's flawed. Like I am either an assassin, a bad person who knows all these assassin tricks and martial arts, or I'm an Asian victim. I mean that's very common.[6]

The contradictory characterizations of "incomprehensible" and "really bright," "below human" and "super human," and "victim" and "assassin" illustrate the *binary structure* of stereotypes, toggling between two polar opposites or occurring simultaneously (Hall, 1997: 263). This binary structure maintains and reinforces the "otherness" of Asian characters (Hamamoto, 1994; Lee, 1999; Moy, 1993). The exoticization of Asian American women is a case in point. Asian American female actors often encounter a "victim"-"vixen" binary structure that combines racial and gender stereotypes to connote sexualized racial exoticism. Routine depic-tions of Asian women as wartime spoils, prostitutes, and madams simultaneously typecast Asian American female actors into exoticized roles and exclude them from lead roles often reserved for white women. Mya, a Korean American female actor with short spiky dyed platinum blond hair, has problems finding roles in film and television because she does not fit into any stereotype. She describes how her "Asian" face makes her "too Asian" to get cast as the "girl-next-door," which usually "casts white." However, her short blond hair makes her "not Asian enough" to get cast for current popular Asian exotic beauty roles, "like Tia Carrera who's all T and A [tits and ass], and dragon ladies like Lucy Liu." Such racially gendered stereotypes serve to limit the role quality and selection for Asian American female actors (Kondo, 1997; Marchetti, 1993; Xing, 1998).

Hollywood also stereotypes Asian characters as the "other" by conflating

U.S-born Asian Americans with foreign-born Asians, depicting them as foreign through particular signifiers such as accented speech (Tuan, 1998; Xing, 1998). Asian American actors are expected to speak English in "Asian" accents regardless of their English fluency and nativity status.[7] According to the actors whom I have interviewed, white executives (producers and casting directors and the like) almost never distinguish Asian Americans from foreign Asians in terms of characterization, and they almost never differentiate one Asian ethnic accent from another. Consequently, Asian American roles—however rare—are deemed "foreign" and are portrayed as such. Lily, a fourth-generation Japanese American actor, comments on a Japanese native who is cast in the lead role of a U.S.-born Japanese American character in *Snow Falling on Cedars*:

> [W]hat was kind of annoying about *Snow Falling on Cedars* was the woman who got cast was from Japan, . . . an up-and-coming Japanese actress. But she's not Japanese American, she's Japanese. She has an accent. The character is supposed to be born in America.[8]

Similarly, the "Asian" accent in English speech that is unique to a particular national-origin group may not be considered "authentic" if it deviates from the Hollywood-designated "Asian" accent. Spencer, an established Japanese American male actor in his early thirties, describes an audition in which the casting director conflates a Japanese with a Chinese accent:

> I remember going in for a role for a Japanese mafia guy and this lady [the casting director] wanted a Japanese accent. So I do this accent like Toshiro Mifune,[9] and she's like, "That's not it!" This forty-three year old Jewish woman is telling me, "Can you do it again and this time in a Japanese accent?" . . . So then on a whim, I start thinking, okay, everything funnels back to Chinese, so I start talking like I'm from Hong Kong, with a sort of Cantonese accent, and she goes, "THAT'S IT! That's the Japanese accent I'm looking for!"[10]

Ji also speaks about her experience performing roles with Korean, Chinese, Japanese, and Vietnamese accents without doing "justice to the original ethnic" speech accent because most people "can never tell" the difference. Even when writers, executives, and casting directors attempt to designate characters specific to Asian ethnicities (such as using surname signifiers), the attempts are often careless, arbitrary, and unverified. For example, Spencer discovers from his white producer—after many years of portraying an Asian character on a successful television series—that the fictional surname of his character ("Kim"—a popular Korean surname) does not match his character's intended ethnicity, which is Chinese.

As these accounts illustrate, Hollywood is both unable and unwilling to realistically represent Asians and Asian Americans. As a result, Hollywood intentionally and unintentionally churns out characters that fit into a racialized and gendered typecasting and, consequently, contributes to misrepresentation.

COPING WITH ADVERSITY ACTIVELY AND STRATEGIZING TO MAKE A CAREER IN CONTEMPORARY HOLLYWOOD

Hollywood creates Asian characters based on racial and gender stereotypes, resulting in a limited number of stereotyped roles for Asian American actors. In response to racialized or racially gendered characterizations, both veteran and aspiring Asian American actors strive to maximize their career opportunities through a variety of strategies.

Accepting Racialized and Racially Gendered Roles: Practicality and Ambivalence

One strategy is to accept available roles despite racialized and racially gendered limitations. Anne, an aspiring second-generation Chinese American actor, sees the practical implications of accepting racially gendered roles. Citing Lucy Liu's immense success as a typecast "dragon lady," Anne considers performing racially gendered roles a necessary part of the professional process for success. She views being typecast as getting a "foot in the door" and a chance to accumulate professional experience because Hollywood executives are not apt to take a chance to start off an actor completely new. Even though Anne, like many other Asian American actors, would prefer to play "normal" roles, such as the "girl-next-door," they are usually reserved for white female actors like "Sandra Bullock and Julia Roberts." Therefore, Anne willfully accepts stereotyped roles like the "vixen" or "dragon lady" and treats them as "stepping stones" to better roles. She explains: "So, typecasting, you've already beaten the system if you get typecast. And that just shows that you know your strengths, you know how to market yourself. So it really is a smart thing to do."[11]

Evidently, accepting stereotyped roles does not necessarily mean passively yielding to racial stereotyping. Anne and many others translate these opportunities into conscious attempts to get a foot in the Hollywood door. For example, many Asian American actors deliberately claim a pan-Asian ethnic identity or fabricate alternative Asian ethnic identities—exploiting the realization that whites cannot tell the difference among

Asian ethnics—in order to increase their chances for ethnicity-specific characters. Anne has played both Chinese and Japanese characters in film and theater and has known Asian American actors to invoke situational and even fictional and multiple ethnicities—"half Chinese and half Korean"—whenever necessary.

Unlike Anne, other Asian American actors feel more ambivalent about accepting racialized and racially gendered roles. For example, Ji, an actor with ten years of experience, politically opposes and is wary of perpetuating stereotypical images of Asian Americans on screen and on stage. However, she finds it difficult to pass on stereotyped roles when she has to "stay alive" professionally and financially. She remarks:

> Well, stereotypical-stereotyped characters don't have any dimension but the superficial thing. It's like wearing a mask, you might as well just wear a mask. I mean granted, as an artist, it's your responsibility to give humanity and depth to that character. But some of the pittance that they give you, that they write, is just so insulting ... there's so much pain that goes in when you have to take on that role.... It's a difficult choice when they give you a role that's, kind of, compromising. But at the same time, you have to stay alive. And you want to continue to act, or you just want to act. And there's always this moral side battling with the artistic side.[12]

"It Was Chinky, but It Was Completely Not": Condemning the Stereotype, Redeeming the Role

Most Asian American actors whom I have interviewed, even those who accept stereotyped roles as potential stepping-stones to stardom, do not view stereotyped roles favorably. In fact, despite recognizing the practical need to accept stereotyped characters for professional reasons, most actors simultaneously condemn the stereotyped characterizations and consciously redeem those roles through their acting. For example, Anne infuses the stereotyped roles she plays with qualities from the "girl-next-door" role she aspires to play. She describes how she alters a recurrent "vixen" character on a popular television daytime soap opera:

> I think they wanted [the role] vixenly. I don't know why they hired me then. But I can be flirty. So it was flirty. It was cute, flirty, bubbly, and so I did that, but I don't think it was vixen enough. I think they wanted a Lucy Liu.... I think they had an idea of what they wanted, and the dialogue that I was saying was just straight out, slut! And here I am this wholesome, this girl-next-door saying these slutty words. I don't think it worked.[13]

Even though Anne portrays a "vixenly" character, she changes it to reflect her "wholesome girl-next-door" personality. Instead of performing the character as a "vixen" with "slutty" dialogue, she performs the character as "cute, flirty, [and] bubbly." Even in her acceptance of racially gendered roles, Anne copes by altering the character to more closely resemble her ideal role.

Like Anne, Ji describes how she redeems a racially gendered character through her performance:

> When I took that massage parlor, young mother, ditched house-wife victim, it wasn't a very good representation of the Korean woman. It was one representation, but it wasn't a complete representation. And because Koreans, or Asians aren't seen very often on T.V., those rare cases when you do see their faces on T.V., that's how people are gonna judge us. And I didn't like that. But I gave it as much humanity as I could. And it actually turned out really, really well. Cause at the end of the show, my character got a lot of respect for being strong.[14]

Ji condemns the character of a "massage parlor, young mother, ditched housewife victim" as an incomplete representation of Koreans (and Asians more generally) that television viewers may "judge [Asians] by." The role connotes many stereotypical characteristics of Asian females such as exoticism and servitude. However, Ji does not allow the stereotyped characterization to deter her from trying to redeem the character through her performance. She bestows the character with as "much humanity as [she] could," countering the superficial exoticism. Furthermore, at the end of the show, the character gains "a lot of respect for being strong," reversing the characteristics of servitude and weakness. Within the confines of the role, Ji changes an Asian female stereotype of exoticism and weakness into humanity and strength through her performance. Ji's transformation of her character displays the ability of actors to challenge stereotypes within a limited context.

Like Ji, Scott also feels ambivalent about portraying a stereotyped character. Accordingly, he constructs an account that simultaneously condemns and redeems a "chinky" (derogatory depiction of the Chinese) role:

> I won't do anything that continues to feed the flames of Asian stereotype.... Though I have to say, if it's an equal opportunity offender movie, like a Howard Stern type of thing, oh hell yeah, I'll do it. I got hired last year to play like the sixth lead in movie X with famous comedic actors A, B, C, D, and E. And it was the chinkiest motherfucker on this planet. But I took chinky and took it way to

the top. And I come in my hair's like this long, I had it bobby-pinned and I came in. It was chinky, but it was completely not. It was the most denigrating thing you could do on this planet, in the traditional sense. But I looked at it, I was like, okay, I will do this because I'm playing opposite of [names of A, B, C, D, and E]. I think it's because I took it to a whole stratospheric level of, was this guy gay? Was he androgynous, was he hetero, was he sane?[15]

Even though the character is "the most denigrating thing" owing to its explicit stereotype, Scott accepts the role because of the professional opportunity to play opposite famous comedic actors. However, Scott reverses the stereotype through satire, layering multiple dimensions of gender, sexuality and ambiguity, something that he considers "completely not [chinky]."

"My Asian Accent Isn't Really an Asian Accent": Challenging and Resisting Stereotypes

Asian American actors who refuse to be pounded into a stereotypical mold often find it difficult to get through the Hollywood door. However, many persist in challenging and resisting stereotypes, with mixed strategies and mixed success. Mya's short, dyed platinum blond hair defies the expected phenotype of an exotic Asian woman with long black hair. Even though she seldom gets roles in film and television because she chooses not to conform to stereotypes, Mya has experienced moderate professional success in commercials. Recent studies show a higher number of Asian American castings in commercials than in film and television (Entman and Rojecki, 2000). My interviewees also report that commercials are more apt to feature racial and ethnic minority actors in nonracialized roles. Moreover, since commercials seem to be less weighty professionally compared to film and television castings, Asian American actors tend to use this space to challenge racialized expectations in commercial castings. Mya talks about her role in a beer commercial that casts against racially gendered expectations:

Like I went blond for a year, and that got me a lot of notice, and I remember a casting for Generic Beer. Apparently they had added like an "Asian" category, and every Asian chick there had hair down her back. . . . The casting description was casual . . . and so I just went in there in T shirt and jeans. These girls were made up, looking like the biggest freakin' hookers, tightest shirts you could possibly find . . . and I was the one who booked it—blond Asian girl with short hair . . . I think a lot of these girls think they have to be in this traditional category. Well how do you figure you're gonna stand out if everybody looks like that?[16]

In this case, Mya's non-Asian appearance—short blond hair and casual T-shirt and jeans—seems to have helped her stand out among her co-auditioners who conformed to the "traditional category" with "hair down their back" and the look of "freakin' hookers." By defying the expected racialized phenotypes and dress, Mya "stands out" from the crowd and successfully obtains the advertisement commercial role.

Some Asian American actors challenge not just racial/gender phenotypes but also behavioral stereotypes. As noted earlier, Hollywood racializes "Asian" characters as "foreign," through accents. Because most Hollywood executives have a perceived inability to differentiate between Asian ethnic accents, Asian American actors creatively subvert this signifier of "Asianness." For example, Scott develops an "Asian accent [that] isn't really an Asian accent" but manages to fulfill the expected Asian accent in Hollywood:

> And the thing about an Asian accent is my Asian accent isn't really an Asian accent, it's just this hybrid weird thing. But the funny thing is, what's great about it is, they can't tell the difference.... My thing is like this mishmash of like Hong Kong British, American slang thing. The reason I do it is because it's technically not really an Asian accent, yet the whole room of white people laugh to death ... cuz you're fulfilling an expectation.

When I asked Scott where he came up with that particular accent, he replied:

> I had to find an accent that could really work, doing full-bore comedy on the stage, which meant a type of accent that could complement the English vernacular.... If you really want to be able to play with people like Billy Crystal, Martin Lawrence, or Mike Myers ... the English language with an Asian accent traditionally cannot facilitate that ... it's very stunted.[17]

Rather than speaking with an authentic Asian accent that will stunt his ability to perform "full-bore comedy," Scott creates an accent that is a "mishmash of like Hong Kong British, American slang thing" that complements his natural speech pattern, the "English vernacular." His invented accent serves to fulfill the expectations of a "whole room of white people" by making them "laugh to death." In essence, Scott cleverly invents an accent that facilitates his comedic performance while fulfilling an expectation. By exploiting the inability of whites to distinguish the difference between an Asian accent and an invented hybrid accent, Scott challenges the usage of the foreign "Asian" accent as a racial signifier of Asianness.

Although Scott succeeds in subverting the Asian accent, he does so within Hollywood's conventions. John, a third-generation Chinese American veteran actor with a repertoire of accents ranging from "Chinese," "Filipino," "Latino," to "Southern," attempts to transcend the stereotypical Asian accent by performing an Asian guest star role on an all-white sitcom set in the U.S. South with a southern drawl. He recalls:

> I played an Asian—kind of a selling, improve yourself kind of— [guy]. But I did him without an accent. You know what was funny, she [the lead actor] was on the set. She came in late, and I was working with the director, and I hadn't met her yet. So I decided to make him [the character] with a southern accent and the director liked it. She came in and said, "No don't do that, I don't like that." She didn't want to be upstaged.[18]

As a signifier of race, the Asian accent is often expected for Asian-specific characters. Therefore, John's portrait of an "Asian" character speaking with a southern drawl challenges both the affiliation of Asian accents with Asians as well as the nonaffiliation of southern accents with Asians. Hence, John's performance of his dialogue with an effective southern accent creates a mismatch of expected racial signifier to performer, which may, in turn, shock viewers. Consequently, because the lead actor fears being "upstaged" by the shock element of his performance, she denies John the opportunity to perform with a southern drawl. This denial reveals the persistence and dominance of such racialized conventions in Hollywood. Despite the defeat, John is able to perform the character with *no* accent, thereby successfully challenging the Asian accent as a racial signifier. While Hollywood may limit the role options of Asian American actors, these actors actively cope by developing myriad work strategies that simultaneously accept, subvert, and challenge racialized and racially gendered expectations.

CREATING A SPACE OF THEIR OWN: CROSSOVER ROLES IN ETHNIC AND MULTICULTURAL THEATERS

On the road to Hollywood, Asian American actors also actively redefine external impositions of racialized and racially gendered characterizations through the pursuit of crossover roles.[19] However, nonracialized crossover roles are rare in Hollywood and are limited to minor roles in film and television or roles in commercials. Even in multiethnic castings where such crossover roles are available, racial categories are often inescapable and salient. For example, Frank, a biracial actor with an Anglo surname, has played characters in film and television originally written as non-Asian characters with non-Asian surnames. Sometimes the surnames are not altered, giving Frank opportunities to portray characters with non-Asian surnames. However, other times, the surnames are altered to "Asian" surnames in order to match his "Asian" face. In other words, despite his own Anglo surname, his self-defined "all-American" look, that is, athletic build and tall stature of 6'1," producers and casting agents frequently box him into an "Asian" character because of his dark hair and almond-shaped eyes.

In response to Hollywood's racialization of Asian characters and the consequent limited crossover opportunities, many Asian American actors etch out alternative spaces in ethnic and multicultural theaters (Kondo, 2000; Kurahashi, 1998; Lee, 1997; Pao, 2000, 2001). Not subject to the same constraints as the profit-driven entertainment industry in Hollywood and many mainstream theaters, ethnic theaters purposefully cast against Holly-wood convention, creating opportunities for racial and ethnic minority actors to portray crossover roles. For example, Essential Theatre, founded in 1999, is a self-defined "Asian American" theater ensemble composed of a group of aspiring and politically conscious Asian American artists, including actors, writers, directors, and producers. The theater group aims to create a professional and political haven for Asian American artists. Professionally, Essential Theatre provides a forum for Asian American artists to participate in all aspects of the theater, including performing crossover roles and expanding their creative autonomy by taking on roles as producers, directors, writers, and technical workers. Politically, Essen-tial Theatre seeks to challenge the one-dimensional and misrepresented stereotypical images of Asian Americans often portrayed by Hollywood and the mass media. By recasting Asian American actors in nonstereo-typed, crossover roles, Essential Theatre allows actors to break out of the mold and perform to their full potential. Anne compares the lead role she portrays in *Neighborhood,* one of Essential Theatre's mainstage plays, to her "vixen" soap opera role on television:

> I really enjoyed playing the female lead of *Neighborhood* only because I loved who my character was. . . . She was finding a sense of normalcy for herself. . . . I've played like the vixen . . . on TV, but those aren't like so complex or deep or anything like that. So I get kind of bored with it.[20]

In contrast to the stereotyped roles thrust upon Asian American actors in Hollywood, most of the roles in Essential Theatre are "normal," sophis-ticated, and multifaceted. Anne contrasts her enjoyment of playing a "complex" character who finds "a sense of normalcy" with her boredom with the television "vixen" role that lacks depth. Essential Theatre serves as a venue for Asian American actors like Anne to portray nonracialized lead roles that are nearly absent in Hollywood.

Essential Theatre also creates opportunities for Asian American actors to portray cross-racial characters. Young, a Korean American in his mid-twenties, who speaks both Spanish and English fluently, plays the part of Juan, the Mexican gardener in *Neighborhood*. An excerpt from my field notes recounts the predominantly Asian American audience's reaction to Young's first half-English, half-Spanish words on stage:

> Young appears on stage in denim overalls. With a small garden shovel in his hand, he begins to "garden" by tapping around flower beds on stage. When a white actor in khakis and a short-sleeved dress shirt comes on stage, Young rises, puffs his chest out, and, in a loud and exaggeratedly cheerful tone, shouts: "Good morning Mister Tim, Buenos Dias Meeester Teeeem!" Young elicits a roar of laughter from the audience composed of predominantly Asian Americans.[21]

The combination of perfect English and Spanish in Young's portrait challenges racialized representations of Asians in the United States as speaking English with Asian accents or only speaking Asian languages. Furthermore, this cross-racial portrayal challenges the use of accents and physical appearance as racial signifiers of "Asian" and "Latino." Young mixes up the conventional associations with these racial/ethnic groups, thereby rendering such signifiers arbitrary. Essential Theatre provides actors such as Young the opportunity to portray a character that crosses racial boundaries and moreover, offers the Asian American community the opportunity to witness a crossover portrait rarely seen in mainstream Hollywood.

Although Hollywood may discourage the use of southern drawls by Asian American actors due to a mismatch in conventional racial signifiers, Essential Theatre freely employs such signifiers in their productions, challenging their non-Asian associations. Essential Theatre's *Judgment Day* is a case in point. This surreal contemporary play challenges racial signifiers through the performances of characters with non-Asian surnames, southern drawls, and country western costumes, by Asian American actors. John, the veteran actor who could not perform his television guest star role with a southern accent, describes not having to "think about race" while playing the lead role of "Mac Winston" in *Judgment Day*. The following field note excerpt describes the crossover performances of the all-Asian American cast:

> As Mac Winston, played by John Lee, walks onto the stage, many actors dressed in jeans, flannel shirts, donning cowboy hats with bandanas tied around their necks arise, zombie-like, from behind stacked crates. Cigarettes in hand, coughing and crawling slowly on the floors, they speak soporifically, with southern drawls,

seemingly enveloped by the surreal smoky country-western setting and the occasional twang of a banjo.[22]

The western setting, a symbol of the frontier and "America," often excludes Asian Americans who are typically affiliated with foreignness. By casting an all Asian American cast to portray a western scene, using southern drawls and donning "jeans, flannel shirts" and "cowboy hats," Essential Theatre effectively challenges the prevailing image of Asian Americans as foreign.

In addition to ethnic theaters such as Essential Theatre, multicultural theaters also act as alternative spaces for actors to perform crossover roles. Some multicultural theaters employ "conceptual casting," or purposeful casting of a nonwhite actor in a cross-racial, and/or cross-gender lead role to give the play greater resonance (Pao, 2000). Multicultural theaters do not ignore an actor's race and gender, but utilize them to subvert and challenge conventions. James, a Korean American actor with extensive classical theater training in Europe, describes a play in which he portrays the "first Korean-American-Jewish-intellectual-New Yorker." The director purposefully challenges racial expectations through his clever staging of James's entrance. James recalls:

> The first image [of my character] is at this funeral, with me with a yarmulke on my head. Head down, the first light cue happens and looks at my face and people were like [James widens his eyes, raises his eyebrows, opens his mouth wide, and lets out a slight gasp].... The only Asian girl I saw that entire time was this girl who saw the play—called me and asked if she could take me out to lunch.... She was so moved. She said she'd never seen an Asian person doing a major role on stage or screen before and she just had this look in her eyes, I'd never forget it, she was like, "Please, whatever you do, do not take any stereotypical parts."[23]

In this conceptually cast role, James challenges racial expectations by contradicting and challenging the phenotype of a "Jewish" man. The audible shock of the audience upon seeing James's face rising from beneath a yarmulke is likely the director's desired effect. The reaction of the Asian American woman in the audience, however, is less shock and more emotion. The woman is "moved" at seeing a "major" nonstereotypical role played by an Asian American actor. In multicultural theaters, actors have greater access to opportunities to portray crossover lead roles usually reserved for whites. Consequently, multicultural theaters challenge stereotyped expectations and create varied effects upon audiences depending partly on their group affiliation.[24]

Some multicultural theater productions cast actors in cross-racial and cross-gender parts. While such productions may utilize racial and gender differences conceptually, they do so in a critical manner that requires audiences to completely suspend conventional categories of race and gender. Mya describes her cross-racial, cross-gender portrayal of Shakespeare's Hamlet in a multicultural, multiracial production:

> I got to play Hamlet. But that's because the director was very open-minded, and it was a woman and she did cross-gender and cross-cultural casting. . . . Guildenstern and Rosencrantz, they were women. . . . The king was black, where the queen was white. So it was a wonderful opportunity for a lot of people who wouldn't get to do these roles. What was great was that I quickly became noticed so that I was able to do leads in the productions. So that gave me a great opportunity to exercise my acting skills. . . . So I've been fortunate overall with the kind of roles that I've played. And I like to stay with what I've done. I've no interest in doing a dragon lady.[25]

Mya regards this multicultural production of *Hamlet* as affording "a lot of people who wouldn't get to do these roles" a "wonderful opportunity," since such opportunities for nonwhite actors to cross over racial *and* gender boundaries are extremely rare in Hollywood. Crossover roles provide actors with professional training during which actors can exercise, develop, and receive attention for their talents. By playing Hamlet, Mya describes how she "quickly became noticed" because of the "great opportunity to exercise [her] acting skills." Therefore, in order to avoid portraying stereotyped parts like the "dragon lady," actors like Mya seek out opportunities to portray crossover roles in multicultural theaters. By participating in ethnic and multicultural theater groups, Asian American actors carve out alternative professional spaces to challenge conventional categories of race and gender.

CONCLUSION

As a major distributor of the mass media, Hollywood helps to create and perpetuate stereotypical images of Asian Americans. More specifically, Hollywood racializes Asian American actors by lumping distinct ethnicities into a single racial category and pounding them into particular molds with racial signifiers such as phenotypes, accents, and distorted behavior characteristics. In response, Asian American actors actively work behind the scenes to contest the racialized and racially gendered stereotypes through various performative and coping strategies. The study reveals the Asian

American actors' conscious attempts to challenge and resist phenotypical, verbal, and behavioral stereotypes. Asian American actors are not inanimate puppets, but agents who actively negotiate Hollywood categorizations and perform race to assert an Asian American identity into mainstream American culture.

Despite the agency displayed by Asian American actors, institutional constraints continue to limit Asian Americans' abilities to drastically change racialized and racially gendered stereotypes. In other words, although Asian American actors may successfully alter characterizations, they can do so only within the established conventions. As a result, regardless of their ability as individuals to challenge such classifications through the development and employment of varied work strategies, Asian American actors still face enormous barriers and are far from overcoming Hollywood's system of racialization. Precisely because of these obstacles, Asian American and other nonwhite actors establish ethnic and multicultural theaters, creating professional and political spaces that cultivate opportunities for crossover roles and alternative representations of people of color.

Since the majority of American consumers of film, television, and theater are non-Asians, the portrayals of Asian Americans in the visual media have a direct effect on how viewers, particularly those with little direct contact with Asian Americans, perceive Asian Americans as a group. Recent studies show that viewers draw from both real world examples and stereotyped characterizations from the media to represent groups to which they belong, but use stereotyped characterizations from the media to "represent groups to which they do not belong and about which they therefore know less" (Entman and Rojecki, 2000: 146). With the widespread global consumption of film and television products, Hollywood plays a potential role in shaping understandings of race both within and beyond the United States. Consequently, Asian American actors and other nonwhite actors increasingly attempt to subvert and contest Hollywood's racialized representations from within and outside of the Hollywood system. In short, representations are neither fixed nor reflective of the "real" world, but instead, are professionally and performatively negotiable, and hence, socially constructed.

Notes

1. Face-to-face interview with Scott by author on November 28, 2001, in Los Angeles
2. I utilize "Hollywood" to describe the Los Angeles-based commercial conglomerate of film, television, and advertisement commercial production studios and all of its affiliate institutions.
3. Nontraditional roles refer to "the casting of ethnic, female, or disabled actors in roles where race, ethnicity or physical capability are not necessarily to the characters' or play's development" (Pao, 2001: 391).
4. I conducted participant observation at Essential Theatre for a period of eight months (December 2000 to August 2001). I attended meetings, auditions, rehearsals, and socialized

with members, most of whom had East Asian (Chinese, Japanese, or Korean) ancestry, were between the ages of 18 and 40, and were born or raised in the United States. I also conducted in-depth, face-to-face interviews lasting two to three hours with eight male actors, one writer, and five female actors. All names, including Essential Theatre, have been altered to preserve anonymity. Because most of the respondents were part of an all-Asian-American theater group, the sampling was nonrandom.

5. Face-to-face interview with Scott.

6. Face-to-face interview with Ji by author on May 12, 2001, in Los Angeles.

7. Asian Americans have an extremely high foreign language attrition rate; for more detail, see Chapter 1 in this volume.

8. Face-to-face interview with Lily by author on August 29, 2001, in Los Angeles. *Snow Falling on Cedar* is a Universal Studios feature film based on David Guterson's award-winning novel published by Vintage in 1995.

9. Toshiro Mifune is a famous Japanese actor who starred in many films by Akira Kurosawa, including *Seven Samurai* (1954).

10. Face-to-face interview with Spencer by author on July 11, 2002, in Los Angeles.

11. Face-to-face interview with Anne by author on May 26, 2001, in Los Angeles.

12. Face-to-face interview with Ji.

13. Face-to-face interview with Anne.

14. Face-to-face interview with Ji.

15. Face-to-face interview with Scott.

16. Face-to-face interview with Mya by author on October 25, 2001, in Los Angeles.

17. Face-to-face interview with Scott.

18. Face-to-face interview with John by author on October 30, 2001, in Los Angeles.

19. In this study, I define *crossover* as those cross-racial roles in which the actor is cast in a role whose perceived race/ethnicity differs from the actual race/ethnicity of the actor, and cross-gender roles in which the actor is cast in a role whose perceived gender differs from that of the actor.

20. Face-to-face interview with Anne.

21. Author field notes taken on May 5, 2001, while being an audience in theater.

22. Author field notes taken in November 2001 while being an audience in theater.

23. Face-to-face interview with James by author on July 20, 2001, in Los Angeles.

24. In this case, the Asian American in the audience, as an in-group member, reads James's performance differently from out-group audiences. Richard Dyer (1986) describes how audiences of different racial groups, such as blacks and whites, may "read" performances by a black performer differently.

25. Face-to-face interview with Mya.

CHAPTER 17

Searching for Home:

Voices of Gay Asian American Youth in West Hollywood[1]

Mark Tristan Ng

I'm comfortable being there, but I don't like being there. I have
nothing to relate to. Other than the fact that I'm gay, everything
else about me is different. Everything about me doesn't fit it. I just
don't relate. I don't feel safe to be different.

Nam, a 25-year-old Vietnamese
Asian American community activist, 1.5 generation[2]

Before being "gay," I was very proud of my Pilipino heritage. I
showed this by the way I'd dress, the jewelry I'd wear. When I first
started going to West Hollywood, not that I was denying my Pinoy
identity, but I was not as showy with it. I didn't wear any trinkets
or anything that showed my (racial) identity. I wanted to fit in.

Rommel, a 22-year-old Pilipino
Asian American community activist, second generation[3]

Paralleling ethnic enclaves, queer enclaves have become increasingly visible
in America's urban landscape. In recent years, some vibrant urban neighborhoods, such as the Castro District in San Francisco and West Hollywood
(WeHo) in Los Angeles, have been established as distinctly queer places.
Much in the same manner that ethnic enclaves such as "Chinatown,"
"Little Tokyo," "Manilatown," and "Little Saigon," defy the classical notion
of a singular American culture, queer places shatter the myth of a universal
sexuality (Reyes, 1996). Indeed, these places have become "home" to queer

Americans. On any given evening, a visitor to any of the hotspots in West Hollywood, such as the Abbey Coffeehouse or Rage Dance Club, will inevitably witness the increase in racial minority men, particularly young Asian American men. The visibility of Asian American gay men, coupled with the emergence of Asian-themed dance clubs (such as Buddha Lounge and Red Dragon) and the growing demand for gay Asian males in personal ads, have perpetuated the myth that West Hollywood is now a "safe space" free of racialization and marginalization pervasive in the larger society.

Is the changing demographic scene of West Hollywood a sign of a community in transformation? Is the "blue-blond-and-buff" paradigm finally reshifting to be more inclusive of the "other"? By virtue of their sexuality, do gay Asian Americans inherently have a space free of racial constraints within West Hollywood? The general assumption that any gay man, regardless of race, would feel safe, comfortable, and at home in a place like West Hollywood may be elusive. I argue that particular physical sites for gay men are important markers upon which social and power relationships are reproduced and that the sense of belonging and community varies by race, even within identifiable queer places.

This chapter examines the issue of "searching for home" among gay Asian American youth. More specifically, it focuses on the social spaces of interaction within West Hollywood and on how these physical sites have become the playground, meeting ground, training ground, and battleground for individuals who identify themselves as gay and strive to establish safe havens for themselves. This chapter considers how gay Asian Americans negotiate identity, confront racialization, and contest marginalization in the complex process of community building. By listening to the voices of the youth though intensive face-to-face interviews, it is possible to critically examine the underlying dialogue and power relationships at two major places of the gay culture—dance clubs and personal ads. With a nonintrusive eye, we can therefore observe gay male interactions and cultural politics at Asian-themed dance clubs. In addition, we analyze the contents of personal advertisements published in gay magazines and West Hollywood's local community newspapers.

GRAPPLING WITH THE COMPARTMENTALIZED SELF

Gay Asian American youth often find themselves leading double lives—the racial versus the sexual. Many live in silence and secrecy, and often find themselves in situations where they are forced to compromise the multiplicity of their identities. Their invisibility and compartmentalized self raise pressing issues. How are queers recognized in Asian American contexts? How are Asian Americans recognized in queer contexts? Must multiple identities be dichotomized into the racial and the sexual, or can they be realized in full harmony with each other? The Asian American does not want to face the queer within himself, and the queer does not want to face the colored within himself. Thus, gay Asian Americans confront the difficulty of affirming a seemingly contradictory identity that has been negated, or simply exists in a space of absence. Such confrontation in this realm of the "borderlands" inevitably begs the question of allegiance (Anzaldua, 1987).

Am I Asian American?

The myth of Asian Americans as a homogeneous and heterosexual (even asexual) "model minority" since the 1960s has worked against the varied nature of sex and gender. Diversity in sexuality is irrelevant or ignored (Leong, 1996). As the "model minority," Asian Americans are expected to conform to and practice the norms and values upheld in mainstream American culture: individualism, self-reliance, hard work, delayed gratification, and discipline, as well as heterosexuality and the married-couple family. In a sense, the model minority myth prescribes a compulsory heterosexuality that does not recognize Asian Americans in any other sexual context except straight. So what now of the queens, the bull dykes, the baklas, the tomboys, the fist-fuckers, the transvestites, and the queers who are undoubtedly Asian American? Invisibility.

Am I Queer?

Within the broader queer community in the United States, racial and ethnic identities are presumed to be subordinated to sexuality and are thus rendered inconsequential, as is evident in most North American studies on sexuality and gender that have largely excluded racial minorities and same-sex sexuality in their analyses and discussions. As a result, the racial/ethnic "other" is reproduced within the context of the sexual "other." Asian Americans who are gender nonconformists are only partially accepted in the broader queer community as tokens of inclusion and remain largely invisible (Leong, 1996). So what now of the Pilipino, the Chinese, the Vietnamese, the Hmong, the Korean, the Japanese, and the Samoans who are undoubtedly queer? Silenced.

Many of the informants interviewed for this study express frustration, difficulty, and strain in attempting to grapple with the compartmentalized self, acknowledging that it is often a question of choosing one or the other. If they choose to root themselves in an Asian American context, they are expected to be straight. If they choose to locate themselves in a gay environment, they are expected to "act white." For instance, Jason, a 24-year-old, 1.5-generation, Pilipino American banker succinctly reflects on this point:

> Being a gay Asian is hard. West Hollywood itself is very white-oriented and it's not really welcoming to Asian crowds. But I'd rather go there than to Legend or 21XL parties [straight Asian clubs] because I ain't even trying to be straight. I don't know . . . it's just hard.[4]

Again, the question remains. Who are gay Asian Americans? Where do they belong? As Eric Reyes (1996: 87) proposes, "[C]onsider which you really want—rice queen fantasies at your bookstore or freedom rings at the checkout stand outside your local Asian market?" Finding the correct answer to either question is nearly impossible unless one learns how to recontextualize the frames of references and how to readjust the lenses through which one has been socialized to view and deal with "complexities." Normative socialization has taught Asian American youth to view every aspect of human experiences in a linear way along a bipolar spectrum—that one can only be either male or female, gay or straight . . . Asian or queer. This linear thinking freezes categories and leaves no room to deal with outer boundaries and borderlands. In reality, Asian Americans have to constantly contextualize and negotiate their multiple identities. As Nam puts it: "I think you can look at comfortability from two different aspects. In terms of my gay identity, I do feel comfortable in West Hollywood. But if we take it in terms of my Asian identity, I don't think I'd ever go to West Hollywood."[5]

DRAGONS AND LANTERNS AND LIGHTS: OH MY!

The emergence of Asian-themed dance clubs, such as Buddha Lounge and Red Dragon, is a recent phenomenon in West Hollywood's gay enclave. Buddha Lounge is the only Asian-themed club located on the West Hollywood Strip, and its prime location enhances its popularity. Red Dragon stands as the largest gay Asian-themed dance club in the United States. The dance club provides thousands of gay Asian men, and their admirers, an "alternative" location to party outside of the main West Hollywood strip. Many Asian American gay men flock to Buddha Lounge every Thursday night and to Red Dragon every second Saturday of the month to party, network, and escape the confines of "straight" reality. For many Asian American gay men, the mere existence of these Asian-themed clubs affirms the formation of a genuine space called "home." As Jason remarks:

> I feel more comfortable in Asian clubs. Maybe because I fit in more or something. I don't feel like I stand out there. When I would go to the Abbey [an Anglo dance club] I would have fun and every-

thing, but I always felt like I stood out. People looked at me like I didn't belong there.[6]

Ray, an 18-year-old first-generation Chinese American student echoes Jason's sentiment: "Yeah, I didn't really feel comfortable around a big group of white people bumpin' into me with no rhythm. I'm much more comfortable here [an Asian dance club] with my brothers."[7]

Asian-themed dance clubs are popular among gay Asian American youth, and they undoubtedly serve as a comfortable place where Asian Americans feel "normal" and "like everyone else" rather than like a stranger or outsider. However, the question remains, do they foster a sense of community? Before tackling this question, one needs to ask for whom these clubs exist—for Asian Americans in particular, gay men in general, or for some other purpose? Much in the same manner in which thriving ethnic businesses in Chinatowns, Little Tokyos, and Little Saigons make the ethnic enclaves novelties or exotic lands within mainstream society and popular culture, similar dynamics occur in the establishment of Asian-themed dance clubs in the context of the larger gay community. Although white Americans may exoticize vibrant ethnic enclaves as a place to frequent for fun and entertainment, they remain marginal to the mainstream society, even though they constitute an inseparable part of American life. Thus, going "there" while remaining "here" is not so much melting as sustaining identifiable boundaries. Within the larger context of West Hollywood, one finds pockets of "color," ethnic-theming that can superficially be translated into the creation of more inclusive "safe spaces" within an increasingly "color-blind" community.

One must, however, be mindful of the broader social and power dynamics of the white hegemony that gets reproduced and played out within these pocket places that are seemingly homey. Ray, who feels comfortable hanging out with Asian brothers at the Asian-themed club, is also critical of these clubs:

> I think it's far from being a true safe space for us. It's just more of a presence. Club promoters want to start new Asian clubs because they're doing so well right now. But even with these places, it's not really a sign of our integration into WeHo. Even Buddha Lounge is not really indicative of any major change in the greater gay community ... it's more of an extension of it.[8]

Ray points to a fundamental difference between a physical space in which Asian Americans can hang out with ease, comfort, and anonymity and a social space in which they can identify as home and feel a sense of belonging.

West Hollywood's Asian-themed dance clubs are mostly owned by non-Asians, and owners intentionally ethnicize their clubs as exotic lands with an eye on profit making rather than on community building for gay Asian Americans. The popularity of Asian-themed clubs reflects a long-standing invention and exploitation of Orientalism for the fetishization and enjoyment of the largely gay white community. According to Edward Said (1995: 87), the Orient is "almost a European invention, and has been since antiquity a place of romance, exotic beings, haunting memories and landscapes, remarkable experiences." Said argues that the *Oriental* has become one of the most recurring images of the *Other* and has helped to define Europe (or the West) in the sense that it sets up a contrasting frame of reference— image, idea, personality, and experience—against which cultural and value judgments are to be made. In other words, Orientalism gives European culture its strength and identity by setting itself off against the Oriental Other. Because it is European culture that has managed and produced the political, social, and ideological nature of "the Orient," Orientalism has become a Western hegemony that dominates, restructures, and controls the entire region of the Orient.

In applying Said's theory of Orientalism, the rise of Asian-themed dance clubs can be seen as the modern materialization of Orientalism in that they give gay white America a hegemonic frame of reference based on the conception of "the Other" while reaping monetary benefits from exploiting exoticized Oriental objects. For the "rice queens" (white men who have an exoticized preference for Asian men) who frequent these clubs, the space was created for their enjoyment (Manalansan, 1994). Gay white men frequent Asian-themed clubs to seek out their exotic objects of desire, which effectively reaffirms the privilege of whiteness and reproduces the hegemonic race relations between whites and the other, namely, racial minorities. Many of the respondents concur with this sentiment, as Nam comments:

> Buddha Lounge is run by a Latino guy who has a preference for Asians. So therefore, it's decked out in "Oriental" garb: rice lanterns, Buddhas, red tassels, fake jade amulets, and red lights. Red lights seem to be a very popular thing as far as what they consider "Oriental." This guy [the manager] probably has not the slightest clue as to what the whole Asian American community is about . . . just what he sees at a Chinese restaurant.[9]

Rio, a 20-year-old first-generation Pilipino American artist adds: "The promoters of these clubs are not Asian American. I see their website and they're totally exploiting Asians. They reinforce this whole Asian passive-submissive thing. I wish more clubs exist where Asians are really in control."[10]

Asian-themed dance clubs serve as important sites of gay culture and as relatively comfortable places for gay Asian American youth to hang out, have fun, and socialize with one another. Yet they are just little more than modern materializations of Orientalism. Hence, these sites are not safe "spaces" for the gay Asian American community. Rather, they are exoticized playgrounds where gay white men can realize their Orientalized fantasies. Even within the general gay enclave in West Hollywood, gay Asian American youth are often aware of their treatment as outsiders. For instance, Frank, a 22-year-old second-generation Korean American dancer, recalled a time when a group of his friends (who happen to be Asian) were walking on the streets of West Hollywood. They ran into a group of young white men who just stared at them and sneered out loud, "Look at those Asians." Rio also recalled a certain time period in the late 1990s when Asian Americans were not welcome in certain dance and sex clubs in West Hollywood because they were considered "just not as popular [as whites]."

PERSONAL ADVERTISEMENTS IN THE ECONOMY OF DESIRE: THE DOMINANT VERSUS THE SUBMISSIVE

Parallel to the club scene, personal ads in gay magazines and local newspapers are other important sites within gay culture that transcend geographical boundaries. They offer a unique place where gay Americans are able to claim both a hidden and an openly gay identity. Despite the stereotypical perception of personal ads as nothing more than a place for the "single and desperate," these sites allow gay men to depart from the more "traditional" ways of meeting other males and to indirectly dialogue with each other about the gay culture and same-sex desire. Personal ads are places of fantasy—places where the relegation of same-sex desire as deviant, abnormal, and taboo is negated and its inverse affirmed.

The economy of desire and the articulation of pleasure mirror the established racial hierarchy of the mainstream society. Because gay white males control the value and currency of this economy, they occupy the dominant and privileged position as the active agents determining and dictating who and what is desirable, how much value there is in an object, and how to pursue that desire. This reality sets up an economy of the gay culture where the sexual identity of Asian males is strongly informed by the white sexual identity and is subordinated to white sexual needs. According to the informants, the only role that gay Asian American men are expected to play in this economy is the stereotypical role of the submissive, exotic, and passive commodified sexual being, much like the way Asian women are depicted in mainstream society. Frank and Ray's comments shed some light on this point. As Frank remarks: "In any picture of an Asian man, the only thing you'll see is his butt. Even the Asian go-go dancers are expected to show off their butts. We're perceived as bottoms, as submissive ... that's what they want us to be."[10] Ray adds:

> Asian men are viewed as asexual, submissive ... not quite as "manly" as White, Black, and Latino men are seen. A lot of the stereotypes projected onto Asian women in straight society are projected to Asian men in gay society. There's definitely a lot of preconceived notions of what and who you're supposed to be.[12]

A close content analysis of personal ads reveals evidence of racialization and marginalization of gay Asian American men. Two popular gay magazines are *Edge Magazine* and *Frontiers Newsmagazine*.[13] In both, an overwhelming number of ads in the personal ads section are generally placed by those desperately seeking gay Asian males (GAMs) or simply "any Asians." The examples selected here are from two categories: those seeking GAMs and those placed by GAMs. The following are selective ads placed by those seeking GAMs:

> For Asians! Very good looking German escort 24 blonde/blue 5'11" 150#, nice smooth chest, friendly playful personality. Jason. Beverly Hills. In/Out

> R*U*VIETNAMESE If so, I am offering $40 sale on a full body massage! White 26 yo & very cute. M–F 4pm out. Call Rob

> *FOR ASIAN MEN* Sensual W/M 6' 170# w/deep blue eyes gives erotic rub

> FREE MASSAGE FOR ASIAN GWM 38 offers free full body massage for a slim Asian 18–32. I'm kind, gentle and discreet & HIV–. No strings attached! Just be nice and clean. Lay back and enjoy!

> I LUV JAPANESE/AMERICAN (mixed heritage guys). U are in shape to 35, romantic, masculine but playful, cuddly, not moody! I'm 46, Tall bear type, brd, gut, GDLK. Very oral. Luv to give/get massage, spontaneous lovemaking

> ASIANS ONLY! HOT WHITE GUY IN s. Bay. 25 brn/blu grt bod.

> FOR ASIANS ONLY 47 wm 150 HOT VGL Asian 25–38 for fun and more and romance. Me 6'1", hairy chest, grn eyes, 195 lbs, good shape professional

> FOR ASIANS very goodlooking masseur, 24, blonde/blue 5'11", table and fine oils

> *ALL ASIANS* WM 30 5'8" 160# friendly, sexy & nude!

By browsing through these selective ads, one can see the general demand for GAMs. Bold headings such as "FOR ASIANS!" "*FOR ASIAN MEN*," "ASIANS ONLY!" "*ALL ASIANS*" may be viewed as indicators of a growing appreciation, and perhaps acceptance, of the gay Asian American man in the larger gay community. Rommel reflects on the sudden popularity of Asian men:

> As of lately, there has been an increasing and overwhelming desire for Asians. I don't know, it's like a trend . . . like a hot thing. I look Latino. Recently, this guy found out that I was Pilipino. All of a sudden, I became like a new commodity or something. It got to the point when this guy said, "Oh my gosh, you're Pilipino. All this time I thought you were Mexican. If I knew you were Pilipino, I would've been on you since day one."[14]

Not every gay Asian man is in demand, only those who fit the stereotypes. The very fact that these ads do not specify any personal characteristics or prerequisites, except for being "Asian," signal a type of epidermal fetishism affecting the Asian American community in both heterosexual and gay contexts. Epidermal fetishism is defined as "exaggerated love or even worship of skin color," a process in which the skin color takes on sexual properties that do not naturally inhere in it (Wolfenstein, 1993: 161). It is a situation in which a person is initially stimulated by skin color and by the various values projected upon it rather than by actions or primary sexual characteristics. What characteristics and sexual properties do gay white males (GWMs) and other non-Asians associate with the term *Asian*? Examining a few more ads placed by those seeking GAMs reveals some clues:

SEEKING HOT ASIAN BOY gdlk GWM 5–11 160#, 40 yo slim, honest, caring, ISO Asian boys under 30 for fun times. Must be cute, slim, sexy, affectionate, HIV–, in-shape bottom.

SEEKING ASIAN PLAYMATE GWM 39 5'10", 185 cute, seeks GAM for kissing, cuddling, massage and creative safe sex. You be 18–35, HIV- with good body + sense of humor. No drugs or s+m. I'm eager to get my hands on you.

ASIAN SONS, NEED DAD-BUDDY? Mature heavy GWM 6' brn/blu dad type seeks asian sons under 35 for dates, dining and affection. Please be honest, enjoy kissing and touching and have good sense of humor. Small, sweet and shy area +++

ISO VERY SISSY bottom. Looking to meet very fem bottoms for hot, no strings pounding. I especially adore cross dressers, Asians and Latins. Your place only.

REAL DAD SEEKS SON/LOVER I'm 5'10" 145# avg lks very attractive/ambitious + into longevity and life regression. You 30s slim/smooth body Asian/Hispanic short and cute.

SEEKING ASIAN in panties. Mixed Black male, handsome, light skinned, 6', 32, works out, professionally educated, seeks exotic, attractive Asian who is tall and intelligent. I want to grind you while you wear your panties. I want to cum on you while you wear a thong.

HOT BLACK TOP needs Asian. Smooth exotic Asian underneath hot Black top. 32 year old mixed Black male, handsome 6', 180 lbs, seeks gorgeous, smooth Asian for friendship and fun. Please be intelligent, down to earth, sensitive, work out and interesting.

BRAT SEEKS ASIAN Black top, handsome, 32, 6', 180 lbs, intelligent, professional, works out, seeks smooth, muscled bottom, Asian, in East LA area. I want to fuck your bubbling thighs.

Even though this set of ads is still under the heading of those placed in search of GAMs, it differs from the first set in that the ads specify particular roles and characteristics demanded from the GAMs. Those in search of GAMs expect them to be exotic "boys," "playmates," "sons," "sissies," and "bottoms." The very language of these personal ads clearly signals the expected role of gay Asian American men to be the passive and submissive partner within these desired sexual relationships. Specifically, the ads placed in search of "boys," "sons," and "sissies" deny the identity of gay Asian Americans as anything but *Men,* subordinating GAMs to the inferior position and to the unknowing and inexperienced objects to be taught and trained by true Men. When asked about this whole "daddy-son" phenomenon, Frank comments, "Asian men don't really get picked up on by these young Caucasian men. The men who are attracted to us are older Caucasian guys.[15] And Rommel adds, "They're [young Caucasian men] not attracted to me because I don't look boyish.[16]

Apparently, the demand side of the economy of desire is dictated by GWMs distorting the sexual and gender identities of GAMs for their own benefits. The supply side—responses on the part of GAMs—simultaneously reproduces the dominant/submissive relationship, and consequently reinforces the system of domination in the gay culture. Understanding the context and values of the economy of desire, many GAMs respond to the market demand on precisely what is expected of them, as revealed in the following personal ads placed by GAMs:

EXOTIC ASIAN MALE attractive boyish GAM w/smooth & sensual body 21 y/o 5'4" 115 iso handsome, fit, romantic GWM under 39 for friendship and more.

SWEET CHARMING ASIAN BABY that holds snuggly in your arms. 24 5'7" 120, slender/fit with cute boyish look. I prefer guys under 32. Butch, stable, fit muscular with all the manly stuff.

NEW IN TOWN ASIAN STUDENT 26 5'11" 155#, in shape. ISO GWM under 35, attractive, horny, patient. Tell me how to be a bottom. I'll do anything for you. PS- all American boy next door look A+.

ASIAN BOTTOM 22y 5'6" 130 29w dark hr/eyes nice bod w/round silky smooth buns.

HANDSOME ASIAN SEEKS GWM I'm 28, 5'7", 135 lbs, good build, no facial hair. I want to meet GWM 20–40, dark hair muscular, masculine for loving and caring relationships, romance, dinner, movies.

MASTER WANTED Novice Asian slave 5'10" 160# yng lkg 40s ISO GWM Master to learn lite BD SM whip dungeon dog slavery. Ontario Mills area

SPICE THAI Full body massage from cute Asian college student, 24 yo, 5'8", 130#, nice and friendly. 1 hr. $60.

JAPANESE BOY Hot Japanese 5'11" 140# 29 w 7" 24 yr, swimmers body gives Deep Tissue full body massage in the nude.

CUTE FILIPINO DEAF MALE Me: Filipino, 24 yr old friendly seeks American 24–26 White guy. Bodybuilder top, clean shaved, haircut, must be health friendly, no drug, no alcoholic, no smoke, HIV–. Enjoy good time together.

In an economy of desire, individuals "sell" themselves according to the values of the market. Recognizing that there is a preestablished market for the context of their desire, gay Asian American men "advertise" themselves accordingly in order to enhance their market value and, in a sense, maximize profit. Judging from the bold headlines of the ads, gay Asian American men "sell" themselves, according to particular market demands, as "exotic," "sweet charming baby," "boys," "bottoms," and "novice Asian slaves." Most of these ads are placed in the category of in search of GWMs. Here, there is some indication that some Asian males conform to the norms expected of them and to the gay culture where white male sexuality provides the direction in which sexual fantasies are created. It is through these personal ads that the economy of desire within the gay community is verbalized and transacted.

CONFRONTING HEGEMONY

For gay Asian Americans, West Hollywood is a place where they feel relatively comfortable. But such a place is by no means equal to the social space to which they feel they belong because the gay enclave is not created by and for the gay Asian American community, nor is it color-blind. Many informants recognize the dominance of the enclave's Eurocentric nature. For example, when asked what a "typical" person in West Hollywood looks like, almost all of the informants visualize someone "tall, blond, and buff." However, when asked to describe this "culture," respondents have difficulty specifying it. However, Rommel's characterization provides a glimpse of it:

> West Hollywood is very white. I don't know how you can explain acting white. It's a very (long pause) ... there's no culture, not to say that white is not a culture. In East L.A. you can see a lot of Cholos, there's a strong sense of cultural identity. But in WeHo there is no culture. It's not a culture, but it is a culture in itself.[17]

Because West Hollywood was established in a white Euro-American gay male context, certain stereotypically preestablished roles and hegemonic relationships are transferred to these created places. As Almaguer (1993: 263) succinctly points out, "White men provided the foundation upon which they could boldly carve out the new gay identity. Their collective position in the social structure empowered them with unique skills and talents needed to create new gay institutions, communities, and a unique sexual subculture." Although gay men do not have the power within the system of social relationships to be homophobic, it is within their full capacity to hold racist beliefs and attitudes. Consequently, the dominance of white gay males has ideologically made its way into the many facets that comprise the larger gay culture, community, and practice.

One significant influence of this racial hegemony is evident in the internalization of marginality in GAMs as shown in the ads and cited responses of GAMs to the market demand. At times, some GAMs feel just-matter-of-factly, as Jason explains:

> I think I fit that whole mold. I'm not aggressive. I'm passive, feminine, and submissive, in a way. But I'm not doing it because I'm just conforming, but I just fit into this mold. It doesn't bother me, but it just sucks. No, there's no pressure. But sometimes I think I do it unconsciously so I kind of fit in, to conform myself ... but I don't feel the pressure to do it.[18]

Rommel adds:

> A lot of my friends conform to these views, but they are not pressured to. I've seen people that will conform to being a bottom for someone they care about. On the whole, Asians really are bottoms to begin with.[19]

While Jason and Rommel deny the invasive and transformative power of racial stereotypes and domination, both choose the word "conform" and are extremely uncomfortable admitting that conformity is inevitably accompanied by pressure. Both stress the fact that GAMs feel no external pressure to conform. The inability to readily acknowledge the pressure appears to be a coping strategy on the part of GAMs to avoid the reality that they are forced into a mold and its consequences. However, almost all of the informants report feeling frustration and embarrassment when they see a fellow GAM openly conforming to the stereotypical roles. As Rio states: "I get mad when I see Asians reinforce this stereotype. Why do they have to act like that? I just want to go up to them and say, 'Do you know what you're doing?'"[20]

GAMs also suffer from a sense of false consciousness, "a systematically distorted understanding of and resistance to corrective learning experience, i.e., from everyday activity" (Wolfenstein, 1993: 2). Consequently, some of the GAMs are buying into these racially hierarchical power relations without question and resistance. Moreover, some gay racial minority men are also affected by this racial hegemony, seeking out GAMs in personal ads in similar ways as GWMs. This is a parallel occurrence to what bell hooks calls "a slave's idea of freedom," that is, the slave whose perception of the ideal free lifestyle is based on the master's way of life (hooks 1981: 156). By illustration, Jason remarks:

> When I think of West Hollywood, I think of white people, yeah. But there are also Asians, Blacks, Latinos who are just like them. It's not just the white people but also a lot of Asians that have this white attitude. But its not just whites ... it's just a West Hollywood thing.[21]

Rommel echoes Jason's opinion: "There's no real race predominant in WeHo, but there's a racial attitude. Even if they're Latino, Pilipino, or Black they have this ... not to stereotype, but they are very (long pause) Caucasian. They act white."[22]

That kind of false consciousness also hinges on the "assimilation" of racial minorities to the GWM-dominated culture of West Hollywood. Because this skewed perspective has become somewhat standard and institutionalized in West Hollywood, the top-down power relation that valorizes the power and privilege of the gay white man stands firm. Consequently, the GWM standard relegates all racial minorities, especially Asian Americans, to the marginalized position of the "other" and impedes the true empowerment of the gay Asian American community. Perhaps the most devastating outcome of the racial hegemony is the resulting indifference, as revealed in the following interviews:

In terms of expressing my sexuality, it [West Hollywood] is a safe place for me. In terms of me being Asian, it's okay ... not too bad.[23]

Even though West Hollywood is not totally safe for gay Asian Americans, I'm just glad it's there.[24]

It's [Red Dragon] a club, that's what a club is ... it plays on fantasies. It's not making a political statement. It's not trying to say, "Hey look! All Asian Americans have dragons and Chinese characters tattooed all over their bodies. Clubs aren't meant to be realistic. It's a club. A club is a club.[25]

Regardless of the indifference, more and more racial minority members—African Americans, Latino Americans, and Asian Americans—are seeking out this unique gay enclave and have started to proactively make this place their own. Meanwhile, the numerical dominance of gay white men is beginning to dwindle. Whether this is due to a greater openness and inclusiveness of mainstream gay culture, the increased socioeconomic status of racial minorities, better marketing strategies of West Hollywood's entertainment businesses, or simply the demographic shift in the metropolitan areas that has brought out the coming-of-age generation of racial minority gay men are questions for future research. But this growing trend signals a need for racial minority gay men to redefine a culture and identity that is both more inclusive and more empowering. As Calvin, a 21-year-old, third-generation Chinese American activist points out:

There's definitely a lot more representation of Asian American men in WeHo now than some years ago. Also, more and more are coming out at an earlier age. I think it's great that there are more Asian American men in WeHo. It gives more people greater awareness of the Asian American culture.[26]

CONCLUSION

This chapter attempts to provide a better understanding of the subjective experiences of gay Asian American male youth in West Hollywood through the interrogation and deconstruction of the *place* as home. West Hollywood has been considered a safe "place" for gay white men, but this study raises the question of whether such a "space" exists for gay Asian Americans. Through an in-depth analysis of the club scene and personal ads, face-to-face interviews, and participant observation, the study investigates the ways in which gay Asian American youth deal with the complex processes of confrontation, contestation, and negotiation in their continual search for the space called home. The findings reveal that a space for the gay Asian American community is far from being established, even though West Hollywood is a relatively safe place for GAMs.

As Reyes (1996: 253) puts it, "[B]y becoming visible, place can be established, but this physical place, discursively or physically ghettoized through an academic discipline or neighborhood, is not enough. For as marginalized individuals whether on the basis of ethnicity or sexuality (or otherwise), we understand how we can be here in this place, but not here in this space." This definition of "space" provides a theoretical alternative that allows researchers to move away from the general tendency of conceptualizing "space" as a basis for analysis, as opposed to "place," a mapped location. Although a separate and exclusive space may not necessarily be what the gay Asian American community should struggle to achieve, community building based on common lived experience is a necessary first step. Only by creating their own space will they be free from the racial hegemony of the gay white male culture.

Notes

1. West Hollywood is a municipality located within the city of Los Angeles and an identifiable gay community. The research on which this study is based occurred primarily on this site. I conducted my face-to-face interviews with a snow-ball sample of seven Asian American gay men aged 19–25 and participant observation at dance clubs and restaurants during the months of September to December 1998. Pseudonyms are used throughout the chapter to ensure anonymity.
2. Face-to-face interview with Nam.
3. Face-to-face interview with Rommel.
4. Face-to-face interview with Jason.
5. Face-to-face interview with Nam.
6. Face-to-face interview with Jason.
7. Face-to-face interview with Ray.
8. Face-to-face interview with Ray.
9. Face-to-face interview with Nam.
10. Face-to-face interview with Rio.
11. Face-to-face interview with Frank.
12. Face-to-face interview with Ray.
13. All the examples are selected from *Edge Magazine* 389 (June 10), 1998 and *Frontiers Newsmagazine* 17 (3), 1998.
14. Face-to-face interview with Rommel.
15. Face-to-face interview with Frank.
16. Face-to-face interview with Rommel.
17. Face-to-face interview with Rommel.
18. Face-to-face interview with Jason.
19. Face-to-face interview with Rommel.
20. Face-to-face interview with Rio.
21. Face-to-face interview with Jason.
22. Face-to-face interview with Rommel.
23. Face-to-face interview with Frank.
24. Face-to-face interview with Calvin.
25. Face-to-face interview with Ray.
26. Face-to-face interview with Calvin.

CHAPTER **18**

Marriage Dilemmas:

Partner Choices and Constraints
for Korean Americans in New York City[1]

Sara S. Lee

Intermarriage is regarded as a benchmark for assimilation, an indication of eroding social and economic barriers between the immigrant group and host society. Milton Gordon (1964) theorized, for example, that a high intermarriage rate is an indication that the racial and ethnic barriers between the minority group and host society are softening and that identification assimilation—wherein prejudice, discrimination, value, and power conflict are diminishing—is taking place. As the children of post-1965 Asian immigrants reach marriageable age, an examination of their marriage preferences can provide a glimpse into their social and cultural assimilation processes. Marriage preferences can also provide insight into the collective and personal identities of Asian Americans, as well as the impact the identities have on the way they navigate their social worlds.

Through the lens of second-generation Korean immigrants living in New York City, this chapter examines the attitudes and opinions that young Asian American adults hold about whom they wish to marry.[2] Where do second-generation Korean Americans draw marriageable boundaries? Who do they regard as the "other," and how do these boundaries intersect with class and gender? This chapter explores the constraints and choices that Korean Americans face in choosing romantic partners and reveals that the marriage dilemmas of young Asian Americans transcend the boundaries of race and ethnicity. Contrary to popular opinion, class and gender complicate their choices and often override race and ethnicity.

RECENT ASIAN AMERICAN MARRIAGE PATTERNS

The Asian American intermarriage rate is relatively high, reaching approximately 25 percent nationwide as of 1990, and it has continued its upward trend into the twenty-first century (Lee, 1996).[3] Although some interpret the high intermarriage rate of Asian Americans as an indication that they are the next in line to become "white," a closer examination of Asian American marriage patterns presents a different and more complicated story about their process of assimilation.

Asian American marriage trends since 1980 indicate that more Asian Americans are marrying interethnically, while fewer are marrying interracially than in the past (Shinagawa and Pang, 1996). In other words, Asian Americans are increasingly marrying one another (e.g., Korean Americans marrying Chinese Americans) rather than members of another race. The growing rate of Asian interethnic marriages, according to Nazli Kibria (1997), indicates that an ethnogenesis—a collective identity shift from being ethnic to being pan-ethnic—is taking place among Asian Americans. Asian Americans are constructing a pan-ethnic, or racial, identity based on their common experiences of being racially labeled as Asian by the host society (Espiritu 1992), resulting in an increase in pan-ethnic marriages.

Larry Hajime Shinagawa and Gin Yong Pang (1996) note, however, that the growing sense of a shared and common racial identity among Asian Americans is facilitated by their shared socioeconomic status as college-educated professionals. The large number and concentration of middle-class Asian Americans—particularly on college campuses—increase the availability of potential in-group partners and provide more opportunities for interpersonal interaction. Although prior studies recognize the importance of class in facilitating pan-ethnic marriages among middle-class Asian Americans, they have largely ignored the effect of class on the marriage preferences of working-class Asian Americans.

Gender differences also prevent us from concluding that Asian American intermarriage patterns reflect an overall trend of a growing pan-ethnic identity. Existing studies have repeatedly shown that Asian women, across generations, tend to out-marry at a higher rate than Asian men (Kitano et al., 1984; Lee and Yamanaka, 1990; Shinagawa and Pang, 1996; Sung, 1990). In short, although a significant presence of Asian military wives has accounted for much of the gender gap among first-generation immigrants, researchers continue to find gender differences in intermarriage rates between native-born Asian men and women (Chow, 2000; Fong and Yung, 1995; Kibria, 1997; Kitano et al., 1984; Shinagawa, 1994). Asian American men and women, it seems, diverge in their desires, options, and/or constraints pertaining to marriage.

STUDY DESIGN AND METHODS

The study is based on 60 open-ended, in-depth interviews of adult second-generation Korean Americans in New York City.[4] It was designed to explore how class and gender impact the racial and ethnic boundary construction processes by comparing the partner preferences of working- and middle-class Korean American men and women. Comparing the dilemmas, choices, and constraints involved in the partner selection processes of working- and middle-class Korean Americans contributes to our understanding of how class intersects with or overrides ethnicity in shaping both marital preferences and ethnic identities. The study also examines the continuing discrepancy in the intermarriage rates between Asian American men and women by assessing whether Korean American men and women have different notions about who they would like to marry. Finally, this study compares the internally and externally ascribed gender stereotypes of Korean American men and women, and examines whether the stereotypes impact their marital preferences.

The interviews were conducted during a 19-month period from March 1999 to October 2000. Each interview averaged two hours in length, during which the respondents were asked about their knowledge and experiences relating to their racial and ethnic membership, culture, and identity, and, in turn, how these affect their preferences for marriage partners. The open-ended questions during the in-depth interviews enabled an understanding of the nuances and subtleties involved in selecting marriage partners.

Given the class- and gender-comparative framework of the study, rather than a random, representative sample of the Korean American population in New York City, a purposive sample of working- and middle-class, male and female Korean Americans was collected in equal numbers. Two sampling methods were used to locate the study's participants: (1) a cluster sample of Korean Americans was located for each class group; and (2) the sample was expanded from the initial clusters by use of the "snowball" sampling method wherein informants were asked to refer other second-generation members who fit the criteria for inclusion in the study method. The initial professional cluster was recruited at a Korean American professional organization called the Young Korean American Network (Y-KAN).[5] The initial nonprofessional sample was recruited from friends and family members of police officers at a New York Police Department precinct that employed several Korean American officers, as well as from friends and family members of those who attended New York City's community colleges.[6] Working-class Korean Americans were sought through community colleges based on two suppositions: first, community colleges largely attract students from working-class backgrounds; and, second, working-class Korean Americans who attend college are much more likely to attend two-year colleges than four-year or private colleges (Kim, 2001). Most of the working-class Korean Americans located through community colleges were working students, who often held full- or part-time jobs while going to school part-time. All of the interviewees were between 21 and 39 years of age at the time of their interviews, with the majority falling in their mid- to late twenties; the median age was twenty-seven.

PARTNER PREFERENCES: INTERSECTIONS OF RACE, ETHNICITY, GENDER, AND CLASS

The respondents' partner preferences fall into one of the following three categories: (1) a preference for a coethnic partner; (2) no racial or ethnic preference; and (3) a preference for a non-Asian partner. In general, the middle-class Korean Americans emphasize their racial and ethnic identities and feel that it is important to marry a coethnic, or at least someone Asian. The working-class Korean Americans, on the other hand, do not regard their racial or ethnic identities to be of primary importance in their lives; thus, they are more flexible about whom they wish to marry. Compared to their middle-class counterparts, working-class Korean Americans are also less concerned about how their parents might react to the possibility of intermarriage. Finally, gender plays a pivotal role in shaping partner preferences; one-fifth of the women in the sample prefer to marry someone who is not Korean or Asian.

Coethnic and Pan-Ethnic Preferences among Middle-Class Korean Americans

Because ethnic identity is central to their lives, the majority of middle-class Korean Americans express a strong preference for a coethnic marital partner (Lee, 2002). These respondents assert that Korean Americans have a common understanding that enables them to bond more easily and deeply. When asked to describe what they mean by a "common understanding," some respondents could not elaborate further, except to invoke a primordial sense of Korean American ethnic identity that is independent of cultural characteristics or even concrete ethnic attachment. For example, when asked whether he has a preference for marrying someone Korean, a second-generation Korean American male explains:

> Yeah, I would like to marry somebody who is Korean just because I think that I treasure the Korean aspect of me. The fact that I speak English and I'm American and all those things are great, but then there are these intangible aspects of who you are that has

more resonance and means more to you than what you do or who you hang out with. And I really want to go with that side, the Korean side—that is, having a Korean wife and having a Korean family.[7]

One of the most frequently cited "Korean" values that middle-class Korean Americans regard as important in marriage is the emphasis on family. Although almost all of the respondents report that their parents want them to marry a Korean American, the respondents who prefer to marry a coethnic are not simply blindly following their parents' wishes. Rather, they indicate that they prefer to marry a Korean American because they believe that it is in the best interest of the family. More specifically, the respondents state that marriage is a union of two families rather than two individuals. Hence, it is important for the partner to be compatible not only with the respondent but also with the rest of the family, especially with the parents who did not speak English very well. For instance, a Korean American male explains that he prefers a coethnic partner because he believes that cultural and linguistic compatibility between his parents and future spouse is important:

I want to make sure that culturally and communicatively [sic] they are going to be able to communicate smoothly with my parents. Being the first son, I have to kind of carry on the family traditions and family name and all that other good stuff, and also make sure that my parents are comfortable. And them being comfortable includes being able to communicate smoothly with everyone in the family. So for me, a serious dating prerequisite is that she has to be Korean. Preferably someone who speaks Korean.[8]

Ironically, although most of the respondents cannot speak Korean very well, they place importance on their partners' ability to speak—or at the very least to understand—Korean.

For the most part, however, cultural compatibility transcends language and denotes broader issues such as having common values. Thus, if middle-class Korean Americans cannot find a coethnic partner, they feel that the "next best thing" to marrying someone Korean American is to marry someone who shares a similar culture—in this case, an Asian American. When asked what cultural aspects they believe Asians have in common, middle-class Koreans cite the following values most frequently: the emphasis on education and family as well as respect for elders. They elaborate that being Asian means being raised with strict parents who are often unfamiliar with American culture. It also means having parents who are extremely emphatic about their children's academic education and performance. However, when probed as to how they define "Asian," most middle-class Korean Americans narrowly define the category to include only East Asians such as Chinese, Japanese, and Koreans. In their view, the term *Asian*, therefore, excludes people from Southeast Asia, such as Vietnam or the Philippines. Some of the respondents reluctantly reveal that the exclusion of Southeast Asians as potential partners stems from their parents' perceptions of Southeast Asians as "lower class," which is consistent with prior research findings (Kibria, 1997; Lee, 1996; Pang, 1994). In fact, their prejudice is so strong that they admit that their parents would actually prefer that they marry someone Caucasian over someone who is Southeast Asian.

Although class plays a central role in shaping the marital preferences of middle-class Korean Americans, they rarely pointed to class distinctions during the interviews. However, class determines where middle-class Korean Americans grow up, attend schools, and work, and consequently, shape their social networks. Many of the middle-class respondents in this study state that they have met and established social and personal networks with other Korean and Asian Americans during college. This affirms the finding that Asian Americans experience growing opportunities to meet and befriend one another in colleges and universities (Shinagawa and Pang, 1996). The respondents repeatedly explained that they established deep and close relationships with the Korean American friends they made during their college years both because they made conscious efforts to do so and because they usually had more in common with one another. For example, one second-generation Korean American female states: "There's an intimacy and a bond and more shared experience with Korean Americans. And there's more empathy in a way—they know where you're coming from. There's more shared experience."

Racial and ethnic organizations and clubs on college campuses such as the Korean Students' Association or the Asian American Students' Association largely foster the affinity that Korean Americans develop with coethnics. These organizations help to instill a sense of ethnic commonality that many of the respondents had not previously experienced while growing up in predominantly white, middle-class neighborhoods. Furthermore, courses that focus on racial/ethnic studies or Asian American studies that are offered at many large, four-year universities provide middle-class second-generation Koreans an opportunity to learn more about their culture, heritage, and history in the United States. Cultural and historical knowledge of their home country and of the coethnic group's experiences in the United States infuse a sense of pride in their racial and ethnic identities, an idea elaborated by a second-generation Korean American:

I liked [the introduction to East Asian Studies]. It was really interesting. It really opened my eyes up to a lot of things. I know more now and I have a lot more respect for Korea. A lot more understanding so it makes me, as I get older, more proud. Because I know that Korea went through a lot of crap and yet they still can hold their heads up high and have such great ideas and be so.... Even the simple things like you shake somebody's hand if they are older than you with two hands. Stuff like that. It's such a beautiful thing and it shows so much respect.[9]

The newfound respect and appreciation for their racial and ethnic heritage, and the intimate bond they develop with other Korean and Asian Americans help to explain why middle-class Korean Americans prefer to date Korean and Asian Americans over other racial groups.

Preferences among Working-Class Korean Americans

Unlike their middle-class counterparts who maintain that their ethnic identity is both central to their lives and paramount in their choice of a partner, many of the working-class Korean Americans articulate vastly different views. Although they indicate that it would be nice if they happened to marry a coethnic, it is certainly not a prerequisite or even a central characteristic in their preference for a partner. For working-class Korean Americans, race and ethnicity hold little significance in forging relationships with friends and acquaintances, including romantic relationships.

Like the parents of middle-class Korean Americans, the parents of working-class Korean Americans are just as insistent that their children marry a coethnic. However, working-class Korean Americans strongly believe that choosing a marriage partner is strictly a personal choice. Hence, unlike their middle-class counterparts, they do not feel the need to please or accommodate their parents' preferences by dating or marrying a fellow ethnic. For example, a working-class Korean American male explains that regardless of the parental pressure he may experience to marry a Korean American woman, he openly dates and will continue to date women of other racial and ethnic backgrounds:

They [my parents] want me to marry Korean. They even make threats. Like my dad will say, "I'll disown you!" But it's like, "Okay, whatever. I don't care." I think that every race is beautiful. I've been out with black women, Latino women, and they tend to be people who are comfortable with themselves or comfortable with me so it has never really been a big thing.[10]

Similarly, another respondent explains:

> If they were attractive enough and you had the same things in common and you were going the same way, then I.... Personally, I'm a very open-minded person so I would consider anything. I really would. To a lot of children, what their parents think is important and I guess making them happy is important. But I think some people let their parents' decisions take precedence over what their own preferences are, and I'm not that way. If I found someone I thought was really good, then I wouldn't necessarily care if my parents were happy or not.[11]

Interestingly, reflections about marital preferences frequently led to discussions about the need for the second generation to define and develop an individual sense of self and identity, independent of the first generation. For example, a second-generation male states:

> It would be nice if I dated some Korean girl, but it's not an issue. (*Question*: So you're not really worried about what your parents think?) During college, yeah [I did]. [But] I reached a point where . . . maybe I am being selfish, but I am trying to figure out what I am and what I want to do as oppose to what I think is the right thing to do. It's time to find my identity.[12]

Others suggest that upon reaching adulthood, it is clear that they need to separate their values and preferences from those of their parents, as elaborated by another respondent:

> I've decided she [my mother] can talk as much as she wants. Before, I was really scared. "Oh my God, what am I going to do?" But I realized that she is going to have to accept that this is the person I'm going to live with and I'm going to have children with and if it's not something she agrees with, she is going to have to accept it eventually, even if at the moment or for the first stages she refused to accept it . . . I think with Korean parents, there are some battles that are worth fighting. There are expectations, and there are issues that your parents will tell you about, but they are battles you just have to fight. You have to say, "I don't care if you don't approve of this. I don't care if this is not what you expect of me. This is who I am and this is what I've decided. Because I'm not a teenager anymore."[13]

It would be a mistake, however, to assume that working-class Korean Americans do not feel a sense of ethnic and cultural distinctiveness or pride; they, too, believe that there is something about being Korean—some sense of connection, historical, cultural, or emotional—that makes them unique. They also elaborate upon aspects of the Korean culture they particularly like and value such as the celebration of the Korean New Year or the respect that Koreans pay to their elders. However, what distinguishes the working-class Korean Americans from their middle-class counterparts is that they do not believe that Koreans necessarily have more in common with one another. Rather, working-class Korean Americans maintain that the concerns and values that stem from their socioeconomic background override their sense of ethnic identity. In other words, because their class status is more salient in their daily lives than their ethnic identity, working-class Korean Americans are more open to dating and marrying across racial and ethnic lines.

For working-class Korean Americans, cultural compatibility means an affinity with socioeconomic class status rather than with race, ethnicity, or language. For example, a female working-class respondent who is dating a Jamaican American reports that she feels closer to him than she did to her previous boyfriend, who was Bangladeshi, because even though her previous boyfriend was Asian, she and her Jamaican boyfriend have something more similar in common—their shared class background. She elaborates, "He [my ex-boyfriend] was always about money this and status that, but Andrew and I aren't like that. We come from the same values, you know? The same ethics about money and what we value in life."

Just as class determines the middle-class respondents' place of residence, schools, and social networks, class also plays a crucial role in shaping the social networks of working-class Korean Americans. Unlike other working-class ethnic members, who typically grow up and live in ethnic enclaves, the working-class Korean Americans in this sample grew up in working-class neighborhoods in Brooklyn and the Bronx with large black and Latino populations and few Asian neighbors to speak of. Moreover, because most working-class Korean Americans typically attend local and community colleges (where the presence of and involvement in ethnic or pan-ethnic organizations is rare), they do not have the opportunity to meet and forge relationships with other Korean Americans. The lack of such opportunities stands in stark contrast to those available to middle-class Korean Americans who normally attend four-year or private universities where ethnic and pan-ethnic organizations and coethnics of similar class status abound. Reflecting both the social and spatial proximity to non-Asians, working-class Korean Americans tend to identify more closely with other working-class individuals with whom they live, work, and attend school rather than with middle-class coethnics or other Asian Americans from more privileged class backgrounds.

THE ASIAN AMERICAN MALE: STEREOTYPES OF RACE AND GENDER

Several male respondents (both working and middle class) explain that their choice of partners is based less on personal preferences and more on constraints and the limited options available to them. Throughout the interviews, Korean American men reiterated that most non-Asian women do not find Asian men attractive, thereby leaving them with little choice but to date fellow ethnics or other Asians. For example, a respondent who grew up in a predominantly white suburb of Virginia remarks:

> I think for me, for Asians in particular, or any minority, it's much harder to date. It's much harder to date especially because of where I am from; I mostly hang out with American [white] people, but I feel like half of the women won't even look at me because I'm Asian.... So right off the bat, half of the girls that I ever meet are out of the question. And then the other half, they have to be really open and only half of them are really super-open to the idea of dating outside of their race. The other half, some of them might be open, but to actually take that step to date is a whole other story. So that rules out even more. So for me, I feel like it's a much smaller pool to choose from.[14]

Another Korean American male explains that Asian males generally do not embody the ideal Western image of masculinity:

> This is my hypothesis, but I think that Asian men are probably the least desired group of males in the whole world. I think that is definitely true.... If you took a typical woman off the street and said, "What kind of a guy do you like?" how many of them would say, "an Asian man?" Some might say, "I want a blonde-hair guy" or "a Latino man." Or some say, "I want a big black guy with muscles." But very, very few (I think the smallest amount if you were to sample the whole country) would want an Asian man.[15]

Although not all of the respondents in the sample agree, the majority of the Korean American men assert that non-Asian women are generally unwilling to date Asian men because the dominant stereotypes of Asian men characterize them as effeminate (frail, meek, and passive) or as sexual deviants.

The negative stereotypes have real consequences in not only limiting the partner choices of Asian men but also in affecting the partner preferences among Asian women, some of whom subscribe to the dominant stereotypes of Asian men as socially awkward and sexually undesirable. Women who grew up with little contact with Asians are especially impressionable to such stereotypes, which they have picked up from movies and television shows. One example that the respondents brought up time and time again is the film *Sixteen Candles*, an iconic film of American teenage culture in the 1980s. *Sixteen Candles* features an Asian exchange student whose national origin is ambiguous. In the movie, the character is from Korea, but his name sounds vaguely Chinese (Long Dok Dong) and he speaks broken English with a heavy Japanese accent. Dong is portrayed as an exotic "Other" who lusts after American girls and, incidentally, ends up with the film's version of the most undesirable and unattractive American girl. Some female respondents admit that the negative media portrayal of Asian men has left them with an indelible imprint during their impressionable and formative adolescent years. These images seared into their consciousness the idea that Asian men are sexually unattractive and make objectionable romantic partners. As one Korean woman explains:

> I don't think I've ever really been attracted to an Asian guy.... I think this is definitely related to media representation of Asian men. And growing up, there was no example of what a sexual Asian man would be like. So I just ... it's a big question mark for me, and I go through phases where I'm like, "I should just try to date an Asian guy. It would be really good for me." But it is weird. It's very strange.[16]

In addition to the externally ascribed sexual stereotypes of Asian men as effeminate and asexual, internally ascribed stereotypes of Korean men also lead Korean women to deliberately choose non-coethnic mates. For instance, several Korean American women are weary of dating Korean men because they believe that Korean men are chauvinistic and sexist. The respondents elaborate that if they were to marry a Korean man, they would have to follow a set of particularly strict, patriarchal behavioral standards and rules of Confucianism that promote obedience and subservience to male authority.[17] Although Confucianism is no longer a vital, manifest religion in contemporary Korea (particularly among the more Westernized Koreans in the United States), Koreans still maintain certain values, particularly those relating to deference to male authority and elders. For example, a Korean American woman explains why she prefers to date non-Koreans:

> I haven't really been attracted to any Korean men and it's more because of attitude than anything else. Because they are very ... they are the kings of their family and they have no reason to change. It doesn't get any better for them than it already is. Whereas change is good for us, as women, because it only gets better from the Korean concept of what a woman is supposed to be.[18]

Another woman expresses a similar view:

> I think subconsciously a lot of Korean men want the kind of woman who will take care of them and will deal with the domestic issues like cleaning and cooking and that sort of thing.... And that's why I don't date Korean men.[19]

The majority of these women, however, have never dated Asian men, and, thus, their rejection of Asian men is based on assumptions and stereotypes to some degree, as well as the gender dynamics they witness in their families or in the Korean community, such as the Korean church. For example, several women in this category feel that their fathers mistreat their mothers, who often perform double duties—working outside the home to earn a living and having to do all of the domestic work.[20] For the American-born and American-educated women, watching their mothers perform a second shift makes an unfavorable impression about Korean gender roles. Several women reveal that their mothers have advised them not to marry a Korean man; one Korean American woman articulates this idea:

> I know a lot of Korean parents who want their children to marry Koreans. But my mother had said that if I married a Korean, it would be good because she could communicate better with the person, but for me, and for my sake, she prefers that I marry a non-Korean person because she felt that Korean men were not as good to their wives.[21]

These women indicate that their mothers want more for their daughters than they have in their own relationships—that is, independence and more equality. As Americans, they believe in gender equality, and thus they express an aversion to the patriarchal aspects of Asian culture.

Conclusion

For working- and middle-class Korean Americans, partner preferences are a result of residential, spatial, and social propinquity, leading to vastly different dating patterns between the two groups. The middle-class Korean Americans in New York prefer coethnic partners because they are socially networked to coethnics and are familiar with the cultural norms, experiences, and sensibilities of Korean Americans, the majority of whom are middle class. By contrast, for the working-class Korean Americans, their class status creates social and geographic distance between them and their more privileged coethnic counterparts. Because they have grown up in more racially and ethnically diverse, working-class neighborhoods, working-class Korean Americans feel closer to other working-class minorities, such as blacks and Latinos, than to middle-class Koreans or Asian Americans. Thus, when issues of marriage are involved, the concerns and values that stem from their socioeconomic background override their ethnicity or race.

Furthermore, gender matters. The cultural perceptions and negative stereotypes of Asian males affect partner preferences and dating patterns among both Korean American men and women. Korean American men feel that the stereotypes circumscribe their choice of partners, and they are not wrong on this count. The negative images are powerful enough to lead some Korean American women to seek non-Asian mates. Fujino (2000) notes that "in the absence of antimiscegenation laws and gender-based immigration policies, the social construction and racialization of media representations play an important role in shaping individual preferences and behaviors." In this regard, television and other media act as "cultural propaganda," powerful social institutions shaping racialized views in both overt and covert ways (Rumbaut, 1997b; also see Chapter 15 in this volume). These "controlling images" also influence Korean Americans to have negative racial views of themselves (Collins, 1990). These findings indicate, therefore, that while we as individuals have the will to choose our mates, social and cultural factors play a significant role in constructing our intimate relationships. Future studies should examine whether the class and gender patterns in this study are generalizable to other Asian ethnic groups.

Notes

1. This research was partly supported by the International Migration Program of the Social Science Research Council, the National Science Foundation Grant SES-0000267, and the Korea Foundation.
2. Throughout this chapter, the terms *second-generation Korean immigrant, Korean second generation,* and *Korean American* are used interchangeably. Because the majority of post-1965 second-generation Asian immigrants are still young and have not married, this study examines their marriage preferences rather than their actual marriage patterns. Pseudonyms are used to ensure anonymity for the study's participants.

3. According to Lee (1996), the rate for Koreans was 32 percent, slightly below the rate for the Japanese (34 percent) but significantly above that of the Chinese (16 percent).
4. For the purpose of the study, I define second-generation Korean American as the children of first-generation Korean immigrant parents who are either native born or came to the United States by the age of six.
5. Y-KAN is a not-for-profit social organization with approximately 200 second-generation Korean American members. The organization's objective is to represent the Korean American community to the broader New York community by providing community services. The organization also aims to provide Korean American professionals with networking opportunities. For many, the organization primarily serves as a social function—it provides a way to meet and befriend other professional Korean Americans in New York City.
6. Because the majority of the Korean immigrant community is in the middle to upper middle class (Kim, 2001), it was relatively easy to find professional Korean Americans. On the other hand, special efforts had to be made to find working-class Korean Americans, who comprise a very small segment of the general Korean American population (Lee, 2002).
7. James Kim, face-to-face interview by author, October 1999.
8. Steve Park, face-to-face interview by author, March 1999.
9. Sang Lee, face-to-face interview by author, September 2000.
10. James Cho, face-to-face interview by author, October 2000.
11. Dan Kim, face-to-face interview by author, November 1999.
12. Joe Shim, face-to-face interview by author, February 2000.
13. Rebecca Kim, face-to-face interview by author, February 2000.
14. John Chung, face-to-face interview by author, April 1999.
15. Sam Kim, face-to-face interview by author, March 1999.
16. Helen Lee, face-to-face interview by author, April 1999.
17. According to Confucian ideology, a woman must obey her father as a daughter, obey her husband in marriage, and obey her eldest son when she becomes a widow. Also, a woman's main duty is in the domestic sphere: being a wise mother and a good wife.
18. Sue Choi, face-to-face interview by author, January 2000.
19. Jessica Park, face-to-face interview by author, May 1999.
20. In many dual-income families, particularly in immigrant families, women work both inside and outside the home. However, their expanded economic role and having this life outside the home do not liberate most of them from the "chains of traditional patriarchy" (Min 1998). Rather, they end up working two jobs—one at home preparing meals, cleaning, washing, and childrearing and one outside the home.
21. Jennifer Kim, face-to-face interview by author, July 1999.

CHAPTER 19

A Commentary on Young Asian American Activists from the 1960s to the Present

William Wei

The emergence of the Asian American movement (hereafter, the Movement) in the 1960s marked a watershed event in the history of Asians in America. The Movement sought to strengthen the political clout of Asian Americans and improve their opportunities in mainstream American society. By redefining Americans of Asian ancestry as Asian Americans and organizing them into a pan-Asian coalition, the Movement was and remains a vehicle for empowering Asians in America. This chapter takes a critical look back at the Movement in the 1960s, specifically reevaluating its organizers, defining their goals, and identifying the issues around which they chose to mobilize. It also focuses on one of the most enduring legacies of the Movement—the creation of Asian American Studies as an academic field. Finally, it assesses what lessons the Movement offers the new generation of Asian American youth, investigates some of the issues around which they organize today, and speculates on the future of Asian American activism at the turn of the twenty-first century.

LOOKING BACK: THE MOVEMENT AND ITS PIONEER ACTIVISTS

The Movement was born during a tumultuous period in American history, a time when dissent challenged the nation's definition of itself as a democratic and pluralist society. As a reform effort, the Movement sought both to identify the inequalities in the existing system and to rectify them. At the same time, it provided a national platform on which the previously sporadic instances of resistance to the racial oppression of Asian

Americans could be solidified. Moreover, it fostered a sense of pan-ethnicity within diverse Asian ethnic groups of varied socioeconomic backgrounds and among geographically dispersed ethnic communities. For Asian Americans, the Movement became the primary vehicle to advocate for their rights in an ethnically pluralist society. It aimed to change the prevailing perception that Asians in America are an inferior race, or at best an exotic foreign group.

Like many young American radicals in the 1960s, Asian American activists emerged as a force inspired both by their African American and Latino peers and by Third World liberation movements and the Cultural Revolution in China. Having played a pivotal role in Asian American political activism, however, the Movement's pioneers have since become mythologized. In discussions on college campuses and in the Asian American community today, Asian American activists of the 1960s are presented to a greater or lesser degree as incarnations of an ideal political archetype rather than as the idealistic individuals that they were.

Looking back on the Movement today, it is difficult to separate the activists from the political ideals they have come to represent. Those who participated in the Movement are divided either by professional interests developed since their years of activism or by their current attitudes toward politics, both theoretical and practical. Furthermore, they continue to be at odds with each other over ideological and political matters. To complicate matters, pioneer activists have aged and in many cases are no longer politically active. They are often uncertain about the meaning of the "sixties" and their role in it—who they were, what their motives were, what they did, and how much they accomplished have all become points of dispute. Although these thorny issues will not be resolved anytime soon, if ever, it is still worthwhile to examine what the young Asian American activist pioneers were like and what their successors have been doing since. Such a consideration necessarily begins with a deconstruction of the political archetype and a discussion of the background of the Asian American activists of the late 1960s and early 1970s.

Activism as a Matter of Class

One of the more fanciful facets of the archetype is that the young Asian American activists were proletarians, that is, working-class men and women. Ideally, these proletarian activists grew up on the crowded streets of Asian ghettos such as Chinatowns in San Francisco and New York City. Although they may not have received much formal education, they were intelligent beyond their years; they were "street-savvy," having learned bitter lessons about the "real world" in which they were forced to live. From experience or intuition, they had a keen understanding of the way in which historical forces created ethnic and class inequities. Most importantly, they held a progressive political stance because of their underprivileged class backgrounds. Although the notion of Asian American activism of the 1960s stemming from proletarian hardships is a romantic and compelling one, it is also an inaccurate one. In fact, the majority of young Asian American activists were college students who grew up in white suburbs or managed to escape ethnic communities.

In reality, relatively few young Asian American activists came from working-class backgrounds; instead, most were from petty bourgeois backgrounds. By the 1960s, most of the U.S.-born generations of Asian Americans—Chinese and Japanese in particular—had moved out of the ethnic enclaves and distanced themselves from Asian immigrants. These middle-class Asians lived in a period dominated by the repressive assimilationist thinking of Anglo-conformity and the anticommunist politics of the 1950s (see also Chapter 6 in this volume). In contrast to this group, most working-class Asian American adults were far too busy trying to make a living and raise a family to direct their time and energy toward political activities. Their children, Asian American working-class youth, were not better equipped to lead the Movement than their parents. Many found themselves trapped in ethnic ghettos and ethnic gangs, roaming the streets in search of alternative, often illegitimate, means of survival.

The Asian Americans who became politically active during the 1960s belonged to a unique and unprecedented generation: they were part of the American baby-boom generation that emerged after World War II at a time of relative affluence. Prior to World War II, few Asian American youths participated in white mainstream activities, since anti-Asian exclusionary laws had prevented most Asian immigrants from establishing families in the United States. Of the precious few who were born into Asian immigrant families, many were unable to attain an adequate education because they were forced to attend inferior or segregated schools. Even if they were fortunate enough to attend college, they were unable to find jobs commensurate with their training in the larger economy (see also Chapter 6 in this volume). The situation changed dramatically during the postwar period as second- and third-generation Asians came of age. By 1970, over 100,000 Asian Americans were enrolled in colleges and universities. It was this generation of college-educated students who were at the heart of the Movement. Except for a few working in the Asian ethnic communities, most of the young Asian American activists of the 1960s came from college campuses across the nation and from upwardly mobile middle-class families.

POLITICS, NEITHER PURE NOR SIMPLE

Another potent component of the archetype is that young Asian Americans were inspired by leftist politics. According to the ideal, during their college years, they studied Marxism-Leninism and Mao Tse-tung Thought (or MLMTT, to use the political shorthand of the period). Through political pamphlets or perhaps the aphoristic *Quotations from Chairman Mao*, they learned about the nature of oppression and power. Having attained a heightened political or "Third World" consciousness, they laid aside their middle-class ambitions and distinguished themselves from apathetic Asian Americans, Asian immigrant workers, and diligent Asian American students whom they viewed as slavishly and selfishly working for only themselves and their families. Instead, the activists were selfless individuals committed to larger goals, namely, the liberation of Asian Americans from an oppressive American society and the founding of a more humane society that was egalitarian and democratic. Inspired by the Maoist slogans "Dare to struggle, dare to win" and "Serve the people," they devoted themselves to organizing others in Asian ethnic communities and engaging in militant, direct action to bring about progressive social change.

To some extent, these characterizations are accurate. Leftist politics was undeniably a factor in the quest of many activists for change, especially for those belonging to the ideologically driven Maoist organizations. (However, whether it was political ideology that initially moved them or whether ideology was something they acquired afterward remains to be seen.) Asian American Maoists personally identified with the militants of the past and with "freedom fighters" waging wars of national liberation in the present, especially those in Indochina resisting American imperialism. They considered the Movement to be one of many liberation movements within and outside the country. They felt themselves to be part of a worldwide struggle against imperialist domination. In reality, however, the Asian American movement and other social movements were never a part of the liberation movements taking place across the globe. On the contrary, they were separate and unconnected phenomena, having more to do with internal rather than external forces.

For most young Asian American activists, however, it was "identity politics" rather than "leftist politics" per se that attracted them, and "ethnic consciousness" rather than a "political consciousness" that spurred them to action. They became activists when the United States experienced major internal upheavals during the 1960s. Like their mainstream counterparts, they, too, were caught up in the important social issues of the period such as opposition to the Vietnam War (1965–1975). Asian Americans, old and young, opposed the war because it was immoral rather than because it was a war that could not be won, as some opponents to the war have argued. They emphasized the racial nature of the war, in part, because mainstream antiwar activists tended to ignore this important element. Asian American antiwar activists were concerned that American soldiers were trained psychologically to hate Asians and by extension, Asian Americans. They believed that it was this racial hatred above all that led to the atrocities committed against Southeast Asian civilians in Indochina. In sum, Asian American activists opposed the Vietnam War because it was both unjust and racist.

As a result of their opposition to the Vietnam War, Asian Americans experienced a unique social transformation. Originally identifying themselves as members of specific Asian ethnic groups or as hyphenated variants such as Chinese-American or Japanese-American, they transcended these traditional ethnic boundaries and fostered solidarity with all Asians in America to oppose the war. In other words, theirs was an ethnic identity that coalesced around the opposition to the Vietnam War. While working with other Asian ethnic groups, including newly arrived immigrants, was difficult, many Asian American activists realized that if they were ever to have a voice in America, they would have to engage in identity politics. Participation in the antiwar movement convinced many that the path to political empowerment was through an inter-Asian coalition based on a pan-Asian identity.

LEGACIES

Asian Communities: Returning "Home" to "Serve the People"[1]

The Movement of the 1960s played a pivotal role in inspiring young Asian Americans to return to their ethnic communities. This return to Asian ghettos was due more to an "ethnic consciousness" inspired by the civil rights and the Black Power movements than to a "political consciousness" based on MLMTT theory and practice. Indeed, for young Asian American activists of the late 1960s and 1970s, working in the Asian ethnic community was an expression of their ethnic identity, of which they felt robbed under the pressure of Anglo-conformity in their suburban middle-class families.

Through their newly developed "ethnic consciousness," many young Asian American activists came to view their college education as meaningless, or, for the more militant, as an act of "selling out to the white establishment." In turn, some abandoned their studies to return "home," devoting themselves to rebuilding their ethnic communities, often in urban ghettos. Equipped with a progressive worldview and political ideas about the efficacy of direct action and mass democracy, they believed that they could bring about social change. They hoped to ameliorate the wretched condition of their ethnic enclaves and politically to empower their fellow Asian Americans. As an article of faith, they established what they called "serve the people" organizations, as opposed to existing nonprofit social services organizations, hoping to arouse working-class Asian Americans' sense of class consciousness and achieve equality through grassroots organizing.

The Asian ethnic communities to which aspiring Asian American youth returned were inner-city ethnic enclaves plagued with poverty and multiple social problems—unemployment, juvenile delinquency, health hazards, and overcrowded housing, among others. With the influx of new Asian immigrants and families following the Immigration Act of 1965, the situation grew worse. Aside from the urgent need to deal with the social problems, there was the additional need to overcome language and cultural barriers in order to deliver public resources and services. Making matters more difficult was the fact that the U.S. government and public institutions largely ignored or severely underserved many Asian communities, justifying their neglect by claiming that Asian Americans were culturally inclined or preferred to be left alone and rely on their own internal community resources. Accordingly, government programs shifted their resources to other ethnic minority communities that were politically more vocal. At the same time, traditional elite groups in Asian communities were either unable or unwilling to try to obtain sources of support outside of government agencies for fear that such support would undermine their power and prestige.

Imbued with idealism and a desire to rediscover their roots, many Asian American college students returned to work in Asian ethnic communities, bringing with them endless enthusiasm and energy. They were the vanguard in founding grassroots organizations, voluntarily working with disenfranchised members of the community such as drug addicts and juvenile delinquents. Unfortunately, most of these grassroots organizations proved to be ephemeral. Those that survived did so because they made the transition to nonprofit social service organizations.

Asian American college students served as cultural brokers between their isolated ethnic communities and mainstream society. They worked voluntarily with other community social service agencies that operated differently from more mainstream American institutions. Many were linguistically competent, culturally sensitive, and professionally trained, providing much needed counseling, welfare assistance, and employment services to recently arrived immigrants. Using their education and understanding of American bureaucracy, young Asian American activists were able to obtain federal and private funds to improve the lives of Asian Americans, especially those from working-class or immigrant backgrounds.

Nevertheless, the impact of the return was short-lived for several reasons. First, young activists adopted idealistic strategies that overemphasized self-reliance in an already impoverished community that needed and deserved government assistance. Second, they experimented with new organizational forms that were based on participatory democracy. While sounding good in theory, it proved to be ineffective in practice because the people they served were members of the working class or noncitizen immigrants whose main preoccupation was survival, with little time to spare for politics. Finally, with the exception of a few dedicated individuals who remained in their communities, many of the original organizers and activists eventually grew tired and left, usually going back to college to obtain their degrees in order to land jobs elsewhere. Even those motivated by a leftist ideology abandoned the people in Asian ghettos that they were serving and redirected themselves toward other political causes. In most instances, living and organizing in the community became a memorable but transitory phase in their lives, albeit a life-altering experience. Some who ventured to make a "second" return to their ethnic enclaves after obtaining a college education and an advanced degree went back to assume different roles— as lawyers, accountants, doctors and health-care workers, teachers, and other professionals.

College Campuses: Establishing the Interdisciplinary Field of Asian American Studies

Although the involvement of young Asian American activists in Asian ethnic communities was relatively short-lived, they left a profound and indelible mark on college campuses across the country. The most significant was the founding of the new interdisciplinary field of Asian American Studies. Influenced by civil rights and Black Power movements, young Asian American college students experienced an ethnic awakening and demanded to know more about their history and culture in America. The well-known Third World Strikes at San Francisco State College (now San Francisco State University) and at the University of California, Berkeley, during the late 1960s were pivotal political movements in which Asian American students and other students of color joined forces to protest the exclusion of their histories from the college curricula. For Asian American youth, these were seminal events. For the first time, they organized politically as a unified force and engaged in collective action in alliance with the Third World Liberation Fronts—coalitions of students of color who identified with the national liberation movements of people in Africa, Asia, and Latin America. Together, they fought for equal access to educational opportunities and demanded that curricula reflect the histories of racial and ethnic minorities. They insisted on courses that were not only developed by but also taught by faculty who were members of racial and ethnic minority groups.

The development of Asian American Studies initially focused on the "sins" of omission and commission in existing college curricula and textbooks, aiming to reclaim Asian American history. Earlier Asian American Studies courses tended to discuss Asian Americans as both an immigrant and a racial group. Besides organizing the history around the various push/pull factors that explained Asian immigration to America, instructors also emphasized an experience of racial oppression parallel to that of other people of color, pointing to similarities between the coolie trade and the African slave trade.

Asian American activists also pointed to a concomitant tradition of racial resistance. Seeking to reclaim earlier examples of Asian Americans' resistance to oppression, activists cited past instances of militancy. Course staples included the Chinese laborers who worked on the Central Pacific half of the Transcontinental Railroad who had gone on strike for equal wages and better working conditions, and the Japanese American "troublemakers" incarcerated in the Tule Lake concentration camp during World War II. In addition to understanding the history of Asians in America, Asian American Studies also focused on reinventing a coherent Asian American culture. Through literature, art, and film, they sought to recover old traditions, customs, and values, and at the same time, develop new sensibilities, perspectives, and connections.

Besides giving definition and depth to an Asian American identity, Asian American Studies participated in (and continues to participate in) the larger cultural war to re-vision America as a multicultural society with a cultural pluralist perspective that accepts Asian Americans as equal members of society. In the final analysis, Asian American Studies has proven to be the enduring legacy of young Asian American activists. At present, many college campuses have established Asian American Studies programs and departments and offer Asian American Studies courses.

THE DECLINE OF ASIAN AMERICAN ACTIVISM

By the late 1970s, there was a perceptible decline in activism among Asian Americans. The most important reason was probably the end of the war in Vietnam and Southeast Asia. Asian American activists, along with a generation of antiwar protesters who had devoted many years to opposing the war, now turned their attention to more mundane matters. In effect, they moved on with their lives, starting families and finding jobs that allowed them to support themselves. Since most were college students with middle-class backgrounds, they found it relatively easy to make the transition from activism to careerism. Many entered professional fields and became incorporated into the mainstream economy, whereas others worked in Asian American communities, bringing with them valuable organizing experience and leadership skills acquired from years of political activism.

Another major reason for the decrease of Asian American activism was the rampant sectarianism that plagued the Asian American movement. Young Asian American activists became disillusioned with the destructive ultra-leftism within and between radical organizations, especially those of a Maoist persuasion. Too often, such conflicts spilled over to community organizations, impeding their ability to perform their practical mission of delivering services and resources to needy Asian Americans. Typically, these sectarian struggles were over ideology and power. Competing for the "hearts and minds" of an ever-dwindling supply of political activists, leftists engaged in sterile debates over MLMTT. In retrospect, the political arguments that seemed so crucial at the time were irrelevant and served only to divorce activists from the reality of Asian America.

By the 1980s, many of the former activists had outgrown their radical youth to become professionals with middle-class concerns, such as the "glass ceiling" that prevents Asian Americans from obtaining leadership positions in large corporations commensurate with their level of education, skills, and years of working experience. To gain access to political power, they traded radical politics for electoral politics and participated in local and national election campaigns. Some of them still adhered to the spirit of the Movement. Acting on their new and now widely accepted identity as Asian Americans, they continue to work for racial equality, social justice, and political empowerment. The struggle has moved, however, beyond the urban Asian ethnic enclaves and onto a national platform. An early issue around which activists organized nationally was anti-Asian violence, a problem that has worsened over the years. Another issue that they embraced was the movement for redress and reparations. This eventually led to the passage of the Civil Liberties Act of 1988, which acknowledged that a grave injustice had been done to the Japanese Americans in incarcerating them in concentration camps during World War II.[2]

The next generation of young Asian American activists joined the pioneers in these efforts, though rarely taking the lead as their predecessors had done. Rather than founding community-based organizations, they tend to join existing national organizations that advocate for Asian Americans and defend their civil rights. In so doing, they have invigorated old groups like the Organization of Chinese Americans, which has adopted pan-Asian policies and perspectives, or one of the many new Asian American organizations that have been established in the last two decades, with their youth and energy.

THE REVIVAL OF ASIAN AMERICAN ACTIVISM

Beginning in the last decade of the twentieth century, there has been a revival of 1960s activism. Signs of this activism are sprouting among the new generation of Asian Americans who are predominantly children of post-1965 immigrants. The revival of Asian American activism has been most visible on several fronts: college campuses, Asian American organizations, and nationwide protests in response to particular events.

On college campuses, activism is channeled into developing or strengthening existing Asian American Studies curricula and fighting for equal educational opportunities. For example, in the mid-1990s, young Asian American students at Princeton University and Northwestern University went on hunger strikes and publicly protested, demanding the establishment of Asian American Studies programs on their campuses. In a show of racial-minority solidarity, black and Latino students supported them. Though reminiscent of the Third World Strikes at San Francisco State College and the University of California at Berkeley during the late 1960s, these student demonstrations took place in a radically different political climate and social context. Perhaps the most important difference is that Asian American Studies of the mid-1990s was no longer an unknown quantity but one with a 30-year history. Also, while many students are interested in taking Asian American Studies courses few pursue it as a major, giving the impression that many of today's Asian American college students are freeloaders on the Movement.

The growth of Asian American Studies has also gained momentum because of the increasing enrollment of Asian American students on college campuses. This is especially evident at the top colleges and universities, from the Ivy League to the Big Ten universities in the Midwest to the University of California campuses. At the University of California at Irvine, for example, nearly 60 percent of the undergraduate student population is Asian American and at UCLA, over 40 percent. However, unlike their Asian American student counterparts of the 1960s, who were unified in their political stance and displayed ethnic solidarity, today's Asian American students are much more diverse in ancestral origin, family socioeconomic background, and political orientation. Among the most diverse are those from the refugee families that fled Southeast Asia after America lost the Vietnam War in 1975. As members of families that sided with America against the communists in Vietnam, Laos, and Kampuchea (a.k.a. Cambodia), they have little sympathy for the so-called progressive political agenda implicit in many Asian American Studies courses.

Collective action has moved beyond university settings and has also appeared within Asian American organizations, where different ethnic groups fight for representation within the field of Asian American Studies itself. The 1998 Yamanaka affair that rocked the field provides a prime example. The controversy began when the awards committee of the Association of Asian American Studies (AAAS) voted to give the best literary book award to Lois-Ann Yamanaka's novel *Blu's Hanging.* Some Asian

American scholars and students charged that *Blu's Hanging* was explicitly racist because it perpetuated negative stereotypes of Filipino Americans as sexual predators. They insisted that the book was damaging to Filipino Americans and exacerbated the discrimination against them. As far as the critics were concerned, giving Yamanaka the award in the first place was a betrayal of one of the original goals of the field—to develop closer ties among various Asian American ethnic groups. This incident symbolized some of the tensions within Asian American Studies: some see it as a strictly academic field; others think it should also promote a political agenda. Rather than evaluating Yamanaka's work from an academic and literary standard, critics judged her work as undeserving of an award since her portrayal of Filipino Americans was not positive. Out of solidarity with the Filipino American community, a majority of the members of the AAAS who attended the association's business meeting approved a resolution to revoke the award that had been given to Yamanaka. The decision also reflected a desire to "take back" the field of Asian American Studies from the "professionals" and return it to the "activists" who had founded it. Although the event was undoubtedly a coup for the activists, it also compromised the credibility of Asian American Studies as a legitimate field of inquiry and served to alienate a segment of the AAAS membership.

Beyond the borders of academe, Asian American youth have recently banded together to stage protests around several recent events that have challenged their identities as Americans. The most visible case of Asian American activism took place in 2001. This was the year that the former Los Alamos nuclear scientist Wen Ho Lee was charged with 59 felony counts of mishandling classified information and violating the Atomic Energy Act. When Lee was charged and arrested, questions immediately surfaced about whether he was secretly a spy for the Chinese government, raising questions about whether Asians are truly American. Lee eventually pleaded guilty to a single felony charge of mishandling classified information after the U.S. government's case fell apart in court. Lee has alleged in court documents that his ethnicity played a role in his being targeted as an espionage suspect at Los Alamos, and Asian American activists fully agreed, as they protested his incarceration and demanded that he be released from prison.

In 2002, another instance of Asian American activism was the protest against a line of tee shirts made by the popular clothing store Abercrombie & Fitch. The tee shirts depicted Asian cartoon characters in stereotypically negative ways—slanted eyes, thick glasses, and heavy Asian accents. One of the tee shirts portrayed a male Asian cook with a caption reading "Wok and Roll"—playing off the stereotypical image that all Asians have accents, are forever foreign, and are not American. Through petitions circulated through the Internet and demonstrations at some Abercrombie & Fitch store locations, Asian American activists quickly came together to boycott the chain. As a result, Abercrombie & Fitch decided to stop selling the offensive tee shirts.

Most recently, in December 2002, Asian Americans responded when the African American superstar center of the L.A. Lakers, Shaquille O'Neal, told a reporter in a sing-song voice, "Tell Yao Ming, 'ching-chong-yang-wah-ah-soh.'" O'Neal was not trying to speak Chinese; he was making a racist jab at the 7'6" rookie center for the Houston Rockets, Yao Ming. While national and local news organizations ignored O'Neal's racist comments, Fox Sports Radio's *Tony Bruno Morning Extravaganza* played a recording of his racial taunt several times to its nationwide audience on December 16 and 17. This incident revealed that racist taunts of Asians are alive and well, and perhaps more crucially, not reprimanded by the media or the American public. However, Asian American activists did not allow O'Neal's comments to disappear without spreading the word. The Internet site AsianWeek.com quickly got the word out to its subscribers, who then forwarded the article to others. Eventually O'Neal admitted that his comment was "stupid."

All of these incidents illustrate that stereotypes of Asian Americans still exist, and moreover, at least some portion of America's population subscribes to them. Would Wen Ho Lee have been charged with 59 felony counts and confined to nine months of solitary confinement if he had been a white rather than a Chinese American? Would Abercrombie & Fitch have depicted African Americans in a similarly negative light and felt that it was not offensive to do so? And would the National Basketball Association (NBA) have tolerated a white sports star who made derisive comments about an African American player? The answer is a resounding no.

The current generation of Asian American activists is distinct from their 1960s predecessors in some significant ways. The most obvious difference is that they are much more heterogeneous ethnically. In addition to the Chinese and Japanese Americans, there are those who belong to the post-1965 wave of immigrants and the post–Vietnam War refugees who came to the United States. They have far fewer reservations about America, having come to this country to escape the economic and political problems of their Asian homelands without having to suffer the indignities associated with past American immigration laws or being interned by the American government during World War II. For many of them, America is the "Promised Land" rather than a hostile land that failed to fulfill the ideals expressed in its founding documents. Indeed, they make no apologies for their middle-class aspirations and avidly pursue the so-called American Dream.

That is why many of them are more conservative politically. They are, for instance, divided over the issue of affirmative action. The spring 2003

Supreme Court case on the University of Michigan's admissions policy is a case in point. Many Asian Americans have come out in support of the University of Michigan's policy because they believe it contributes to a diverse student body.[3] Moreover, they feel that the outcome of the case will affect affirmative action not only in higher education but also in areas of employment and promotion, contracting, and K-12 education. Others, however, are opposed because they believe that race-sensitive admission policies can be used to exclude groups such as Asian Americans who are perceived as overrepresented at colleges and universities.[4] They are unwilling to support such policies for underrepresented groups at the expense of the Asian American community.

For them, solidarity with other people of color has little meaning, in part, because of the interethnic conflicts that they experienced during the last decade of the twentieth century. The Los Angeles riots in 1992, when much of the violence was directed against Korean Americans and other Asian Americans, is a major example.

As the responses to the Wen Ho Lee, Abercrombie & Fitch, and Shaquille O'Neal incidents cited above indicate, young Asian American activists are willing to defend themselves and their community against those who question their American identity or deprive them of it. They recognize that, regardless of differences in ethnicity, generation, socioeconomic status, and political orientation, they are often lumped into a homogeneous category and regarded by some of their fellow Americans as forever foreign or not fully American. Hence, they feel the need to work actively against such pervasive and persistent problems as racial profiling and racial stereotyping. In this regard, the young Asian American activists of today and the old Asian American activists of yesterday have much in common.

CONCLUSION

The young Asian American activists of the 1960s have been romanticized for several reasons. The romanticization may be due in part to the "Camelot" phenomenon in which people remember them as participants in a noble quest. More likely, it is because the image serves the purpose of implicitly providing Asian Americans and others with moral, educational, and political examples for emulation. If that is indeed the case, then the idealized figures more closely resemble the larger-than-life figures in the colorful yet unrealistic and unconvincing Maoist posters of heroic workers, peasants, and soldiers that adorned the apartments of 1960s youth, rather than the real Asian American activists of yesterday.

Without doubt, these pioneer activists belonged to an idealistic generation that experienced an unprecedented "ethnic awakening," and they successfully developed a common pan-ethnic identity as Asian Americans. As Asian Americans, they were able to transcend the limitations implicit in being a member of a particular Asian ethnic group and to identify with the fate of all Asians in America. By engaging in identity politics, they have been able to approach mainstream society on the basis of greater equality, an empowering step.

But what can be said about the current generation of young Asian American activists? With the dawning of the twenty-first century, there is every reason to be optimistic about them. Although the problem of racism remains, today's Asian American activists are in a better position than their predecessors of the 1960s to deal with it, whenever it appears. Simply stated, they have a more sophisticated understanding and knowledge of racism in America, and they have greater access to institutional resources on college campuses and in the Asian communities to assist them in combating it. In the future, young Asian American activists will continue to be involved in the identity politics of an increasingly multicultural America.

Notes

1. "Serve the People" is the title of an essay written by Mao Tse-tung in 1944, which became highly popular during the Chinese Great Cultural Revolution. The essay eulogized a devoted, selfless Red Army soldier Chang Szu-teh. Asian American activists who performed ordinary tasks in these organizations likened themselves to heroes like Chang and also dedicated themselves to the liberation of the people, working selflessly in the people's interest.

2. Passage of the Civil Liberties Act notwithstanding, there are those, including government leaders, who continue to believe that the internment was the right thing to do. For example, on a radio call-in show on February 5, 2003, Representative Howard Coble (R—NC), chair of the House Judiciary Subcommittee on Crime, Terrorism and Homeland Security, said that interning the Japanese Americans in internment camps was the right thing to do. After public protests by the Japanese American Citizens League and other Asian American organizations, Coble offered what S. D. Ikeda aptly described as a "non-apology-apology" two days later. Coble said,"I apologize if I offended anybody. I certainly did not intend to offend anybody," but insisted, "I still stand by what I said … that, in no small part [internment], was done to protect the Japanese Americans themselves." Furthermore, "I don't think I said anything that calls for an apology." On February 10, Coble finally admitted, "Today we can certainly look back and see the damage that was caused because of this decision. We all now know that [FDR's internment policy] was in fact the wrong decision and an action that should never be repeated." S. D. Ikeda, Asian-American Village, "On Coble: 'It's the Leadership, Stupid!'" http://www.imdiversity.com/article_detail.asp?Article_ID=15132

3. Asian American organizations have signed on to the amicus brief to the Supreme Court submitted by the National Asian Pacific American Legal Consortium (NAPALC) in support of the University of Michigan, for example.

4. The Asian American Legal Foundation, for example, has come out in support of the plaintiffs in the University of Michigan case.

CHAPTER **20**

Conclusion:

Reflections, Thoughts, and Directions for Future Reseach

Jennifer Lee and Min Zhou

The study of youth and youth culture in the United States has a history that dates back to the early work of scholars in the Chicago School at the turn of the twentieth century. From the time when Talcott Parsons coined the phrase "youth culture" in 1942 to recent years, this line of research has progressively developed to include more youth-centered approaches. However, it still remains constrained, to a certain extent, by the conventional frameworks of criminology and deviance. Since the youthful revolts in the late 1960s, research on youth and youth cultures has ranged from work that documents and interprets the histories, activities, value systems, and multifaceted lived experiences of American youth, particularly as they developed in schools and peer groups. Later studies linked youth cultural expression, consumption, and production to socioeconomic outcomes, including both direct and indirect effects on upward or downward mobility (Bennett, 2000; Bielby, 2003; Coleman, 1961; Griffin, 1985; Jensen and Rojek, 1992; Redhead, 1993; Scarpitti and Datesman, 1980; South, 1999; Wooden and Blazak, 2001).

Although past research has moved far past its roots in deviance and delinquency, it has largely overlooked at least two significant aspects of youth and youth culture: race and gender. Not only did prior research center on whites (especially working-class whites), rendering racial minority youth invisible, it also focused heavily on males, consequently relegating females to the margins. While the white, male-dominant focus stemmed, in part, from the power and privilege of whites in the larger society, it also resulted from the bias of white, male researchers who felt that the gendered pattern of girls' leisure activities did not constitute a distinctive form of youth culture (Griffin, 1985; McRobbie, 2000; McRobbie and Garber, 1976). In sum, much of the prior research on youth culture concentrated on working-class, heterosexual white males, deviance, delinquency, and resistance to authority, thereby providing a one-dimensional portrait of youth and youth culture.

In this volume, we have gone far beyond the discussion of deviance, resistance, and male activities, and have adopted a more comprehensive approach to the study of youth culture. Focusing on Asian American youth, we posit that the study of youth culture should focus on the diverse practices of young people and that our task as social scientists is to uncover the values that underlie their activities and behavior. Moreover, we contend that the study of youth culture should be defined not only by class but also by race/ethnicity and gender. Finally, we claim that there is more cultural agency in the study of youth than previous work has acknowledged (Austin and Willard, 1998; Wulff, 1995). By more broadly investigating Asian American youth—both young men and women—we argue that they play a pivotal role as actors, agents, producers, distributors, and consumers of a distinctive youth culture of their own.

Asian American youth have actively created their own culture, often by negotiating between "American" and "Asian" traits and mixing elements of both worlds to produce an "emergent culture of hybridity." The results of their grassroots cultural production take the form of new practices, products, spaces, identities, and ethnicities that are uniquely Asian American. Although Asian Americans have been active agents in the production of a distinctive youth culture, we would like to reiterate that its development is the product of opportunities and choices on the one hand, and of structural and historical constraints on the other. This is precisely because any consideration of Asian American youth should be examined within the broader history and context of Asians in the United States. As the chapters in this volume illustrate, the processes of acculturation, assimilation, socialization, intermarriage, multiracial identification, community and political development, sexual and ethnic identification are dialectical—meaning that they are two-sided, involving both Asian American youth and outsiders. This volume also reflects the ambiguity felt by many Asian American youth who sense that they are both a part of and yet apart from mainstream America.

As we bring this volume to a close, we return to the debate with which we have been engaged from the beginning—that is, whether *Asian American* is a meaningful analytical category, especially given the diversity of the ethnic cast that comprises it. Our answer is yes. Second, synthesizing the work of the authors in the volume, we depict how Asian American youth have successfully created alternative spaces and negotiated new identities for themselves. Third, we illustrate how Asian American youth culture is distinct from other minority youth cultures, and we detail how the culture emerges as a reaction from both their parents' restrictive norms and various modes of exclusion. As Asian American youth come of age in large numbers, we hope that our readers take this volume as a point of departure and venture beyond what we have initiated. Finally, in the closing pages, we seek to offer motivating ideas and new directions for future research in this vibrant and still underexplored terrain.

ASIAN AMERICAN AS A SALIENT AND MEANINGFUL ANALYTICAL CATEGORY

As Min Zhou's chapter illustrates, Americans of Asian ancestry are composed of more than 20 different national origin groups that are diverse with regard to their mode of entry into the United States, mode of incorporation, class background, educational attainment, generational status, and American reception. The majority of Asian American youth today come from immigrant families whose parents were peasants, urbanites, laborers, professionals, entrepreneurs, transnationals, or refugees. Their varied immigrant and class backgrounds are intertwined with the process of racialization in the United States to profoundly influence their mobility outcomes. Like their immigrant parents, some will continue on the traditional bottom-up route to social mobility; others will bypass the bottom rung and move directly into mainstream American society; and still others will be trapped in poverty with dim prospects for upward mobility (Portes and Zhou, 1993). The different origins and destinies among Asians result in varied experiences in growing up American among the children of immigrants. Given the diversity of experiences across class and ethnic lines, we revisit the question of whether the category "Asian American" is analytically meaningful and useful.

Class differences among and within Asian ethnic groups are critical in shaping Asian American cultural practices, as many of the chapters in this volume illustrate. For instance, class differences play out in the marriage market, as Sara Lee poignantly reveals in Chapter 18. She notes the sharp differences in the dating patterns and partner preferences of middle- and working-class Koreans, with the middle class exhibiting a stronger preference for coethnic partners compared to their working-class counterparts who openly date across racial and ethnic boundaries. Furthermore, Linda Trinh Võ and Mary Yu Danico find that class rather than ethnicity is more important in determining the customer base of the cyber cafés that have come to dot southern California's landscape. Although Asian American patrons hail from a variety of ethnic backgrounds, they are largely from working-class households with little disposable income, few resources, and no structured after-school activities in which they actively partake. Because cyber cafés provide an inexpensive form of entertainment, working-class youth readily flock to them.

Although ethnic differences abound and class differences are pivotal in shaping the experiences of Asian American youth, we reiterate that "Asian American" remains a useful analytical category for several reasons. First, although Asians are a heterogeneous group, certain aspects of the culture transcend ethnic, class, geographic, and generational boundaries, leading to pan-ethnic alliances and practices. By illustration, Shirley Lim's chapter (Chapter 6) on the youth consumer culture of Asian American women describes the activities of Asian American sororities that included both Chinese and Japanese American members during the post–World War II era; these practices often mixed Asian ethnic and American cultural traits, resulting in hybridity. Furthermore, Victoria Namkung's study of the import car racing culture in Chapter 10 shows that while most racing crews are divided along ethnic lines, a few pan-ethnic crews have emerged onto the racing and show scenes. Similarly, Rebecca Kim's work (Chapter 15) on evangelical churches documents the emergence of pan-ethnic congregations among Asian American youth, a clear divergence from the immigrant parents' generation.

Second, Asian is a useful category because pan-ethnic alliances remain critical for political mobilization. As William Wei's chapter (Chapter 19) clearly establishes, Asians set ethnic differences aside in their fight to create the field of Asian American Studies, one of the most enduring legacies of the Asian American Movement in the 1960s. Furthermore, pan-ethnic alliances remain essential in effectively combating offensive incidents based on race and ethnicity. Wei's chapter details some of the recent incidents that led Asian American youth to collectively protest, such as the production of the offensive Abercrombie & Fitch tee-shirts that depicted Asians in a stereotypically negative light and Shaquille O'Neil's ludicrous remarks about fellow NBA player Yao Ming, who is from China. These incidents transcend ethnic boundaries and are offensive to all Asians, regardless of ethnicity, nativity, geography, and generational status.

Finally, because ethnic identity is a dialectical process—one that involves both internal and external perceptions and processes—while Asian Americans may try to assert a distinct ethnic identity, others often racialize them into a monolithic racial category (Nagel, 1994). As Nancy Yuen's study of Asian American actors in Los Angeles illustrates (in Chapter 16), Hollywood racializes Asian Americans by lumping distinct ethnic groups into a single racial category and pounding them into narrow, stereotypical molds. Even when writers, executives, and casting directors attempt to designate characters specific to Asian ethnicities (such as using surname signifiers), the attempts are often careless, arbitrary, and unverified. Moreover, as Mark Ng's research of the West Hollywood scene illustrates (see Chapter 17), Asian American gay males—regardless of ethnicity or nativity—are expected to play the stereotypical role of submissive, exotic, and passive commodified sexual beings. For Asian American youth, ethnic identity is not simply a matter of choice but one of constraint in which external forces strongly shape ethnic and racial identities.

Although ethnicity may be symbolic for whites who have the luxury of picking and choosing which aspects of their ethnic identity they wish to embrace and which to discard, ethnicity is not similarly optional for Asian Americans (Gans, 1979; Waters, 1990, 1999). As Gloria Chun's research (Chapter 7) illustrates, while U.S.-born Chinese youth adopted vastly different identities before and after World War II, their identities could hardly be considered voluntary or optional. Rather, in both periods, they were bound by social, economic, legal, and geopolitical constraints that forced them to assume two radically different ethnic options: self-asserting Chinese in the 1930s; and self-hating, sycophantic worshipers of white America in the 1950s. Moreover, Sabeen Sandhu's research in Chapter 8 underscores the nonoptional nature of Asian Indian ethnicity as she reveals that while it may be chic for Westerners to wear *mehndi*, adorn a *bhindi*, and practice yoga, it is considered foreign and traditional rather than fashionable when Asian Indian youth adopt these practices. Unlike the ethnic options enjoyed by whites, the ethnic identities of Asian Indian youth are not symbolic, but concrete and consequential.

As Jennifer Lee and Frank D. Bean's work (Chapter 3) reminds us, racial and ethnic identities are not primordial, but rather social and cultural constructions that have changed throughout our nation's history. In the year 2000, 12.4 percent of Asians claimed a multiracial background, and by the year 2050, social scientists project this figure to rise to 35 percent. Moreover, 40 percent of third-generation Asians intermarry today, largely to whites, and the children of these unions have the option to identify as "white." The high rate of Asian intermarriage combined with the option to identify multiracially or as white begs the question of whether Asian American youth are the next in line to become white (see also Lee and Bean, 2004 and Zhou, 2004 for further elaboration). Although this is certainly one possibility, continued immigration from Asia and the racial stereotypes that Asian Americans face present serious obstacles to this scenario. Hence, whether Asians—or at least some Asian ethnic groups—are the next in line to become white still remains to be seen.

At the moment, Asian American youth are certainly not white, nor do they enjoy the privileges of white ethnicity. Ethnicity is not symbolic, costless, or optional. Moreover, the negative (and positive) facets of one Asian ethnicity are often transferred to another. For instance, as William Wei notes, when Wen Ho Lee was charged with espionage, stereotypes of Asian Americans (not just Chinese Americans) as un-American, unpatriotic, and forever foreign immediately surfaced, a theme that also resonates in Gloria Chun's work. For Asian Americans, ethnic stereotypes easily and often transcend ethnic boundaries and become racial stereotypes. In sum, although *Asian American* undoubtedly masks enormous ethnic and class differences, we argue that it remains a salient and meaningful analytical category today.

CREATING ALTERNATIVE SPACES AND NEGOTIATING NEW IDENTITIES

As we speak of Asian American youth culture, it is important to note how it differs from distinctive youth cultures created and practiced by other racial minority youth, notably African Americans and Latinos. We posit that the Asian American youth culture has emerged in response to the exclusion from predominantly white mainstream society, as well as from other minority institutions with which they sometimes feel they have little in common. The Asian American youth culture also developed in response to their parents' immigrant culture, which many youth perceive as unbearably strict, foreign, and un-American. Because most of today's Asian American youth are either immigrants or the children of immigrants, their conflicts with their parents stem from differences not only in generation but also in language, culture, and customs. And unlike their native-born African American counterparts, they must navigate between two different worlds and cultures. Moreover, unlike most of their native-born Latino counterparts, they must constantly battle the stereotypical image of rootless foreigners from remote, alien cultures.

As this volume reveals, Asian American youth have had to strike a balance between these two cultures—that of their parents and that of their host country—and in the process, they have created unique cultural forms and practices. For example, Valerie Matsumoto's chapter (Chapter 5) shows how under the watchful eyes of the immigrant community, young Nisei women established and sustained dating practices on their own terms. Within the tightly knit immigrant community—where female behavior and family reputation were closely linked and carefully scrutinized—Nisei women actively organized a variety of girls' and women's clubs where a great deal of romantic socializing and courtship took place. In a similar vein, Arleen de Vera's work (Chapter 4) reveals how some Rizal Day Queen contestants expressed their own desires for self-fashioning, display, and behavior that were intended to shock the dominant leadership and parental generation more generally.

Asian American youth today continue to develop cultural practices in response to their parents' restrictive beliefs about appropriate youth behavior. For instance, in Sody Lay's chapter (Chapter 14) on Cambodian youth, he details how Cambodian culture is extremely constraining with regard to premarital romance: marriages are traditionally arranged; dating is not permitted; and social interaction with the opposite sex is frowned upon. Hence, Cambodian American parents often prohibit their children from participating in activities such as parties and dances, causing Cambodian American youth to be indignant as they witness others freely engage in these typically American teenage activities. Perhaps not surprisingly, one appeal of gang membership for Cambodian youth is that they provide a vehicle through which the teens can participate to some degree in popular American youth culture such as dating and parties.

The emergence of Asian American youth culture is in part a reaction to their parents' rigid rules and standards, and in part a response to their discomfort and/or exclusion from predominantly white and other minority social spaces. As Victoria Namkung illustrates in Chapter 10, Asian American youth were excluded from the V-8, Anglo-dominated muscle car culture of the 1970s and 1980s, and hence decided to start their own races and shows with their own cars. However, it is a mistake to assume that the exclusion stems only from white-dominant institutions and cultures; Asian American youth also experience exclusion from other ethnic scenes. For instance, since its inception, hip-hop youth culture has been dominated by African American youth, but as Lakandiwa de Leon's work (Chapter 12) shows, it was not until Filipino DJs emerged on the scene that Filipino American youth gained entry into this culture.

Moreover, the research by Diego Vigil and his colleagues and Lay (Chapter 13 and Chapter 14) illustrates that Cambodian and Vietnamese youth gangs initially emerged in response to their ostracization and repeated victimization in school by some of their classmates and members of other ethnic gangs. As their work poignantly details, in gangs, one finds opportunities for companionship, protection, excitement, a sense of identity, and not least of all, acceptance—all-too-scarce resources in a culture that deems these Asian American youth as outsiders. Both Lay and Vigil and his colleagues argue that gang formation and participation is a response to the exclusion that some Asian American youth experience from school, home, and society at large.

The theme of exclusion and the consequent creation of alternate spaces has historical roots among Asian American youth. de Vera's work (Chapter 4), for instance, shows that at a time when Filipinos were excluded from white American institutions and social scenes, Rizal Day Queen contests offered Filipino Americans a safe space to convene and socialize with coethnics. Moreover, Matsumoto's study shows that the courtship rituals among Nisei women were complicated by the structure of prewar race relations on the West Coast as well as the racial discrimination that they faced from the larger society. What is also important to note here is that young women have played a critical role in the development of Asian American youth cultural practices, a factor largely ignored in prior work on youth culture.

As producers, distributors, and consumers of these new forms of culture, Asian American youth actively created new social and cultural spaces for themselves and in the process negotiated new identities. In doing so, Asian American youth also actively challenged the enduring ethnic and racial stereotypes that too often constrain them. For instance, as Christy Chiang-Hom's work (Chapter 9) illustrates, immigrant youth develop social support networks and adopt in-group biases and out-group derogation to buffer the effects of discrimination. By remaining actively engaged in ethnic cultural practices, immigrant youth successfully create a familiar space for themselves that reaffirms a sense of ethnic pride, self-worth, power, and control in their new environment. Moreover, Yuen's chapter shows that while Hollywood may attempt to box Asian American actors into a one-dimensional mold, the actors make conscious attempts to challenge the phenotypical, verbal, and behavioral stereotypes in order to assert an Asian American identity that is more complex and multifaceted. Hence, while Asian American youth face constraints and exclusion, they work to actively create new cultural forms, expressions, products, and identities on their own terms.

MODES OF EXCLUSION

Exclusion also operates in both directions. Asian American youth are not only the recipients of racial exclusion, but they, too, are active agents who exclude other groups—including other racial/ethnic groups, other Asian ethnic groups, and even their less acculturated coethnic peers. For example, Sara Lee's discussion of the marriage preferences of middle-class second-generation Koreans reveals that while they strongly prefer to marry co-ethnics, their next preference would be mates who are "Asian." However, the way middle-class Koreans define "Asian" is narrowly circumscribed to include only East Asians such as Chinese, Japanese, and Koreans; excluded from the category are Southeast Asians such as Vietnamese and Filipinos who they and their parents deem as lower in social status. So strong is their parents' prejudice against Southeast Asians that they would prefer that their children marry a Caucasian before choosing a Southeast Asian partner.

The diversity and implicit stratification within "Asian" reminds us once again that it is a socially constructed category that masks differences in national origin, ethnic identification, and class.

Lee's work also touches upon one of the unspoken yet implicit divides among Asians—that between East and Southeast Asians. Chinese, Japanese, and Korean American youth may feel they have little in common with or feel no fictive kinship with Vietnamese, Filipinos, Cambodians, Hmong, and Asian Indians, and vice versa. Furthermore, East Asians are phenotypically distinct from South and Southeast Asians; Southeast Asians generally tend to be darker-skinned—a nontrivial physical characteristic in a country in which skin color has been associated with class, status, opportunity, and mobility (Davis, 1991; Haney-López, 1996; Keith and Herring, 1991; Massey and Denton, 1993). This divide also manifests in the different types of youth culture in which these groups choose to participate. For instance, Filipino and Asian Indian youth are more likely to gravitate toward the hip-hop scene than are Chinese, Japanese, or Korean Americans. Although we can only speculate at this point, what may emerge in the future is a bifurcated Asian category that places East Asians closer to whites and Southeast Asians closer to other racial and ethnic minorities such as African Americans and some Latino groups. A divide along these lines would provide further evidence of the emergence of a new racial hierarchy split between blacks and nonblacks, as Lee and Bean discuss in Chapter 3 (see also Lee and Bean, 2004).

Asian American youth not only exclude other ethnic groups, but they also discriminate within one's ethnic group, as Chiang-Hom's work on immigrant youth poignantly illustrates. She finds that immigrant youth who immigrate as adolescents find themselves derided as "F.O.B.s" (fresh off the boat) by their U.S.-born and -raised peers, including their acculturated coethnics who view them as "too Asian" and embarrassingly unassimilated. Interestingly, rather than internalizing the negative stereotypes that U.S.-born youth hold of them, immigrant youth remain critical of American culture and do not subscribe to the belief that becoming American is necessarily positive or desirable. Compared to the second generation, immigrant youth are less anxious about their inability to "fit in" with the cool crowd, less troubled by their treatment as newly arrived immigrants, and less affected by discrimination.

Although immigrant youth may have acquired a repertoire of strategies to rebuff the hostility and discrimination that they experience from their American peers, the tension between immigrant youth and Asian American youth who were born and raised in the United States is real. Rather than feeling an obligation to help the newly arrived Asian immigrant youth navigate America's cultural maze or invite them into their social circles, U.S.-born and -raised Asian Americans choose to distance themselves from their less acculturated coethnics. Exactly why this is the case is a question open to debate, but we conjecture that second-generation Asian American youth disparage and distance themselves from their less acculturated counterparts because the newly arrived are a blatant symbol and glaring reminder of the negative stereotype of Asians as "forever foreign." By distancing themselves from foreign-born youth, the more acculturated 1.5 and second generations attempt to actively assert an identity that is diametrically opposed to the "forever foreign" stereotype—one that is unquestionably "American."

This still leaves the question of why Asian American youth should feel a need to distance themselves from their less acculturated coethnics in order to assert an "American" identity. Here, we posit that the greater proportion of foreign-born Asians in the United States casts an "immigrant shadow" on all Asians that marks them as foreign. Because Asian American youth realize that negative consequences are associated with foreign-born status, they choose to disassociate themselves from all newly arrived immigrant youth, including their fellow ethnics. Just as middle-class blacks must often confront the stigma of race and the negative stereotypes of the underclass on a regular basis, native-born Asian American youth must often confront and combat the stigma of foreignness for reasons of race alone (Franklin, 1991). The presence of an "immigrant shadow" reminds us that for Asian American youth, the lived experiences of race are real, consequential, and at times, costly.

DIRECTIONS FOR FUTURE RESEARCH

Although the study of youth culture has historically focused on outcomes, such as crime, deviance, juvenile delinquency, and educational failure, this volume takes a step in moving the research agenda forward by focusing on youth processes, and studying youth as cultural agents in their own right who create, consume, and diffuse new forms and distinctive cultures. Future research on the study of youth culture should continue in this vein. Another historical trend in the study of youth culture has been its traditionally male focus, but as Chapters 4, 5, and 6 illustrate, females have been and continue to be active agents in the production of youth culture. Because female youth have been marginalized in previous studies of youth culture, there is still much ground that can be covered in this regard, both historically and contemporaneously.

In this volume, we have also shown that Asian American youth create a distinctive Asian American youth culture and identity that is the product and consequence of historical and contextual factors, their parents' restrictive beliefs about appropriate youth behavior, and various modes of exclusion. Regardless of the way in which exclusion operates—whether overt or covert, intended or unintended, and who does the excluding—exclusion itself may pave the way for the emergence of new forms of culture. There are many other facets of Asian American youth culture that we have not tapped into in this volume; future research could further identify these, while paying close attention to the structural and historical forces that give rise to them.

Future research could also study youth culture through a lens that compares Asian Americans with other groups such as African Americans and Latinos. The comparative perspective could help to illuminate how different historical experiences, structural constraints, and opportunities give rise to the distinctiveness and differences in expressions and forms of youth culture. This approach would also allow us to identify the interracial and interethnic differences and similarities that emerge among the groups.

It is also important to consider that Asian is a heterogeneous category that masks differences in ethnicity, nativity, and generational status. Although we have argued that some cultural practices have adopted pan-ethnic forms, we are keenly aware that others are uniquely ethnic. Studying which cultural practices span ethnic boundaries and which remain within ethnic lines and why are also important questions for future research. In addition, given the possibility of the emergence of a divide that separates East and Southeast Asians, with East Asians aligning themselves more closely to whites and Southeast Asians moving closer to blacks, will we see evidence of the emergence of a black-nonblack divide, as proposed by Lee and Bean in Chapter 3? Furthermore, if Asian American youth bifurcate along these lines, it will be interesting to study whether new cultural forms also split along similar lines. Moreover, as Lee and Bean underscore, racial boundaries have shifted in the past and are bound to expand yet again. It will be critical to study how the rising rates of intermarriage and multiracial identification among Asian Americans will affect youth culture, ethnicity, and identity.

Finally, as Zhou reminds us, the Asian American youth population is still a very young one, with many of the second generation still in their pre-teen and early teen years. As this population reaches maturity and enters adulthood, future research should note which cultural practices pass from one generation to the next, which fade into the background, and what new cultural forms develop. In the introductory chapter, we borrowed William Bielby's term *grass roots cultural production* to describe how Asian American youth carve out a space and culture of their own (Bielby, 2004). As Bielby suggests, conceptualizing youth culture in terms of "grass roots cultural production" is sociologically interesting on three levels: as a status attainment process; as processes of institutionalization and organizational change; and as a cultural commodity that is consumed, appropriated, and reinterpreted in a way that provides meaning in people's lives.

Like all forms of youth culture, Asian American youth culture will continue to evolve as Asian American youth mature and as historical contexts change. Future research may engage with a number of pressing and unanswered questions regarding the effect of Asian American youth culture on Asian Americans' school performance, transition to adulthood, and adult experiences. It will also be noteworthy to study how Asian American youth culture affects American institutions such as schools, the workplace, and other economic, political, and social organizations. Will Asian American youth culture have an enduring impact on these larger institutions? Moreover, Asian American youth are beginning to establish cultural institutions of their own such as theaters, film and music production companies, music bands, nightclubs, and magazines. Will later generations still find these institutions personally reflexive and socially meaningful and continue to use them for their own cultural expression, innovation, production, and consumption? Alternatively, newer generations of Asian American youth may not find current cultural forms, practices, and institutions relevant in their lives, thereby allowing them to fade away and die. Even if current cultural practices eventually fade into the twilight, it still remains to be seen whether they will become cultural commodities that hold special significance for the generation of youth who grew up in this era (like rock 'n roll and hip hop). In other words, when today's Asian American youth reach their forties and fifties and look retrospectively at their youth, will they feel that it was worth their effort to create and practice a youth culture that was distinctively of their own making?

Although the questions are endless, one thing is certain: as newer cohorts of Asian American youth succeed one another, older cultural forms will evolve and newer ones will develop. However, what is also worth pursuing in future research is which forms will persist, what these persistent forms will look like as opposed to the newly emergent ones, how they will affect the generation coming of age as compared with the grown-up generation, and who will decide what forms are to be kept or let go. In closing, we would like to reiterate that the historical and structural circumstances in which Asian American youth grow up will prompt a new generation of youth to create, adopt, and consume different forms of youth culture, stimulating new research opportunities that extend far beyond today's generation of youth.

Bibliography

Abrams, Mark, *The Teenage Consumer* (London: London Press Exchange, 1959).

Adeva, Manuel A., "Filipino Students in the United States," *Mid-Pacific Magazine* 44 (1932): 119–123.

Agbayani-Siewert, Pauline, and Linda Revilla, "Filipino Americans," in *Asian Americans: Contemporary Trends and Issues,* ed. Pyong Gap Min (Thousand Oaks, CA: Sage Publications, 1995), 134–168.

Alba, Richard D., *Italian Americans: Into the Twilight of Ethnicity* (Engelwood Cliffs, NJ: Prentice Hall, 1985).

———, *Ethnic Identity: The Transformation of White America* (New Haven, CT: Yale University Press, 1990).

Alba, Richard and Victor Nee, "The Assimilation of Immigrant Groups: Concept, Theory, and Evidence," *International Migration Review* 31 (1996): 826–874.

Allen, James P. and Eugene Turner, *The Ethnic Quilt: Population Diversity in Southern California* (Los Angeles: The Center for Geographical Studies, California State University of Northridge, 1997).

Allen, Rebecca and Harry Hiller, "The Social Organization of Migration: An Analysis of the Uprooting and Flight of Vietnamese Refugees," *International Migration Review* 22 (1985): 439–451.

Almaguer, Thomas, *Chicano Men: A Cartography of Homosexual Identity and Behavior* (New York: Routledge, 1993).

Almirol, Edwin B., "Rights and Obligations in Filipino American Families," *Journal of Comparative Family Studies* 13 (1982): 291–306.

Alsaybar, Bangele D., "Deconstructing Deviance: Filipino American Youth Gangs, 'Party Culture,' and Ethnic Identity in Los Angeles," *Amerasia Journal* 25 (1999): 116–138.

Alumkal, Antony, "Scandal of the Model Minority Mind?: The Bible and Second-Generation Asian American Evangelicals," Paper presented at the 2000 *Asian and Pacific Americans and Religion Research Initiative,* Santa Barbara, CA: June 2000.

Anderson, Benedict, *Imagined Communities: Reflections on the Origin and Spread of Nationalism* (London: Verso, 1983).

Anzaldua, Gloria, *Borderlands, La Frontera: The New Mestiza* (San Francisco: Aunt Lute Book Company, 1987).

Arakas, Irini, "Strike a Pose," *Vogue Magazine.* August (2002): 136–143.

Arbetter, Lisa, "Indian Summer," *InStyle Magazine* 6, no. 6 (1999): 79.

Austin, Joe and Michael Nevin Willard, eds., *Generations of Youth: Youth Cultures and History in Twentieth Century America* (New York: New York University Press, 1998a).

Austin, Joe and Michael Nevin Willard, "Introduction: Angels of History, Demons of Culture," in *Generations of Youth: Youth Cultures and History in Twentieth-Century America*, ed. Joe Austin and Michael Nevin Willard (New York: New York University Press, 1988b), 1–20.

Ave, Mario P., "Characteristics of Filipino Organizations in Los Angeles" (Master's Thesis, University of Southern California, 1956).

Azuma, Eiichiro, "Walnut Grove: A Japanese American Farm Community in the Sacramento River Delta, 1892–1942" (Master's Thesis, Asian American Studies Interdepartmental Degree Program, University of California, Los Angeles, 1992).

Baba, Y., "Vietnamese Gangs, Cliques and Delinquents," *Journal of Gang Research* 8 (2001): 2:1–20.

Bach, R.L. and J.B. Bach, "Employment Patterns of Southeast Asian Refugees," *Monthly Labor Review* 103 (1980): 31–38.

Back, Les, *New Ethnicities and Urban Culture: Racism and Multiculture in Young Lives* (New York: St. Martin's Press, 1996).

Baguioro, Luz, "Manila Kids Skip Class to Play Counter-Strike," *Straits Times* (Singapore), January 27, 2002.

Bailey, Beth L., *From Front Porch to Back Seat, Courtship in Twentieth-Century America* (Baltimore: Johns Hopkins University Press, 1988/1989).

Baker, Michael, "Internet Fad Grips Korean Youth Culture," *Courier Mail*, May 6, 2000, p. 21.

Baldassare, Mark, *California in the New Millennium: The Changing Social and Political Landscape* (Berkeley: University of California Press, 2000).

Banet-Weiser, Sarah, *The Most Beautiful Girl in the World: Beauty Pageants and National Identity* (Berkeley: University of California Press, 1999).

Bangkok Post [online], "Internet: Youths Lost in Profitable World of Cyber Games; Café Owners Rush to Lure More Children," Copyright FT Asia Africa Intelligence Wire, August 20, 2001.

Bankston, Carl L., III and Min Zhou, "Effects of Minority-Language Literacy on the Academic Achievement of Vietnamese Youth in New Orleans," *Sociology of Education* 68 (1995): 1–17.

———, "Valedictorians and Delinquents: The Bifurcation of Vietnamese American Youth," *Deviant Behavior: An Interdisciplinary Journal* 18 (1997): 343–364.

Banner, Lois, *American Beauty* (New York: Alfred A. Knopf, 1983).

Batra, Sumita and Liz Wilde, *The Art of Mehndi* (New York: Penguin Studio Group, 1999).

Bean, Frank D. and Gillian Stevens, *America's Newcomers and the Dynamics of Diversity* (New York: Russell Sage Foundation, 2003).

Bearman, Peter S., Jo Jones, and J. Richard Udry, The National Longitudinal Study of Adolescent Health: Research Design [WWW document published in 1997 and viewed on December 15, 1999, at http://www.cpc.unc.edu/projects/addhealth/design.html.

Beck, Aaron. T., C.H. Ward, M. Mendelson, J. Mock, and J. Erbaugh, "An Inventory for Measuring Depression," *Archives of General Psychiatry* 12 (1961): 57–62.

Beck, Aaron. T., Robert A. Steer, and Margery G. Garbin, "Psychometric Properties of the Beck Depression Inventory: Twenty-Five Years of Evaluation," *Clinical Psychology Review* 8 (1988): 77–100.

Becker, Howard, *Outsiders: Studies in the Sociology of Deviance* (New York: Free Press, 1963).

———, *Art Worlds* (Berkeley: University of California Press, 1982).

Bennett, Andy, *Popular Music and Youth Culture: Music, Identity and Place* (New York: Palgrave, 2000).

Benson, J., *The Rise of Consumer Society in Britain, 1880–1980* (London: Longman, 1994).

Berg, Charles Ramirez, *Latino Images in Film: Stereotypes, Subversion, Resistance* (Austin: University of Texas Press, 2002).

Berger, Peter L., *The Sacred Canopy* (New York: Anchor, 1967).

Bielby, William T., "Rock in a Hard Place: Grass-Roots Cultural Production in the Post-Elvis Era," *American Sociological Review* 69 (2004): 1–13.

Blackman, S.J., *Youth: Positions and Oppositions: Style, Sexuality and Schooling* (Aldershot: Avebury Press, 1995).

Blanc-Szanton, Cristina, "Collision of Cultures: Historical Reformulations of Gender in the Lowland Visayas, Philippines," in *Power and Difference: Gender in Island Southeast Asia*, ed. Jane Atkinson and Shelly Errington (Stanford, CA: Stanford University Press, 1990), 345–383.

Bloch, Louis, *Facts about Filipino Immigration into California* (San Francisco: California State Printing Office, California Department of Industrial Relations, Special Bulletin No. 3, 1930).

Boggs, Grace Lee, *Living for Change: An Autobiography* (Minneapolis: University of Minneapolis Press, 1988).

Bogle, Donald, *Toms, Coons, Mulattos, Mammies, and Budks* (New York: Continuum, 1989).

Bonus, Rick, *Locating Filipino Americans: Ethnicity and the Cultural Politics of Space* (Philadelphia: Temple University Press, 2000).

Bourdieu, Pierre, "Cultural Reproduction and Social Reproduction," in *Power and Ideology in Education*, ed. A. H. Halsey and Jerome Karabel (New York: Oxford University Press, 1977), 487–511.

Boyle, Gregory J., "Victimizers Call Us to Compassion, Too," *Los Angeles Times*, September 29, 1995, B4.

Brake, Michael, *Comparative Youth Culture: The Sociology of Youth Cultures and Youth Subcultures in America, Britain, and Canada* (New York: Routledge, 1985).

Brodkin, Karen, *How Jews Became White Folks and What That Says about Race in America* (New Brunswick, NJ: Rutgers University Press, 1998).

Brody, J., "Vietnamese: Statistics Belie the Image of the Superachiever," *Orange County Register*, May 12, 1986, p. A5.

Busto, Rudy V., "The Gospel According to the Model Minority?" *Amerasia Journal* 22 (1996): 133–147.

Butler, Judith, *Gender Trouble: Feminism and the Subversion of Identity* (New York: Routledge, 1990).

Cannell, Fennella, *Power and Intimacy in the Christian Philippines* (Cambridge: Cambridge University Press, 1999).

Carvajal, Doreen, "Trying to Halt 'Silent Exodus,'" *Los Angeles Times*, May 9, 1994, Part A.

Chai, Karen, "Competing for the Second-Generation: English-Language Ministry at a Korean Protestant Church," in *Gatherings in Diaspora: Religious Communities and the New Immigration*, ed. R. Stephen Warner and Judith G. Wittner (Philadelphia: Temple University Press, 1998).

Chan, Jeffrey Paul, Frank Chin, Lawson Fusao Inada, and Shawn Wong, eds., *Aiiieeeee!: An Anthology of Asian American Writers* (New York: Penguin, 1974).

Chan, Sucheng, *Asian Americans: An Interpretive History* (New York: Twayne Publishers, 1991).

Chang, Carrie, "Amen. Pass the Kimchee: Why Are Asian Americans on College Converting to Christianity in Droves?" *Monolid: An Asian American Magazine for Those Who Aren't Blinking* 1, no. 1 (2000): 1–9, http://www.monolid.com/articles1.html, viewed on December 12, 2000.

Chao, Julie, "The Parachute Blues," *San Francisco Examiner*, July 6, 1997, A13 & A15.

Chatterjee, Partha, *The Nation and Its Fragments: Colonial and Postcolonial Histories* (Princeton, NJ: Princeton University Press, 1993).

Cheng, Lucie and Philip Q. Yang, "Asian: The 'Model Minority' Deconstructed," in *Ethnic Los Angeles*, ed. Roger Waldinger and Mehdi Bozorgmehr (New York: Russell Sage Foundation, 1996), 305–344.

Children Now, *Fall Colors 2001–2002 Prime Time Diversity Report* (Children Now, 2000).

Chin, Frank, "Come All Ye Asian American Writers of the Real and the Fake," in *The Big Aiiieeeee!: An Anthology of Chinese American and Japanese American Literature*, ed. Jeffrey Paul Chan, Frank Chin, Lawson Fusao Inada, and Shawn Wong (New York: Penguin Books, 1991), 1–92.

———, *Bridging the Pacific: San Francisco Chinatown and Its People* (San Francisco: Chinese Historical Society of America, 1989).

Chinn, Thomas, "A Historian's Reflection on Chinese-American Life in San Francisco, 1919–1991" (Interviews conducted by Ruth Teiser, Oral History Office, The Bancroft Library, Berkeley, California: Regents of the University of California, 1993).

Chow, Sue, "The Significance of Race in the Private Sphere: Asian Americans and Spousal Preference," *Sociological Inquiry* 70 (2000): 1–29.

Choy, Bong-young, *Koreans in America* (Chicago: Nelson-Hall, 1979).

Christopher, Jason, "Madonna Newswatch," [database on-line]; available at http://www.Singnet.com.sg/'a12345/madnew35.htm, September 21, 1998.

Chun, Gloria Heyung, "Of Orphans and Warriors: Inventing Chinese American Culture and Identity" (Ph.D. dissertation, Department of Ethnic Studies, University of California, Berkeley, 1993).

————, *Of Orphans and Warriors: Inventing Chinese American Culture and Identity* (New Brunswick, NJ: Rutgers University Press, 2000).

Clarke, John, "The Skinheads and the Magical Recovery of Community," in *Resistance through Rituals: Youth Subcultures in Post-War Britain,* ed. Stuart Hall and Tony Jefferson (Hutchinson, UK: Hutchinson University Library in association with the Centre for Contemporary Cultural Studies, University of Birmingham, 1976), 99–102.

Clarke, John, Stuart Hall, Tony Jefferson, and Brian Roberts, "Subcultures, Cultures, and Class," in *Resistance through Rituals: Youth Subcultures in Post-War Britain,* ed. Stuart Hall and Tony Jefferson (Hutchinson, UK: Hutchinson University Library in association with the Centre for Contemporary Cultural Studies, University of Birmingham, 1976), 9–79.

Cohen, Albert, *Delinquent Boys: The Culture of the Gang* (New York: Free Press, 1955).

Cohen, Colleen Ballerino, Richard Wilk, and Beverly Stoeltje, eds., *Beauty Queens on the Global Stage: Gender, Contests, and Power* (New York: Routledge, 1996).

Cohen, Robert, *Acting Professionally: Raw Facts about Careers in Acting* (Mountain View, CA: Mayfield Publishing Company, 1990).

Coleman, James S., *The Adolescent Society: The Social Life of the Teenager and Its Impact on Education* (New York: Free Press, 1961).

Collins, Patricia Hill, *Black Feminist Thought: Knowledge, Consciousness, and the Politics of Empowerment* (New York: Routledge, 1990).

Conzen, Kathleen Neils, David A. Gerber, Ewa Morawska, George E. Pozzetta, and Rudolph J. Vecoli, "The Invention of Ethnicity: A Perspective from the U.S.A.," *Journal of American Ethnic History* 11 (1992) 3–41.

Cooper, J., "Refugees Have Made It a Remarkable 15 Years." *Los Angeles Times,* May 3, 1990, p. B11.

Cordova, Dorothy, "Voices from the Past: Why They Came," in *Making Waves,* ed. Asian Women United of California (Boston: Beacon Press, 1989), 42–49.

Cordova, Fred, *Filipinos: Forgotten Asian Americans* (Dubuque, Iowa: Kendall/Hunt Publishing Company, 1983).

Cornell, Stephen and Douglas Hartmann, *Ethnicity and Race: Making Identities in a Changing World* (Thousand Oaks, CA: Pine Forge Press, 1998).

Cressey, Paul G., *The Taxi-Dance Hall* (New York: Free Press, 1932).

Cross, Brian, *It's not about a Salary … Rap, Race and Resistance in Los Angeles* (London: Verso, 1993).

DaCosta, Kimberly, "Remaking the Color Line: Social Bases and Implications of the Multiracial Movement" (Unpublished Dissertation, University of California, Berkeley, 2000).

Danico, Mary Yu, *The 1.5 Generation: Becoming Korean American in Hawaii* (Honolulu: University of Hawaii Press, 2004).

Davis, F. James, *Who Is Black? One Nation's Definition* (University Park: Pennsylvania State University Press, 1991).

Davis, Kingsley, "Intermarriage in Caste Societies," *American Anthropologist* 43 (1941): 376–395.

de Leon, Felipe M., Jr., "The Filipinos'Colonized Psyche'," *The Philippine News,* Week of September 27–October 3, 1995, A10.

De Vera, Arleen, "The Tapia-Saiki Incident: Interethnic Conflict and Filipino Responses to the Anti-Filipino Exclusion Movement," in *Over the Edge: Remapping the American West,* ed. Valerie J. Matsumoto and Blake Allmendinger (Berkeley: University of California Press, 1999), 201–214.

Dre, Dr., DJ Quick, and Truth Hurts, "Addicted," *Interscope Records,* 2002.

Dunn, Robert, "In America Lies My Future," *Chinese Digest,* May 15, 1936, p. 3.

Dyer, Richard, *Heavenly Bodies* (Basingstoke, UK: Macmillan, 1986).

Efron, S., "Sweatshops Expanding into Orange County." *Los Angeles Times,* November 26, 1989, p. A1.

Eng, Alvin, *Tokens?: The NYC Asian American Experience on Stage* (New York: Asian American Writers' Workshop, 1999).

Enloe, Cynthia, *Bananas, Beaches and Bases: Making Feminist Sense of International Politics* (Berkeley: University of California Press, 1989).

Entman, Robert M. and Andrew Rojecki, *The Black Image in the White Mind: Media and Race in America* (Chicago: University of Chicago Press, 2000).

Epstein, Jonathon, *Youth Culture: Identity in a Postmodern World* (Oxford, UK: Blackwell, 1998).

Eschbach, Karl, "The Enduring and Vanishing American Indian: American Indian Population Growth and Intermarriage in 1980," *Ethnic and Racial Studies* 18 (1995): 89–108.

Espiritu, Yen Le, *Asian American Panethnicity: Bridging Institutions and Identities* (Philadelphia: Temple University Press, 1992).

Farley, Reynolds, "Identifying with Multiple Races: A Social Movement That Succeeded but Failed?" Research Report No. 01–491 (Ann Arbor, MI: Population Studies Center, University of Michigan, 2001).

Fass, Paula, *The Damned and the Beautiful: American Youth in the 1920's* (New York: Oxford University Press, 1977).

Fenton, Steve, *Ethnicity: Racism, Class and Culture* (Lanham, MD: Rowman & Littlefield, 1999).

Firmat, Gustavo Pérez, *Life on the Hyphen: The Cuban-American Way* (Austin: University of Texas Press, 1994).

Foner, Nancy, *From Ellis Island to JFK: New York's Two Great Waves of Immigration* (New Haven, CT and New York: Yale University Press and Russell Sage Foundation, 2000).

Fong, Colleen and Judy Yung, "In Search of the Right Spouse: Interracial Marriage among Chinese and Japanese Americans," *Amerasia Journal* 21 (1995): 77–98.

Foronda, Marcelino A., Jr., "America Is in the Heart: Ilokano Immigration to the United States (1906–1930)," De La Salle University, Occasional Paper No. 3 (Manila: Philippines, 1976).

Foucault, Michel, *The History of Sexuality, Volume I: An Introduction* (Harmondsworth: Penguin Books, 1981).

Franklin, Raymond S., *Shadows of Race and Class* (Minneapolis: University of Minnesota Press, 1991).

Frith, Simon, *The Sociology of Youth* (Ormskirk, Lancashire: Causeway Press, 1984).

Fujino, Diane C., "Structural and Individual Influences Affecting Racialized Dating Relationships," in *Relationships among Asian American Women*, ed. J.L. Chin (Washington, DC: American Psychological Association, 2000), 181–210.

Fuligni, Andrew J., "The Adjustment of Children from Immigrant Families," *Current Directions in Psychological Science* 7 (1998): 99–103.

Gamalinda, Eric, "Myth, Memory, Myopia: Of, I May Be Brown But I Hear America Singin'," in *Flippin': Filipinos on America*, ed. Luis H. Francia and Eric Gamalinda (New York: Asian American Writers Workshop, 1998).

Ganguly, Meenakshi, "Indian Stunners," *Time.com: Time Magazine*, July 31, 2000, pp. 1–3.

Gans, Herbert J., *The Urban Villagers: Group and Class in the Life of Italian-Americans* (New York: The Free Press, 1962).

———, "Symbolic Ethnicity: The Future of Ethnic Groups and Cultures in America," *Ethnic and Racial Studies* 2 (1979): 1–20.

———, "Second-Generation Decline: Scenarios for the Economic and Ethnic Futures of the Post-1965 American Immigrants," *Ethnic and Racial Studies* 15 (1992): 173–192.

———, "The Possibility of a New Racial Hierarchy in the Twenty-First Century United States," in *The Cultural Territories of Race*, ed. Michèle Lamont (Chicago and New York: University of Chicago Press and Russell Sage Foundation, 1999), 371–390.

Gelder, Ken, "Introduction to Part Two: The Birmingham Tradition and Cultural Studies," in *The Subcultures Reader*, ed. Ken Gelder and Sarah Thornton (New York: Routledge, 1997), 83–89.

Gelder, Ken and Sarah Thornton, eds., *The Subcultures Reader* (New York: Routledge, 1997).

Gerstle, Gary, "Liberty, Coercion, and the Making of Americans," in *The Handbook of International Migration*, ed. Charles Hirschman, Philip Kasinitz, and Josh DeWind (New York: Russell Sage Foundation, 1999), 275–293.

Gibson, Margaret A., *Accommodation without Assimilation: Sikh Immigrants in an American High School* (Ithaca, NY: Cornell University Press, 1989).

Gilbertson, Greta, Joseph F. Fitzpatrick and Lijun Yang, "Hispanic Intermarriage in New York City: New Evidence from 1991," *International Migration Review* 30 (1996): 445–459.

Glenn, Evelyn Nakano, *Issei, Nisei, War Bride: Three Generations of Japanese American Women in Domestic Service* (Philadelphia: Temple University Press, 1986).

Godfrey, Brian J., *Neighborhoods in Transition: The Making of San Francisco's Ethnic and Nonconformist Communities* (Berkeley: University of California Press, 1988).

Goffman, Erving, *Stigma: Notes on the Management of a Spoiled Identity* (Englewood, NJ: Prentice Hall, 1963).

Gold, Steve J. and Nazli Kibria, "Vietnamese Refugees and Blocked Mobility," *Asian and Pacific Migration Review* 2 (1989): 27–56.

Gonzalves, Theodore S., "The Day the Dancers Stayed: On Pilipino Cultural Nights," in *Filipino Americans: Transformation and Identity,* ed. Maria P.P. Root (London: Sage, 1997).

Goodwin, Jin, "Come out of Chinatown," *Chinese Press,* April 18, 1950, p. 6.

Gordon, Milton M., *Assimilation in American Life: The Role of Race, Religion, and National Origins* (New York: Oxford University Press, 1964).

Graham, Jefferson, "Cyber Cafés Serve an Explosive Brew," *USA Today,* February 7, 2002, p. 10.

Gramsci, Antonio, *Selections from the Prison Notebooks* (New York: Lawrence and Wishart, 1971).

Grant, B., *The Boat People* (Sydney, Australia: Penguin Books, 1979).

Grant, Kathryn E. and Bruce E. Compas, "Stress and Anxious-Depressed Symptoms among Adolescents: Searching for Mechanisms of Risk," *Journal of Consulting & Clinical Psychology* 63, no. 6 (1995): 1015–1021.

Gray, Herman, *Watching Race: Television and the Struggle for "Blackness"* (Minneapolis: University of Minnesota Press, 1995).

Griffin, Christine, *Typical Girls? Young Women from School to the Job Market* (Boston: Routledge and Kegan Paul, 1985).

———, *Representations of Youth: The Study of Youth and Adolescence in Britain* (Cambridge, UK: Polity Press, 1993).

Hall, Kathleen, "There's a Time to Act English and a Time to Act Indian: The Politics of Identity Among British-Sikh Teenagers," in *Children and the Politics of Culture,* ed. Sharon Stephens (Princeton, NJ: Princeton University Press, 1995), 243–264.

Hall, Stuart, "The Spectacle of the 'Other'," in *Representation: Cultural Representations and Signifying Practices,* ed. Stuart Hall (London: Sage, 1997), 225–279.

Hall, Stuart and Tony Jefferson, eds., *Resistance through Rituals: Youth Subcultures in Post-War Britain* (Hutchinson, UK: Hutchinson University Library in association with the Centre for Contemporary Cultural Studies, University of Birmingham, 1976).

Hamamoto, Darrell Y., *Monitored Peril: Asian Americans and the Politics of TV Representation* (Minneapolis: University of Minnesota Press, 1994).

Hamilton, Denise, "Chinese-American Leaders Call for Action on 'Parachute Kids'," *Los Angeles Times,* July 29, 1993a, p. B3.

———, "A House, Cash—and No Parents," *Los Angeles Times,* June 24, 1993b, p. A1.

Haney-López, Ian F., *White by Law: The Legal Construction of Race* (New York: New York University Press, 1996).

Hanser, Ernest O., "Chinaman's Chance," *Saturday Evening Post,* December 7, 1940, p. 85.

Harker, Kathryn, "Immigrant Generation, Assimilation and Adolescent Psychological Well-Being," *Social Forces* 79 (2001): 969–1004.

Harris, Kathleen M., "The Health Status and Risk Behavior of Adolescents in Immigrant Families," in *Children of Immigrants: Health, Adjustment, and Public Assistance,* ed. Donald J. Hernandez (Washington, DC: National Academy Press, 1999), 286–347.

Harter, Susan, "Causes and Consequences of Low Self-Esteem in Children and Adolescents," in *Self-Esteem: The Puzzle of Low Self-Regard,* ed. Roy F. Baumeister (New York: Plenum Press, 1993), 87–116.

Harter, Susan and Nancy R. Whitesell, "Multiple Pathways to Self-Reported Depression and Psychological Adjustment among Adolescents," *Development and Psychopathology* 8 (1996): 761–777.

Hemminger, Carol, "Little Manila: The Filipino in Stockton Prior to World War II," *The Pacific Historian* 24 (1980): 207–220.

Hicks, Jerry, "Cyber Café Crackdown Looms," *Los Angeles Times,* January 21, 2002, p. B1.

Hirata, Lucie Cheng, "Free, Endentured, Enslaved: Chinese Prostitutes in Nineteenth-Century America," *Signs* 5 (1979): 3–29.

Hirschman, Charles, Richard Alba, and Reynolds Farley, "The Meaning and Measurement of Race in the U.S. Census: Glimpses into the Future," *Demography* 37 (2000): 381–393.

Ho, Fred, "Identity: Beyond Asian American Jazz: My Musical and Political Changes in the Asian American Movement," *Leonardo Music Journal* 9 (1999): 45–51.

Hom, Christy L., "The Academic, Psychological, and Behavioral Adjustment of Chinese Parachute Kids" (Ph.D. dissertation, Department of Psychology, University of Michigan, Ann Arbor, 2002).

Hong, Kaye, "Go West to China," *Chinese Digest,* May 22, 1936, p. 3.

Hong, Maria, "Introduction," in *Growing Up Asian American: Stories of Childhood, Adolescence, and Coming of Age in America, from the 1800s to the 1990s—by 32 Asian American Writers,* ed. Maria Hong (New York: Avon Books, 1993), 13–17.

Hong, Peter Y., "The Changing Face of Higher Education," http://www.aac.sunysb.edu/asian americanstudies/changingface.htr, viewed on December 12, 2000.

hooks, bell, *Ain't I a Woman: Black Women and Feminism* (Boston: South End Press, 1981).

Hsia, Jayjia and Marsha Hirano-Nakanishi, "The Demographics of Diversity: Asian Americans and Higher Education," *Change: The Magazine of Higher Learning* (November/December, 1989): 20.

Hua, Vanessa, "We All Scream for Chinoiserie," *San Francisco Examiner,* February 6, 2000, p. 10.

Hunt, Darnell, "Prime Time in Black and White: Making Sense of the 2001 Fall Season," *The CAAS Research Report,* vol. 1, no. 1 (Los Angeles: UCLA Center for African American Studies, 2002).

Hurh, Won Moo and Kwang Chung Kim, "Religious Participation of Korean Immigrants in the United States," *Journal for the Scientific Study of Religion* 29 (1990): 19–34.

Hwang, Sean-Shong and Rogelio Saenz, "The Problem Posed by Immigrants Married Abroad on Intermarriage Research: The Case of Asian Americans," *International Migration Review* 24 (1990): 563–576.

Ignatiev, Noel, *How the Irish Became White* (New York: Routledge, 1995).

Ima, Kenji and Jean Nidorf, "Characteristics of Southeast Asian Delinquents," in *Struggling to Be Heard: The Unmet Needs of Asian Pacific American Children,* ed. Valerie O. Pang and Li-Rong L. Cheng (Albany: State University of New York Press, 1998), 89–104.

Iwasaki, Naomi, "Don't Play Yourself," *Gidra* 1, no. 3 (1999): 21–22.

Jacoby, Tamar, "An End to Counting Race?" *Commentary* 111, 6 (June 2001): 37–40.

Jensen, Gary F. and Dean G. Rojek, eds., *Delinquency and Youth Crime* (Prospect Heights, IL: Waveland Press, 1992).

Kalmijn, Matthijs, "Patterns in Black/White Intermarriage," *Social Forces* 72 (1993): 119–146.

Kang, Connie, "Church Provides One-Stop Center for Koreans' Needs," *Los Angeles Times,* October 23, 1992, A1.

Kao, Grace and Marta Tienda, "Educational Aspirations of Minority Youth," *American Journal of Education* 106 (1998): 349–384.

Kasindorf, Martin, "Orphaned for Educational Opportunity," *USA Today,* March 2, 1999, p. 5A.

Keith, Verna M. and Cedric Herring, "Skin tone and stratification in the Black community," *American Journal of Sociology* 97 (1991): 760–778.

Kelly, G., *From Vietnam to America: A Chronicle of the Vietnamese Immigration to the United States* (Boulder, CO: Westview Press, 1977).

Kelley, Robin D. G., *Race Rebels: Culture, Politics, and the Black Working Class* (New York: The Free Press, 1994).

Kent, D.R. and G.Y. Felkenes, *Cultural Explanations for Vietnamese Youth Involvement in Street Gangs* (Westminster, CA: Westminster Police Department, Office of Research and Planning, 1998).

Kibria, Nazli, *Family Tightrope: The Changing Lives of Vietnamese Americans* (Princeton, NJ: Princeton University Press, 1993).

———, "Not Asian, Black or White? Reflections on South Asian American Racial Identity," *Amerasia Journal* 22 (1996): 77–86.

———, "The Construction of 'Asian American': Reflections on Intermarriage and Ethnic Identity among Second-Generation Chinese and Korean Americans," *Ethnic and Racial Studies* 20 (1997): 522–544.

———, *Becoming Asian American: Second Generation Chinese and Korean Identity* (Baltimore: Johns Hopkins University Press, 2002).

Kim, Dae Young, "Immigrant Entrepreneurship and Intergenerational Mobility among Second-Generation Korean Americans in New York" (Ph.D. Dissertation, Department of Sociology, City University of New York, 2001).

Kim, David Kyuman, *Becoming: Korean Americans, Faith, and Identity—Observations on an Emerging Culture* (Master's of Divinity thesis, Harvard Divinity School, 1993).

Kim, Kwang Chung and Shin Kim, "Ethnic Meanings of Korean Immigrant Churches," Paper presented at the Sixty North Park College Korean Symposium, Chicago, October 12, 1996.

Kim, Won Moo and Kwang Chung Kim, "Religious Participation of Korean Immigrants in the United States," *Journal for the Scientific Study of Religion* 29 (1990):19–34.

Kimmel, Michael S., "Masculinity as Homophobia: Fear, Shame, and Silence in the Construction of Gender Identity," in *Theorizing Masculinities*, ed. Harry Brod and Michael Kaufman (Thousand Oaks, CA: Sage Publications, 1994).

Kingston, Maxine Hong, *The Woman Warrior: Memoirs of a Girlhood among Ghosts* (New York: Alfred A. Knopf, 1976).

Kirshenblatt-Gimblett, Barbara, "Objects of Ethnography," in *Exhibiting Cultures: The Poetics and Politics of Museum Display*, ed. Ivan Karp and Steven D. Lavine (Washington, DC: Smithsonian Institution Press, 1991), 386–443.

Kitano, Harry H., W.T. Yeung, L. Chai, and H. Hatanaka, "Asian American Interracial Marriage," *Journal of Marriage and the Family* 46 (1984): 179–190.

Kitwana, Bakari, *The Hip Hop Generation: Young Blacks and the Crisis in African American Culture* (New York: Basic Books, 2002).

Klein, Malcolm, *The American Street Gangs* (New York: Oxford University Press, 1995a).

———, "Deference to Gangs Makes Them Kings of the Roost," *Los Angeles Times*, September 19, 1995b, B3.

Kleiner, Carolyn, "Mind-Body Fitness, Yoga Booms in Popularity as a Way to Heighten Flexibility, Improve Breathing, and Gain Sanity," *Usnews.com*, May, 13. 2002, pp. 1–3.

Kondo, Dorinne, "(Re)visions of Race: Contemporary Race Theory and the Cultural Politics of Racial Crossover in Documentary Theatre," *Theatre Journal* 52, no. 1 (2000): 81–107.

———, *About Face: Performing Race in Fashion and Theater* (New York: Routledge, 1997).

Krohn, Marvin D., Alan J. Lizotee, and Cynthia M. Perez, "The Interrelationship between Substance Use and Precocious Transitions to Adult Statuses," *Journal of Health and Social Behavior* 38 (1997): 87–103.

Kurahashi, Yuko, *Asian American Culture on Stage: The History of East-West Players* (New York: Garland, 1998).

Kurashige, Lon, *Japanese American Celebration and Conflict: A History of Ethnic Identity and Festival in Los Angeles, 1934–1990* (Berkeley: University of California Press, 2002).

Laguio, Perfecto E., *Our Modern Woman: A National Problem* (Manila: Philaw Book Supply, 1931).

Lam, Julie Shuk-yee Lam, *Chinese America: History and Perspectives, 1987* (San Francisco: Chinese Historical Society of America, 1987).

Lawcock, Larry A., "Filipino Students in the United States and the Philippine Independence Movement: 1900–1935" (Ph.D. dissertation, University of California, Berkeley, 1975).

Lee, Jennifer, "Striving for the American Dream: Struggle, Success, and Intergroup Conflict among Korean Immigrant Entrepreneurs," in *Contemporary Asian America: A Multidisciplinary Reader*, ed. Min Zhou and James V. Gatewood (New York: New York University Press, 2000), 278–296.

———, *Civility in the City: Blacks, Jews, and Koreans in Urban America* (Cambridge, MA: Harvard University Press, 2002).

Lee, Jennifer and Frank D. Bean, "Beyond Black and White: Remaking Race in America." *Contexts* (2003): 26–33.

———, "America's Changing Color Lines: Immigration, Race/Ethnicity, and Multiracial Identification" *Annual Review of Sociology* 30 (2004): 221–242.

Lee, Joann Faung Jean, *Asian American Actors: Oral Histories from Stage, Screen, and Television* (London: McFarland, 2000): 221–242.

Lee, Josephine, *Performing Asian America: Race and Ethnicity on the Contemporary Stage* (Philadelphia: Temple University Press, 1997).

Lee, Robert G., *Orientals: Asian Americans in Popular Culture* (Philadelphia: Temple University Press, 1999).

Lee, Rose Hum, "The Decline of Chinatown in the United States," *American Journal of Sociology* 54 (1949): 422–432.

———, "Your Job and You," *Chinese Press*, August 11, 1950, p. 4.

———, *The Chinese in the United States of America* (Hong Kong: Hong Kong University Press, 1960).

Lee, Sara, "Racial and Ethnic Identities of Second-Generation Korean Immigrants in New York City" (Ph.D. Dissertation, Department of Sociology, Columbia University, 2002).

Lee, Sharon M. and Keiko Yamanaka, "Patterns of Asian American Intermarriage and Marital Assimilation," *Journal of Comparative Family Studies* 21 (1990): 287–305.

Lee, Sharon M. and Marilyn Fernandez, "Patterns in Asian American Racial/Ethnic Intermarriage: A Comparison of 1980 and 1990 Census Data," *Sociological Perspectives* 41 (1998): 323–342.

Lee, Spencer, "The Import Car Scene," *Yolk* 5, no. 4 (1999): 30.

Lee, Stacey J., *Unraveling the "Model Minority" Stereotype: Listening to Asian American Youth* (New York: Teachers College Press, 1996).

Leonard, J., "Orange County Violence on Rise at Central O.C. Cyber Café of Crime: Police Say Weekend Slaying at PC Café in Garden Grove Is the Latest in a String of Assaults at Teen Hangouts," *Los Angeles Times*, January 1, 2002, p. B5.

Leong, Karen, "The China Mystique: Mayling Soong Chiang, Pearl S. Buck, and Anna May Wong in the American Imagination" (Ph.D. dissertation, University of California, Berkeley, 1999).

Leong, Russell, "Introduction: Home Bodies and the Body Politic," in *Asian American Sexualities: Dimensions of the Gay and Lesbian Existence*, ed. Russell Leong (New York: Routledge, 1996).

Li, Wei, "Anatomy of a New Ethnic Settlement: The Chinese Ethnoburb in Los Angeles," *Urban Studies* 35 (1988): 479–501.

Liang, Zai and Naomi Ito, "Intermarriage of Asian Americans in the New York City Region: Contemporary Patterns and Future Prospects," *International Migration Review* 33 (1999): 876–900.

Lieberson, Stanley and Mary C. Waters, *From Many Strands: Ethnic and Racial Groups in Contemporary America* (New York: Russell Sage Foundation, 1988).

Lieu, Nhi, "Remembering 'the Nation' through Pageantry: Femininity and the Politics of Vietnamese Womanhood in the Hoa Hau Ao Dia Contest." *Frontiers* 21, no. 1–2 (2000): 127–151.

Lim, Shirley Jennifer, "Girls Just Wanna Have Fun: The Politics of Asian American Women's Public Culture" (Ph.D. dissertation, University of California, Los Angeles, 1998).

———, "Contested Beauty: Asian American Women's Cultural Citizenship during the Early Cold War Era," in *Asian Pacific American Women's History*, ed. Shirley Hune and Gail Nomura (New York: New York University Press, 2003).

Lin, Justin (Director), *Better Luck Tomorrow*, Hollywood, CA: Paramount Pictures, 2003.

Lipsitz, George, "We Know What Time It Is," in *Microphone Fiends: Youth Music and Youth Culture*, ed. Andrew Ross and Tricia Rose (New York: Routledge, 1997).

———, "The Hip Hop Hearings: Censorship, Social Memory, and Intergenerational Tensions among African Americans," in *Generations of Youth: Youth Cultures and History in Twentieth-Century America*, ed. Joe Austin and Michael Nevin Willard (New York: New York University Press, 1998), 395–411.

Liu, W.T., *Transition to Nowhere: Vietnamese Refugees in America* (Nashville, TN: Charter House Publishers, 1979).

Loewen, James, *The Mississippi Chinese: Between Black and White* (Prospect Heights, IL: Waveland Press, 1988).

Los Angeles Times [staff], "Home Alone—Up Market L.A. Style," *Los Angeles Times*, June 27, 1993, p. M4.

Louie, Vivian, "'Becoming' and 'Being' Chinese American in College: A Look at Ethnicity, Social Class, and Neighborhood in Identity Development," in *The Place of Identity: Interdisciplinary Perspectives on Subjectivity and American Migrations*, ed. Colin Wayne Leach and Donna R. Gabaccia (New York: Routledge, 2001).

Lowe, Lisa, *Immigrant Acts: On Asian American Cultural Practices* (Durham, NC: Duke University Press, 1996).

Lum, Ethyl, "Chinese during the Depression," *Chinese Digest*, November 22, 1935, p. 10.

Mabalon, Dawn, "History: Filipino American," *Psst! Magazine* 2, no. 1, October–November 1997.

Maira, Sunaina Marr, *Desis in the House: Indian American Youth Culture in New York City* (Philadelphia: Temple University Press, 2002).

Malhotra-Singh, Angelina, "Brownsploitation!" *India Currents Magazine* 13, no. 3 (1999): 38–40.

Manalansan, Martin, "Searching for a Community: Filipino Gay Men in New York City," *Amerasia Journal* 20 (1994): 59–73.

Maram, Linda Nueva España, "Negotiating Identity: Youth, Gender, and Popular Culture in Los Angeles's Little Manila, 1920s–1940s" (Ph.D. dissertation, Department of History, University of California, Los Angeles, 1996).

Marchetti, Gina, *Romance and the "Yellow Peril"* (Berkeley: University of California Press, 1993).

Mariano, Honorante, "The Filipino Immigrants in the United States" (Master's thesis, University of Oregon, 1933).

Marriot, Michel, "The Sad Ballad of the Cyber Café," *New York Times on the Web*, April 16, 1998.

Marsh, R.E., "Socioeconomic Status of Indochinese Refugees in the United States: Progress and Problems," *Social Security Bulletin* 43 (1980): 11–12.

Massey, Douglas S. and Nancy A. Denton, *American Apartheid: Segregation and the Making of the Underclass*. (Cambridge, MA: Harvard University Press, 1993).

Matsumoto, Valerie J., "Redefining Expectations: Nisei Women in the 1930s," *California History* (1994): 44–53, 88.

May, Elaine Tyler, *Homeward Bound: American Families in the Cold War Era* (New York: Basic Books, 1988).

Maybelline Cosmetics, "Cosmic Edge," *Jane Magazine* 3, no. 5 (1999): 14.

McRobbie, Angela, *Feminism and Youth Culture* (New York: Routledge, 2000).

McRobbie, Angela and Jenny Garber, "Girls and Subcultures: An Explanation," in *Resistance through Rituals: Youth Subcultures in Post-War Britain*, ed. Stuart Hall and Tony Jefferson (Hutchinson, UK: Hutchinson University Library in association with the Centre for Contemporary Cultural Studies, University of Birmingham, 1976), 209–222.

McWilliams, Carey, *Brothers under the Skin* (Boston: Little, Brown, 1951).

Mehta, Gita, *Karma Cola: Marketing the Mystic East* (New York: Vintage International, 1979).

Melendy, H. Brett, *Asians in America: Filipinos, Koreans, and East Indians* (Boston: Twayne Publishers, 1951).

Meñez, Herminia Quimpo, *Folkloric Communication among Filipinos in the United States* (New York: Arno Press, 1976).

Merton, Robert K., "Intermarriage and the Social Structure: Fact and Theory," *Psychiatry* 4 (1941): 361–374.

———, *Social Theory and Social Structure* (New York: Free Press [1949], 1968, 2nd ed.).

Messner, Michael, *Power at Play: Sports and the Problem of Masculinity* (Boston: Beacon Press, 1992).

Min, Pyong Gap, "The Structure and Social Functions of Korean Immigrant Churches in the United States," *International Migration Review* 26 (1992): 1370–1394.

———, *Changes and Conflicts: Korean Immigrant Families in New York* (Boston: Allyn and Bacon, 1998).

Mok, Teresa A., "Asian American Dating: Important Factors in Partner Choice," *Cultural Diversity and Ethnic Minority Psychology* 5 (1999): 103–117.

Moy, James S., *Marginal Sights: Staging the Chinese in America* (Iowa City: University of Iowa Press, 1993).

Mullins, Mark, "The Life-Cycle of Ethnic Churches in Sociological Perspective," *Japanese Journal of Religious Studies* 14 (1987): 321–334.

Nagel, Joane, "Constructing Ethnicity: Creating and Recreating Ethnic Identity and Culture," *Social Problems* 41 (1994): 152–171.

Nakano, Mei, *Japanese American Women: Three Generations, 1890–1990* (Berkeley: Mina Press Publishing/San Francisco: National Japanese American Historical Society, 1990).

Nee, Victor G. and Brett de Bary Nee, *Longtime Californ': A Documentary Study of an American Chinatown* (Stanford, CA: Stanford University Press, 1986 [1972]).

Nguyen, L.T., and A.B. Henkin, "Vietnamese Refugees in the United States: Adaptation and Transitional Status," *Journal of Ethnic Studies* 9 (1984): 101–116.

Ni, Ching-Ching, "Dens of the Cyber Addicts," *Los Angeles Times*, June 28, 2002, pp. A1, A4, and A5.

Niiya, Brian, ed., *Japanese American History, An A-to-Z Reference from 1868 to the Present* (Los Angeles: Japanese American National Museum, 1993).

Nishi, Setsuko Matsunaga, "Japanese Americans," in *Asian Americans: Contemporary Trends and Issues*, ed. Pyong Gap Min (Thousand Oaks, CA: Sage Publications, 1995), 95–133.

Office of Refugee Resettlement, *Report to Congress* (Washington, DC: U.S. Department of Health and Human Services, Family Support Administration, 1988).

Okamura, Jonathan, "Situational Ethnicity," *Ethnic and Racial Studies* 4 (1981): 452–465.

Omi, Michael and Howard Winant, *Racial Formation in the United States from the 1960s to the 1980s* (New York: Routledge, 1994).

Osumi, Megumi Dick, "Asians and California's Anti-Miscegenation Laws," in *Asian and Pacific American Experiences: Women's Perspectives*, ed. Nobuya Tsuchida (Minneapolis: Asian/Pacific

American Learning Resource Center and General College, University of Minnesota, 1982), 1–37.

Padilla, Amado M., Yuria Wagatsuma, and Kathryn J. Lindholm, "Acculturation and Personality as Predictors of Stress in Japanese and Japanese-Americans," *Journal of Social Psychology* 125 (1985): 295–305.

Padilla, Felix M., *The Gangs as an American Enterprise* (Piscataway, NJ: Rutgers University press, 1992).

Pai, Young, Delores Pemberton, and John Worley, *Findings on Korean American Early Adolescents* (Kansas City: University of Missouri School of Education, 1987).

Palladino, Grace, *Teenagers: An American History* (New York: Basic Books, 1996).

Pang, Gin Yong, "Attitudes toward Interracial and Interethnic Relationships and Intermarriage among Korean Americans: The Intersections of Race, Gender and Class Inequality," in *New Visions in Asian American Studies: Diversity, Community, Power*, ed. Franklin Ng, Judy Yung, Stephen S. Fugita, and Elaine H. Kim (Pullman: Washington University Press, 1994), 111–124.

Pao, Angela C., "Recasting Race: Casting Practices and Racial Formations," *Theatre Survey* 41 (2000): 1–21.

———, "Changing Faces: Recasting National Identity in All-Asian(-) American Dramas," *Theatre Journal* 53 (2001): 389–409.

Park, Lisa Sun-Hee, "Asian Immigrant Entrepreneurial Children" in *Contemporary Asian American Communities: Intersections and Divergences*, ed. Linda Trinh Võ and Rick Bonus (Philadelphia: Temple University Press, 2002), 161–177.

Park, Robert, *Race and Culture* (Glencoe, IL: Free Press, 1926 [1950]).

Parker, Andrew, Mary Russo, Doris Summer, and Patricia Yeager, eds., *Nationalisms and Sexualities* (New York: Routledge, 1992).

Parson, Talcott, *Essays in Sociological Theory* (Glencoe, IL: Free Press, 1949).

———, "Age and Sex in the Social Structure of the United States," *American Sociological Review* 7 (1942): 604–616.

Pascoe, Peggy, "Race, Gender, and Intercultural Relations: The Case of Interracial Marriage," *Frontiers* 12, no. 1 (1991): 5–18.

———, "Miscegenation Law, Court Cases, and Ideologies of 'Race' in Twentieth-Century America," *Journal of American History* 83 (1996): 44–69.

———, "Race, Gender, and the Privileges of Property: On the Significance of Anti-Miscegenation Law in the U.S. West," in *Over the Edge: Remapping the American West*, ed. Valerie Matsumoto and Blake Allmendinger (Berkeley: University of California Press, 1999), 215–230.

Petersen, William, "Success Story, Japanese-American Style," *New York Times Magazine*, January 9, 1966, pp. 20–21, 33, 36, 38, 40–41, 43.

Peterson, J., "Saigon U.S.A.: Exploring Orange Country's Vietnamese Community," *Orange Coast Magazine*, November (1988): 123–128.

Pido, Antonio J., "Macro and Micro Dimensions of Pilipino immigration," in *Filipino Americans: Transformation and Identity*, ed. Maria P.P. Root (London: Sage, 1997).

Polenberg, Richard, *One Nation Divisible: Class, Race, and Ethnicity in the United States since 1938* (New York: Penguin Books, 1980).

Portes, Alejandro, "Economic Sociology and the Sociology of Immigration: A Conceptual Overview," in *The Economic Sociology of Immigration: Essays on Networks, Ethnicity, and Entrepreneurship*, ed. Alejandro Portes (New York: Russell Sage Foundation, 1995), 1–41.

Portes, Alejandro and Dag MacLeod, "What Shall I Call Myself? Hispanic Identity Formation in the New Second Generation," *Ethnic and Racial Studies* 19 (1996): 523–547.

Portes, Alejandro and Min Zhou, "The New Second Generation: Segmented Assimilation and Its Variants," *Annals of the American Academy of Political and Social Science* 530 (1993): 74–96.

Portes, Alejandro and Rubén G. Rumbaut, *Immigrant America: A Portrait*, 2nd ed. (Berkeley: University of California Press, 1996).

———, *Legacies: The Story of the Immigrant Second Generation* (Berkeley: University of California Press, 2001).

Posadas, Barbara, *The Filipino Americans* (Westport, CT: Greenwood Press, 1999).

Prashad, Vijay, *The Karma of Brown Folk* (Minneapolis: University of Minnesota Press, 2000).

Qian, Zhenchao, "Breaking the Racial Barriers: Variations in Interracial Marriage between 1980 and 1990," *Demography* 34 (1997): 263–276.

Rams, Bill, "Slaying Spurs Cybercafe Scrutiny," *Orange County Register*, January 2, 2001, p. 1.

Redhead, Steve, ed., *Rave Off: Politics and Deviance in Contemporary Youth Culture* (Brookfield, VT: Avebury, 1993).

Revilla, Linda, "Filipino American Identity," in *Filipino Americans: Transformation and Identity*, ed. Maria P. P. Root (London: Sage, 1997).

Reyes, Eric, "Strategies for Queer Asian Pacific Islander Spaces," in *Asian American Sexualities: Dimensions of the Gay and Lesbian Existence*, ed. Russell Leong (New York: Routledge, 1996).

Rizal, Jose, *Noli Me Tangere* (Honolulu: University of Hawai'i Press, 1997).

Roediger, David, *The Wages of Whiteness* (New York: Verso, 1991).

Rose, Charlie, "Interview with Mira Nair," *The Charlie Rose Show*, May 1, 2002.

Rose, Tricia, *Black Noise: Rap Music and Black Culture in Contemporary America* (Hanover, NH: Wesleyan University Press, 1994).

Rotheram-Borus, Mary J., "Biculturalism among Adolescents," in *Ethnic Identity: Formation and Transmission among Hispanics and Other Minorities*, ed. Martha E. Bernal (Albany: State University of New York Press, 1993), 81–102.

Ruddick, Susan M., *Young and Homeless in Hollywood: Mapping Social Identities* (New York: Routledge, 1995).

Ruíz, Vicki L., "The Flapper and the Chaperone: Historical Memory among Mexican-American Women," in *Seeking Common Ground: Multidisciplinary Studies of Immigrant Women in the United States*, ed. Donna Gabaccia (Westport, CT: Greenwood Press, 1992), 141–158.

———, *From Out of the Shadows: Mexican Women in Twentieth-Century America* (New York: Oxford University Press, 1998).

Rumbaut, Rubén G., "The Agony of Exile: A Study of the Migration and Adaptation of Indochinese Refugee Adults and Children," in *Refugee Children: Theory, Research, and Services*, ed. Fredrick L. Ahearn, Jr. and Jean L. Athey (Baltimore: Johns Hopkins University Press, 1991), 53–91.

———, "Ties That Bind: Immigration and Immigrant Families in the United States," in *Immigration and the Family*, ed. Alan Booth, Ann C. Crouter, and Nancy Landale (Mahwah, NJ: Lawrence Erlbaum Associates, 1997a), 3–46.

———, "The Crucible Within: Ethnic Identity, Self-Esteem, and Segmented Assimilation among Children of Immigrants," *International Migration Review* 28 (1997b): 748–794.

Rumbaut, Rubén and Alejandro Portes, ed., *Ethnicities: Children of Immigrants in America* (Berkeley: University of California Press; New York: Russell Sage Foundation, 2001).

Rumbaut, Rubén and Wayne A. Cornelius, ed., *California's Immigrant Children: Theory, Research, and Implications for Educational Policy* (La Jolla, CA: Center for U.S.-Mexican Studies, University of California, San Diego, 1995).

Rutter, Michael, William Yule, Michael Berger, B. Yule, J. Morton, and Carl Bagley, "Children of West Indian Immigrants: I. Rates of Behavioral Deviance and of Psychiatric Disorders," *Journal of Child Psychology and Psychiatry and Allied Disciplines* 15 (1974): 241–262.

Saenz, Rogelio, Sean-Shong Hwang, Benigno E. Aguirre, and Robert N. Anderson, "Persistence and Change in Asian Identity among Children of Intermarried Couples," *Sociological Perspectives* 38 (1995): 175–194.

Said, Edward, *Culture and Imperialism* (New York: Vintage Books, 1994).

———, "Orientalism," in *The Post-Colonial Studies Reader*, ed. Bill Ashcroft, Gareth Griffiths, and Helen Tiffin (New York: Routledge, 1995).

Scanlon, Jennifer, *Inarticulate Longings: The Ladies' Home Journal, Gender, and the Promises of Consumer Culture* (New York: Routledge, 1995).

Scheer, R., "New National Monument: The Jailhouse," *Los Angeles Times*, August 27, 1995, B3.

Screen Actor's Guild, "Screen Actors Guild Employment Statistics Reveal Increases in Total TV/Theatrical Roles and Increases for All Minorities in 2000." http://www.sag.org/diversity/castingdata.html viewed on August 27, 2002, published in 2000.

Sefton-Green, Julian, *Digital Diversions: Youth Culture in the Age of Multi-Media* (New York: Routledge, 1998).

Sermon, Eric and Redman, "React," *Label J Records*, 2002.

Shah, Nayan, *Contagious Divides: Epidemics and Race in San Francisco's Chinatown* (Berkeley: University of California Press, 2001).

Shih, Hsien-ju, "The Social and Vocational Adjustments of the Second Generation Chinese High School Students in San Francisco" (Ph.D. dissertation, University of California, Berkeley, 1937).

Shih, Tzymei, "Finding the Niche: Friendship Formation of Immigrant Adolescents," *Youth and Society* 30 (1998): 209–240.

Shin, Eui Hang and Hyung Park, "An Analysis of Causes of Schisms in Ethnic Churches: The Case of Korean-American Churches," *Sociological Analysis* 49 (1988): 234–248.

Shinagawa, Larry Hajime, "Intermarriage and Inequality: A Theoretical and Empirical Analysis of the Marriage Patterns of Asian Americans" (Ph.D. Dissertation, Department of Sociology, University of California at Berkeley, 1994).

Shinagawa, Larry Hajime and Gin Yong Pang, "Asian American Panethnicity and Intermarriage," *Amerasia Journal* 22 (1996):127–152.

Skelton, Tracey and Gill Valentine, eds., *Cool Places: Geographies of Youth Cultures* (New York: Routledge, 1998).

Skinner, K., "Vietnamese in America: Diversity in Adaptation," *California Sociologist* 3 (1980): 103–124.

Smith, Christian, *American Evangelicalism: Embattled and Thriving* (Chicago: University of Chicago Press, 1998).

Smith, James P. and Barry Edmonston, *The New Americans* (Washington, DC: National Academy Press, 1997).

Sodowsky, Gargi R. and Edward W. M. Lai, "Asian Immigrant Variables and Structural Models of Cross-Cultural Distress," in *Immigration and the Family: Research and Policy on U.S. Immigrants*, ed. Alan Booth, Ann C. Crouter, and Nancy Landale (Mahwah, NJ: Lawrence Erlbaum Associates, 1997), 211–236.

Song, J., "Law Enforcement in the United States," *Justice Quarterly* 9, no. 4 (1992): 703–717.

Song, Jason, "Fast Times at the Cybercafe," *Los Angeles Times*, September 10, 2001, p. E1.

Song, Minho, "Towards the Successful Movement of the English-Speaking Ministry within the Korean Immigrant Church," Paper presented at *Katalyst 1994*, Sandy Cove, MD, March 21–24, 1994.

South, Nigel, ed., *Youth Crime, Deviance, and Delinquency* (Brookfield, VT: Ashgate, Dartmouth, 1999).

Spencer, Jon Michael, *The New Colored People: The Mixed-Race Movement in America* (New York: New York University Press, 1997).

Spickard, Paul R., *Mixed Blood: Intermarriage and Ethnic Identity in Twentieth-Century America* (Madison: University of Wisconsin Press, 1989).

Stein, B.N., "Occupational Adjustment of Refugees: The Vietnamese in the United States," *International Migration Review* 13 (1979): 25–45.

Steinberg, Laurence, *Beyond the Classroom: Why School Reform Has Failed and What Parents Need to Do* (New York: Simon and Schuster, 1996)

Stephan, Cookie White and Walter G. Stephan, "After Intermarriage: Ethnic Identity among Mixed-Heritage Japanese-Americans and Hispanics," *Journal of Marriage and Family* 51 (1989): 507–519.

Sullivan, John, "PC Bangs a Hit with Local Kids," *Newsday New York,* August 7, 2001, p. A13.

Sung, Betty Lee, *Chinese American Intermarriage* (New York: Center for Migration Studies, 1990).

Takaki, Ronald, *Strangers from a Difference Shore: A History of Asian Americans* (New York: Penguin Books, 1989).

Thomas, Maria, "A Long Way from Home: Thinking about International Students," *Psychodynamic Counseling* 1 (1995): 343–362.

Thrasher, Frederick M., *The Gang* (Chicago: University of Chicago Press, 1927).

Toop, David, *Rap Attack 2: African Rap to Global Hip Hop* (London: Pluto Press, 1994).

Trinidad, Elson, "City of Los Angeles Dedicates Historic Filipinotown," viewed at www.pinoylife.com on August 5, 2002.

Tsering, Lisa. 2002. "HMV Sues 'Truth Hurts Label for $500M." *India-West* 16 (2002): C1–10.

Tuan, Mia, *Forever Foreigners or Honorary Whites? The Asian Ethnic Experience Today* (New Brunswick, NJ: Rutgers University Press, 1998).

U.S. Immigration and Naturalization Service (USINS), *Statistical Yearbook of the Immigration and Naturalization Service, 2000* (Washington, DC: U.S. Government Printing Office, 2002).

U.S. News & World Report, "Success Story of One Minority in the U.S.," December 26, 1966, pp. 73–78.

Valen, Terry, "The Bus Stop: An Event by the Balagtasan Collective," *Critical Planning* 6 (1999): 5–6.

Vigil, J.D., *Barrio Gangs: Street Life and Identity in Southern California* (Austin: University of Texas Press, 1988).

———, A *Rainbow of Gangs: Street Cultures in the Mega-City* (Austin: University of Texas Press, 2002).

Vigil, J.D. and S.C. Yun, "Vietnamese Youth Gangs in California," *Gangs in America*, ed. C.R. Huff (Newbury Park, CA: Sage Publications, 1990), 146–162.

Waldinger, Roger and Jennifer Lee, "New Immigrants in Urban America," in *Strangers at the Gates: New Immigrants in Urban America*, ed. Roger Waldinger (Berkeley: University of California Press, 2001), 30–79.

Wang, Grace W., "A Speech on Second-Generation Chinese in U.S.A.," *Chinese Digest*, August 7, 1936, p. 6.

Waters, Mary C., *Ethnic Options: Choosing Identities in America* (Berkeley: University of California Press, 1990).

———, *Black Identities: West Indian Immigrant Dreams and American Realities* (Cambridge, MA: Harvard University Press, 1999).

———, "Immigration, Intermarriage, and the Challenges of Measuring Racial/Ethnic Identities," *American Journal of Public Health* 90 (2000): 1735–1737.

Wei, William, *The Asian American Movement* (Philadelphia: Temple University Press, 1993).

Weikel, D., "Crime and the Sound of Silence," *Los Angeles Times*, October 21, 1990, p. A1.

Welborn, L., "Prosecutor Uses Unusual Doctrine in Gang Slaying," *Orange County Register*, March 22, 2002, p. B1.

White, Nate R., "Chinese in America," *Christian Science Monitor*, February 1, 1941, p. 4.

Whyte, William Foote, *Street Corner Society: The Social Structure of an Italian Slum* (Chicago: University of Chicago Press, 1943).

Williams, Kim, "Boxed In: The United States Multiracial Movement" (Ph.D. Dissertation, Cornell University, 2001.

Williams, Raymond Brady, *Religions of Immigrants from India and Pakistan* (New York: Cambridge University Press, 1988).

Wilson, Bryan, *Religion in Sociological Perspective* (Oxford: Oxford University Press, 1982).

Wilson, William J., *The Truly Disadvantaged: The Inner City, the Underclass, and Public Policy* (Chicago: University of Chicago Press, 1987).

Witzel, Michael Karl and Kent Bash, *Cruisin': Car Culture in America* (Osceola, WI: Motorbooks International Publishers and Wholesalers, 1997).

Wolfenstein, Victor, *The Victims of Democracy: Malcolm X and the Black Revolution* (New York: Guilford Press, 1993).

Wong, Bernard P., *Chinatown: Economic Adaptation and Ethnic Identity of the Chinese* (New York: Holt, Rinehart, and Winston, 1982).

Wong, Deborah, "Just Being There: Making Asian American Space in the Recording Industry," in *Music of Multicultural America: A Study of Twelve Musical Communities*, ed. Kip Lornell and Anne K. Rasmussen (London: Schirmer Books, 1997), 287–316.

Wong, Eugene Franklin, *On Visual Media Racism: Asians in the American Motion Pictures* (New York: Arno Press, 1979).

Wong, Sau-ling Cynthia, "Ethnicizing Gender: An Exploration of Sexuality as Sign in Chinese Immigrant Literature," in *Reading Literature of Asian America*, ed. Shirley Geok-lin Lim and Amy Ling (Philadelphia: Temple University Press, 1992).

Wood, James Earl, Papers archived at the Bancroft Library University of California, Berkeley.

Wooden, Wayne S. and Randy Blazak, *Renegade Kids, Suburban Outlaws: From Youth Culture to Delinquency*, 2nd ed. (Belmont, CA: Wadsworth, 2001).

Writers Guild of America, "The 1998 Hollywood Writers' Report Executive Summary," viewed at http://www.wga.org/manuals/Report/ExecutiveSummary.html on September 2, 2002, published in 1998.

Wu, Judy Tzu-chun, "'Loveliest Daughter of Our Ancient Cathay!': Representations of Ethnic and Gender Identity in the Miss Chinatown U.S.A. Beauty Pageant," *Journal of Social History* 31 (1997): 5–32.

Wulff, Helena, "Introducing Youth Culture in Its Own Right: The State of the Art and New Possibilities," in *Youth Cultures: A Cross-Cultural Perspective*, ed. Vered Amit-Talai and Helena Wulff (New York: Routledge, 1995), 1–18.

Xie, Yu and Goyette, Kimberly, "The Racial Identification of Biracial Children with One Asian Parent: Evidence from the 1990 Census," *Social Forces* 76 (1997): 547–570.

Xing, Jun, *Asian America through the Lens : History, Representations, and Identity* (Walnut Creek, CA: Altamira Press, 1998).

Yablonsky, Lewis, *Gangsters: Fifty Years of Madness, Drugs, and Death on the Streets of America* (New York: New York University Press, 1998).

Yancey, William, Richard Juliani, Eugene Erikson, "Emergent Ethnicity: A Review and Reformulation," *American Sociological Review* 41 (1976): 391–403.

Yi, Daniel, "At Cyber Cafés, Playing Games Can Turn Serious," *Los Angeles Times*, June 16, 2002, pp. B1 and B14.

Ying, Yu-wen, "Cultural Orientation and Psychological Well-Being in Chinese Americans," *American Journal of Community Psychology* 23 (1995): 893–911.

Ying, Yu-wen and Lawrence H. Liese, "Emotional Well-Being of Taiwan Students in the U.S.: An Examination of Pre- to Post-arrival Differential," *International Journal of Intercultural Relations* 15 (1991): 345–366.

Yoo, David, *Growing Up Nisei: Race, Generation and Culture among Japanese Americans of California, 1924–1949* (Urbana-Champagne: University of Illinois Press, 2000).

Yu, Henry, *Thinking Orientals: Migration, Contact, and Exoticism in Modern America* (New York: Oxford University Press, 2001).

Yu, Renqiu, *To Save China, to Save Ourselves: The Chinese Hand Laundry Alliance in New York* (Philadelphia: Temple University Press, 1992).

Yung, Judy, *Unbound Feet: A Social History of Chinese Women in San Francisco* (Berkeley and Los Angeles: University of California Press, 1995).

Zhao, Xiaojian, *Remaking Chinese America: Immigration, Family, and Community, 1940–1965* (New Brunswick, NJ: Rutgers University Press, 2002).

Zhou, Min, "Growing Up American: The Challenge Confronting Immigrant Children and Children of Immigrants," *Annual Review of Sociology* 23 (1997): 3–95.

———, "'Parachute Kids' in Southern California: The Educational Experience of Chinese Children in Transnational Families," *Educational Policy* 12 (1998): 682–704.

———, "Coming of Age: The Current Situation of Asian American Children," *Amerasia Journal* 25 (1999): 1–27.

———, "Straddling Different Worlds: The Acculturation of Vietnamese Refugee Children," in *Ethnicities. Children of Immigrants in America*, ed. Rubén G. Rumbaut and Alejandro Portes (Berkeley: University of California Press, 2001), 187–227.

———, "Chinese: Once Excluded, Now Ascendant," in *The New Faces of Asian Pacific America: Numbers, Diversity and Change in the 21st Century*, ed. Eric Lai and Dennis Arguelles (Los Angeles: UCLA's Asian American Studies Center and the Coalition for Asian Pacific American Community Development, 2003a).

———, "Negotiating Culture and Ethnicity: Intergenerational Relations in Chinese Immigrant Families in the United States," Paper presented at the conference on Intergenerational Relations in the Family Life Course, Academia Sinica, Taiwan, March 12–14, 2003b.

———, "Are Asian Americans Becoming White?" *Contexts* 3(2004): 29–37.

Zhou, Min and Bankston, Carl L., III., *Growing Up American: How Vietnamese Children Adapt to Life in the United States* (New York: Russell Sage Foundation, 1998).

Zhou, Min and James V. Gatewood, *Contemporary Asian America: A Multidisciplinary Reader* (New York: New York University Press, 2000).

Zhou, Min and Xiyuan Li, "Ethnic Language Schools and the Development of Supplementary Education in the Immigrant Chinese Community in the United States," *New Directions for Youth Development: Understanding the Social Worlds of Immigrant Youth*, (Winter 2003): 57–73.

Contributors

EDITORS

Jennifer Lee is an associate professor in the Department of Sociology at the University of California, Irvine. She earned her B.A. and Ph.D. degrees from Columbia University and was a fellow at the Center for Advanced Study in the Behavioral Sciences at Stanford (2002–2003). She is the author of *Civility in the City: Blacks, Jews, and Koreans in Urban America* (Harvard University Press, 2002). Her current research project with Frank D. Bean examines how immigration and racial/ethnic diversity affect multiracial identification. Using data from the 2000 Census combined with in-depth interviews, Lee and Bean study the way interracial couples identify their children and multiracial adults negotiate their identities. Her research interests include immigration, the new second generation, race and ethnic relations, and multiracial identification.

Min Zhou is a professor in the Department of Sociology and chair of Asian American Studies Interdepartmental Degree Program at the University of California, Los Angeles. She earned her Ph.D. in sociology from the State University of New York at Albany. Her main areas of research are immigration; Asian Americans; race and ethnicity; and urban sociology. She is the author *of Chinatown: The Socioeconomic Potential of an Urban Enclave* (Temple University Press, 1992); co-author of *Growing up American: How Vietnamese Children Adapt to Life in the United States* (Russell Sage Foundation, 1998); and co-editor of *Contemporary Asian America* (New York University Press, 2000).

CONTRIBUTORS

Frank D. Bean is a professor in the Department of Sociology and co-director of the Center for Research on Immigration, Population, and Public Policy at the University of California, Irvine. He earned his Ph.D. from the Department of Sociology at Duke University and is a demographer with specializations in Mexican migration to the United States, international migration, family and fertility, the demography of racial and ethnic groups, and population policy. Some of his books include *America's Newcomers and the Dynamics of Diversity* (2003, with Gillian Stevens); *The Hispanic Population of the United States* (1987, with Marta Tienda); *At the Crossroads: Mexico and U.S. Immigration Policy* (1997, edited with Rodolfo de la Garza, Bryan R. Roberts, and Sidney Weintraub); *Help or Hindrance? The Economic Implications of Immigration for African Americans* (1998, co-edited with Dan Hamermesh); and *Immigration and Opportunity: Race, Ethnicity and Employment in the United States* (1999, co-edited with Stephanie Bell-Rose). His current research focuses on various determinants and consequences of U.S. immigration patterns and policies, changes in patterns of Mexican migration to the United States, the implications of immigration for labor market structures and processes, and the implications of immigration for racial/ethnic groups in the United States.

Jesse Cheng is a doctoral student in the Department of Anthropology at the University of California, Irvine, and also earned a law degree from Harvard University. His research focuses on the intersection of the social construction of crime and childhood.

Christy Chiang-Hom earned her Ph.D. in clinical psychology from the University of Michigan and is currently a postdoctoral fellow at Children's Hospital of Orange County. Her research interests include parachute kids, immigration issues, and American adolescents' values and psychological adjustments. She also has both clinical and research experience working with Asian American families and children with developmental disabilities.

Gloria Heyung Chun is the director of Graduate Diversity for the Social Sciences in the College of Letters and Science at University of California, Berkeley. She earned her Ph.D. in comparative ethnic studies from the University of California, Berkeley and an M.A. from the Union Theological Seminary in New York. She has taught at California State University at Long Beach, Princeton, Columbia, and Bard College. She is the author of *Of Orphans and Warriors: Inventing Chinese American Culture and Identity* (Rutgers University Press, 2000).

Mary Yu Danico is an associate professor in the Psychology and Sociology Department at California State Polytechnic University, Pomona. She earned her Ph.D. from the University of Hawai'i. She is the author of *The 1.5 Generation: Becoming Korean American in Hawai'i* (University of Hawai'i Press, 2004) and co-author of *Asian American Issues* (Greenwood Press, 2004).

Lakandiwa M. de Leon is a freelance film/video editor and documentarian residing in the Los Angeles area. He is the co-creator of "Beats, Rhymes, and Resistance," a documentary that explores the Filipino hip-hop experience in Los Angeles. As part of the *Balagtasan Collective*, he also documents the lives of young poets, artists, and organizers in the Los Angeles and San Francisco Bay areas. An avid record collector, DJ, and musician, he has facilitated presentations and workshops throughout the country about hip-hop history and culture. He is currently a Masters candidate in the Department of Asian American Studies at the University of California, Los Angeles.

Arleen de Vera is an assistant professor in the Department of History and the Asian and Asian American Studies Program at the State University of New York at Binghamton. She earned her Ph.D. in History from the University of California, Los Angeles. Her research interests center on nationalist movements, colonial studies, race, gender, and sexuality. She has taught courses on Asian American history, the history of the American West, U.S. twentieth-century history, Philippine history, and modern Southeast Asia.

Rebecca Y. Kim is an assistant professor in the Department of Sociology at Pepperdine University, Malibu. She earned her Ph.D. in sociology from the University of California, Los Angeles. Her research interests include race and ethnicity, religion, immigration, and education. She is currently working on a book on Asian American evangelicals on college campuses.

Sody Lay earned his B.A. in Philosophy and Political Science from the University of California, Los Angeles, and a Juris Doctorate from Columbia University School of Law. He has worked as a legal analyst for an international radio program, and taught "The Cambodian American Experience" at UCLA, University of California, Irvine, and California State University, Fullerton, as well as "Cambodian American Culture and Community" at the University of Massachusetts in Boston. He is a former board member and vice president of the Cambodian Family, a social service organization helping refugees of all ethnic backgrounds. He is also a founder and former executive director of the Khmer Institute.

Sara S. Lee is an assistant professor of Sociology at Kent State University of Ohio. She earned her Ph.D. in Sociology from Columbia University and her B.A. from the University of California, Berkeley. Her research interests include race and ethnicity, international migration, and social inequality. She is currently working on a book that examines the racial and ethnic identities of working- and middle-class, second-generation Korean immigrants in New York City.

Shirley Jennifer Lim is an assistant professor in the Department of History at the State University of New York at Stony Brook. She earned her Ph.D. from the University of California, Los Angeles. She is currently working on a book manuscript titled *Girls Just Wanna Have Fun: The Politics of Asian American Women's Public Culture, 1930 to 1960*. The book examines how Japanese American, Chinese American, and Filipina American women used movies, magazines, sorority membership, and beauty pageants to claim American cultural citizenship during an era of racial segregation and immigration exclusion.

Valerie J. Matsumoto is an associate professor in the Department of History and Asian American Studies at the University of California, Los Angeles. She earned her Ph.D. from Stanford University. She is author of *Farming the Home Place: A Japanese American Community in California, 1919–1982* (Cornell University Press, 1993) and co-editor of *Over the Edge: Remapping the American West* (with Blake Allmendinger, University of California Press, 1999). She is currently writing a book on Nisei women and on the creation of urban youth culture in Los Angeles during the Jazz Age and the Great Depression.

Victoria Namkung earned her M.A. in Asian American Studies from the University of California, Los Angeles in 2000 and is currently a Los Angeles-based print journalist. Her work has been published in more than 20 magazines and newspapers, including the *Los Angeles Times Magazine, In Style, Los Angeles, Asian Week, Women's Wear Daily*, and *Daily Variety*, among others. She has taught undergraduate courses at the University of California, Santa Barbara and UCLA.

Mark Tristan Ng earned his B.A. from UCLA and his Master's in Public Affairs (MPA) from Princeton University. He has worked and volunteered for several community organizations including: Search to Involve Pilipino Americans (SIPA), the Policy Institute of the National Gay and Lesbian Task Force (NGLTF), and is the co-founder of a conference for LGBT Filipinos. He is currently a marketing consultant with Wells Fargo Bank, responsible for devising and implementing the bank's strategy to target multicultural markets.

Sabeen Sandhu is a doctoral student in the Department of Sociology at the University of California, Irvine. She earned her B.A. at the University of California, Berkeley. Her research interests include immigration, the new second generation, and race and ethnicity. She is currently working on her dissertation, which explores the migration and economic incorporation of highly skilled Asian Indian immigrants in Los Angeles and the Silicon Valley.

James Diego Vigil is a professor of social ecology in the Department of Criminology, Law, and Society at the University of California, Irvine. He earned his Ph.D. in anthropology at UCLA. As an urban anthropologist focusing on Mexican Americans, he has conducted research on ethnohistory, education, culture change and acculturation, and adolescent and youth issues, especially street gangs. This work has resulted in the publication of books such as *From Indians to Chicanos: The Dynamics of Mexican American Culture*, 2nd edition (Waveland Press, 1998); and *Personas Mexicanas: Chicano Highschoolers in a Changing Los Angeles* (Harcourt Brace, 1997 [Belmont, CA: Thomson Pub., 2003]); *Barrio Gangs* (University of Texas Press, 1988). His new book, *A Rainbow of Gangs: Street Cultures in the Mega-City* (U. Texas, 2002) addresses cross-cultural themes among the street gangs of Los Angeles. Current research activities include fieldwork in Chiapas, Mexico, tracing peasant adaptation to the city, and continuing data collection focusing on schooling and academic achievement among high school students in East Los Angeles.

Linda Trinh Võ is an associate professor in the Department of Asian American Studies at the University of California, Irvine. She is the author of *Mobilizing an Asian American Community* (Temple University Press, 2004). She has edited a special issue on "Vietnamese Americans: Diasporas and Dimensions" for *Amerasia Journal* (July 2003) and has co-edited three books, *Contemporary Asian American Communities: Intersection and Divergences* (Temple University Press, 2002); *Asian American Women: The "Frontiers" Reader* (University of Nebraska Press, 2004); and *Labor versus Empire: Race, Gender, and Migration* (Routledge, 2004).

Nancy Wang Yuen is a doctoral student in the Department of Sociology at UCLA. She earned her B.A. in English, with a specialization in creative writing, from the University of California, Los Angeles. She was the recipient of the prestigious National Science Foundation Graduate Fellowship.

Her current research interests include race, ethnicity, media studies, cultural studies, and language code-switching.

Steve C. Yun is a physician in private practice in southern California. He earned a B.S. in anthropology from the University of Wisconsin-Madison and an M.D. from the University of Southern California. He has collaborated with James Diego Vigil on a number of projects involving ethnographic fieldwork with Vietnamese youths.

William Wei is professor in the Department of History and director of the Sewall Academic Program at the University of Colorado, Boulder. He earned his Ph.D. in 1978 from the University of Michigan at Ann Arbor, and is an authority on modern Chinese history and Asian American Studies. He is the author of *Counterrevolution in China: The Nationalists in Jiangxi during the Soviet Period* (University of Michigan Press, 1985), *The Asian American Movement* (Temple University Press, 1993), and many other publications. The University of Colorado awarded him the Eugene M. Kayden Faculty Book Manuscript Prize for *Counterrevolution in China*. He has held several national research awards, including the Rockefeller Foundation Research Fellowship, Mellon Fellowship for Advanced Study and Research from the American Council of Learned Societies, and Fulbright-Hays Research Fellowship. Recently, the University of Colorado honored him with the Robert L. Stearns medal for extraordinary achievement in research, teaching, and service.

Index